Untying the Gordian Knot

Contemporary Whitehead Studies

Edited by Roland Faber, Claremont School of Theology, and Brian G. Henning, Gonzaga University

Contemporary Whitehead Studies, co-sponsored by the Whitehead Research Project, is an interdisciplinary book series that publishes manuscripts from scholars with contemporary and innovative approaches to Whitehead studies by giving special focus to projects that: explore the connections between Whitehead and contemporary Continental philosophy, especially sources, like Heidegger, or contemporary streams like poststructuralism; reconnect Whitehead to pragmatism, analytical philosophy and philosophy of language; explore creative East/West dialogues facilitated by Whitehead's work; explore the interconnections of the mathematician with the philosopher and the contemporary importance of these parts of Whitehead's work for the dialogue between sciences and humanities; reconnect Whitehead to the wider field of philosophy, the humanities, the sciences, and academic research with Whitehead's pluralistic impulses in the context of a pluralistic world; address Whitehead's philosophy in the midst of contemporary problems facing humanity, such as climate change, war and peace, race, and the future development of civilization.

Recent Titles in this Series

Untying the Gordian Knot

Process, Reality, and Context

Timothy E. Eastman

LEXINGTON BOOKS

Lanham • Boulder • New York • London

Published by Lexington Books
An imprint of The Rowman & Littlefield Publishing Group, Inc.
4501 Forbes Boulevard, Suite 200, Lanham, Maryland 20706
www.rowman.com

6 Tinworth Street, London SE11 5AL, United Kingdom

British Library Cataloguing in Publication Information Available

Library of Congress Control Number: 2020945463
ISBN 978-1-7936-3916-5 (cloth)
ISBN 978-1-7936-3918-9 (pbk)
ISBN 978-1-7936-3917-2 (electronic)

This work is dedicated to my life partner, Carolyn Thompson Brown, core of a beloved community, whose unlimited love, support and superb editorial skills made its completion a real possibility and finally an actualized fact.

Contents

Acknowledgments

This highly integrative work would not have been possible without the prior accomplishments and publications of a vast community of scholars over the centuries. In many cases, research that led to dead-ends has been just as valuable as work resulting in promising new and productive approaches. In particular, I acknowledge the valuable contributions of contemporary scholars, particularly in the fields of quantum physics, American and European philosophy, process philosophy, semiotics and biosemiotics, and information and complex systems.

I am indebted to a wide range of scholars with whom I have dialogued in person including, among others, (Science, philosophy of science) Ian Barbour, Jesse Bettinger, Jeffrey Bub, Reginald Cahill, Geoffrey Chew, Terrence Deacon, Joseph Earley, George Ellis, Lawrence Fagg, David Finkelstein, Leonard Garcia, David Grinspoon, Gary Herstein, William Kallfelz, Stuart Kauffman, Hank Keeton, John Jungerman, Ruth Kastner, Wolfgang Kundt, Eric Lerner, Roland Omnès, Anthony Peratt, Hilton Ratcliffe, Joe Rosen, Robert John Russell, Henry Stapp, and Robert Valenza; (Humanities) George Allen, Randall Auxier, Joseph Bracken, James Bradley, Søren Brier, Milič Čapek, Philip Clayton, John B. Cobb, Jr., David Christian, Herman Daly, Ronny Desmet, William Desmond, Roland Faber, Evan Fales, Lewis Ford, Arran Gare, Herman Greene, David Ray Griffin, John Haught, Brian Henning, George Lucas, Jr., Farzad Mahootian, Derek Malone-France, Leemon McHenry, Thomas Mikelson, Robert Neville, Jorge Luis Nobo, Nicholas Rescher, Franz Riffert, Johanna Seibt, Robert Spitzer, Marjorie Suchocki, Yutaka Tanaka, Thandeka, Michel Weber, Paul Weiss, and Alan White.

Above all, I wish to especially acknowledge the groundbreaking research work of Michael Epperson and Elias Zafiris, whose insights in quantum physics and philosophy directly inspired the current work. These advances in turn were earlier made possible by partial support through the Fetzer-Franklin Fund, including critical research and workshops, thanks to coordination efforts by Paul Gailey and Jan Walleczek. And, finally, I am deeply thankful to George Shields of the University of Kentucky for several extended dialogues, during the late stages of this work, that inspired notable improvements in the first dozen drafts.

I am further indebted to my direct human heritage, parents and ancestors, to whom I owe my very existence, and to the loving support of my wonderful children, siblings, in-laws, and their families. Further, I'm indebted to the innumerable persons, institutions, teachers and mentors that enabled my growth, education, and career including, among many others, the University of Minnesota, University of Colorado, Los Alamos Scientific Laboratory, University of Alaska Geophysical Institute, University of Iowa, University of Maryland, NASA Headquarters, National Science Foundation, NASA Goddard Space Flight Center, ADNET Systems, Inc., and Atmospheric Plasma Solutions. Finally, I wish to thank various members of the Fetzer Institute of Kalamazoo, Michigan, for their helpful input and encouragement.

My resources for research were critically dependent on the Library of Congress, especially its John W. Kluge Center which, for over a year, provided research space for my wife, Carolyn T. Brown, following her retirement as director of the Center. We very productively shared that space.

Chapter 1

Quest

AWAKENING

I was about thirteen years old that seemingly ordinary late May day when I walked down a beautiful hillside overlooking Big Stone Lake in Minnesota. My childhood self was blissfully unaware of my own complexity (10^{26} atoms, 10^{15} cells, 10^{10} neurons, etc.)[1] and of the wider context (gravitational field, electromagnetic field, ecosystems, etc.) in which I was immersed. I was naturally quite clueless about the breadth and depth of the world. Breathing in the fresh woodland air and gazing across the lake to the Dakota hills, beautifully lit by the morning sun, I was seized by a distinct spiritual experience: a sudden awakening to a sense of awe and greater consciousness of the immensity of the natural world; a new recognition of my radical finiteness and humility before an infinite cosmos; and a commitment to learning and understanding what all of this was about.[2] That moment initiated my quest to understand the fundamental nature of the universe and sparked the inquiry that would ultimately result in this book.

Feeling the soil and grass below me, I felt the throbbing life of insects, worms, and plants, and wondered how was I fundamentally like or different from such creatures? How was my radically limited self connected to various possible levels of this wondrous whole? In that unique event, I experienced a heightened awareness of our shared radical contingency, of the immensity of alternative possibilities, of the overwhelming possibility of not existing at all, of the unlikely privilege of being a healthy, sentient entity able to self-reflect, and of being able to examine my privileged perspective in ways far beyond that available to the insects and worms. I meditated on my own ignorance and fears, my radical givenness, and the unlimited possibilities going forward.

Looking back with maturity through a philosophical lens, I see my younger self then as a radically finite, contingent being of limited perspective looking out over an equally contingent lake. I was a subject with respect to all things available as objects (including my immediate past self), a self giving rise to inevitable object-subject (cognition-dependent) relationships emerging from such finite perspectives, and yet a self acknowledging a universe of cognition-independent "things" beyond any practical reach. At the time, I desperately wanted to be given some "God's eye view" perspective that transcended my own tiny existence,[3] just as my own feeble perspective far surpassed the views of insects and worms.

Sitting in that lakeshore woodland, struggling with my own limitations, and filled with an abundance of sense impressions, I unknowingly had stumbled into my lifelong quest, a quest not just for enhanced awareness, not just for understanding the physical world, but ultimately a quest for meaning. Initially I thought that science would provide the key to answering my still inchoate questions and concerns,[4] even while some intuitive part of myself suspected that I might require a broader set of tools. While still in high school I was somehow self-motivated to read through the entire, quite sophisticated section of Western philosophy in the Carnegie Library in Ortonville, Minnesota.

In college at the University of Minnesota, with my bachelor's degree in physics close at hand, I was unclear as to whether I should go on to graduate school in physics or philosophy. My philosophy of science professor, a former member of the famed Vienna Circle of logical positivism, Herbert Feigl, advised me that if I wanted to engage the philosophy of physics, I should first learn the physics and the philosophy could come later. Wise advice! I went to graduate school in space physics, ultimately obtaining a doctoral degree from the University of Alaska. My specialty, space plasma physics, indeed helped me understand the physical world in a practical way. Yet through my college years, both undergraduate and graduate, I nurtured my passion for philosophy by taking courses in philosophy and frequently attending lectures in that field.

As my career unfolded, although pushed to the periphery of my immediate concerns, my lakeside aspirations were never far from the surface. Over the decades I continued to study philosophy as well as many areas of science and the humanities.[5] Although I never obtained a degree in philosophy as such, this runaway avocation led to my giving presentations at philosophy conferences, editing two books, and publishing over thirty papers in the field, most peer reviewed, all while continuing my career in space science.

As a young person, I did not know that a God's eye view is impossible for finite creatures. Indeed, each and every sentient organism (insect, worm, etc.) generates a world-as-perceived *umwelt* (after Uexküll[6]), which requires any perceiving entity to generate some type of stimulus-response modeling of its particular complex of object-subject relationships. We may treat such models and associated *umwelts* as effectively "local," but there is always an implicit movement beyond the local to a more inclusive context. This more inclusive context is only beginning to be incorporated into the worldview of those who, via intellectual work and abstract conceptualization (e.g., space scientists), are able to access a far more inclusive framework that goes beyond a species-specific *umwelt*. Yet such endeavors still do not really provide a God's eye view, except in model-centric abstractions.

Real-world interactions always involve context, and some local-contextual framing inevitably occurs. Whereas scientific description and approximations very often strip away context and so enable discrete measurement results and simple input-output pairings (dyads), real-world interactions always require triads, cycles of input-output-context, or, at least, some inevitable reference to a third. Limiting any given analysis to only standard pairings or dyads necessarily involves some degree of approximation; likewise any measurement necessarily involves error, thus requiring error estimates in any full analysis.[7] Thus, both some forms of approximation and triadic logic are necessary for understanding the complex whole of the real world.

My youthful notions and hopes about the scientific method were faulty from the beginning. I imagined early on that science could support aspirations for a God's eye view of the world. I hoped that it could not only help me to understand quantitative measurement and physical models, but also enable me to address the full range of quantitative plus qualitative properties, including the full reality of human experience. Instead, the better path was to follow my earlier intuition that philosophy, which could provide critical help in handling context and in understanding other humanistic disciplines, was essential in fully interpreting the world and in effectively advancing my quest.

This book is my attempt to satisfy my naive but profound youthful aspiration to find a framework that could articulate the full experience of that moment, the material, the interactive and aesthetic, and the spiritual.

Any framework that aspires to completeness is doomed to failure before it begins. We human creatures are radically limited in our capacity to know. Here I offer a speculative framework grounded on the work of others in a wide variety of fields and perspectives, not with the expectation that it will be complete, but rather with the more modest hope that this proposal will encourage new ways of seeing the world, and will provide a new perspective on its complexities, one that will open new spaces for further inquiry.

WAYS OF KNOWING

Rather than limit myself from the beginning to a subset of experience, as do most attempts at a comprehensive framework, I have tried to take into account an extremely wide range of tools and topics available. These include the analytic, reductionist tools of the scientific method (here focused on the method and not the always-incomplete findings), the domains of science, the interpretive, aesthetic dimensions of human experience, and those elements which, at least until the past two centuries, most peoples across the globe considered as spiritual or belonging to the realm of the ultimate. Further, although rooted in the Western philosophical tradition, a metaphysics that approaches reality from these fundamental human experiences may suggest new ways of bridging philosophical assumptions across cultures. Paths along the multiple ways of knowing are effectively without limit, but human experience suggests three fundamental ways of knowing.

(1) The *way of numbers:* a focus on context independence and quantitative representation (as with some claimed "theories of everything," which often presume a science-only approach); also including the way of signs (semiotics);

   A much less restricted framing would be one associated with humanistic studies:

(2) The *way of context:* roughly the domain of arts and humanities; fully affirming qualitative dimensions that, in turn, also include semiotics;

   Finally, to truly incorporate an unrestricted domain of discourse:

(3) The *way of spirit:* addressing reference to ultimate boundaries, ultimacies, and spiritual experience.

These three primary ways can be thought of as addressing ways of knowing that are, respectively, (1) context independent,[8] then (2) context dependent, and finally (3) ultimate context. Such reference to context is one important way in which the modes of knowing (epistemology) are interrelated with the nature of being or becoming (ontology). I will address in chapter 2 the centrality of relations and triads and how these generalizations apply to context itself, and will revisit these ways of knowing in later chapters. In my analysis of complex systems (chapter 4), I will show that although the way of numbers (i.e., science) and the way of context (i.e., arts and humanities) are distinct in goals and emphasis, these modes of knowledge discovery are complementary and synergistic. The importance of inference and knowing is emphasized by Phillip Stambovsky, who affirms "the truth of that metaphysical dictum of [Oliva] Blanchette's . . . namely, *knowing is of being*" (Stambovsky 2009, 289). Finally, in chapter 8, I will argue that reference to both multilevels of context and ultimate context is unavoidable and, further, that this result has important implications for both the notions of values and meaning, and for the spiritual dimension of experience.

PROBLEM-SOLUTION-GOALS APPROACH

"One of the main challenges for today's popularizers," reports Anthony Gottlieb, is that "scientific theories are getting weirder" (Gottlieb 2016). Yes, there are real challenges and difficulties; indeed, it can be argued that nearly all technical specialties in the past century have developed such complex levels of terminology, concepts, and application, that specialists in one field encounter serious difficulty and most often do not attempt to learn multiple disciplines. The age of the true multidisciplinary scholar, who is able to understand nearly all known fields, came to an end more than two centuries ago. Further, the creation of new understandings, knowledge, and relatively reliable facts inevitably involves complex "actor-networks" within which, as Bruno Latour states, "facts remain robust only when they are supported by a common culture, by institutions that can be trusted, by a more or less decent public life, by more or less reliable media" (Latour 2018). Such complexities and context are never properly superseded by claims for "facts" discovered from some *View from Nowhere* as Thomas Nagel has labeled it (Nagel 1986).

The principal issue here concerns the wholesale and often unnoticed and unstated migration of modern scientific methods into a domain of thought that is essentially interpretive, and where improved acts of inquiry aim at clarifying and realizing a notion of the good, rather than at simply sifting quantifiable and ostensibly value-neutral information. However limited in implementation, in this work I strive to forward a humanist-interpretive framework, as advocated by Thomas Pfau, in contrast to "strictly naturalist (or deterministic and reductionist) models of human agency" (Pfau 2015, 17). I propose that the most fundamental notions can be inferred from normal human experience; that concepts of contemporary science and philosophy can be woven together in a way that cuts through claims of quantum weirdness; that these concepts reveal a deeper reality that comports well with basic human experience and intuition; and that they move us from a very particular human quest and journey to a promising new synthesis—natural, existential, spiritual.

"Gordian knot" is a metaphor for a seemingly intractable cluster of related problems that can be solved only by thinking creatively in new ways. This book is my attempt to cut through or untie a Gordian knot of multiple fundamental philosophical problems. Although I do not claim to have solved any one of these foundational problems, I propose a preliminary sketch arising from a confluence of research developments (both in science and humanities, especially philosophy) that points to a new, inclusive view of reality. I call this the relational (*Logoi*) framework.[9] My "aha" moment came recently as an insight that numerous fragments of contemporary knowledge are coalescing in a coherent way. After decades of reflection and more than five years of concentrated research, I experienced a stunning sense of discovery.

The *Logoi* framework represents a synthesis of several key ideas that each have a long heritage but have not been previously integrated in the way here proposed—a creative synthesis built upon the works of numerous scholars over the centuries. Given the complexity of recent advances in philosophy and science, identifying some unifying framework has appeared more remote than ever, except for those who claim to reduce everything to science and further reduce "reality" to one core equation or a set of Platonic forms.[10] Arguably, such reductions, even if taken at face value, effectively address only a limited domain of discourse. In contrast, the present work attempts to wrestle with all reality—an unlimited domain of discourse.

Going beyond the simplistic reductions of scientism,[11] many scholarly works struggle with the full complexity of the real world, and understandably encounter innumerable complications that are both the glory and the curse of cutting-edge scholarship. These complications have led to a cornucopia of scholarly specialties in science, arts, and humanities over the past centuries, and especially over the past half century. Drawing on some advances achieved within this vast literature, the present work attempts to frame a viable systematic philosophical framework, the *Logoi* framework. I here adopt Alan White's preference for using "systematic" instead of "speculative"as a label for this approach.[12] As Alfred North Whitehead, the British-American scientist-philosopher stated, "Speculative [systematic] Philosophy is the endeavor to frame a coherent, logical, necessary system of general ideas in terms of which every element of our experience can be interpreted" (Whitehead 1978, 3). Similarly Arran Gare, referencing C. D. Broad, states that "the goal of speculative philosophy is to take into account the whole range of human experience—scientific, social, ethical, aesthetic and religious, and to develop a coherent conception of reality that does justice to all of these" (Gare 2017, 113). I will inevitably fail to reach this lofty goal; however, in a spirit of adventure, I will attempt to see how far I can push this quixotic enterprise.

Integrative efforts are too often left to reductionists,[13] who tend to neglect broader scholarly advances, and who frequently deploy ever more complex exotica, such as multiple universes, which inevitably depend on, typically unstated, philosophical presuppositions. In contrast, my approach toward a new synthesis is to ask, once again, given the full range of human experience and the universe at large, and given a truly unlimited domain of discourse, can we obtain a relatively simple set of conjunctively coherent fundamental notions that can do the job of integration? That is, can we recursively and dynamically generate from such hypothetical notions a next order set of basic concepts enabling, in turn, the full array of concepts needed to integrate the best of contemporary scholarship? In addition, can these most fundamental notions be empirically grounded in basic human experience without initial appeal to highly abstract concepts that are not directly utilized or reflected in such experience? My very preliminary answer to this question is "yes,"[14] provided we follow Whitehead's sage advice: "Seek simplicity and distrust it" (Whitehead 1920, 163). As "tentative formulations of the ultimate generalities," (Whitehead 1978, 8) any such framework of systematic philosophy, including hypotheses about such fundamental notions, is highly fallible. I stress such fallibility because I am a simple sentient being limited to a small planet in a remote neighborhood of an average galaxy at a particular juncture of history. Thus, I offer these suggestions with all humility before the awesome vastness and daunting complexity of the cosmos.

This work is subject to the same kinds of limitations in awareness, much less of knowledge, that Whitehead acknowledged in his defense of systematic philosophy. I strive to focus on inferences from immediate experience, deploying a methodology of testable inferences, scientific method,[15] and when appropriate, more generally scholarly analysis, while always recognizing the limits of deduction, induction, and Peircean abduction.[16] My research has led me to see the inevitable need for philosophical analysis and inference, yet with enhanced sensitivity to problems with globalized claims (e.g., onto-theology, logocentrism, Platonic realms, spatializing, and various "-isms"— see Robert Corrington (2013)) as well as various forms of reduction, both with respect to substance and process (for *substance* forms of reduction, as articulated by Hilary Putnam, see Randall Auxier (2015); for *process* forms of reduction, see Johan Siebers (2002)). Whitehead was persistent in criticizing the false certainties of philosophy: "The chief error in philosophy is overstatement" (Whitehead 1978, 7). Likewise, Isabelle Stengers promotes both moderately deconstructive and constructive conversations, through the exemplars of Gilles Deleuze and Whitehead, in a sustained critique of any one unitary framing (Stengers 2014).

Despite our very human limitations, tendencies for error and overstatement, and frequent entrapment by globalized claims, Auxier and Gary Herstein point out that, nevertheless, we always retain a commitment to some form of realism: "Scientists are almost universally realists" (Auxier and Herstein 2017, 204). Such commitment suggests the need to affirm "that *concrete existence explains the abstract aspects of experience* [such being Charles Hartshorne's credo] and not vice versa. The unexpected characteristic of our experience is that it abstracts from the flux, not that it flows concretely, which we expect" (Auxier and Herstein 2017, 2). George Lucas, Jr. points out that this emphasis on concrete experience was shared as well by both Ludwig Wittgenstein and Whitehead in the form of an "endorsement of common sense and the wisdom of common language and common life" (Lucas 1989, 137). Evan Fales as well emphasizes the centrality of experience: "Whatever conceptual distinctions we later impose as we theorize in order to assemble our experiences into a coherent or unified picture, we must begin here, with the experiences themselves" (Fales 1990, 220). Similarly, Whitehead stated that "you may polish up commonsense, you may contradict it in detail, you may surprise it. But ultimately your whole task is to satisfy it" (Whitehead 1917, 112).

The basic approach taken in my quest for understanding, therefore, is to focus on candidate fundamental notions that are empirically based, simple, and intuitive. As an example of a nuanced set of fundamental notions, Gare has offered the following list: "activity, order and becoming; process, structure and event; cause; and spatio-temporal position" (Gare 1994, 313). Inspired by Gare, my method is primarily abductive in contrast to the typical focus on deduction, and includes the goals of coherence, consistency, and applicability, adopted from Whitehead. Nicholas Maxwell argues for a very similar methodology, with emphasis on coherence and the empirical (Maxwell, 2017). All too often, false projections, dualities, or "perfections" (e.g., Platonic forms) are promoted as starting points whether, for example, as "absolute" laws, Big Bang initial conditions, or mathematical Platonism. Various versions of a metaphysics of perfection have a long and continuous history (reflected in both classical theism and much scientific speculation) from Plato's forms and Euclid's geometry to René Descartes's certainty, on to scientism and scientific "theories of everything." As Auxier argues, "The tradition of associating logical (or mathematical), psychological (or cognitive), and ontological necessity with one another, which I call the 'unholy trinity,' was the basis for claiming [necessary] ontological knowledge from Aristotle up to the mid-nineteenth century. As the last 150 years have unfolded, the old assumptions about all types of necessity have come unraveled" (Auxier 2013, 54). As we shall see in chapter 8, this statement is overly strong; it would be more accurate to reference here "numerous claimed necessities" instead of "all types of necessity." Nevertheless, Auxier continues, "Although most philosophy departments have not gotten the news, rationality today is based on the structure of possibility and probability, not on the structure of necessity, and knowledge today does not require necessity of any kind—logical, psychological-cognitive, or ontological" (Auxier 2013, 55). Supporting such skepticism, Lucas has shown how both Wittgenstein and Whitehead "place a heavy emphasis on fallibility" (Lucas 2003, 83). Auxier's disclaimer above arguably applies to numerous claimed necessities, but clearly does not apply to the deductive rigor of much formal logic and does not apply to certain fundamental metaphysical propositions. Overall, however, my approach is consistent with Auxier's skepticism about certainties and leverages the power of sampling alternatives and evolutionary process—harnessing diversity, error, failure, and approximation.

Finally, the present work overall applies a *problem-solution* approach with the problems being those of the Gordian knot set, and the solution set being this draft proposal of the *Logoi* framework. This framework may also be thought of as an ecological vision, a concept applied by John B. Cobb, Jr. and Wm. Andrew Schwartz (2018), because it emphasizes the interrelatedness of processes at multiple levels.

FROM DUALISTIC THINKING TO A NEW VISION

A major impediment toward achieving a deeper understanding of our world is the tendency toward dualistic thinking, which sets up problems as simplistic "either-or" choices among abstract opposites (mind-body, self-other, black-white, etc.). Of course, there are numerous dualities that we encounter in our everyday world, as J. A. Scott Kelso and David Engstrom have documented; especially notable is their table of complementary pairs (Kelso and Engstrom 2006, 36–37). However, to insist on a particular one-dimensional view of such dualities yields reified dualisms that almost always move us from helpful distinctions to dysfunctional abstractions. Whether analyzing the binaries of the *polis* or Descartes's mind-body distinction, one is well advised to attend to Murray Code's emphasis on how such dualisms often lead to cul-de-sacs of thought.

> Not the least of the problems that the aspiring cultural therapist must tackle, then, concerns the tendency of modern philosophers to turn useful conceptual contrasts (such as body-mind, subject-object, and so on) into vicious dualisms. (Code 2007, 244)

In *Truth and Historicity*, Richard Campbell lays out the historical background for the deep strain between Greek metaphysics and biblical thinking which, although maintained concurrently, albeit fitfully, for over 1,500 years, finally fractured by the seventeenth century. This fracture "decisively occurred with the distinction between real and nominal essences, articulated by Locke" (Campbell 1992, 170) (see *On the Failure of Actualism and Nominalism* in chapter 4). Continuing, Campbell states that

> as a consequence of this split, philosophy from the seventeenth century onwards has been plagued by a series of systematically related dichotomies: of mind over against body (Descartes); of nominal essence over against real essence [nominalism] (Locke); of relations of ideas over against matters of fact (Hume); of the analytic over against the synthetic (Kant and also the positivists); of phenomena over against things-in-themselves (Kant again); of thought and language over

against reality (almost everyone); of values over against facts (again almost everyone). (Campbell 1992, 170)

For any duality, there is always some broader framing, environment or framework, an added dimension that can put that duality in a more inclusive context. Thus, a better strategy is to consider non-dual approaches, as per discussions by David Loy (1988) and Milton Scarborough (2011). In addition, by building on the works of Ken Wilber, Dustin DiPerna (2014), and others, Steve McIntosh lays out helpful strategies for overcoming the limitations of dualistic thinking (McIntosh 2007). As I explained in an earlier work, my method is to apply non-dualistic strategies to various dualities in our experience (Eastman 2004), which helps one to overcome their limitations or, at least, to make explicit the approximations imbedded in the use of a particular dual description.

Often combined with dualistic thinking is the common fallacy of what Teilhard de Chardin termed the "analytical illusion" whereby a proper and reductive methodological strategy is converted into an ontological claim. Instead, the needed perspective is artfully articulated by John Haught.

Scientific materialists try to understand the universe by breaking down every physical entity, including life and mind, into elemental components that, according to the materialist worldview, have been blindly gathered by aimless physical laws and processes into more complex aggregates during the course of time. The materialist and atomist metaphysics of the past, however, fails to *see* what is going on in the larger movement of the universe, and it deliberately leaves human subjectivity out of its vision of nature. Our anticipatory perspective, on the other hand, views human consciousness not as an exception to, but as an intensification of, what has always been going on in the universe . . . The recent arrival of human beings endowed with minds and moral aspiration is a heightening of being, an intensification of the enduringly anticipatory quality of nature, not a clean break from it. (Haught 2015, 142)

Consistent with Haught's quote above, chapter 4 on *Causation, Emergence, and Complex Systems* demonstrates how recent scholarly work in philosophy and science points to a type of anticipatory perspective that I incorporate within the *Logoi* framework. With a focus on the scientific understanding of complex natural systems, Robert Rosen has argued extensively for the importance of anticipatory dynamics (Rosen 2012).[17] Over the past two centuries, there have been several pendulum swings regarding the relevance and importance of science for society. The last of these was the dramatic rise of nuclear and high energy physics after World War II, which continued for a half century without significant disruption. But then, as noted by Daniel Sarewitz, the failure of the superconducting super-collider project appeared for some to signal the end of the age of physics (Sarewitz 1996). In spite of these ups and downs, it appears to me that there have been overall advancements in both science and engineering, and in the relevance and importance of these for societal needs. Indeed, this is confirmed by the fact of the Industrial Revolution of the nineteenth century and the scientific and communication revolutions of the twentieth century. What may yet be in question is whether these scientific advances are really for the common good (Robert Reich 2018) or whether they just help to exacerbate extremes in inevitable better-worse cycles, as featured in the intense dialogues of the Munk Debates as reviewed by Steven Pinker et al. (2016).

Numerous post-modern and other "post-"framings, as Mikhail Epstein has pointed out, have focused on contemporary problems. "The magic of this prefix allowed theoreticians to put any concept under the sign of its transcendence, relegating the term to the past. This conceptual mode, however, was ambivalent and, in a certain sense, self-defeating, because it presumed the concept's dependence on the existing one" (Epstein 2012, 24). Very often, the term "post-modern" has presumed a de-constructive thrust, a way of negating deleterious impacts of "modern" life and the "modern" world. David Ray Griffin has vigorously given voice to the message that efforts toward constructive post-modern frameworks are more positive and forward looking than de-constructive versions of the post-modern (Griffin 1992). Epstein as well notes that "We live not so much after (modernity, structuralism, or Communism) as in the very beginning of a new epoch whose features must now be more positively defined in terms of 'proto-' rather than 'post-': [for example] proto-global" (Epstein 2012, 25). Santiago Sia summarized this perspective: "The hope for society's advance . . . is rooted in the very nature of creativity (or creative synthesis), especially in its human form . . . creative synthesis points the way for us to really *transform* society. In other words, it is a vision of society that forges and substantiates a mission for all of us. It presents us with a challenge—and the capability—to meet the challenges of living in society" (Sia 2014, 248).

PROPOSED FRAMEWORK AS CREATIVE SYNTHESIS

My proposed *Logoi* framework is not post-anything but a proto-worldview, an ecological vision, a visionary rough sketch which attempts to leverage progress on key conceptual issues over the past few centuries. In addition to a confluence of scientific and technological advancements that have profoundly transformed civilizations (admittedly with much less, if any, progress in ethical or aesthetic dimensions), there has been a dramatic increase in both the extent and range of humanistic scholarship. One proxy for such increase is the change in size, and access to, information content, the latter greatly enhanced by new computer and network technologies. Presently, anyone with a computer and internet access has available a vast range of information, which completely dwarfs that available to any scholar prior to the mid-twentieth century. Epstein notes that "in the past 30 years, more new information was produced than in the previous 5,000 years. A single daily edition of the *New York Times* contains more information today than an average person in the seventeenth century encountered in a lifetime" (Epstein 2012, 160).

My approach is to build a creative synthesis, based on what I view as the accomplishments of scholars over the centuries, primarily in philosophy and science. A primary goal of the present methodology is to build on the best of prior thinking and models, incorporate their strengths as much as possible, and formulate a new model that enables greater explanatory power through a constructive approach that incorporates such prior models. Such a new model can hopefully explain both the successes of prior models and their limitations. An important exemplar for such progressive model development is the way in which the strengths and limitations of classical physics have been fully incorporated into modern physics, which also provides explanations of both its own limitations and limitations of the prior model. The present work builds as well on lessons learned from the failure of many scholarly efforts over the past few decades and centuries. For example, a cornucopia of failures in understanding just the concept of time is laid out masterfully by Raymond Tallis (2017). Examples of instructive dead-ends are simplistic forms of monism, dualism, materialism, idealism, nominalism, actualism, and scientism, among others. Indeed, I have come to be skeptical of almost any -ism. One route beyond such dead-ends is that of a pragmatic strategy that is yet realistic, as exemplified in the works of Nicholas Rescher (Pihlstrom 2017). Cheryl Misak summarizes this point about Rescher's oeuvre:

> His kind of pragmatism is an objective truth-and-inquiry oriented pragmatism, rather than a subjective "anything-goes" pragmatism. According to Rescher, the contingency and fallibility of knowledge and belief formation do not entail that our beliefs are simply what our community decides or that truth and objectivity are spurious notions. That is, he offers us a real chance of understanding how it is that beliefs can both be the products of human inquiry and nonetheless aim at the truth. (Misak 2017, ix)

Some criteria for meaning are useful, most often as a critique of abstraction; as Charles Hartshorne stated so concisely, "verifiability (liberally enough construed) is valid as criterion of meaning in general; and falsifiability is valid as criterion of empirical meaning" (Hartshorne 1970, 21–22). An even more subtle issue concerns the, often unstated, context and presuppositions of concepts deployed in model making. Nicholas Maxwell stated it well: "Untestable metaphysical[18] [and philosophical] ideas . . . form a vital, integral part of the intellectual domain of science. It's important that such ideas, now implicit, be made explicit within science, so that these ideas can be critically assessed and improved" (Maxwell 1999, 27).

INFLUENCES AND PERSPECTIVES

My primary intellectual influences are broadly process and American philosophy, natural science, and semiotics. My more specific influences include, among others, epistemology, logic and analytic philosophy, metaphysics, intellectual history, empirical observation, and data and information systems. This work is set in context of efforts to grapple with an unlimited domain of discourse, drawing on the structural-systematic philosophy of Alan White and Lorenz Puntel (White 2014) and Charles Hartshorne's neoclassical metaphysics as fleshed out by Donald Viney and George Shields (2020) including integrative metatheories such as those summarized by Paul Marshall (2016) and various ontologies (e.g., Nicolai Hartmann (2013), Roberto Poli, and Johanna Seibt (2010)); philosophy and metaphysics (e.g., Richard Campbell (1992), George Shields (2003), and Raymond Tallis (2018)). In various areas of scholarship, my particular influences include the following: American philosophy and process philosophy (e.g., Nicholas Rescher (2017) and David Ray Griffin (2007)); speculative naturalism (e.g., Leon Niemoczynski (2011), Lawrence Cahoone (2014), and Arran Gare (2017)); information theory and semiotics (e.g., Robert Logan (2014) and Paul Cobley (2010)); and European philosophy (e.g., Richard Kearney (2003) and William Desmond (1995)). More specific areas of influence include biosemiotics (e.g., Jesper Hoffmeyer (2009)), complex systems (e.g., Robert Rosen (2000)), physics (e.g., Roberto Unger and Lee Smolin (2015), and George Ellis (2016)), and mathematics and logic (e.g., Murray Code (1995) and Nicholas Rescher (2014)), among many others.[19]

Raymond Nogar has characterized two important modes of understanding in terms of "picture people" versus "drama people":

The first looked for a picture of things in order, a cosmic and personal worldview; the second looked for a drama unfolding. The first were restless until they felt that they had grasped something timeless, some eternal verity, and had placed themselves securely into changeless order. The second were impatient and distrustful until they found themselves in the space-time story of reality unfolding, a drama in which they had a part. They wanted to be involved; dynamically identified with all reality. But the picture people wanted just the opposite: detachment, escape from the effort and effect of the sorrows and joys of biographical and temporal existence. (Nogar 1966, 16–17)

Contemporary physical cosmology is often summarized by a picture person, one who seeks and emphasizes cosmic order but in a way that tends to spatialize cosmic systems with tendencies for thing-oriented versus functional descriptions (Eastman 2016). In contrast, some drama people have repackaged their narratives into a cosmic creation story; for example, Brian Swimme's creation story (Swimme 1984) that is part of some "Big History," the latter being explicit about a human role in that story; see David Christian (2019), or William Grassie's applications of Big History (Grassie 2018).

The *Logoi* framework works with both of these perspectives yet endeavors to avoid any simplistic God's eye view framing. In both "picture" and "drama" (or story form), my quest has become both a systematic philosophical framework and an *Adventure of Ideas* (Whitehead 1933).

SUMMARY OF CHAPTERS

In this first chapter, Quest, I have laid out the motivation for this study and sketched my own half-century journey, from a childhood enlightenment experience, through decades of readings and research in philosophy, physics, space science, and related fields, to the realization of a possible new synthesis that has the promise of untying a Gordian knot of problems. Recommended readings for each chapter are provided in Appendix 1. The core of the proposed approach, the *Logoi* framework, as sketched in chapter 2, is the notion of process from the Latin *processus*—a going forward or advance. Process incorporates succession—"one darn thing after another"—and partners with two other fundamental notions: logic and relations. Each of these fundamental notions has at least two aspects: process (local/global; imbedded), logic (binary/nonbinary; triadic), and relations (part/whole; internal/external, extension, information,[20] semiotics[21]). Key components of the *Logoi* framework are the models of Relational Reality[22] inspired by recent developments in quantum physics, as discussed in depth by Michael Epperson and Elias Zafiris (2013), and augmented by Ruth Kastner and colleagues (Kastner, Kauffman, and Epperson, 2018) and Hans Primas (2017); along with process-based theories of required basic concepts, suitably updated for multiscale processes, emergence, and complex systems, especially as discussed by Campbell (2015), Seibt (2004), Siebers (2002), and Auxier and Herstein (2017). Several cross-cutting concepts are introduced along the way, including, among others, how our world is permeated by both information and signs.

The Gordian knot set of problems is laid out in chapter 3, and the *Logoi* framework is applied to suggest possible approaches to resolving these problems. Resolving the critically important Gordian Knots can only be accomplished through both humanistic scholarship (here, especially philosophy) and science, not science alone. As both Ludwig Wittgenstein and Alfred North Whitehead argued, "scientism" is specifically rejected.[23]

Building on this approach, I lay out tentative solutions in chapter 4 for the fundamental problems of causation, physical relations (aka "law"[24]), and emergence. Chapter 5 summarizes the intellectual history that ties together information and semiotics, the theory of signs, with process thought and speculative [systematic] naturalisms. It is important to note that the *Logoi* framework is not a logocentric metaphysics, which Jacques Derrida criticized, and which, Arran Gare points out, is "the quest for an origin or foundation in truth, reason, or the Logos . . . to find some fixed, permanent center, a transcendental signifier that will give meaning to all other signs" (Gare 2002, 42–43). Instead, my approach seeks to leverage the deconstructive critique of such modernism, opening space for a third way[25] that incorporates both fundamental logic and a semiotic and relational perspective. That is, my approach is neither modernism or simplistically post-modern, but rather seeks a coherent and integrative positive philosophy, such as that characterized by Friedrich Schelling, as argued by Gare, in his speculative naturalism (Gare 2002, 38). Gare also argues for the importance of applying such speculative naturalism in current efforts to address the environmental crisis. Finally, the *Logoi* framework incorporates elements of both Western and Eastern culture, both rational order and aesthetic order, both rational thinking and correlative thinking, both abstract relations and concrete particulars—all these imbedded in a most general science of order which, as noted by David Hall and Roger Ames with respect to the Chinese tradition of thought, can be characterized as the "art of contextualizing."[26] Arguably, there is a correlation as well between the above distinction of rational thinking and correlative thinking with the distinction of sequential and nonsequential modes of knowing (per Primas's discussion). These latter modes of knowing are based on complementarity in quantum physics which, in turn, reflects the distinction between two fundamental kinds of logic, Boolean and non-Boolean (Primas 2017), which are discussed in detail in chapter 2.

Chapter 6, which addresses the complex whole, both incorporates multiple ways of knowing and attempts to provide a philosophically grounded synthesis. My way of framing the complex whole is inspired, in part, by recent attempts to be both compatible with recent scientific results, yet skeptical of any scientific "theory of everything." The essential triadic logic that permeates the several fundamental notions is brought out as a centerpiece for chapter 7, which discusses a convergence of Peirce's triads and Whitehead's process, especially as outlined by Campbell (2015) and Auxier and Herstein (2017).

The final chapter provides reflections on the overall quest and focuses on the questions of ultimate context and meaning. I argue for the immense value of scholarly research in a wide variety of fields that could contribute to enhanced human self-awareness, other-awareness, and deeper understandings of reality.[27] This final chapter 8 connects new scientific results to that humanistic scholarship, which is yet again expanding the human context, historically, humanistically, and spiritually. These recent developments clearly indicate the need for updated worldviews[28] that can avoid the nihilism of mechanistic materialism and simplistic reductionisms, and that can open up space for new perspectives on human meaning and the spiritual dimension. Taken together, such research has the potential to overcome the tendency toward false dualities, false -isms,[29] made-up facts, scapegoating, racism, and the resulting strife and wars, all being largely preventable illnesses of the human condition. At a time of reduced support for the humanities, as a scientist I concur with Epstein's persuasive argument (Epstein 2012) about the singular importance of humanistic discourse in enabling the transformative work that is so critically needed.

NOTES

1. Powers of 10 are typically represented as an exponent of 10 so that 10^6 represents 10 multiplied by itself 6 times to yield one million. The number 10^{26} is an inconceivably large number for which we require abstract representation.

2. My most vivid spiritual experiences have been rare; in contrast, as documented by Kathleen Duffy, Pierre Teilhard de Chardin's spiritual experiences were frequent and well integrated into his life journey (Duffy 2014).

3. For the purpose of this work, in general, I am not distinguishing "existence" and "reality," broadly interpreted. Philosophical analyses of these terms is essential but varied; see Milton Munitz (1974).

4. Science is a highly diverse enterprise that, at its core, aspires to develop quantitative, context-independent models of natural systems. At the same time, there is a vast network of practices of science that incorporate context dependence, normative constraints of policy, resources and domains of reference that often transcend science issues *per se*; for example, see Stephen Norton and Frederick Suppe (2001).

5. Unless otherwise specified, "philosophy" in this work refers primarily to Western philosophy, even while recognizing that there are great schools of philosophical inquiry in East Asia, South Asia, and Persia, among others.

6. John Deely argues that for Jacob von Uexküll the *umwelt* is above all "a lattice and network of ontological relations between organism and environment, elevating

the latter to the level of the animal's awareness," and this *umwelt* always incorporates a biologically under-determined modeling system (Deely 2004, 29).

7. For further notes on the basic elements of science, including approximation, see the *Symmetry in Science* section in chapter 4.

8. The goal of identifying parameters that are context independent is essentially identical to the scientific goal of finding symmetries in nature. This is because context independence enables immunity to a possible change, which defines symmetry (see *Symmetry in Science* section in chapter 4).

9. *Logoi* is Greek for rational principle, ratio, proportion, or relation; *logos* is most often associated with problem-solving modes of action and language. My focus here on *logoi* (plural form of *logos*) is not intended to deny the importance of aesthetic and mythic domains, including art and poetry in their contribution to problem-solving modes of action and language. I intend *logoi* as a pointer to an ecological vision of the world, interrelated and multilevel, distinct from most theological uses of the term yet overlapping with how Maximus the Confessor applies an integral, ecological framing; see Radu Bordeianu (2009).

10. The term "Platonic forms" refers to patterns or structures of relations that are inferred to have some reality distinct from the actualizations of our given world; such were introduced by the Greek philosopher Plato in the 4th C. BCE.

11. Scientism refers to the belief that all meaningful propositions can be reduced to only scientific propositions. This is equivalent to the metaphysical claim that science's particular domain of discourse is all inclusive.

12. Philosophical approaches that deny the quest for some final, or "perfect" truth are sometimes denoted "speculative"; they are also fallibilistic, progressive and open-ended. However, to affirm their systematic intent, I will mostly use the term "systematic" versus "speculative"; see Alan White (2014).

13. Reduction of complex systems to more simple, basic parameter representations is central to the model making that characterizes all science; however, such methodological reduction does not support ontological claims of "reductionism," the claim that all things are, in some sense, "nothing but" aggregates of the reduced terms. As Mario Bunge states, such "metaphysical fundamentalism is dangerous because it leads to postulating the final simplicity of some form of experience or some kind of substance thereby barring any inquiry into their structure" (Bunge 1966, 85).

14. This affirmation is sustained as well by Daniel Athearn in his extensive defense of narrative causal explanation in physics (Athearn 1994).

15. The "scientific method" is sometimes described as focused on deductive or inductive methods; however, science is broader and includes abductive reasoning as a key component (see Brian Haig 2005). Indeed, actual scientific practice is highly varied, and the analysis of the "scientific method" itself is a subject for the philosophy of science, which varies from traditional affirmations of such method to the consideration of multiple layers of meaning indicating "that there is no distinctly scientific method" (James Blachowicz 2016, 1).

16. Peircean abduction, through an emphasis on coherence of explanation versus deduction, strives to infer explanatory hypotheses that can best explain currently observed conditions (see Paul Thagard and Cameron Shelley 1997); also Jaakko

Hintikka (2007). By comparison, induction is the inference of a generalized conclusion from particular instances.

17. Robert Rosen states that "an anticipatory system is one in which present change of state depends on future circumstances, rather than merely on the present or past . . . biology is replete with situations in which organisms can generate and maintain internal predictive models of themselves and their environments and utilize the predictions of these models about the future for [the] purpose of control in the present" (Robert Rosen 2012, v).

18. Metaphysics is that branch of philosophy which analyzes fundamental concepts, principles and prior assumptions of the greatest degree of generality, including a focus on such abstract concepts as causation, temporality, being and becoming. Metaphysics also evaluates alternative fundamental ways to view the world (worldview or *weltenschaung*) and rules to be followed in their formulation (see Jorge J. E. Gracia 1999).

19. My recognition of significant influences should not be interpreted as agreement between them; for example, Rescher rejects Griffin's approach, based on Whitehead, of treating actual occasions as temporal atoms.

20. Information is comprised of dynamic, symbolic elements, a key part of the symbolosphere, whose meaning is given by the processes that interpret it, a measure of distinctions that make a difference (Robert Logan 2014).

21. Semiotics concerns the theory and application of sign, broadly interpreted as more inclusive than language dependence. Chapter 5 on *Information and Semiotics* provides details on this important concept.

22. Michael Epperson first introduced Relational Reality and the Relational Realism interpretation of quantum physics in 2009 with a paper in the peer-reviewed journal *Process Studies* (Epperson 2009). For details, see *The Relational Reality Model* in chapter 2.

23. Details about problems and failures of scientism are provided by Joseph Margolis (2003); Murray Code (1997); Richard Williams and Daniel Robinson (2014).

24. In this work, "physical relations" will be often used in place of the common term "law" because the latter tends to be understood in simple dyadic, entailment form, and is thus inadequate for representing more general, triadic physical relations. Further, law carries problematic metaphysical baggage based on its origin in 18th C. deism and the laws of God—see chapter 4. If current usage were not so entrenched, I would leave law to lawyers. However, given present realities, we should inform readers of scientific materials that law (in its scientific usage) denotes highly probable correlations within constraints, and should not be taken to require entailment.

25. SUNY has published over twenty volumes in its Series in Constructive Postmodern Thought, overall consistent with Gare's call for a third way (e.g., David Ray Griffin et al., 1992).

26. In the essay "Issues and Methods of Analytic Philosophy" Yiu-Ming Fung questions any strong distinction between Chinese correlative thinking and Western rational modes of thinking, arguing that many elements of the latter are present in the Chinese philosophical tradition (Yiu-Ming Fung 2016). In the same volume, Roger

Ames attempts to demystify the distinction by pointing out that Peirce's abductive reasoning is "a more familiar form of correlative thinking" (Ames 2016, 40).

27. When discussing levels of reality, Basarab Nicolescu distinguishes the real, which is always hidden, from reality "that *resists* our experiences, representations, descriptions, images, and mathematical formulations" (Nicolescu 2014, 105). Here I simply use the term "reality" to refer to that which exists and resists, independently of ideas concerning it, without any hypothesis about ultimate hiddenness.

28. Worldviews are fundamental conceptual frameworks for human interaction, most often not articulated. They can range from core philosophical presuppositions to active models for world encounter. A Christian worldview and some alternatives have been summarized by James Sire (2014) and J. P. Moreland and William Lane Craig (2003). Mehdi Golshani has recently articulated why "Science Needs a Comprehensive World View" (Golshani 2020). My use of the term is independent of any particular religious or philosophical framework—everyone by definition has a worldview, including atheists and agnostics.

29. Standard -isms often depend on false dualities or partial framings of basic philosophical positions. In particular, the *Logoi* framework does not fit any of the standard "-isms" typically discussed as, for example, in *The Ism Book* by Peter Saint-Andre (2017).

Chapter 2

Relations—*Logoi*

In this chapter, I will introduce core elements of the *Logoi* framework, first using a phenomenological analysis of immediate experience, second laying out fundamental questions and complementary philosophical analyses, and third leveraging recent interpretive advances in contemporary science, especially quantum physics. For the latter, quantum physics is our most fundamental theory concerning the nature of matter and energy. Further, it is the most successful theory ever formulated, rigorously tested for almost a century. Unresolved issues are primarily matters of interpretation, which I will address in this and the next chapter.

FROM EXPERIENCE TO MULTILEVEL CONTEXT

The immediacy of my youthful, lakeside spiritual experience inspired in me a strong intuition of elemental succession in the universe. I felt this experience to be radically contingent, just one among a near infinity of possibilities, most of which excluded any account of my very being. Thus, I directly felt and affirmed possibility as part of reality[1] along with the actuality of my hands clutching the grass and soil of the hillside.[2] Simultaneously, I felt the radical finiteness and localness of my perspective on the world, my world-as-perceived—my *umwelt*. Yet that highly localized perspective was not merely self-contained; it felt clearly linked to a larger context. Over the years, through both scientific research and personal experience, I have come to affirm that such local-contextual framings have a basis in reality, reflected in any and all input-output-context relationships. Scientific description and approximations, and various tools of model making, frequently employ simple input-output pairings because that methodology is useful and effective.

However, as I noted above, real-world interactions, considered in their ontic fullness, always involve sequences of triads (input-output-context).

Applying a phenomenological analysis to my lakeside experience suggests the following fundamental notions: (1) process—succession,[3] (2) logic of both actuality and potentiality,[4] and (3) relation, including local-global relations,[5] all associated with the concept of process. Eva Brann, who studied the particular Greek usages of the term *logos*, as well as its particular Greek origins, argues in her work, *The Logos of Heraclitus*, that for her *logoi* implies both flux (process) and relations (Brann 2011). Tallis points out that "there are many translations of *Logos* . . . The register of its tentacular meanings would include ratio, proportion, principle, standard; reasoning power; hypothesis, grounds for belief or action . . . to gather together, to arrange, and to put in order . . . that which results in a world picture" (Tallis 2018, 32). My *Logoi* framework works with all of these meanings and in multiple ways, and can be characterized by a term that William Desmond has emphasized, *metaxu*,[6] the Greek word for "between."[7]

> Metaxological philosophy holds that to be is to be between. Nothing is defined purely through itself alone; all that is is in relation; this relatedness encompasses being in relation to other things, as well as self-relation. Metaxology refers us to a logos of the between. The between is hospitable to plural intermediations. (Desmond 2016, 423)

The elements of experience articulated by the *Logoi* framework are so fundamental that they may, as Griffin argues, represent cases of hard-core common sense (Griffin 2007), that is, concepts that are presupposed in practice. Does anyone ever have an experience—without a concurrent sense of succession?—without some sense of alternative possibilities?—without some awareness, however indirect, of a more encompassing global context for that immediate local experience?

ELEMENTS OF THE *LOGOI* FRAMEWORK

Succession can be simply thought of as "one darn thing after another." Consider then all events as asymmetric sequences of discrete actualizations ordered by a definite logic (two-valued, Boolean logic[8]). "That production is an asymmetric relation," as Fales states, "is something we experience. We do not merely experience forces as having location, magnitude, and direction. We experience them as acting upon something—in the case at hand, upon our bodies" (Fales 1990, 34). For the *Logoi* framework, the overall context for succession depends on *both* the above standard (Boolean) logic of actualizations (Latin *res extensae*) *and* a logic of potentialities (Latin *potentia*, plural—*potentiae*), which is multivalued, non-Boolean logic.[9] As Randall Auxier has stated, "The actual and possible together effectively form what [Josiah] Royce means by the 'real,' and the order we hypothesize for those relations is the universally mediating relation of time. The 'possible' is associated with the future and the 'actual' with the past, while the present moment is an indefinite duration that links what is actual to what is possible in overlapping . . . nested hierarchies of time-spans" (Auxier 2013, 59). Fundamental process incorporates such hierarchies of events through relentless input-output succession within context (constraints and *potentiae*), and such process is both local and contextual, a multilayered whole, the "local-global." Emergent temporality is built into such process and mediates the temporal modalities by providing basic ordering relations.

Potential Relations (potentiae)—Most importantly, the "real" is constituted by both the actual and the possible or, more fully expressed, potential relations (*potentiae*). This distinction has a long history for, as Michael Epperson points out, "Aristotle held that potential and actuality are two species of reality . . . that actualities give rise to *potentia*, which give rise to actualities" (Epperson 2016, 62). Ronny Desmet highlights the Whiteheadian idea, going back to the *Organization of Thought* (1917), that "all thought—common sense thought, scientific thought, and mathematical thought—is propositional, and always involves both concrete actuality and abstract potentiality, even though the share of the former component decreases, while the share of the latter component increases, as we shift from common sense to science to mathematics" (Desmet 2010a, 152). In his work *Logic in Reality*, Joseph Brenner shows in multiple ways how the real is both the actual and the possible (Brenner 2008). To appreciate the reality of potential (yet not actualized) relations, consider how the many paths that you did not follow are important for who you are now; consider the multiple scenarios (some that you consciously filter out; many that you don't) under which you would have hit an oncoming car with just a small, careless change of steering. Such alternative scenarios indicate how paths not taken can make a "real" difference. Paths not taken are effectively infinite; actualized paths are finite, unique, and sequential.

The concept of relations, whether actual or potential, incorporates part/whole, internal/external, relations of relations, and algebras of relations, this last concept being addressed in contemporary mathematics through category theory (for details, see five sections below beginning with *The Relational Reality Model*, and the section on *A Theory of Relations for Modeling and Process—Category Theory* in chapter 6). Fundamental relations are either triadic (semiotics) or dipolar (part/whole—mereology). As Duane Voskuil states, "Any whole/part relation is necessarily dipolar—one side of a dipolar contrast is the inclusive pole characterizing the whole; the other side is the included pole, and characterizes the parts in a whole" (Voskuil 2016, vxiii). Further, in the real world (versus simple human abstraction), any dyad is always imbedded in some context (input-output-context), thus necessarily contained within a triadic logic. Such a triadic logic of relations was first explicitly formulated by John Poinsot in 1632, as shown by Mauricio Beuchot and John Deely (Beuchot and Deely 1995; Deely 2001) and later by Charles Sanders Peirce, as surveyed by Thomas Lloyd Short (2007, 326). These developments, in turn, inspired major, international scholarly efforts in semiotics (the theory of signs) and, more recently, biosemiotics (see chapter 5). The inevitability of context for finite knowledge is expressed by Whitehead, in his essay "Mathematics and the Good" as follows, "The notion of the complete self-sufficiency of any item of finite knowledge is the fundamental error of dogmatism. Every such item derives its truth, and its very meaning, from its unanalyzed relevance to the background which is the unbounded Universe" (Whitehead 1948, 78). As well, as part of a critique of analytic epistemologists, the logician Bernard Bosanquet stated already in 1920 that "every inference involves a judgment based on the whole of reality, though referring only to a partial system which need not even be actual" (Bosanquet 1920, 4).

The three fundamental bridging notions above (process, logic, and relations) exemplify these desiderata in multiple ways, as will be shown in what follows. Further, the three fundamental ways of awareness and knowing (numbers, context, and spirit) help to clarify both applicability and adequacy, and the logic and coherence of the *Logoi* framework. This foundational epistemology is expressed in the *Ways of Knowing* section of chapter 1 above, namely the ways of context-independence (numbers, *à la* science), context-emphasis (context/semiotics, *à la* arts and humanities), and ultimate context (spirit, *à la* spiritual "dimension"), and these arguably correlate with the three fundamental orders of ontology—the order of actualizations, the order of *potentiae*,[10] and the order of ultimacies.[11] Finally, this triad correlates with James Bradley's three basic questions concerning the nature of difference (dyadic input-output—numbers/quantification), order (triadic order—context/semiotics—*qualia*), and origin (spiritual "dimension"—ultimacies) (Bradley 2009, 169).

The most basic definition of *semiotics* is that it is the theory of signs. To be more precise, as Daniel Chandler explains the concept, "Semiotics involves the study not only of what we refer to as 'signs' in everyday speech, but of anything which 'stands for' something else" and such study informs both "how meanings are made and how reality is represented" (Chandler 2002, 2). By applying a broad interpretation of semiosis and an evolutionary perspective, Marcello Barbieri emphasizes the importance of three thresholds, that is three developmental stages, associated with the evolution of semiosis in life forms:

(1) "the origin of organic semiosis (the semiotic threshold),
(2) the origin of interpretive semiosis (the hermeneutic threshold), and
(3) the origin of linguistic semiosis (the cultural threshold)" (Barbieri 2008, 596).

In addition, Barbieri attempts a deep historical account of these basic thresholds:

> The origin of organic semiosis and the origin of interpretation were separated by three billion years of cellular evolution, because interpretation is dependent on internal models of the world, and probably evolved only in animals. The origin of language came after another five hundred million years . . . The history of semiosis, in conclusion, was a process that started with context-free codes and produced codes that were more and more complex. (Barbieri 2009, 239)

Chapter 4 provides further discussion on thresholds and issues of multiscale emergence, illustrated here above with Barbieri's insight into code complexification.

Summarizing the above, I hypothesize that all reality, taken inclusively, includes both actuality and *potentiae*, which enables all emergent phenomena, including the multiscale emergence pointed to above. Affirmation of the reality of both *potentiae* as well as actualized "dynamic particulars"[12] is correlated with the reality of fundamental relations; and these foundational relations in turn enable the emergence of physical law out of the realm of *potentiae* (via general constraints on *potentiae*, which are then revealed by minimization principles like the principle of least action—see below; also chapter 4).

My approach specifically denies nominalism, which is the theory that only individuals and no abstract entities exist (whether essences, classes, propositions, or even *potentiae*).[13] Indeed, nominalism fails both in terms of mathematical practice, as noted by David Corfield (2010) and fails in terms of certain speculative physics claims, such as multiple universes, in which actualism[14] is presupposed and relational possibilities lack any grounding (Auxier and Herstein 2017, 208). Further details about why nominalism fails are provided in chapter 4. In contrast, the *Logoi* framework, along with contemporary field theory,[15] and alternatives and constraints enabled by *potentiae*, bypasses the numerous problems generated by nominalism.

Fundamental process arises from never-ending successions of events, as both Jorge Nobo (2004) and Leemon McHenry (2015) have argued, and each event is constituted by a combination of immediate physical inputs, physical relationships, and *potentiae* for their realization—all features foundational to contemporary field theory in physics.[16] Temporality and spatiality are coextensive with such process, and the asymmetry of time emerges from the inevitable successiveness of such process. Arguments for the bidirectionality of time are based on models, effectively of pre-space trajectories in *potentiae*, not directly on measured physical parameters.[17] Symmetry applies to pre-space *potentiae* and trajectories but the measurement process and successive actualizations break such symmetry.

Alternative *potentiae*, framed in terms of alternative trajectories in pre-space, which can be thought of as "pre-space paths," can be modeled as sums of action parameters. Optimizing such sums (either to obtain a minimum or a maximum, depending on the representation used) enables the derivation of most physical relationships (laws of physics)[18] (for details, see *"Law"—From Entailment to Constrained Processual Histories* section in chapter 4). I am here speculatively expanding on the constraint interpretation for emergence, which James Blachowicz proposed to encompass the emergence of all physical relations (Blachowicz 2012, 205).

Process/logic/relations are the most fundamental notions; physical relations, although basic (for science), are derivative relative to this most fundamental (philosophic) level. Nevertheless, very high levels of predictability can arise from such probabilistic law with constraints (boundary conditions, initial conditions, context), but they are not entailments (viz., involved by necessity) as in deductivist accounts.[19] The ultimate basis of such physical relations, within multiple levels of constraint on *potentiae*, may be revealed when further imbedded in constraints of metalogic. For example, recent research in fundamental logic by Nick Rossiter and Michael Heather (2005, 2018) indicates that the "arrow" in category theory[20] is a promising key concept for an ultimate logic. In turn, this result is compatible with both fundamental triadicity and the above discussion of fundamental notions focused on process, logic, and relations, as well as inevitable context.

Summarizing once again, this time in terms of logic, one can conclude from the fundamental theory of relations (category theory), and semiotics, that triadic relations (e.g., input-output-context) are most fundamental and that dyadic relations (e.g., input-output only) are derivative even though they often provide useful abstractions and approximations. "Symmetry is immunity to a possible change," as Joe Rosen stated (1995, 2), and many dyadic relations can be represented in a symmetric way. Yet adding a third term to create a triad will most often create an asymmetry. This important result arises from fundamental logic as shown by logician George Shields.

The *most* definitive of functions, the only functions capable of defining all others in singular fashion, are the Sheffer functions, which possess a triadic asymmetry that yet *includes* dyadic symmetry . . . symmetry *within* an all-embracing asymmetry. (Shields 2003, 20)

This result is supported as well by Rosen, a leading expert on symmetry theory in physics. Reflecting on Hartshorne's identification of an ultimate pattern of "symmetry within an all-embracing asymmetry," Rosen states that "asymmetry is a necessary condition for symmetry. For every symmetry there is an asymmetry tucked away somewhere in the world" (Rosen 2004, 134). Further details are provided in the *Symmetry in Science* section of chapter 4.

As part of the *Logoi* framework, I hypothesize that these results point to the conclusion that dyadic relations do not, in fact, ever exist in the real world (versus the world of abstract modeling) because of the inevitable involvement of context; thus, the triad input-output-context is completely general.[21] Importantly, this result, as well as other elements of the *Logoi* framework, effectively denies key metaphysical claims of scientism,[22] which Don Ross, James Ladyman, and David Spurrett (2007) argue for in their work *In Defense of Scientism* as part of a naturalistic metaphysics. However, they presuppose actualism and their discussions of the basic physics fail to include reference to the Boolean/non-Boolean logic distinction, which is central to my analysis and, arguably, central to quantum physics itself. Further, they call "the synthesized empiricist and materialist—and resolutely secularist—stances the scientistic stance" (ibid. 64). They argue that living out this stance "requires, most importantly of all, paying close attention to the actual progress of science" (ibid. 65). Yet, ironically, this "scientistic" practice should cause them, in light of the fact that the domain of the real encompasses both the actual and *potentiae* (given the latest developments of quantum physics), to re-think such materialist and scientistic commitments!

Potentiae, or potential relations, characterize all domains of process. My overall argument for the *Logoi* framework correlates with three roles for *potentiae*:

1. *potentiae* or potential relations, along with actuality, is an essential component of the "real"; this hypothesis derives from both human experience and philosophical analysis, with their multiple forms of creative emergence, and from recent results of quantum physics;
2. *anticipatory logic*, associated with such *potentiae*, enables important new understandings in the analysis of causation, physical relations, biological anticipatory systems, and human experience (see *Complex Systems* section of chapter 4);
3. *correlations of potentiae* can enable the coherence of physical relations as observed at astronomical scales (the "principle of universality"[23]) (see chapter 4); among human systems, such coordination could even help us to understand evidence for archetypal phenomena (see Harald Atmanspacher

and Christopher Fuchs, 2014) and certain psychic phenomena (see Griffin, 1997) including anomalous cognition (see chapter 8).

The *Logoi* framework incorporates both fundamental principles of relation and concepts relating both the contingent, as focused on naturalistically by William Wimsatt (2007) and more theologically by Hartshorne (Viney and Shields 2020) and Roland Faber (2018), as well as the non-contingent dimensions of being and becoming, which is Lorenz Puntel's focus (2008). The contingent dimension includes both the entirety of Boolean logical actualizations and non-Boolean *potentiae*. Yet, as we will see in chapter 8, it is impossible for everything to be simply contingent. Augmenting such argument, Whitehead's ontological principle affirms that any reality that accords to an abstraction must depend on actual entities upon which it is composed or grounded. By this principle, only actual things can act; thus, *potentiae*, although demonstrably real, can only act via some embodiment in one or more actual things. From this we infer that there must be some ground for *potentiae*; concurrently this provides a basis for both logical truths, mathematical forms and ethical norms, potentially solving fine-tuning problems as well as both the Platonic and the Benacerraf problems[24]—see Griffin (2007, 56) (also the *Systematic Philosophy and Ultimacies* section of chapter 8).

The importance of metaphysical possibility is also emphasized by Nicholas Rescher as follows:

> To account for the being of contingent existence at large, one has to impose the burden of explanation on something that is itself entirely outside the realm of contingent existence and of existential fact. But where can one possibly look for explanatory resources if the realm of actuality, of "what there is," is not available? The answer is clear: we must look to the realm of possibility, of what *can possibly be*. For if reality is to have a basis, then *possibility* is the only available prospect . . . What is thus called for here is a principle of explanation that can effect a transit from possibility to actuality. (Rescher 2017, 15–16)

The *Logoi* framework enables this transit from possibility to actuality in multiple ways, via our analyses of time and causation, and quantum physics, among others. Indeed, such transitions are reflected as well in our fundamental tools for analysis. As Ronny Desmet points out, Whitehead "conceived both algebra and logic as symbolic tools to support the mathematician's essential activities of recognizing, entertaining, and applying relational patterns; and that both led Whitehead to disentangle pure and applied mathematics, and to illuminate that the essential pure-applied interplay of mathematics and physics is a high-level expression of the potential-actual dialectics of human thought" (Desmet 2010b, 225). As the fundamental tool for the analysis of pattern, mathematics works basically with potential relations (*potentiae*) in combination with supporting hypotheses about modeling the world and correlating measurements.

LEVERAGING INTERPRETIVE ADVANCES
IN CONTEMPORARY SCIENCE

As noted above, the *Logoi* framework is leveraging a combination of scholarly advances that includes, among others, progress in understandings of quantum physics, logic, philosophy, and semiotics. Such progress has clarified the concepts of physical relations, functions, temporality, causal orders, and logics, including the distinction of the logic of actualization and the logic of *potentiae* in terms of the Boolean/non-Boolean logic distinction. Advances have been made as well in understanding local-global relations and multilevel relations of input-output-context (see section *Causal Orders, Form and Fact, Potentiae and the Actual* later in this chapter).Up through the nineteenth century, it was plausible to take the sequence of events as just that,

> a simple sequence, and to map such onto rulers or the number line, thus, effectively spatializing time and presuming simple entailment. The multiple problems with spatializing time have been systematically raised by Milič Čapek (1991) and more recently surveyed by Tallis (2017). Further, with the advent of James Clerk Maxwell's field theory, and modern physics based on such field theory (indeed, the core of modern physics), the interpretation of both the concept of mathematical function (for physics) and thus the understanding of sequences in nature (and of time) have required a much richer conception that involves process and relations at multiple levels, as John Jungerman (2000), Leemon McHenry (2015), and others have argued. As Tim Maudlin states, "Contrary to common belief, relativity does not *spatialize time*, it rather *temporalizes space*" (Maudlin 2016).

The mathematical function is a concept central to modern physics, and such is notably exemplified in Whitehead's work as a mathematical physicist, initially in his 1884 thesis at Cambridge University on Maxwell's new field theory, and continuing through his *Principles of Relativity* (Whitehead, 1922). Whitehead recognized in his work three key features of relation in general, namely, activity (~*potentiae*), differentiation (~actualization), and ordination (~law-like relation). Further, physical relations can arise from optimizations in *potentiae* "space," as with the principle of least action[25] (see discussion on physical "law" in chapter 4.) In addition, these three key features map as well to the Peircean triunity (firstness, secondness, thirdness).[26] Thus, the heart of modern physics, which includes the mathematical concept of function, and modern field theory, builds into itself a framework of relation that is highly flexible regarding the nature of the variables deployed. Indeed, Bradley's generalized functional analysis enables a "universal account of instantiation in terms of three, irreducible or subsistent, elements, which are necessarily nonconceptual in nature because they are the irreducible elements of activity: namely, infinite mapping activity, free difference or singularity, and free synthesis or individuality" (Auxier and Herstein 2017, 79). Using the notion of an iterative map,[27] Bradley explains this framework of relation in more detail as follows:

> The principle of iterative mapping activity can thus be regarded as a ontological generalization and constructivist reinterpretation of the Plato-Frege theory of numbers as serial relations or connectives in series. Its general significance can be stated this way: subject and object, as well as subject and predicate, are not here fixed ontological opposites. They are not fundamentally different in nature or kind. Rather, they are the basic states or sequential relations of finite instances of iterative mapping. For in the infinitely iterative, threefold series of mapping, a finite instance switches roles from being a successor mapping, or synthetic subject, to being the predecessor, object, or basis, and thus the predicate, of those mappings which are its successors and for which it has the role of a genetic or environmental domain or inheritance. (Bradley 2003a, 82)

Bradley's treatment of iterative mapping activity is analogous to how I, as "subject," presently experience objects in my environment in addition to the "object" of my immediate past self. A moment later, that "subject" switches roles and becomes the immediate past self (now as "object") of my immediate successor self as "subject." We will see later in this chapter, in *The Relational Reality Model*, how this process of succession is embodied in fundamental quantum process and includes all three elements of Bradley's generalized functional analysis (mapping activity, difference, and synthesis).

In addition to the Relational Reality model, discussed immediately below, this ontological generalization of the function as a mapping activity is another component of the *Logoi* framework, which is now seen as inclusive of both quantum process and fundamental mapping activity, augmented as well with both the modeling schema and anticipatory functionality of complex systems (see *Complex Systems* in chapter 4; also Robert Rosen, 2012).

PROBLEMS OF REDUCTION AND SCALE

The methodology of science is basically that of careful observation, experimentation, and model making, and the goal of the latter is to identify effective quantitative representations of physical relationships; for example, mappings of variables, functions, and equations. Building on the proper and important reductive methodology of science, many interpreters mistakenly extend such methodological or epistemological reduction to a problematic ontological reduction,[28] either in substance or process, the former exhibited by those who assume reductive materialism and the latter by some expositors of process philosophy. Alternatively, instead of presuming that Whitehead's term "actual entity" or, equivalently, Hartshorne's term "dynamic particular," is uniquely micro-scale, Auxier and Herstein argue that this concept is best interpreted as a metaphysical "quantum of explanation" whose exemplars, even if mostly micro-scale, can in principle be of any scale (Auxier and Herstein 2017). A similar conclusion is also worked out by F. Bradford Wallack (1980), Siebers (2002), and Campbell (2015). Micro-scale reductive explanations, whether in science or metaphysics, provide simplicity and apparent explanatory power, but most often at the expense of inclusiveness or contextual factors. As Harald Atmanspacher has pointed out, multilevel context-driven explanatory frameworks sacrifice simplicity, but then can achieve greater inclusiveness and coherence (Atmanspacher 2007). Another benefit of such explanatory frameworks is that they enable critical rapprochement between the discourse of science and the discourse of everyday life, between the physicists' account of a chair and the chair as normally perceived. As Nicholas Rescher describes it, "The latter is solid and filled with material. The former is largely empty space and is replete with electromagnetic phenomena" (Rescher 2017, 35).

When treating the question of individuation,[29] Didier Debaise agrees with Deleuze that Whitehead's *Process and Reality* represents a philosophy of events, as developed in detail by Leemon McHenry in *The Event Universe* (2015), but Debaise then goes on to ask *"where to situate events?"* (Debaise 2017, 54) [author's italics] Debaise interprets Whitehead as not viewing actual entities as events, which instead are the more accessible entities that Whitehead calls "societies." Debaise argues that we should not confuse

actual entities with societies, two things that *Process and Reality* basically opposes to one another. The former are essentially "abstract," corresponding to nothing in experience; their level is "microscopic." The latter are "concrete events," events we experience in perception, in our sensations, our desires and so on. They comprise a "macroscopic" plane. The philosophy of individuation always takes place on a "microscopic" scale, a scale that can in no way be an object of our experience, either in the form of an empirical or an intentional object. (Debaise 2017, 55)

From a broader scientific standpoint, I would say that only some entities of very roughly middle dimension are directly available to human sensation for empirical access. All else requires the augmentation of special tools (microscopes, telescopes, etc.). I suggest at least four levels: microscopic, mesoscopic, macroscopic, and astronomical. Both microscopic and astronomical levels are not directly accessible (or, at most, barely accessible) and require substantial augmentation by special tools for empirical access. Thus, both are, in Debaise's treatment, "essentially abstract." *Mesoscopic* could then refer to objects of very small to mid-range scale that are directly accessible, and *macroscopic* could denote objects of mid-range to planetary scale that are directly accessible to human perception. Except for elemental, quantum events, these directly accessible systems are all societies in Whitehead's terminology. The philosophical issues of individuation and relations can be applied at multiple scales as proposed by Auxier and Herstein; however, fundamental quantum events have a key role in grounding societies at whatever scale, thus providing some support for Debaise's argument. Nevertheless, real complex systems at multiple scales tend to undermine any simplistic ontology, which suggests that the best strategy for metaphysical work is to avoid dependence on any particular scale, which also accords with the importance of scale-free processes in many physical systems (e.g., space plasmas). Further, as questioned by Geoffrey Chew (2004), we may ask about what is the proper scale associated with fundamental quantum process—is it at nuclear scale or at Planck scale ($\sim 10^{18}$ times smaller)? A deep philosophical analysis should not depend on the answer to such complex and unresolved scientific questions.

THE RELATIONAL REALITY MODEL

Since the beginnings of quantum physics a century ago, a central problem has been how to understand the prominent feature of indeterminacy within that theory. A major approach has been to adopt Niels Bohr's Copenhagen Interpretation[30] within which indeterminacy effects are mostly assigned to epistemic limitations (i.e., limitations of knowledge) and questions about more fundamental "reality" are set aside. By mid-century a seemingly viable model for explaining indeterminacy effects in terms of underlying (not directly accessible) "hidden variables" was proposed by David Bohm.[31] Following that, for the latter half of the century, interpretations of quantum physics were a major part of the growing field of philosophy of physics and, at the same time, many thinkers were seeking viable "realist" interpretations. This proliferation of realist quantum physics interpretations has continued unabated. One pattern that emerges in many of these interpretations (whether affirming indeterminism or not) is that the domain of the "real" is presumed to be entirely the "actual"—actual measurement outputs, quantum states and variables (hidden or not), correlations of such, and so on. In many cases, a common underlying metaphysical claim (often unstated) is that of determinism with its corollary assumption that the "real" is fully reducible to determinate actualities and unique trajectories (in the relevant phase spaces). In response to this claim, I ask why should we consider the "real" as needing to be so narrowly constructed?

Real consequences derive from a much broader set of real relations as argued above in *Elements of the Logoi Framework*. In particular, consider the many alternative choices that you did not make within the past few days, consider the innumerable alternative ways whereby you could have been hit by a passing car, or consider the alternative scenarios that you are constantly processing when driving, fully aware that just a small, careless change of steering (by you or the driver of an oncoming car) could lead to an accident or your own untimely death. Such alternative scenarios are major inputs to our actual choices and help us to drive safely. Such safe driver methods show how paths not taken can make a real difference. Paths not taken are effectively infinite; actualized paths are finite, unique and sequential. For those who insist that the real is reducible to nothing but the actual and introduce some actual "hidden variables" to satisfy the requirements of quantum measurements, how can we properly test such hidden variables that are entirely excluded from any direct measurement—are manipulations of theory alone sufficient to overcome these limitations? Such problems continue to haunt both physicists and philosophers.

The essence of my book and the *Logoi* framework is to challenge such actualist presuppositions and consider what consequences and solutions follow from that intellectual shift. I will now argue against the presupposition associated with the pattern noted above: namely the presupposition that the "real" is nothing but the "actual," or actualism.[32] Recent convergence in research (theory and experiment) in quantum measurement has yielded progress in both the standard Copenhagen interpretation and the decoherence interpretation.[33] Combining these results with new developments in mathematics (especially category theory, an algebra of relations), and in philosophical analysis enables an interpretive framework for quantum physics that provides viable interpretations for all known quantum experiments and does so without introducing new physics beyond basic, highly tested quantum physics.

This Relational Reality approach,[34] pioneered by Epperson (2009), and Epperson and Elias Zafiris (2013), a central component of the *Logoi* framework, in addition to independent research by Ruth Kastner (2013) and along with independent work by Hans Primas (2017), shows the need to make the distinction, as discussed above, within the conception of full ontological reality of *both* actualizations *and potentiae* (Kastner, Kauffman, and Epperson,

2018). Actualizations have the essential characteristics of givenness and place; *potentiae* provide a needed basis for physical relationships through the application of optimization principles in possibility "spaces" (*potentiae*) (e.g., to minimize an action variable in physics when applying the principle of least action;[35] for details, see *"Law"—From Entailment to Constrained Processual Histories* section in chapter 4). In previous work, these researchers independently developed quantum interpretations that emphasized the importance of this distinction and, in that sense, their approaches are complementary. The Relational Reality model, in particular, requires this distinction between the logic of actualizations (standard Aristotelian or Boolean logic) and a non-Boolean logic for *potentiae*; real-world applications of these logics necessarily require as well (at least implicitly) three components (overall a triadic logic), covering input-output-context.

In summary, the Relational Reality approach accommodates the highly successful Copenhagen interpretation as applicable to the logic of actualizations, with epistemological emphasis, and adds a category-theory-enhanced realist treatment, building on the decoherence interpretation, capable of handling the logic of *potentiae* as well. In this way, we can avoid the presupposition of actualism, which has arguably been a major impediment to understanding the basis for indeterminacy in quantum physics.

The past century's flirtation with actualism is now being superseded by several new results in both philosophy and quantum physics. In addition to potentiality, as pointed out by Nathan Houser and Christian Kloesel, Peirce also extensively treated issues of context-bound reasoning and abduction, all relevant to these new developments (Houser and Kloesel, 1992). For quantum physics, as Epperson and colleagues state, "local Boolean measurement contextuality is not merely an epistemic coordination, but rather an ontologically significant, 'logical conditioning' of *potential* outcome states such that they can evolve, through coherent integration, into *probable* outcome states—a conditioning that *always* occurs in quantum mechanics" (Epperson et al. 2018). Several scholars have analogously argued for the physical reality of *potentia*. Early work on triadic logic, or the "included third," as Basarab Nicolescu documents, was carried out by Stéphane Lupasco (1900–1988), a philosopher of scientific formation (Nicolescu, 2015). Jeffrey Bub references various works in quantum logic from the late twentieth century that address the question of non-Boolean logics (Bub 1997). Extending early work by Yuri Orlov on the logical origins of quantum mechanics (Orlov 1994) and working with Clifford algebra, Elio Conte argues for a triadic logic basis for quantum physics, which he interprets as involving self-referential processes that enable "a transition from potentiality to actualization" (Conte 2011, 115). As stated by Epperson and colleagues, "Unlike the classical, *bipolar dualism* of physical objects and conceptual objects (e.g., Cartesian matter and mind), which are mutually exclusive categories of reality, actuality and potentiality are understood as a *dipolar duality* in quantum mechanics: they are mutually implicative categories of reality in that neither can be defined in abstraction from the other" (Epperson et al. 2018). This is because, ontologically, fundamental quantum process comprises both the logic of actualization (Boolean logic) and the logic of *potentiae* (non-Boolean logic), and separating these components always involves some form of abstraction, model making, or approximation, however precise may be the approximation (e.g., taking precise measurements, inevitably involving approximation, of quantum states at two distinct times for a quantum physics application).

CAUSAL ORDERS, FORM AND FACT, *POTENTIAE* AND THE ACTUAL

Constraints on the causal order will be further discussed in chapter 4. However, I here focus on principal concepts of the Relational Reality model, and recommend Epperson and Zafiris's pioneering work for its detailed exposition (Epperson and Zafiris 2013) augmented by concise summaries by each author, published later in an edited volume (Epperson 2016; Zafiris 2016). Essential for quantum physics are both the causal order, viz., the physical causal order, sometimes termed "efficient" cause, and the logical order, an order that is logically conditioned.[36] Quoting Epperson and Zafiris:

> The correlation of the asymmetrical relationship depicted by "cause-effect" statements with the asymmetrical relationship depicted by "if-then" statements has been an infamous philosophical problem since the time of Plato because while it is easily demonstrated, it cannot be proven by derivation or deduction from some more fundamental principle. Even classical mechanics provided philosophers of the early modern period with no readily discernible indication of why the physical order of causal relation correlated with the conceptual order of logical implication. As Hume famously argued, one cannot ever "directly observe" causal connection, any more than one can directly observe logical implication; rather, we infer causal connection only after directly observing system states in conjunctive relation—e.g., before and after a measurement interaction. (Epperson and Zafiris 2013, 58–59)

The mutual implication of the causal and logical orders discussed here interrelates the logical orders of actualizations and *potentiae* and further emphasizes the limitations of direct observation. For any scientific work, from successive measurements and theory, we "infer causal connections" that we inevitably cannot "directly observe." Decades of such inference, model making, theoretical work, and testing has led to the highly successful quantum physics that we now inherit and struggle to properly interpret. The Relational Reality model, building on the unparalleled practical success of quantum physics, utilizes this distinction of the causal order and logical order, including the associated logics of actualization (Boolean) and *potentiae* (non-Boolean), to provide a highly productive and intuitive interpretation.

Within this approach, any and all particular measurement outcomes, or data, may be direct observations of particular actualizations that we can represent in Boolean propositions. From such data, we can reasonably infer causal connections, logical implications, superposition, or entanglement effects that cannot be directly observed. Such inductive or abductive inference is a standard part of the scientific process. Epperson and Zafiris continue:

> Quantum mechanics . . . provides a strong indication that the asymmetry of the order of causal relation presupposes the asymmetry of the order of logical implication, yet cannot in any way be reduced to the latter; for its fundamentally indeterministic nature, both at the level of theory and empirical practice, utterly precludes any such sheer assimilation of contingency to necessity—e.g., in the spirit of Spinoza or Leibniz. Rather, quantum causality's necessary presupposition of the logical order entails simply that the causal and logical orders are properly understood as mutually implicative at the level of fundamental physics. Again, it is an essential presupposition of quantum mechanics that universally, every local measurement context is structurally Boolean—that is, every local context can be represented mathematically as a Boolean subalgebra, or alternatively as an equivalence class of Boolean subalgebras. It is by this presupposition that all local contexts are globally relatable coherently and consistently (as is presupposed by every physical theory whose laws are presumed to hold universally). (Epperson and Zafiris 2013, 59)

Here, Epperson and Zafiris emphasize the importance of distinguishing the orders of causal relation and the order of logical implication, in turn the Boolean order of contingent actualizations versus the non-Boolean order of *potentiae* and local to global coordination, a "logical causality." Here we witness local-global linkages (see below) as well as why the claim that any "assimilation of contingency to necessity" (as presumed in claims of absolute determinism) is fundamentally in error, both because of the indeterministic features of quantum physics, based on both theory and experiment, and because of the critical distinction of the causal and logical orders.

As an example of the Relational Reality model, and in the spirit of Whitehead's analysis of an actual entity but here updated to accommodate new developments in quantum physics, I here outline the workings of fundamental quantum process without reference to any particular scale. Consider then the process associated with an actual entity or "dynamic particular" (DP) (using Hartshorne's expression). First, there are the several inputs of the causal order: input particulars (i.e., past DPs, especially the immediate "past self" DP and input fields (various quantum fields, electromagnetic fields, etc.)), these being the focus of most mainstream physics accounts. Second, there are the constraints and considerations affecting both the causal order and the logical order (boundary conditions, initial conditions, structures of Boolean context), being a focus of George Ellis's book on *How Can Physics Underlie the Mind?* (Ellis 2016). Third, there are real effects of *potentiae* and non-Boolean context, which are emphasized in Epperson and Zafiris's monograph, that include all three of these modes affecting fundamental process. In the Relational Reality model, successions of DPs are sequences of fundamental process input-output functional pairings, always within an input-output-context triad. The output of one individuated, Boolean actualized DP is necessarily part of the input to the successive next DP (but never the sole input due to the triadic fundamental structure of such process). Specific space-time or DP outputs are part of actualized, Boolean characterizations of such process, but as such never enable a full account however much they may represent useful ways to portray dynamical system trajectories, quantum field interactions, and output measurables. Inevitably, the logical order and associated *potentiae* have real effect on DPs. Further, complexes of DPs may themselves individuate in multiple ways and multiple levels, and the innumerable possibilities for such complex relations enable complex systems emergence as described by complex systems theory (see *Complex Systems* in chapter 4). The *form* of things is constituted by constraints of context, *potentiae* and the logical order; *facts* arise from individuated, actualized dynamic particulars. Both form and facts are essential; any nominalistic facts-only account is necessarily incomplete (see *On the Failure of Actualism and Nominalism* in chapter 4). As another example of the Relational Reality model, and in application to describing electrons, Epperson and Zafiris state that,

> the electron, in other words, is always observed as actualized, in either one state or another, in satisfaction of PNC [Principle of Non-Contradiction], and never *observed as potentialized*—i.e., as a superposition of potential states in violation of PNC. In this way, superpositions are properly understood as relations of successive actual states, initial and final, via an appropriate measurement interaction.
>
> In quantum mechanics, this relation is fundamentally describable as an evolution of: [1] a pure state of *potential* outcome states (these are not mutually exclusive and can violate PNC), to [2] a mixed state of *probable* outcome states that are [a] mutually exclusive (satisfying PNC, i.e., "*at most* one outcome state will be actual upon measurement") and [b] exhaustive, in that the probability valuations,

by definition, must sum to unity (satisfying PEM, i.e., "*at least* one outcome state will be actual upon measurement"). (Epperson and Zafiris 2013, 37)

Immediately following this articulation of fundamental quantum process as applied to successive electron states, Epperson and Zafiris highlight how some theorists, committed to actualism, look for explicit, actualized, deterministic sequences from input to output and, not finding such, proclaim an essential incompleteness in quantum physics. Instead, Epperson and Zafiris highlight what is presupposed in quantum evolution.

> Though this logically conditioned evolution of potential to probable outcome states is a fundamental feature of quantum mechanics (Von Neumann formalized the mathematics of this evolution as his "Process 1"), it is important to emphasize that quantum theory *presupposes* this evolution. The theory does not, in other words, entail any physical dynamical mechanism that "generates" the evolution of potentiality to probability. Likewise, the theory also presupposes the evolution of probable outcome states to unique actual outcome state, in satisfaction of PEM [Principle of Excluded Middle]. These are both aspects of the "problem of state reduction" in quantum mechanics, which many theorists have cited as evidence of the incompleteness of quantum theory—that it presupposes [1] the existence of the actualities it measures, and [2] that its measurements will satisfy PNC and PEM…neither of these presuppositions can be reasonably assessed as a theoretical deficiency, since both are necessarily presupposed by the scientific method itself—the method by which quantum theory was initially conceived and validated, and by which it continues to be developed and implemented. (Epperson and Zafiris 2013, 37–38)

This analysis shows that the actual/*potentiae* distinction, and associated causal/logical order distinction, combined with careful attention to presuppositions, avoids imposing a unitary physical mechanism that would exacerbate the quantum measurement problem. It is an entirely reasonable logical requirement that the electron is observed or actualized in one state or another and never "observed as potentialized." Further, we can reasonably envision the evolution as being from a wide range of potential outcomes states, followed by a more limited set of probable outcome states, and finally to a specific, actualized outcome state. Each of these steps exhibits distinct logical constraints (PNC, PEM) that are practically presupposed in the analysis, and being presupposed, the associated analysis should not be considered as deficient for its stated purpose.

As a key part of the actualization process for any DP is the "logically conditioned evolution" of *potentiae* discussed in the quote above. Such logically conditioned evolution, including the effects of initial and boundary conditions, is often neglected in standard causal accounts. Mereology is the study of whole-part relations and such study is focused on the relations of Boolean actualizations. In contrast, by using concepts of topology, the more general theory of relations, including spatial relations,[37] it is now possible to reconceive fundamental relations in quantum physics. Utilizing the new field of mathematical category theory, an algebra of relations that applies topological principles to various fields, Epperson and Zafiris's monograph provides important advances with their application of category theory to quantum physics, thus enabling a clear path beyond standard mereology along with clarifying many otherwise puzzling aspects of quantum physics. As part of this application, they discuss Boolean subalgebras (i.e., algebras limited to a specific, local Boolean context) and how the overlapping of such Boolean subalgebras enables a proper global description that includes both Boolean and non-Boolean features.

First, in arguing for the importance of topology in addressing local and global relations, Epperson and Zafiris highlight the need to understand asymmetric internal relations, and relations of relations, in quantum physics.[38]

> Quantum theory's signature replacement of classical local-global mereology with the concept of "inducing the global" via overlapping local contextual Boolean subalgebras, where *potential* measurement outcomes in one context are always internally related to *actual* measurement outcomes in others, is central to the argument that topology is the proper means by which to formalize quantum mechanical relations, given their underlying asymmetrical logical order. This is because quantum mechanical relations . . . are not properly understood as relations of independently extant *objects*; rather, they are *asymmetrical internal relations of relations considered objectively.* (Epperson and Zafiris 2013, 65)

Thus, whereas classical mechanics involves relations as only external relations involving independent things or objects, quantum physics involves as well internal relations, and relations of relations, the latter being a structure-preserving form of things. Epperson and Zafiris continue:

> Thus, as object relata, quantum mechanical internal relations are *always structure preserving*, as can be depicted topologically (i.e., mereotopologically via category theory) allowing for inductions like overlapping Boolean subalgebras to have ontological and not merely epistemic significance. By contrast, the conventional metrical approach to quantum mechanics, with its adherence to classical mereology, is incapable of depicting structure preserving "relations of relations" in this way. In the conventional set theoretic framework, for example, "elements"—the framework's fundamental object relata—are only relatable externally, never internally; there is no formal means by which to depict an

element's "internal relational structure"—i.e., its internal relations to other elements and their relations. (Epperson and Zafiris 2013, 65)

Here we witness the introduction of the critical distinction of internal relations versus external relations in the application of quantum physics, in contrast to classical mechanics which is often characterized as only requiring external relations of isolatable substance and trajectories in classical phase spaces. If a complex system is characterized only by external relations, then one can conceivably support a substance-oriented, facts-only nominalist description. Indeed, Bertrand Russell rejected internal relations as inevitably leading to a problematic monism, and promoted a nominalistic logical atomism whereby the world consists exclusively of independently existing things in external relation. Instead of Russell's stark contrast of external vs. internal relations as pluralist versus monist extremes, McHenry highlights Whitehead's third approach. "Crucially, Whitehead's view of prehension does not treat the relations as abstractions, as entities in their own right, but rather as concrete functions of actual occasions. The relation is the present occasion's absorption of past actual occasions in its process of self-creation. In this manner, the unity of the universe grows from bottom-up. This marks the most radical departure from the position Russell advanced" (McHenry 2017, 325). Details on Whitehead's concept of prehension are given in chapter 4, sections *Unified Process Approach to Causation and Emergence* and *Generalizing the Function*.

Whitehead's third approach is supported by quantum physics for which, in the inevitable combination of local and global relations, along with "asymmetrical internal relations of relations," we now have requirements for both internal and external relations involving both form and fact. Further, the standard set theory, classical local-global mereology is displaced here with category theory mereotopological relations that are capable of handling the concept of "inducing the global" via contextual Boolean subalgebras, and structure-preserving relations between alternative contexts.

Several issues of local context, internal and external relations, and global system are brought together in quantum measurements, which always involve a certain level of self-actualization. Epperson and Zafiris express this as follows:

The "choice" of any particular measurement context for any particular actual occasion in the global system cannot simply be derived in the classical sense of an experimenter choosing a particular device. The most one can say is that every quantum actual occasion has its own particular local context, which is constitutive of itself . . . This "self-determination" of an actual occasion's subjective standpoint/ local context is a signature feature of Whiteheadian metaphysics. But it is also the case in both Whiteheadian metaphysics and quantum mechanics that the local measurement context of a novel actual occasion-in-process, though not externally determined, is nevertheless internally conditioned by virtue of its internal relatedness to its dative world. In quantum mechanics, this is evinced by the fact that the presupposed global logical structure is defined by a Boolean localization scheme, where compatible local Boolean contexts overlap, and the indexical local measurement context must be part of this overlap. (Epperson and Zafiris 2013, 164–165)

Here the result that "local measurement context must be part of this overlap" points to how any specific dynamic particular (DP), encompassing both fact and form, involves both internal and external relations at multiple levels, local and global, such that, directly and indirectly, any DP is imbedded in a multilevel web of relations. In practice, most such relations can be neglected in approximations and models for (methodological) reductive analysis but, ontologically, for any truly in-depth scientific *and* philosophical analysis, the world is incredibly interrelated.

The Relational Reality model provides explicit synergy between the extension of the local to the global, and restriction of the local by the global. Epperson and Zafiris provide details about such mutually implicative local-global relations as follows (setting aside category-theoretic and other mathematical details):

the fundamental dipolar process in which this framework is anchored—the essential process of quantum mechanics—is [1] the asymmetrical internal relation of a *global outcome state* to locally contextualized measurement outcomes (i.e., *extension of the local to the global*); [2] the asymmetrical internal relation of locally contextualized measurement outcomes to the *global initial state* (i.e., *restriction of the local by the global*). Again, it is a fundamental principle of quantum mechanics per the Kochen-Specker theorem that this dipolar process excludes the possibility of global Boolean contextualization, either synthetically via extension, or analytically via restriction. (Epperson and Zafiris 2013, 57)

This key passage reveals the fundamental reason why any and all God's eye view framings are incorrect, or at least misleading—it is because, by working only with two-valued Boolean algebra, unique global Boolean contextualization is prohibited. In other words, there is no unique specification of the global, and we must work with the coordination of multiple local Boolean frameworks. Epperson and Zafiris further emphasize this critical result as follows:

The constituent facts of this totality, in other words, are not determinate; they cannot *all* be assigned definite bivalent truth values (i.e., *either* true or false) such that PNC and PEM are satisfied among *all* possible relations of these facts. This totality, then, is not only epistemically indeterminate globally; it is ontologically indeterminate locally—that is, as locally *constitutive* of the particular quantum measurement event internally related to it . . . it is via this dipolar process of asymmetrical internal relation that manifold local Boolean contextualized facts can be coherently and objectively integrated nonlocally—even if not comprehensively as a global Boolean totality—such that PNC and PEM condition causal relations not only *within* local Boolean contexts, but also *across* these contexts, even when measured systems are spatially well-separated. It is via asymmetrical internal relation, in other words, that a global totality of facts can be *coherently* internally constitutive of a local quantum process. (Epperson and Zafiris 2013, 57–58)

As we would expect for the diversity of *potentiae*, characterizing the global is inevitably not univocal, and such totality is "epistemically indeterminate." As well, due to the inevitable successiveness (input-output-context) of quantum process, including both dynamic particulars and *potentiae*, all quantum process is not causally closed but "ontologically indeterminate locally." Nevertheless, in spite of these indeterminacies, it is yet possible, by using asymmetrical internal relations, to properly characterize how a "global totality of facts" contributes to ongoing quantum process. Within the Relational Reality framework, this is the basis for the entanglement phenomenon of quantum physics.[39]

The importance of triads in fundamental process, and the inevitable triad of input-output-context or, as often expressed in application to quantum experiments, system-detector-environment, is emphasized by Epperson and Zafiris as follows:

the inclusion of environmental relations in the quantum measurement formalism is not only justified; it is arguably prescriptive if quantum mechanics is to be considered a fundamental physical theory rather than merely a methodology. This is because "system," "detector," and "environment" are always formally entangled in quantum mechanics, such that their partitioning is purely arbitrary. (Epperson and Zafiris 2013, 69)

We have discussed above the importance of succession as part of fundamental process, and that such is more fundamental than space-time description. This succession has aspects of both logical order and causal order, and this distinction provides a useful introduction to the famed EPR argument in which Albert Einstein, Boris Podolsky, and Nathan Rosen (thus, EPR) claimed to have shown how quantum physics (without such distinction and assuming classical conditional probabilities) must be incomplete. Epperson and Zafiris frame it this way:

It is crucial . . . to distinguish between "logical antecedence" and "temporal antecedence" here, for these are often casually assimilated. Temporal antecedence refers to an asymmetrical *metrical* relation of events—that is, a "distance" relation of events as *objects* according to the parameter of time (or more accurately, space-time). Logical antecedence, by contrast, refers to an asymmetrical logical super-session of events which are *themselves* internal relational structures—that is, an internal relation of relations, such as that implied by the notion of conditional probability or more broadly, propositional logic, operative quantum mechanically. For example, in a classical conditional probability P(B|A), "the probability of B given A," there is no requirement that A's logical conditioning of B be understood as a supersession of events A-B since classical conditional probabilities are purely epistemic; that is, as classically conceived, conditional probabilities presuppose that all observables have precise values at all times, such that any logical dependency of B upon A is reflective only of one's knowledge of A and B as already extant facts. The historical significance of the EPR argument and its modern experimental incarnations is the definitive demonstration that this classical conception of conditional probabilities is entirely invalid in quantum mechanics, where measurement must be understood as generative of novel facts (measurement outcome events) and not merely revelatory of already extant facts. (Epperson and Zafiris 2013, 75–76)

Here we witness a direct failure of actualism, which requires that measurement is simply about the recording of already established facts and which claims that logical and temporal antecedence are distinguished only epistemically. Instead, Epperson and Zafiris highlight how,

Thus in quantum mechanics, logical dependence depicted by a conditional probability like P(B|A) can only be understood as a Boolean logical conditioning of potential measurement outcomes at B by an actual measurement outcome A, such that P(B|A) depicts a supersession of ontological events and their asymmetrical logical relation.

In this way, the traditional conflation of temporal and logical antecedence, and more generally, the causal and logical orders—a conflation that has dominated the philosophy of nature since the Enlightenment—has been definitively invalidated by quantum mechanics. (Epperson and Zafiris 2013, 76)

This failed conflation of temporal and logical antecedence correlates with the false duality of presuming that fundamental reality must be either discrete or continuous, which is overcome in the Relational Reality model by demonstrating requirements for both actual and potential relations, both causal/temporal and logical orders, both internal and external relations, and both discrete and continuous features. As articulated by Epperson and Zafiris,

although the quantum actual occasions themselves are discrete, their *potential relations* are continuous and therefore metrically describable in terms of their extensive features. Thus, in the same Aristotelian sense that potentia always pre-suppose actualities, the continuous metrical descriptions of extension deriving from these potential relations presuppose a discrete, mereotopological extensive order of actual facts. But at the same time, in the relational realist philosophical scheme it is also true that actualities always presuppose potentia, since potential relations are always generative of novel actualities—viz., the quantum mechanical evolution of potential fact to probable fact to novel actual fact. In this regard, the various attempts by the physical sciences to depict physical reality as either fundamentally discrete or fundamentally continuous (reflected, for example, by the tension between quantum mechanics and general relativity) neglect the fact that quantum actual occasions cannot be abstracted from, or even defined without reference to, their actual *and* potential relations, both logical/mereoto-pological and extensive/metrical. Potentiality and actuality are thus mutually implicative in the relational realist philosophy, whose fundamental objects are quantum mechanical units of logico-physical relation rather than simply units of physical relata. Objects are therefore always understood as relata, and likewise relations are always understood objectively. (Epperson and Zafiris 2013, 169)

Finally, as part of a concise summary that correlates these new concepts with Whitehead's framework, Epperson and Zafiris note that

the relational realist scheme of internal relation among dipolar quantum actual occasions thus reflects a correlation of the order of logical implication and the order of causal relation—what Whitehead terms, respectively, the "genetic division" and the "coordinate division" of the predicative fact/actual occasion. (Epperson and Zafiris 2013, 173)

FUNDAMENTAL QUANTUM PROCESS

In summary, the Relational Reality model, whose focus is diachronic, articulates four stages of fundamental quantum process. For technical details, in addition to the primary volume by Epperson and Zafiris (2013), see also Epperson's more concise essay "Bridging Necessity and Contingency in Quantum Mechanics" (2016).

(1) actual initial state/global, uncontextualized *potentiae*;
(2) potential states/locally contextualized;
(3) probable states/probability valuation/conditionalization of *potentiae* / restriction of local by global/local relevance of global/decoherence;[40]
(4) actual outcome state/actualization of *potentia*/extension of local to global /global relevance of local.

Actual outcomes or actualizations ("facts"—both *res extensa* and *res qualia*) are inevitably input states as well, combined with *potentiae*, for future successions of such process—bootstrapping the world. Jorge Nobo provides a detailed discussion of the concept of succession within a process framework (Nobo, 2004). Referring to items 1–3 above, (1) the initial stage, via the non-Boolean order of *potentiae* (represented by the "pure state" in quantum physics) is inevitably delimited by (2) potential outcome states [where neither the Principle of Non-Contradiction (PNC) nor the Principle of Excluded Middle (PEM) hold]; indeed, for this stage, PNC and PEM are inapplicable because *potentiae* are ontologically "fuzzy."[41] Finally, for items (3) and (4), a system further evolves in its conditionalization of *potentiae* via local Boolean contextualization, including restriction of the local by the global, to a reduced integration of probable outcome states that satisfy PNC and PEM, ultimately terminating in an actual outcome state or actualization. As Epperson and Zafiris state,

> Although individual local measurement contexts are Boolean, any attempt to relate multiple local measurement contexts together in a single measurement—a normative function of quantum physics—yields non-Boolean potential relations across these contexts because the variously contextualized observables do not commute. (Epperson and Zafiris 2013, 43–44)

Unlike the presumed symmetry of such relations in classical physics,[42] such non-commutativity entails a fundamental asymmetry. Thus, as pointed out by Epperson and colleagues, "Quantum [physics] clearly exemplifies an asymmetrical, internal relational, event-ontological structure" (Epperson et al. 2018, 30). This asymmetry is most clearly shown in Werner Heisenberg's matrix algebra (fully equivalent to Erwin Schrödinger's wave formalism), which is clearly non-commutative.[43]

Formulating a concatenation of all local contexts to directly frame a global context is allowed in classical physics but disallowed in quantum physics, which is one fundamental way in which the whole is greater than the sum of the parts.[44] As Primas states, "The globally non-Euclidean theory of general relativity is an apt analogy for the locally Boolean behavior of globally non-Boolean descriptions . . . algebraically, Boolean contexts play an analogous role as Euclidean spaces play for geometric manifolds" (Primas 2017, 16). As a simple illustration of this point, consider your local coordinates, which can be closely represented by a two-dimensional (2D) map, in contrast to the spherical coordinates required to represent the overall spherical Earth. However useful such 2D maps are, there is no direct mapping between such 2D maps and the overall 3D Earth surface—transformation to some type of spherical coordinate system is required—a global context for your local maps.

Although quantum physics disallows a simple aggregative view of systems, or a related reductionist view of part-whole relations (mereology), research in algebraic formulations of quantum physics have shown how Boolean structures, for sets of actualizations of specific local contexts (represented by Boolean subalgebras), can be extended globally where these subalgebras overlap. Technically, as a proxy for the ontology, these algebraic methods enable an articulation of the constraints and restrictions that apply to efforts toward global extension. For details, see Epperson and Zafiris (2013) and Atmanspacher and Primas (2017) and Primas (2017). Overall, as Epperson and colleagues argue,

> quantum physics is a synthetic process whereby measurement outcomes are not merely revelatory of extant facts, but generative of novel facts . . . a bidirectional, mutually implicative relationship between local and global states . . . enabling extension of the local to the global (locally contextualized measurements have their global relevance) . . . and restriction of the local by the global whereby global actualities (i.e., those environmental to the local measured system) condition local measurement contextualization. (Epperson et al. 2018, 33–34)

This local-global interplay provides a central hypothesis of the *Logoi* framework in which the combination of the two fundamental logical orders, the logic of actualization (Boolean) and the logic of *potentiae* (non-Boolean), correlated with facts/actualizations, and possible relations, respectively, along with the bidirectional, mutually implicative character of local-global relationships, provides a deep grounding for considering all input-output relationships as always in a context (also argued in this chapter above). Thus, given the fundamentality of quantum process, the ontological process accords with a full generalization, at multiple scales (synchronic emergence) and stages (diachronic causative process), of the triad input-output-context, from fundamental logic and quantum physics to high-level complex systems (see chapter 4). These fundamental relations also provide a grounding for multiple levels of emergence and hierarchy (not some ultimate ontological reduction to components of such).

Thus, as part of our *Logoi* framework, I propose reframing both causation and physical relationships to focus on how both actuality and *potentiae* (both components of the real and involving, respectively, Boolean and non-Boolean logic) are intimately joined. This approach then provides a basis for optimizing pre-space *potentiae* (via minimization techniques such as the principle of least action) along with constraints on physical process (emergent law, but not via entailment).[45] Combining each and every event creation with its fundamental successiveness, that is, with its incorporation of past fields and "particles" and pre-space *potentiae*, when coordinated through local-global correlations, then actively creates a particular, individuated new event actuality. Such fundamental, diachronic process is similar to Whitehead's concept of prehensive unification, including both actuality and *potentiae*, but without requiring his concept of eternal objects, at least not with a Platonic emphasis—see McHenry (2015).

In such fundamental process, we move from symmetry (applicable to pre-space *potentiae*) to broken symmetry; as well there is the ongoing emergence of temporality (physical time) and extension (space). In this way, the combination of multilevel (active) causation and general constraints on *potentiae* (physical relationships, or Peircean "generals" being a byproduct), in combination with local-global relations, enables multi-scale emergence (see *Unified Process Approach to Causation and Emergence* in chapter 4). The genuine newness, the novelty of emergence, then arises from pre-space *potentiae*, filtered through multiple levels of process, with both diachronic and synchronic (structural) aspects. Only actual states are fully particular in contrast to *potentiae*, which are not actualized particulars but are yet real (in denial of nominalism), and always to some degree "general."

LOCAL-GLOBAL RELATIONS

As described in detail by Epperson and Zafiris, "*locally*, every measurement context must be Boolean . . . this presupposition of local Boolean contextuality, yielding mutually exclusive outcome states . . . is a necessary prerequisite for the probability evaluation of these alternative outcome states (the Born rule), which is a categorical presupposition of quantum mechanics" (Epperson and Zafiris 2013, 60). If we limit ourselves to such local measurement context, then measurement procedure comports with the Boolean restrictions of classical physics as emphasized correctly by Niels Bohr in his Copenhagen interpretation.[46] However, Epperson and Zafiris point out that "*globally* (when local contexts are brought into nonlocal relation), intra-contextual Boolean material implication (that is, *within* individual local measurement contexts) must be relatable inter-contextually *across* these local contexts (i.e., 'globally'). In quantum mechanics, this is expressed as a tensor product relationship of potential outcome states" (ibid.).

A dramatic example of the importance of multilevel context is the phenomenon of quantum entanglement, which concerns how local processes get entangled with certain distant processes. Within quantum physics, this phenomenon is discussed in terms of quantum states. Several experimental confirmations of entanglement have now been completed (Krenn et al. 2014; Hensen et al. 2015). In the Relational Reality model, this confirmation of non-local effects in quantum physics is a signature of the combination of *potentiae* and local-global relations. This contrasts with how "Almost all correlations between independent observers known in science are local," as noted by Nicolas Gisin and Rob Thew (2007, 166). Such confirmation of entanglement, pointing to real non-local relations, thus both local and local-global relations, is an exceptionally important, yet recent result of quantum physics research. Gisin explains that entanglement goes beyond our normal application of space-time metrics, namely "that nonlocal correlations seem to emerge somehow from outside of space and time in the sense that no story taking place in space as time goes by can account for the way nature produces such correlations" (Gisin 2014, 105). So long as we stay within the confines of the logic of actualization, that is, the Boolean logic of space-time metrics, measurement outcomes, and their space-time correlations, we will remain unable to understand these non-local correlations. We need to evaluate approaches that incorporate the logic of *potentiae* (non-Boolean logic) arising from pre-space fundamental process. Concerning the latter, recent research in quantum field theory indicates both that there is a fundamental succession of quantum process and, Jesse Bettinger argues, based on theoretical work by Erik Verlinde, that such process is prior to the abstraction of space-time metrics (Bettinger, 2015).

Category theory, which is a general algebra of relations, has emerged in modern mathematics; and in application to quantum physics, Elias Zafiris has shown how category theory reveals the importance of both local field relations and local-global relations in explaining successions of quantum events (Zafiris, 2010). Combined with local-global connections, the handling of physical relations in the Relational Reality model exhibits non-local connectedness (entanglement) as inevitable and as logical constraints on *potentiae* (not as some "spooky action-at-a-distance"—an *aporia* arising from the presumption of actualism). The use of local-global here applies either to the inevitable reference to *potentiae* or, at least, to some expanded context, which generates the inevitable triad of input-output-context. Another effort toward a realist interpretation of quantum physics is shared by Dennis Dieks, who states "that from a realist viewpoint, quantum contextuality naturally leads to 'perspectivalism' [in which a] context—or perspective—is needed to define the value of a physical quantity, in accordance with the core of the Kochen and Specker results" (Dieks 2019, 629, 643).[47]

LOGOI FRAMEWORK IN A NUTSHELL

Let me sketch some ways that the *Logoi* framework opens up new avenues of thought, from basic physics to values, meaning and ultimate context. We have started with the fundamental notions of process, logic, and relations, and the three ways of knowing. The concept of relation is foundational for both basic science and humanities as illustrated in all scholarly fields. Semiotics is the study of relations and signs, indeed the study of anything that stands for something else (see chapter 5). However useful we find the approximation of symmetric dyadic relations, in the real world such relations are inevitably set within a triadic asymmetry, viz., input-output-context, the latter being either general (as within domains of *potentiae*) or particular (e.g., symmetry breaking upon a particular measurement outcome in quantum physics).

Augmenting these notions with the Relational Reality model leads to understanding fundamental process as woven, web-like with fundamental succession, including two basic types of logic, Boolean and non-Boolean, which correlate with a logic of actualizations (causal order) and a logic of *potentiae* (logical order), respectively. Then, instead of the usual dependence on God-given "law" and deductive entailment, the fundamental basis of physical relations is grounded in relations of relations in *potentiae* (*à la* potentiality "spaces" or pre-space), which can be determined in part by minimization principles such as the principle of least action. In this way, constraints on *potentiae* enable the generation of physical law with universal scope, or universality, and such process has both diachronic and synchronic aspects, exhibited, respectively, by fundamental quantum process (viz., causation) and multilevel emergence of systems with increasing complexity.[48] Multilevel process (coextensive with Peircean triads of input-output-context and Auxier's quanta of explanation) combined with local-global relations and *potentiae* enable multiscale emergence.

If one holds on to actualism or nominalism, then one abandons any fundamental basis for *potentiae*, quantum fields and other higher-level concepts essential to human understanding; likewise abandoned is any basis for human free will or meaning (see *On the Failure of Actualism and Nominalism* in chapter 4). In contrast, without arbitrarily invoking miracles or some abstract belief system (whether atheistic or theistic), the *Logoi* framework provides a systematic framework from which emerges a viable basis for mind and consciousness. To see how this is possible, building on elements of the *Logoi* framework, I propose that mental processing is distinct from brain actualizations, and has the capability to reflexively contrast "that which is" with "that which could be" and to make decisions among alternative possibilities. Here note that conventional "brain states" are outputs captured by the logic of actualization alone, whereas I hypothesize that mental processing and the inference of "mind" involves both the logic of actualization and the logic of *potentiae*. Such an expanded concept of mind and consciousness is developed in *On the Emergence of Consciousness and Mind* within chapter 7.

Combining such local-global connectedness with biosemiotics (accounting for enhanced information and dynamical depth, see Koutroufinis 2014) enables multilevel frameworks of increasing semiotic complexity with values and meaning (arising from multiple levels of context), and ultimately consciousness, language, and spiritual awareness (enabling enhanced access to *potentiae* and anticipatory capabilities) (see chapter 8, and *Biosemiotics and Anticipatory Systems* within chapter 5). As James Bradley expresses it, this only becomes fully intelligible and self-explanatory with full inclusion of the "self-actualizing activity of recursive subjects" and communities of such (Bradley 2003b, 150). Such high-level functionality only appears in self-aware beings imbedded in multiscale physical and biological systems.

Eventually, with the emergence of consciousness, such self-aware beings evolve to become aware of their ultimate context, not just of multiscale contingencies (worlds-upon-worlds) but also aware of the noncontingent ground of contingency, which may be (or is sometimes characterized as) the spiritual dimension (see chapter 8). At the level of ontology alone, such beings can only be confident of the way of numbers (science) and, to varying degrees, the way of context, or the way of signs (humanities, and semiotics). Going beyond these two ways through the recognition of ultimacies and unrestricted domains of discourse would logically lead to an ultimate basis for closure and meaning, transcending the anthropomorphic, and this in turn leads to the way of spirit (spirituality; the religious dimension). This progression completes the three fundamental ways of awareness for finite beings (the way of numbers, of context/signs, of spirit). These three ways of awareness are also interwoven with two basic modes of knowing, as explained by Primas, the sequential and the non-sequential (Primas 2017, 68), which have corollaries with complementarity[49] in quantum physics, grounded in the distinction of Boolean and non-Boolean logics as argued by Primas (2017, 69), in linear versus correlative thought in Chinese culture (Hall and Ames 1998), and in partial hemispheric specialization of the human brain (left hemisphere tending to emphasize temporally sequential and analytic knowledge; right hemisphere tending to emphasize temporally nonsequential holistic knowledge—see Levy-Agresti and Sperry (1968).

ON *POTENTIAE* VERSUS SOME ALTERNATIVES

The Relational Reality model affirms the ontological reality of *potentiae*. This important distinction of actuality and *potentiae* as both aspects of the "real," understood inclusively, has a long history going back to Aristotle. "In 1890 *The Century Dictionary of the English Language* devoted two columns to definitions of potential and potentiality—many of them written by Charles

Peirce" (Edward Moore 2012, 179). Shortly after Peirce's work, a classic treatise that emphasizes this distinction is that of Whitehead's *Process and Reality* (Whitehead 1929, 1978). Recently, Stuart Kauffman and Arran Gare also emphasized this distinction (Gare 2015). Along with a concise argument for objective chance, Mario Bunge points out that

> Spinoza drew a sharp distinction between *natura naturans* (nature in the making or creating) and *natura naturata* (nature made or created). The pairs possibility/actuality, past/future, input/output, and probability/frequency belong in the study of the *naturans/naturata* duality, whereas the notion of present or now is not only an egocentric particular, as Bertrand Russell pointed out, but also a hinge between *naturans* and *naturata*. (Bunge 2018, 243)

Despite such exceptions, the notion of potentiality no longer receives the attention it once did. As Edward Moore noted, "Twentieth century philosophy has been a philosophy of the actual" (Moore 2012, 179). Ironically, some leading philosophers, desiring to avoid Bunge's objective chance and inspired by both nominalism and the analytic tradition, dominant in twentieth-century philosophy, are trying to be ever more metaphysically parsimonious through reductionist, deflationary ontologies (see Amie Thomasson's *Ontology Made Easy* (2014)).[50] In parallel to such deflation, some leading scientists and philosophers, committed to reductionism and actualism, have invoked multiple worlds and universes (multiverses) to explain recent experiments in quantum physics—thus proposing new forms of inflationary ontology; indeed, highly inflationary "deflations!"[51] These scientific speculations appear to continue unabated even when, as noted by Peter Woit, they go beyond any possibility of falsification (Woit 2007). Another theory-centric strategy is to reduce everything to mathematics, a modern Platonism, one argued by Max Tegmark (2014), which is a strategy that Raymond Tallis thoroughly debunks (Tallis 2017, 187–188). Yet another effort to grapple with interpretive problems of modern physics is Gerard 't Hooft's effort, admitted by the author as rather incomplete, to retain ontological determinism through a cellular automata theory of quantum physics ('t Hooft 2016). (Note: Both Tegmark and 't Hooft are excellent mathematical physicists, but here we are focused on philosophical issues for which physicists in general are not well versed.). Essentially all such alternatives presume a form of reductive substance philosophy combined with actualism and the givenness of certain deductive laws of physics, which itself remains a mystery because we now lack (for generally accepted philosophic procedure) the law-giver available to eighteenth-century deists.

Here I strive to avoid such extremes in reduction, deflation, or inflation, and work to identify a set of basic notions, principles, and ontology that can meet our desiderata of adequate explanation for systematic philosophy and human experience, at multiple levels.

BERGSON, EINSTEIN, AND THEIR
FAMOUS DEBATES OF 1922

The reality of time and whether or not reality is open or deterministic constituted the focus of the famous Bergson-Einstein debates of 1922. Jimena Canales, in *The Physicist and the Philosopher* (2015), provides a very engaging account of these debates, and how they contributed to the rift between science and the humanities later documented by Charles P. Snow in his 1959 Cambridge lecture (Snow, 1963). The famed philosopher Henri Bergson argued that time should not be exclusively understood through scientific means, and that fully understanding the concept of time requires intuitive and philosophical perspectives as well. In contrast, in promoting his new relativity theory, Albert Einstein insisted that "the time of the philosophers does not exist" (Canales 2015, 19). During the debates, Einstein affirmed that his theory had not only formal or mathematical significance but further supports strong claims about what is real. In turn, Bergson emphasized that he had no question about the soundness of Einstein's theory, but argued that Einstein's focus was only on objective measurement, combined with treating every system as real and declaring all physical times of equal value, and as such he neglects important contextual issues, both semiotic and philosophical. In contrast to Einstein's deterministic outlook, as shown in detail by Čapek (1971), Bergson argued that such considerations show that the future is nevertheless open and indeterminate, considerations further elaborated by Vesselin Petrov in his review of Čapek's work (Petrov 2016). Canales points out that, secure in Bergson's chair at the Collège de France, philosopher Maurice Merleau-Ponty later argued, like Bergson, against a scientism that overrules experience, for which, "by excluding our actually perceived environment . . . modern science had lost touch with reality. What would science look like if it reintroduced the world as seen, heard, and felt? For decades, he dedicated himself to answering these questions" (Canales 2015, 49).

By applying my *Logoi* framework and, within that, the Relational Reality model for the interpretation of quantum physics, a resolution of the Bergson-Einstein debates is relatively straightforward. By insisting that only objective measurement outputs are real, Einstein was effectively making the metaphysical claim that the real is nothing but the (Boolean) order of actualization, such actualism being a core claim of scientism (see footnote and critique in the *Potential Relations* (*potentiae*) subsection above). In contrast, Bergson accepted Einstein's scientific claims but effectively denied his metaphysical claim of actualism.

In many ways, the contemporary debate on the passage of time remains tied to assumptions surrounding the 1922 Bergson-Einstein debates as reviewed by Emiliano Boccardi (2016). Breaking out of this impasse, in addition to my critique of physicalism (see chapter 4, *On the Failure of Physicalism),* I propose that the Boolean/non-Boolean distinction is the key scientific basis for the philosophical claim that the real, considered inclusively, is both the actual and the possible; namely the *Logoi* framework's critical distinction of the order of actualization and the order of *potentiae.* With this distinction now available, we can see how both Bergson and Einstein were correct within their limited frameworks. Einstein was correct that his relativity theory gave proper correlations among measurement outputs associated with the dynamics of systems in relative motion and, for that purpose, time measurements could be treated as merely markers of coordinate values within a space-time metric. At the same time, Bergson and Merleau-Ponty were correct to insist that there is more to reality than the tabulation of measurements and their correlations. The scope and implications of this "something more" is the focus of my *Logoi* framework, which is developed throughout this book (e.g., see chapter 4, Gordian knot #4 temporality, and response). When considering semiotics, emergent phenomena, and multiple levels of context, there emerges the full range of ways of knowing, introduced in chapter 1, including humanistic and philosophic discourse as championed by Bergson. Indeed, leaving aside his earlier strong reductionist claims, Einstein advanced his own humanistic concerns, especially through his efforts toward nuclear disarmament.[52]

COMPARISON OF CLASSICAL MECHANICS AND QUANTUM PHYSICS

Some of the very best physics and many of the most productive inventions of the past three centuries have emerged from applying Newton's classical physics, especially with its important nineteenth-century augmentations of the Lagrangian and Hamiltonian formalisms, and Maxwell's electrodynamics. With these powerful tools in hand, the dynamics of systems can be well described from just above atomic scale to macroscopic and astronomical scales. However, at the atomic scales and below, the approximations of classical physics begin to fail. In referring to the time of Newton and the outstanding success of classical physics, as noted above, I here use "classical physics" (CP) to designate the proper classical approximation that it represents relative to quantum physics (QP); in turn classical mechanics (CM) here denotes the same physics but added to that are some common presuppositions based on an overlay of mechanistic-materialist metaphysics. These added elements of presuppositions and ontology commonly associated with classical mechanics are presented in the two right-hand columns of table 2.1, which provides a concise summary of the Relational Reality model by contrasting its framing of quantum physics with key characteristics of the earlier, yet highly successful classical mechanics model. I recognize the limitations of this table or any simplistic comparison of classical and quantum physics. Comparisons of technical, scientific details are reasonably straightforward, which is reflected in the columns pertaining to prime focus and epistemology. However, inferences about presuppositions and ontology are less established; my table here is simply intended to point to common assumptions and trends, not final characterizations. One can point to examples where classical physics is used to study asymmetries or irreversible systems (as with thermodynamics), and yet it is most commonly presumed that such analysis involves underlying symmetries and reversibility. Similarly, quantum physics is often used to evaluate conditions of symmetry and possible hidden variables, yet more fundamentally, as we have seen, context and asymmetry are yet more fundamental, and hidden variable claims most often arise when researchers remain limited to actualism and determinism.

Notwithstanding some limitations in the relatively simple characterizations utilized in table 2.1, in many cases, when shifting from CM to QP, it represents an augmentation from a feature X to a more complex framework involving both X *and* Y. Thus, we transition from dyads, input-output, external relations, symmetry, reversibility, continuity, and Boolean logic for CM, to dyads *and* triads, input-output *and* context, external *and* internal relations, symmetry *and* asymmetry, reversibility *and* irreversibility, continuity *and* discontinuity, and Boolean *and* non-Boolean logic for QP. In many cases, the great practical success of classical physics has lured us into accepting the presuppositions and ontology of CM that go beyond classical physics, which shares with CM only its prime focus and epistemology (see columns 2 and 3 of the table). Unfortunately, as I have discussed in an earlier work, such classical metaphysics when applied to interpretations of QP can result in many quantum puzzles (Eastman, 2008). The resolution of these puzzles depends on identifying and removing classical metaphysics assumptions (presuppositions and ontology for CM) and then deploying the more inclusive interpretive framework enabled by QP (presuppositions and ontology for QP, see table lower right). My candidate for this purpose overall is the *Logoi* framework, which includes the Relational Reality model described above.

A fundamental CM claim is that preexistent imposed law results in strict entailments from causes to effects such that effects are, for all practical purposes, contained in their causes and there is strict deterministic entailment. However, this constitutes a speculative claim that has both scientific

Table 2.1 A Comparison of Classical Mechanics and Quantum physics

Physics Model	*Prime focus*	*Epistemology*	*Presuppositions*	*Ontology*
Classical Mechanics (CM)	measurements and data imposed "law"	dyads input-output measurement as revealing extant "facts" facts (empiricism)	context "hidden" external relations (without history) symmetry reversibility continuity	preexistent law logic of actualizations (Boolean only) effects *in* cause (determinism) input to output entailments
Quantum Physics (QP)	measurements, data, *and* environments filtering of *potentiae* emergent relations of relations	dyads *and* triads input-output *and* context process as generative of novel facts both fact *and* form	context affirmed external *and* internal relations (with history) symmetry *and* asymmetry reversibility, yet fundamental process as irreversible continuity *and* discontinuity	emergent 'law' logics of *both* actuals (Boolean logic) *and potentiae* (non-Boolean logic) effects *in* cause, *and* cause *in* effect; cause-effect as mutually implicative phases of fundamental quantum process

and metaphysical dimensions; namely, that the fundamental ontology of the world can be ordered fully by a Boolean-only logic of actualizations, and that the real is nothing but the actual. The latter is a metaphysical claim most often simply presupposed yet, occasionally, such actualism is made explicit, such as with Samuel Kimpton-Nye's thesis in analytic metaphysics. Along with a complex argument about supporting the reality of possibilities and potencies in a metaphysics of modality, he states that,

> concrete objects and their properties are plausibly the sorts of things that sci-
> ence can tell us about and since the claim is that it is those very objects that
> ground facts about metaphysical modality, hardcore actualism places *scientific*
> methods at the centre of the epistemology and methodology of modal meta-
> physics. Modal metaphysics is no longer primarily concerned with abstracta or
> possibilia, which, by definition, are *not* accessible via empirical scientific meth-
> ods. Hardcore actualism thus constitutes a significant step towards achieving
> continuity between natural science and metaphysics. (Kimpton-Nye 2018, 32)

In contrast to how the application of such "hardcore actualism" in analytic circles tends to presuppose just Boolean-only thinking (with epistemic potencies but not ontic *potentiae*),[53] our results show how quantum physics itself points to an ontic duality of fundamental context because of its need for both Boolean and non-Boolean logics. In this way, modal metaphysics (past-present-future analysis) can fully partner with forefront scientific and philosophical analysis; ironically, physics results themselves undermine the metaphysical claim that the real is merely the actual (actualism).

As shown above, recent research in quantum physics and philosophy has led several research groups to recognize that the real is *both* the actual *and* potential relations or *potentiae*; in turn, there is *both* a (Boolean) logic of actualization *and* a (non-Boolean) logic of *potentiae*. In contrast with narrow, Boolean-only treatments in contemporary analytic metaphysics, this more complex logical space is both more consistent with the science and with basic human experience. As expressed by Epperson and Zafiris, causes and effects are mutually implicative.

A standard CM claim is that measurement merely reveals already extant facts (sometimes suggesting a God's eye view that transcends modal distinctions), and that proper theory must always remain grounded in such empirical facts, such being the logic of actualization (arguably this was the core of nineteenth–twentieth-century empiricism). In contrast, although limited (epistemologically) to measurements of input-output, the theoretical framework of QP, along with careful philosophical analysis and theory of measurement, enables inference and application of both the logic of actualization and the logic of *potentiae*. This provides a robust alternative basis for understanding potential relations and abstractions in ways that go beyond simple reference to properties, dispositions, and potencies within a nominalistic framework.

For CM, the methodological goal of context independence was often converted into an ontological claim of context independence and full isolation of the input-output dyadic. In contrast, for QP, its theory of measurement always includes reference to the measurement process (input-output), measurement outcomes (data), and the measurement environment (laboratory, systems, context); thus, the input-output-context triad (see chapters 4, 5, and 7). Going beyond the context-free external relations presumed by CM, the applications of QP involve multilevels of such process enabling emergent relations of relations (both external and internal, see chapter 4).

Although some QP formalisms exhibit time-reversible structure (e.g., the Schrödinger equation), fundamental quantum process is irreversible due to symmetry breaking as arises during its phases of succession (discussed in the section *Fundamental Quantum Process* above); thus, both symmetry and asymmetry are integral aspects of QP. Finally, users of CM most often presume that law is simply a given—preexistent, whereas the status of law itself is an open question with QP. One way to understand quantitative physical relations (law) is in terms of constraints on *potentiae*—this approach is detailed in the section *"Law"-From Entailment to Constrained Processual Histories* in chapter 4.

SUMMARY OF KEY *LOGOI* FRAMEWORK TERMS AND CONCEPTS

The *Logoi* framework incorporates the Relational Reality model and yet goes beyond it, in the spirit of systematic philosophy, to add some fundamental notions that are either presupposed or function as grounding elements of that model. A few common concepts are conspicuously absent in the *Logoi* framework's core metaphysics because they are here suggested to be derivative notions, and not truly fundamental, however much they may be essential to measurement and scientific applications. Among others, these derivative notions are physical law (vs. constraints on *potentiae*), causality (as having an epistemic focus vs. ontic causation), time (vs. temporality), space (vs. fundamental extension), and space-time metric (vs. quantum field theory constraints on fundamental extension).[54]

A concise summary of the hypothesized fundamental notions of the *Logoi* framework, and their place in a theory of actualization, is as follows:

Process/succession: input-output succession within context (constraints/*potentiae*); continuous-discrete;

Logic: logic of actualizations (two-valued Boolean logic) and a logic of potential relations, or *potentiae* (multivalued logic, non-Boolean);

Relations: constitutive of process (part-whole; local-global; internal-external), including relations of relations/semiotics, as well, extension;[55]

Potentiae: potential relations within a non-spatialized fundamental level of reality (pre-space), ordered by a multivalued non-Boolean logic; input to every fundamental quantum event;

Local-global relations: relations affecting every fundamental quantum event, which can be discussed as either the broader context of the input-output-context triadic, or linkages with the order of *potentiae* that enable entanglement phenomena;

Structure of relations: real-world interactions always involve sequences of triads (input-output-context); dyads of simple input-output are always approximations;

Fundamental ontology: dimensions of both contingent and non-contingent being/becoming;

Ways of knowing: way of numbers (science), way of context/semiotics (arts/humanities), way of spirit (religious dimension);

Basic modes of knowing: sequential and non-sequential (linear vs. correlative thought, as in Chinese culture), such duality correlated with complementarity in quantum physics, which is grounded in the distinction of two fundamental logics, the logic of actualization and the logic of *potentiae*.

From the above fundamental notions of the *Logoi* framework, we now lay out in chapter 3 a Gordian knot of classic philosophical problems for which the above conceptual toolkit can be productively applied.

NOTES

1. Such direct awareness and immediacy of experience could be thought of as a kind of "*a priori* empiricism" after Friedrich Schelling (John Laughland 2016); more fully, as an exemplar of Whitehead's radical empiricism (Auxier and Herstein 2017). Indeed, Michael Grant points out that "Tallis believes that human discourse—in contrast with animal responses to present actualities—is predominantly about *possibility:* possible states of affairs which may or may not be realised. It is this, he argues, that makes language the supreme means by which explicitness may be elaborated and new meanings created" (Michael Grant 2000, 110). Unfortunately, a focus on language can undermine proper metaphysical analysis because, as Michel Weber expresses it, "Language, like sight, prefers clear-cut distinctions, independent entities, external relationships" (Weber 2013, 109).

2. The reliability of immediate, direct feeling, and even the concept of "feeling," has a long history of controversy in philosophy. This is a worthy philosophical debate,

but one that I will not engage for my present effort. For detailed discussions about this issue, see Susan Langer (1953), Charles Birch (1995), and Antonio Damasio (1999).

3. Jorge Luis Nobo has carried out a systematic analysis of the succession concept, developed both in his landmark book on Whitehead's metaphysics (Nobo 1986), and a later essay that suggests scientific implications (Nobo 2004).

4. For issues of modal logic, a type of formal logic that can handle the notion of possibility, Timothy Williamson argues that the actualism-possibilism debate is better addressed by a focus on the necessitism-contingentism debate (Williamson 2013, 22; 2016). As will be shown, possibility here is grounded in experience, philosophical analysis, and analyses of quantum measurement. In the present work, in general, "potentiality" will be more often used to avoid confusion with 'possibility' in possible-worlds semantics, which often presupposes actualism (effectively the denial of an ontological actuality-potentiality distinction).

5. Local-global relations are here defined explicitly in terms of their logical relations in quantum physics. Locally, every measurement context must be Boolean (see first footnote in the next sub-section), whereas "observables contextualized by multiple local measurement contexts do not commute" (Epperson and Zafiris 2013, 64) (e.g., reversing the sequence produces a different outcome). This "global" set of contexts itself is non-Boolean—it is not possible to deduce a "global" Boolean algebra. The terms "local" and "global" are entirely relative; "global" could refer to two different laboratory measurement contexts within the same city or on different planets (see the explanation of local-global later in this chapter).

6. Throughout this work, my use of the word "logos" is intended to be in this sense of *metaxu*, or between, within an inclusive search for consistency and coherence, not the connotation of the purely rational over against ambiguity or mystery.

7. The late 19th C. logician Rudolph Lotze highlighted a "between" in reflective thinking but, as noted by Phillip Stambovsky (2009, 157), Desmond takes this notion further and beyond any limitation to human consciousness.

8. Boolean logic is a simple two-valued logic, involving discrete no/yes (or 0/1) responses to well-defined propositions, which traces back to Aristotle's works, and which was articulated in modern form by George Boole in the mid-nineteenth century. This standard logic is the logical basis of modern computing and networking systems.

9. Non-Boolean logic allows for three-valued logical analysis and enables a logic of potentiality, not just actuality. See Epperson (2016) and Primas (2017) for a comparative discussion of both Boolean and non-Boolean logic.

10. The designation of *potentiae* as an order does not represent an affirmation of Whiteheadian eternal objects, or some externalized domain of Platonic forms, even when augmented with a nuanced modal conception as articulated by David Weismann (1977). Here we envision these orders as distinct yet interwoven (see chapters 6–8).

11. These elements are formally included in mathematician Granville Henry's Prolog program implementation of Whitehead's core logic as presented in his major work *Process and Reality* (Whitehead 1929; 1978); see Henry (1993).

12. "Dynamic particular" is the term used by Hartshorne in place of Whitehead's "actual entity" (see Viney and Shields, 2020). For this book, except for quotes, I will frequently use "dynamic particular" (DP) as a replacement for the term "actual entity."

13. In general, I will avoid the particular-universal dichotomy so imbedded in standard substance views and nominalism; instead, I encourage attention to the break-through works of Johanna Seibt that promote generic processes that transform this classical philosophical debate; see Richard Campbell (2015, 79).

14. A brief history of actualism in contrast with real possibility is provided in chapter 19 on possibility in Robert Doyle's book *Metaphysics* (2016).

15. One demonstration of the reality of fields is the Aharonov-Bohm effect as argued by David Bohm and Basil Hiley (1979).

16. For details about the relationship of physical inputs, relationships, and *potentia,* based on a category theory analysis applied to contemporary quantum physics, see Zafiris (2016).

17. Pre-space here denotes a non-spatialized fundamental level of reality such as, for example, Whitehead's extensive continuum; see C. Papatheodorou and Basil Hiley (1997).

18. These technical methods and their philosophical interpretation are developed by Vladislav Terekhovich (2018); also see *Feynman's Thesis* (Laurie Brown 2005).

19. The standard deductivist, or entailment, account of law has its origin in medieval conceptions of classical theism, and the associated 17–18th century (often deistic) metaphysics of European philosophy that accompanied the beginnings of modern science; see Milič Čapek's classic work *The Philosophical Impact of Contemporary Physics* (1961).

20. Category theory provides a powerful and very general algebra of relations; see entries in the *Stanford Encyclopedia of Philosophy* on "The Algebra of Logic Tradition" (Stanley Burris 2015) and "Category Theory" (Jean-Pierre Marquis 2014).

21. Many scholars emphasize the practically unlimited importance of context, e.g., Carlos Gershenson (2002) and Harald Atmanspacher (2007).

22. Five key claims characterize scientism: (1) that the "real" is nothing but the "actual" (i.e., "actualism"); (2) that such reality is fully captured by quantitative laws of entailment; (3) scientific models can, in principle, achieve completeness through dyadic relations alone; (4) reality conforms to causal closure of the physical; and (5) mechanistic systems can assume a single causally conditioning context. Within this book, I show how all of these claims are ultimately false, although the last item can be practical within approximation even if failing philosophic finality.

23. The principle of universality and its scientific and philosophic dimensions are developed in detail by James Trefil (1989, 1).

24. Benacerraf's problem is an argument against Platonism that highlights a fundamental problem in reducing entities (such as abstract objects) that are not spatially or temporally localized to entities (such as mathematicians) that are spatially or temporally localized. This argument suggests that such relations cannot have an ontologically Platonic nature; see Leon Horsten (2017).

25. The principle of least action is a variational principle, based in quantum physics, that can be used to obtain the equations that describe the dynamics of physical systems.

26. Categories are supplements to reasoning designed to resolve equivocations and prepare for the application of logical laws. Peirce claimed that only three categories are sufficient for this purpose (see chapter 5).

27. An iterative map is one that is applied repeatedly to an object or sequence of such. Iteration or recurrence are standard mathematical and simulation tools. Generally, for mathematics, mapping is a synonym for a function or morphism; see Eric Weisstein (2020).

28. Such ontological reduction commits one to an "analytical illusion" as described by Teilhard de Chardin (2017, 139).

29. Individuation concerns the problem of how to uniquely distinguish one entity from everything else. As shown by Doyle (2019), problems of individuation have a long history in philosophy.

30. The Copenhagen interpretation focuses on Niels Bohr's correspondence principle and Max Born's statistical interpretation of the wave function; see Jan Faye (2019).

31. Details about Bohmian mechanics are documented by Sheldon Goldstein (2017).

32. The problematic philosophical claim of "actualism" is that the domain of the real and the actual are one and the same, thus excluding *potentiae* from the domain of the real.

33. The decoherence interpretation of quantum physics focuses on the loss of a system's information into its environment; without such loss, a quantum state could maintain coherence.

34. Hereafter, in this volume, reference to the Relational Reality model is intended to acknowledge reference to Michael Epperson's initial introduction of the "Relational Realist Interpretation" of quantum physics (Epperson 2009), and to the in-depth monograph *Foundations of Relational Realism* (Epperson and Zafiris 2013) coauthored with mathematical physicist and category theory expert, Elias Zafiris. Going beyond standard epistemic or actualist approaches, as stated by Epperson, "the relational realist interpretation of quantum mechanics is a *praxiological* interpretation; that is, these physical and logical relations are *ontologically active relations*, contributing not just to the epistemic coordination of quantum actualizations, but to the process of actualization itself" (Epperson 2009, 355).

35. The Principle of Least Action is a basic variational principle that uses an optimization method to obtain a system's dynamical trajectory "by imagining all possible trajectories that the system could conceivably take, computing the action (a functional of the trajectory) for each of these trajectories, and selecting one that makes the action locally stationary (traditionally called 'least'). True trajectories are those that have least action." An equivalent concept is Hamilton's principle, which is set up to "emphasize a particular constraint on the varied trajectories" (Chris Gray 2009).

36. Epperson and Zafiris' deployment of logical causality and a distinct logical order emerged from their work in interpreting quantum physics. Their concept of logical causality may be considered as a type of logic in reality as argued by Joseph Brenner in his work *Logic in Reality* (2008).

37. "In mathematics, topology is concerned with the properties of a geometric object "in which two objects are considered equivalent if they can be continuously deformed into one another" such as by stretching, twisting, crumpling and bending, but not gluing or tearing apart (Stephan Carlson 2017). As Vesselin Petrov states,

"Whitehead . . . can rightly be considered as one of the leading topologists of his time, as one of the originators of contemporary topology" (Petrov 2017, 163).

38. An internal relation is "a relation that is involved in or essential to the nature of the thing related" whereas an external relation is "one that does not affect its relata or is not a part of its relata" (Merriam-webster.com, 2020).

39. Quantum entanglement, experimentally demonstrated in multiple ways, is a phenomenon of quantum physics that *"implies the existence of global states of composite systems which cannot be written as a product of the states of individual subsystems."* As a consequence, pairs or groups of particles can potentially interact even when separated by a large distance (Horodecki et al. 2009, 865).

40. In physics, classical systems have unique, univocal states at a given time whereas quantum systems retain superpositions of states. A decoherence process brings a quantum system approximately into an apparently classical state by shifting the treatment of basic interactions to systems larger than what can be directly observed in standard quantum experiments.

41. Kastner, Kauffman and Epperson point out that a tacit assumption behind PEM is "that of actualism: the doctrine that only actual things exist," whereas in quantum physics, PNC and PEM "together evince the ontological significance of both actuality and potentiality" (Kastner et al. 2018, 161).

42. Here I am using "classical physics" to designate the proper classical approximation that it represents, relative to quantum physics; in turn "classical mechanics" here denotes the same physics but added to that are some common presuppositions based on an overlay of mechanistic-materialist metaphysics (see Čapek 1961; later in this chapter, see *Summary of the Relational Reality Model*).

43. An excellent introduction to quantum physics, including explicit examples of both the matrix and wave approaches, is provided by Steven Holzner (2012).

44. "One reason the global can never be deduced from the local quantum mechanically, but only induced, is that observables contextualized by multiple local measurement contexts do not commute; and as Kochen and Specker have shown, it is impossible even in principle to imbed local contextual Boolean subalgebras into a 'global' Boolean algebra . . . the ontological significance of the Kochen-Specker theorem with respect to relating local and global states is intimately related to the logical problem of predicating totalities" (Epperson and Zafiris 2013, 64-65).

45. An analogous suggestion has been made by Poli "to introduce propensities instead of forces, where the former should be regarded, not as simple possibilities, but as physical realities, as real as forces or fields . . . Forces and causes are the isolated, individualized versions of propensities. The latter apply to complex situations taken as wholes" (Poli 2010, 773).

46. Within Bohr's Copenhagen Interpretation, two sets of quantum system description are taken to be complementary. Initially, this was framed in terms of particle and wave properties, but later refined to focus on space-time descriptions (kinematic properties) or claims of causality (dynamic properties). As stated by Faye, "In general, Bohr considered the demands of complementarity in quantum mechanics to be logically on a par with the requirements of relativity in the theory of relativity. He believed that both theories were a result of novel aspects of the observation problem, namely the fact that observation in physics is context-dependent" (Faye 2019).

47. See Carsten Held's essay "The Kochen-Specker Theorem" in the *Stanford Encyclopedia of Philosophy* (Held 2018).

48. In the study of complex systems, one studies how parts of a system lead to collective behaviors of the system, and how the system interacts with its environment. Complex systems are discussed in chapter 4.

49. Complementarity is both an experimental and theoretical result of quantum physics, which holds that objects have certain pairs of complementary properties (particle-wave, position-momentum, etc.) that cannot be observed simultaneously. The concept of complementarity is central to the highly influential Copenhagen interpretation of quantum physics introduced by Neils Bohr. In general, its application is focused on epistemological considerations, and its apparent ontic consequences remain controversial; see discussion by Adam Becker (2018). However, Becker's book takes no account of the Boolean-non-Boolean logical distinction utilized by the *Logoi* framework, which readily explains complementarity from a more fundamental standpoint.

50. A detailed critique of analytic philosophy is provided by Robert Hanna in works featuring the importance of Kant's theories of the epistemological, metaphysical, and practical foundations of the sciences (Robert Hanna 2006; 2020).

51. In contrast to standard multiverse arguments, compatible with the modal realism of David Lewis in which all possible worlds are real, Whitehead's cosmic epochs are different stages of what is ultimately one unified reality similar to what is hypothesized by Roberto Unger and Lee Smolin in their work *The Singular Universe and the Reality of Time* (2015); see also McHenry's essay on the multiverse conjecture (McHenry 2011).

52. The Russell-Einstein Manifest of July 9, 1955, is available through the *Atomic Heritage Foundation* (atomicheritage.org, accessed June 30, 2020).

53. Details of contemporary debates within analytic metaphysics are beyond my current scope, which emphasizes fundamental ontology. In general, such debates focus on epistemology and constraints of linguistic reference. These debates most often emphasize the importance of properties, issues of individuation, and possible attributions of causal powers, among other features; for example, see Lorenzo Azzano (2014). A detailed critique of analytic epistemologies is provided by Phillip Stambovsky (2009).

54. Arguments for such derivative status and various aspects of these contrasts are presented in chapters 2–4.

55. Inspired by Whitehead's work, Auxier and Herstein state that, "in the *idea* of extension, *undivided divisibility*, we have a whole to which all the possibilities, including unrealized possibilities, belong, under the condition that we not speak of cosmic epochs beyond our own, except conjecturally" (Auxier and Herstein 2017, 150).

Chapter 3

Gordian Knot to *Logoi* Framework

Many challenging philosophical problems have arisen out of science including, among others, causality, emergence, continuity, temporality, and potentiality. These fundamental issues impact numerous ongoing debates. For example, the free will debate is dependent on presuppositions related to causality, emergence, and potentiality; and the determinism debate is dependent on these same presuppositions and more. The results of addressing this class of interrelated problems one by one have thus far been unsatisfactory because the issues are interconnected and mutually implicative. An integrated, systematic philosophical framework is required, whether the *Logoi* framework here proposed or some other analogous framework (see *Integrative Frameworks and Methodology*, chapter 8). In addressing these problems via some version of strong reductionism, many thinkers often make unrecognized, generally implicit, philosophical claims that a part can appropriately represent the whole, and that such part-whole mereology obeys simple mappings and a single logic. A more productive way of interpreting the insights of contemporary physics would approach these challenges from a more empirical systems approach, which at its core posits that a local event is not only embedded in a more global context but is in part constituted by its history and processual context and so cannot be removed from such context without error or distortion. Focusing on isolated parts is a powerful methodological tool for science, but it can only result in ontological approximations, however practical and operationally effective. Complementing the scientific process, integrative, systematic philosophical frameworks are needed to clarify fundamental presuppositions in addition to interpretive and contextual relations.

My *Logoi* framework offers a comprehensive vision for addressing a Gordian knot of problems arising out of both the discoveries of modern science and more than two millennia of philosophical debate. Although I do not claim to have achieved definitive solutions, this framework does seem to solve, or at least open up new ways of solving a set of complex, interrelated puzzles.

Below is a baker's dozen (13) of problems that the *Logoi* framework reconceives.

THE GORDIAN KNOT OF PROBLEMS

1. Measurement—Quantum systems can have many values at once for an observable, but upon measurement, such systems "collapse" to only one value. When and how does this happen?
2. Potentiality—Are possible relations (*potentiae*) part of the real (having some ontic status), or do they merely have some pragmatic or epistemic status?
3. Continuity—How are the discrete and continuous aspects of the world to be reconciled? In particular, how can one reconcile quantum physics (whose fundamental structure consists in discrete topological and logical relations) with theories of relativity (whose fundamental structure consists in continuous metrical relations)?
4. Temporality—Is the experience of time (and of temporality) an illusion or does it have some ontic basis in the real world?
5. Causal relations—Is our inference of causal relations only based on epistemic or pragmatic considerations (as with Hume's habits of association), or is there a more fundamental ontic basis for causation?
6. Law—What is the ultimate basis for physical relationships? What enables the uniformity of physical relationships across the universe (i.e., universality)?
7. Emergence—What is emergence? Is it epistemic only, via supervenience, or does it arise by means of some ontic, multilevel creation of genuinely new processes or entities?
8. Information and Knowledge—How is knowledge grounded if not solely in information?
9. Induction—How can we justify inductive inference from the observed to the unobserved? Are there objective regularities enabling an effective and intuitive solution?
10. Access—Are the abstract realms of logic and mathematics distinct yet inaccessible (as with Plato's allegory of the cave), or are such features a deeply imbedded aspect of reality?
11. Matter-symbol problem—What is the fundamental relationship of knower and known?

12. Mind-body problem—How does the physical brain enable processes of consciousness?
13. Problem of meaning—What is the fundamental basis for values and meaning, which appear to lack any scientific basis?

Each and every one of my Gordian knot problems has been discussed before at length, the problems articulated in multiple ways, and afforded a broad array of suggested solutions, but their seeming intractability has been so extensive that scholars often suggest that philosophy is somehow incapable of making any real "progress" as, arguably, science and technology surely can. This question of progress in philosophy has been confronted by David Chalmers (2015) and Nicholas Maxwell (2017) and also in Part IV of a festschrift for Peter van Inwagen (John Keller 2017).

As noted briefly above, the *Logoi* framework provides critical leverage to effectively unravel this Gordian knot of problems. This new interpretive framework strives to yield such results by providing promising routes to solution, and enable progress, not just for one or two of these foundational problems but, directly or indirectly, by enabling possible routes to solution for the entire suite of these interrelated problems. The *Logoi* framework strategy here proposed may be the first attempt to simultaneously unwind this entire Gordian knot set of problems.

CRITERIA FOR AN ADEQUATE SYSTEMATIC FRAMEWORK

Building on Whitehead's defense of systematic (or speculative) philosophy, my integrative, systematic approach is centered on his two rational criteria, these being logic and coherence, and two empirical criteria, those of applicability and adequacy.[1]

Philosopher James Bradley argued that an adequate theory of actualization needs to address three basic questions.

> These are the questions of the nature of origin, difference and order...[an adequate theory] requires an account of that activity which is in some sense prior to difference and order because it is the condition of difference and order. In the second place, [it] requires an account of the actualization of difference or individuality, of the nature of differentiation. And in the third place, such a theory requires an account of the actualization of order. (Bradley 2009, 169)

My fundamental framework provides a way to apply these criteria and address these basic questions through *potentiae*, its distinct logic along with a logic of actualizations, and a theory of relations, including relations of relations (the meta-level). Details of how this is carried out within the *Logoi* framework are provided throughout this work. An alternative tripartite schema, somewhat analogous to Bradley's, is that of form, dynamics, and unification which, John Berthrong argues, can provide a bridge between philosophical frameworks, West and East, from Whitehead and Robert Neville to the neo-Confucian Chu Hsi (Berthrong, 1998).

THE *LOGOI* FRAMEWORK

Based on a confluence of recent scientific research results, philosophical analysis, and human experience, my proposed *Logoi* framework incorporates the Relational Reality model for quantum process, which is concisely summarized below. Along with this summary, I also highlight some implications of this *Logoi* framework, which are explained in greater detail in subsequent chapters. The *Logoi* framework is a systematic philosophical framework based on a complex synthesis that leverages advances in multiple disciplines, especially quantum physics and philosophy, information and semiotics, and complex systems theory. My efforts in multi-pronged analysis, multilevel synthesis, and the development of integral wholes is consonant with Roberto Poli's study of both part-whole and whole-whole connections within which he demonstrates how reductive methods alone inevitably lose relevant information (Poli 2009).

The most fundamental notions are process, logic, and relations as explained in chapter 2. Closely associated with these are the fundamental notions of succession (*à la* process), *potentiae* (domains of non-Boolean logic), and local-global relations, and relations of relations or meta-levels. These notions all reflect basic human experience and correlate very well with concepts inferred from quantum process and results of both modern science and humanistic scholarship. Based on experimental results and analysis in quantum physics, and from phenomenological analysis, I hypothesize that all reality, taken inclusively and at all levels, consistent with the "quanta of explanation" per Auxier and Herstein (2017), includes *res extensa, res qualia*, and *potentiae* (latin, respectively, for "real extension," "real qualitative relations," and "potential relations"). Fundamental process arises from never-ending successions of events, each of which is constituted by a combination of its immediate fields and "particle" inputs and *potentiae* for their actualization. Temporality and spatiality are co-extensive with such process; that is, they arise as part of the process itself (i.e., they are not pre-existing space-time structures functioning as containers for process). While the pre-space relations of the logic of *potentiae* exhibit full symmetries of physical theory, various broken symmetries arise upon the actualization process, especially the asymmetry of time that emerges from the inevitable successiveness of such process.

Many antinomies in understanding the concept of time, as detailed, for example, by Tallis (2017), can be readily resolved within the *Logoi* framework. Alternative paths in possibility pre-space can be modeled as sums of certain physical parameters over *potentiae* (e.g., Feynman sums over histories). Using minimization techniques, including symmetry principles, many central laws of physics can be derived (see discussion about physical relations in chapter 4). Relation is a fundamental notion[2] and, in addition to modern field physics, relations of relations in *potentiae* pre-space give rise to non-local (local-global) connectedness [topology, category theory (an algebra of relations)]. Such local-global linkages provide context for any complex system and enable multiscale emergence, in turn giving rise to multilevel frameworks of increasing complexity.

THE RELATIONAL REALITY MODEL

The Relational Reality model, introduced in chapter 2, is a central component of the *Logoi* framework. Within the conception of full ontological reality for both the logic of actualizations and the logic of *potentiae*, this model makes a critical distinction in associating the former with standard Aristotelian or Boolean logic, and linking the latter with a non-Boolean logic.

The scientific basis for this distinction of logics arises from a recent convergence in three quantum physics research programs that have yielded a breakthrough in the understanding of fundamental quantum process. In particular, in their paper "Taking Heisenberg's Potentia Seriously," Ruth Kastner, Stuart Kauffman, and Michael Epperson combine their three approaches, each comprising a decade or more of substantial research and publication, to show why quantum *potentiae* should be considered as having ontological reality, and why that concept is uniquely capable of solving a complex set of quantum problems (Kastner et al. 2018). Further, both Kastner (2013) and Epperson and Zafiris (2013) have independently proposed specific solutions for the problem of quantum measurement transition that is "grounded in the ontological interpretation of quantum potentiae" (Kastner et al. 2018, 162). Independently of the Kastner et al. collaboration, Christian de Ronde has argued as well for the distinct reality of quantum possibility in a modal interpretation that emphasizes modality and contextuality (de Ronde 2007) with more details provided in a later PhD dissertation and paper, although this insightful philosophical work does not directly address non-Boolean logic and category theory as carried out by Epperson and Zafiris (see de Ronde 2011, 2015). Gregg Jaeger has further clarified uses of *potentia* by Aristotle and Werner Heisenberg (Jaeger, 2017). Elio Conte also argues for a triadic logic basis for quantum physics, which he interprets as involving self-referential processes enabling "such transition from potentiality to actualization" (Conte 2011, 234). These approaches, emphasizing *potentiae,* contrast with conventional approaches, most often invoking the metaphysical claim of actualism (almost always as an unstated presupposition; see extended critique of actualism by Kastner et al. (2018, 161–163)), which either adds some new, untested physics to enable resolution, or hypothesizes vast realms of actualized possible worlds (as with the many-worlds interpretation, or multiverses), leaving Ockham's razor not just dulled, but surely crushed.[3]

It is especially significant that the combined efforts of Epperson and Zafiris, Kauffman, and Kastner, keeping in mind complementary philosophical work by de Ronde and others, achieve this advance by adding interpretive nuance but without introducing any new physics, which enables their complementary approaches to fully leverage the century-long success of the standard formulation of basic quantum physics. For the purpose of the *Logoi* framework, I focus on the Relational Reality model of Epperson and Zafiris (2013), which is part of the Kastner et al. integration, because their model handles both the issue of distinct logics for the realms of actualization and *potentiae*, and also local-global features. Their approach is unique in its focus on category theory analyses for quantum physics issues. Their work demonstrates the necessity of making the philosophical distinction, within full reality, of both actualizations *and potentiae*, the former as essential to givenness and place, the latter potential relationships as providing a needed basis for fundamental indeterminacy and for physical relationships (see *"Law"–From Entailment to Constrained Processual Histories* in chapter 4). As Auxier and Herstein state, "Epperson's and Zafiris' insistence that relations should be treated as having a genuine standing of their own, and not as merely parasitic upon their relata, makes their work one of the most important contributions in the philosophy of physics in recent years." (Auxier and Herstein 2017, 21) Let me rephrase the key point above for emphasis: the Relational Reality model requires a distinction between the logic of actualizations (standard Aristotelian or Boolean logic) and a non-Boolean logic for *potentiae*; real-world application of these logics necessarily requires three components; these are input-output-context with context most often designated as "environment" in quantum physics applications.

Quantum theorist Hans Primas affirms this position. He states that "modern physics proves that the description of matter requires a theory with a non-Boolean logical structure, with the consequence that any description of a universe of discourse including the material world needs to be non-Boolean . . .

A partial Boolean algebra is a family of Boolean algebras whose operations coincide on overlaps so that it is *locally Boolean, yet globally non-Boolean"* (Primas 2017, 3). Several key issues, central to the *Logoi* framework, such as the fundamental logical orders, domains of discourse, and context, are reflected in Primas's detailed exposition.

> The family of Boolean contexts plays a privileged role since a sound theory should be able to describe intersubjectively communicable empirical propositions. Therefore the overall non-Boolean framework must have a locally Boolean logical structure. This guarantees that aspects of reality can be perceived by projections onto empirically accessible Boolean reference frames.
>
> The requirement that empirical propositions have to be truth-definite can only be achieved by deliberately suppressing irrelevant features . . . *Objectivity* in the modern sense is enforced by the requirement that an empirically meaningful statement has to belong to a Boolean domain of discourse.
>
> In order to describe aspects of an overall non-Boolean reality we have to ignore particular global features such that the remainder separates into facts. Inevitably, such a description is valid only within the adopted partition of the world, that is, within the *chosen context*. Every locally Boolean description suppresses correlations between Boolean domains. (Primas 2017, 4)

In this framework, the overall non-Boolean reality also includes the pre-space realm of potential relations (*potentiae*), in addition to measurement outcomes (facts), which by themselves are necessarily limited to an adopted partition of the world, that is, a chosen context. In this way, measurement outcomes are restricted to an objectivity and, within such constraints, limited to particular Boolean domains of discourse (i.e., sets of actualizations).

By applying recent developments in mathematical category theory to quantum physics, in ways complementary to Primas's focus on algebraic quantum theory, the Relational Reality model shows how to correlate these two logical orders, Boolean and non-Boolean or, equivalently, the logic of actualizations and the logic of *potentiae*. A key starting point is the recently achieved recognition that quantum physics exemplifies the fact that physical extensiveness (viz., the grounding for standard space-time description) is fundamentally topological rather than metrical, with its proper logico-mathematical framework being category-theoretic rather than set-theoretic. By this thesis, as Epperson and Zafiris argue (2013, 64–65), extensiveness fundamentally entails not only relations of objects, but also relations of relations; thus fundamental quanta are properly defined as "units of logico-physical relation" rather than merely "units of physical relata," the latter being presumed as exclusive by both materialism and the broader presupposition of actualism. Objects are, in this way, always understood as relata, and likewise relations are always understood objectively. Objects and relations, in other words, are coherently defined as mutually implicative. This approach coheres well with contemporary research in semiotics (see chapter 5), and with John Deely's treatment of "things" and real processes (not mind dependent) in addition to objects (as mind-dependent entities) (Deely 2009).

In their seminal work, Epperson and Zafiris demonstrate that a revised decoherent histories interpretation of quantum mechanics, involving both local and global system histories, structured within a category-theoretic topological formalism, provides a coherent and consistent conceptual framework by which local quantum events can be globally and internally related, both causally and logically (Epperson and Zafiris 2013, 25). Further, this Relational Reality model enables a quantum physical description of spatiotemporal extension that is highly compatible philosophically with the model proposed by Whitehead, considered through the non-reductive lens of Auxier and Herstein (2017) and Campbell (2015), refining and enhancing Whitehead's model by elevating it from a set-theoretic basis to a category-theoretic one; that is, from simply sets of things, however complex, to relations of relations, an algebra of relations. Albeit a speculative ontological project, the conceptual framework of the Relational Reality model incorporates a rigorous mathematical formalism yielding uniquely powerful solutions to several critical problems of quantum physics, and does this by integrating their solutions within a coherent and intuitive ontological scheme.

The central thesis of the Relational Reality model is that the classical, conventional conception of the relationship between physical objects and their presumed direct mapping to discrete facts must be reconceived such that physical things are understood as the outcome of real histories of quantum events. This requires a reconceptualization of ontological and contextual properties as mutually implicative features of every quantum event (thus, inevitably, the triad of input-output-context). In this Relational Realist framework, quantum events are identified as measurement outcomes that refer to corresponding physical observables. The theory then provides the means of relating these events. In this respect, the conceptual complexity of any ontological interpretation of quantum theory stems from two factors:

(1) The actualization of a measurement outcome event representing the state of a quantum system, though always globally objective, can only be predicted probabilistically and contextually—that is, relative to a particular local Boolean measurement context of a selected observable (i.e., a context wherein measurement outcomes can be expressed as mutually exclusive and exhaustive true/false propositions). It is always via such local Boolean contextuality that the universe is decomposed into the triad of system, measuring apparatus, and environment with their respective

state vectors.[4] Equally important, the probability valuations can be affirmed only retrodictively, after a measured result (i.e., a novel fact/ unique actualization of a potential outcome state) has been registered by the corresponding measuring apparatus.

(2) The totality of events related to the behavior of a quantum system cannot be represented within the same local Boolean measurement context due to the property of non-commutativity of quantum observables.[5]

These two factors together necessitate a thorough rethinking of our conceptual and mathematical representation of the notion of a physical continuum suited to the quantum domain of discourse. The first factor illustrates the prominent role that potential relations play in the process of quantum measurement. Quantum physics always entails the evolution[6] of (a) potential outcome states that cannot be integrated in terms of classical Boolean logic (e.g., Schrödinger's cat is both alive and dead) into (b) probable outcome states that can be integrated in terms of classical Boolean logic (Schrödinger's cat is alive with probability x, or dead with probability y); and since $x + y = 1$, one and only one of these unique outcomes must occur. Unless the full measurement context is taken into account, the proper evolution of *potentia* to probability cannot ensue. This evolution is the very heart of quantum physics, without which locally contextualized events cannot be integrated into the globally objective, logically consistent histories ubiquitous to experience.

The second factor likewise illustrates the contextual significance of the empirical requirement of preparation procedures for the evaluation of observables via quantum measurement. These measurement procedures determine the initial actual state of the system, and the measuring apparatus establishes the local context that constrains the final actual state associated with the final measurement. This presupposed contextual correlation is typically understood as an instrumental consideration rather than a philosophical one—that is, a desideratum satisfied via an ad hoc conceptual intervention arbitrarily imposed upon the standard formalism (viz., von Neumann's projection postulate[7]).

Epperson and Zafiris show that these particular instrumental considerations can be more effectively interpreted, both philosophically and mathematically, as necessarily presupposed features of quantum physics when these contextual correlations are depicted topologically—viz., a topological localization of quantum observables with respect to local Boolean contexts (viz., sets of actualizations) (Epperson and Zafiris 2013). An equivalent summary is provided by Primas as follows:

Two Boolean descriptions are said to be *complementary* if they cannot be embedded into a single Boolean description . . . The binary "either-or" thinking of the Boolean worldview is a prejudice that prevents us from new ways of thinking. The development of quantum physics throughout the 20th century has shown that an all-encompassing description of the universe does not have a Boolean logical structure with the law of the excluded middle. Consequently, *the strictly Boolean worldview of classical science has to be given up*. This implies the necessity to use different, incompatible, sets of concepts for different contexts. This incompatibility does not just express a cognitive, or epistemic, limit, but is a fundamental feature of the world. (Primas 2017, 17)

To address this new quantum understanding about different contexts of observation, Primas also points out that Niels Bohr introduced the notion of complementarity to handle incompatible classical concepts, which alone presuppose the completeness of the Boolean order of actualizations for the purpose of characterizing the fullness of reality. The requirement of complementarity is made technically explicit by stating that "two Boolean descriptions are said to be *incompatible* if they cannot be embedded into a single Boolean reference frame" (Primas 2017, 16).

The above quantum perspective, as articulated by both Primas (2017) and Epperson and Zafiris (2013), shows how classical mechanics,[8] despite being an excellent approximation for many practical applications, is not only technically incorrect about the predictions of atomic spectra and other quantum effects. Even though marvelously successful in enabling practical calculations for most macroscopic systems, classical mechanics, introduced by Isaac Newton over 300 years ago, encourages a faulty mechanistic-deterministic metaphysics that is directly falsified by the above requirement of two fundamental logical orders, Boolean and non-Boolean, the order of actualizations and the order of *potentiae*. Albert Einstein's relativity theories, special and general, being of classical form and focused on space-time relationships, do not address this issue (see chapter 6).

By employing rich conceptual, philosophical, and mathematical frameworks, and taking advantage of their systematic coherence, Epperson, Kastner, Kauffman, Primas, Zafiris, and colleagues have accomplished major steps toward the formulation of a realistic ontological interpretation of quantum physics that avoids the paradoxes, inconsistencies, and counterintuitiveness typical of many alternative interpretations.

UNTYING THE GORDIAN KNOT WITH THE *LOGOI* FRAMEWORK

The *Logoi* framework, in combination with advances enabled by the Relational Reality model in understanding quantum process, including the complementary integration of this and related models, systematically breaks the Gordian knot problem set by denying key presuppositions, or by resolving impediments that generate these problems. In particular, my tentative (admittedly incomplete) responses[9] for each problem within the Gordian knot are briefly explained below; subsequent chapters offer more full explanation. This latest effort at untying the Gordian knot leverages the work of numerous scholars who have advanced the relevant research. The unique power of the *Logoi* framework lies in reconceptualizing both problems and potential solutions and in leveraging and synthesizing such prior work to augment the framework. For most knots, further discussion is provided in chapter 4, with the exception of knots 8 (information and knowledge) and 11 (matter-symbol problem) (see chapter 5), and knot 13 (problem of meaning) (see chapter 8).

1. *Measurement*—Quantum systems can have many values at once for an observable, but upon measurement, such systems "collapse" to only one value. When and how does this happen? What is the meaning of wave function collapse in quantum physics, and what is the role of measurement contextuality in determining objective outcomes?

   Response: The Relational Reality model leverages new developments in category theory, decoherence theory in quantum physics, and philosophy to resolve this quantum theory of measurement problem, utilizing as well the concept of partial Boolean algebras. The introduction of *potentiae* as part of full reality is a key to solving problems of interpreting quantum physics, illustrating as well the fundamental distinction between the orders of actualizations (Boolean logic) and *potentiae* (non-Boolean logic); wave function collapse is a transition between these orders. Objective outcomes pertain to the order of actualization whereas the ontological ground of context and possibility in the world arises from the creativity of pre-space *potentiae*.

2. *Potentiality*—Are possible relations (*potentiae*) part of the real (having some ontic status), or do they merely have some pragmatic or epistemic status?

   Response: Both actualizations and *potentiae* are part of the real, built on affirming the reality of both non-Boolean (possibility) logic and standard Boolean (actualization) logic as essential to contemporary quantum physics. Thus, the *Logoi* framework treats *potentiae* as genuinely real (ontic, not just epistemic). Indeed, such a reality is arguably presupposed in practice via human choice and action, thus the importance of recognizing a distinct order of *potentiae*.[10]

3. *Continuity*—How are the discrete and continuous aspects of the world to be reconciled? In particular, how can one reconcile quantum physics (whose fundamental structure consists in discrete topological and logical

relations) with theories of relativity (whose fundamental structure consists in continuous metrical relations)?

Response: Both discreteness (quantization as fundamental in quantum actualizations) and continuity (real and continuous wave functions in non-Boolean possibility space; that is, pre-space *potentiae*) are essential to the fullness of reality. For example, the Relational Reality model reconciles quantum physics (with its quantization of observable outcomes via *discrete* topological and logical relations) with relativity theories, which involve only continuous variables, and whose fundamental structure consists in *continuous* metrical relations. Further, such metrical relations, instead of being simply assumed as in standard theory, are here hypothesized to be derivative and emergent from continuous pre-space structures and fundamental quantum process.

4. *Temporality*—Is the experience of time (and of temporality) an illusion or does it have some ontic basis in the real world?

Response: Temporal passage and temporality are real emergents from fundamental quantum process as each and every quantum event involves passage from alternative possible outcomes, given particular input of fields and "particles," to particular and discrete actualizations; asymmetric temporal passage is coextensive with such quantum process. Symmetry in variables pertains to non-Boolean possibility space constraints (of pre-space *possibiliae*) and not to particular, discrete actualizations, which always exhibit symmetry breaking and have the asymmetry of input-output-context, however effective the local approximation of (context independent) symmetry may be. For the Relational Reality model, topological relations of inclusion yield an asymmetrical logical order (*à la* the arrow in category theory)—the logical asymmetry of this process is reflected temporally as the one-way arrow of time. Temporal order is a derivative and emergent metrical-extensive relational feature of fundamental quantum process. In short, certain abstract models may suppose (incorrectly) that time is mere illusion, but fundamental succession and temporal passage are real emergents. This resolves the apparent conflict exhibited by *Bergson, Einstein, and Their Famous Debates of 1922* (see chapter 2).

5. *Causal relations*—Is our inference of causal relations only based on epistemic or pragmatic considerations (as with Hume's habits of association), or is there a more fundamental ontic basis for causation?

Response: Causal relations represent real relations within pre-space *potentiae*, and correlations in the passage from potentiality to actuality for each and every quantum event; physical relations represent general constraints on such process imbedded in highly correlated non-Boolean *possibiliae*. Within the Relational Reality model, global information conditions the generation of individual local potential facts and such local facts incorporate aspects of the global totality as input, and, in turn, become part of a new totality. Regarding the common presupposition in physics of causal closure (i.e., physical causal completeness within finite systems), Relational Reality's approach to the local/global framework and part/whole relations, which includes both physical causality and logical causality, is free from the paradoxes of self-reference[11] and the imposition of a classically conceived spatiotemporal continuum. Thus, no ultimate closure is available for finite systems and, even for the universe as a whole, because ever new facts break such closure (thus, a corollary for finite physical systems to Kurt Gödel's proof in logic). Further, the fundamental distinction of the Boolean and non-Boolean logical orders (i.e., the order of actualizations and *potentiae*, respectively) denies simple causal closure of the physical.[12]

6. *Physical Relationship*—What is the ultimate basis for physical relationships? What enables the uniformity of physical relationships across the universe (i.e., universality)?

Response: Fundamental process arises from never-ending successions of events, each of which are constituted by a combination of their immediate fields and "particle" inputs and *potentiae* for their realization. Temporality and spatiality are co-extensive with such process, and the asymmetry of time emerges from the inevitable successiveness of such process ("one darn thing after another"). Alternative paths in pre-space *potentiae* can be modeled as sums of certain physical parameters ("action") over *potentiae* (Feynman "sums over histories"). Most laws of physics can be derived using this technique (utilizing the Principle of Least Action (PLA), including symmetry principles); in particular, electromagnetism, quantum physics, and quantum field theory with time-space metric and gravity as emergent (see *"Law"–From Entailment to Constrained Processual Histories* in chapter 4). Relation is a fundamental notion and, in addition to PLA and modern field physics, relations of relations in pre-space *potentiae* give rise to quantum entanglement deriving from non-local (local-global) connectedness [topology, category theory (an algebra of relations)]. Pre-space *potentiae* are properly characterized by symmetry conditions due to the inclusiveness of potential relations, which enable approximate context independence, whereas asymmetry arises from actualizations of quantum process, which impose context dependence (viz., input-output-context). Finally, non-local connectedness (via local-global constraints enabled by global topological phase, etc.—the entanglement phenomena of quantum physics) enables uniformity of physical relationships across the universe, which constitutes the principle of universality.

7. *Emergence*—What is emergence? Is it epistemic only, via supervenience, or does it arise by means of some ontic, multilevel creation of genuinely new processes or entities?

   Response: potentiae + process + local-global; fundamental quantum process always involves a transition from potential relations (*potentiae*) to actuality, with an associated range of possible outcomes; full reducibility to constraints of pre-given actualities is a limiting condition upon highly restricted initial conditions, boundary conditions, and constraints. Determinism and entailment are logical and physical limits, most often imbedded in complex networks of constraints, often not known or visible—not fixed and inevitable God-given law as presumed in classical metaphysics. The Relational Reality model incorporates the creativity of ontic possibility (*potentiae*), which enables genuine, ontic emergence in context of local and global histories of logically conditioned events; further, this model makes possible the emergence of a metrical continuum (space-time) from more fundamental quantum, topological-logical structure via pre-space (equivalently, Whitehead's extensive continuum). Complementary to diachronic quantum process, such multiscale emergence is synchronic, and the associated "actual entities" can, in principle, be of any scale.

8. *Information and knowledge*—How is knowledge grounded if not solely in information?

   Response: Knowledge (based on information—a sequence of symbols that can be interpreted as a message) cannot be framed with symbols alone—the "symbol grounding problem." For the *Logoi* framework, information is fundamentally a logical notion, which is locally formulated by the Relational Reality model in terms of Boolean algebraic logic (i.e., a logic of measurement outcomes/actualizations). Symbol references, context, and thereby knowledge are grounded in relational information exchange (having both epistemic and ontic components). In addition, such context-boosted information is coextensive with input-output-context triadicities of an inclusive semiotics, which go beyond the local, Boolean limitations of information; this correlates with the distinction highlighted by Robert Logan between syntactics (Shannon information) and full semantics (see chapter 5) (Logan, 2014).

9. *Induction*—How can we justify inductive inference from the observed to the unobserved? Are there objective regularities enabling an effective and intuitive solution?

   Response: The inevitable encoding and decoding framework of complex physical systems points to an ontological (not just epistemological) basis for induction. Further, local-global interrelations formulated in the Relational Reality model point to a physical grounding for both emergence and inductive processes; such interrelations are reinforced by recent research, as summarized by Ellis, supporting top-down causal relations and constraints (Ellis, 2016). Such complex systems and local-global features provide a uniform basis for objective regularities and consistent mappings from the observed to the unobserved.

10. *Access* of mathematical entities—Are the abstract realms of logic and mathematics distinct yet inaccessible (as with Plato's allegory of the cave), or are such features a deeply imbedded aspect of reality?

    Response: The Relational Reality model clarifies, via its handling of *potentiae* and local-global relations, the fundamental basis for the causal efficacy of certain mathematical entities; that is, as symbols for relations of relations in pre-space, the order of *potentiae*. Unlike the asymmetry of actualizations (or measurement outcomes) via quantum process, such real "relations of relations in pre-space" are symmetric, which explains the importance of symmetry in physical relations even though the fundamental quantum process itself and the emergent lived world incorporate fundamental asymmetry. In the real world, the context independence required for full symmetry is, at best, an approximation because of the unavoidable role of context (i.e., the inevitable input-output-context triadic).

11. *Matter-symbol problem*—What is the fundamental relationship of knower and known?

    Response: As Howard Pattee states, "Epistemology by its very meaning presupposes a separation of the world into the knower and the known . . . the knowledge vehicle cannot be in the same category as what it is about . . . the epistemic cut." (Pattee 2010, 525) The knower-known relation always maps to some form of input-output, and this in turn always involves both an input-output-context triadic and fundamental quantum process, which bridges the logic of *potentiae* and the logic of actualization. The epistemic cut and matter-symbol problem emerge from the distinction of standard input-output logics, and they are overcome through the interplay of triadic forms and these fundamental processes. In this way, the knower-known distinction, the epistemic cut, and the matter-symbol issue have interrelated epistemic and ontological components.

12. *Problem of consciousness*—How does the physical brain alone enable consciousness?

    Response: The hundreds of attempts to solve the mind-body problem, what Arthur Schopenhauer called the "world-knot," have all failed. The *Logoi* framework provides a new way to potentially transform the formulation of this complex problem. Consciousness is an emergent capability of the mind, distinct from brain actualizations (Boolean outputs), with the capacity to reflexively contrast "that which is" with "that which could be" and make decisions among alternative possibilities, which derive from non-Boolean *potentiae* associated with fundamental quantum process. Self-conscious awareness and its subjective feelings arise from non-linear feedback between such contrasts and active selection, quantum process *potentiae* to actualizations; channeling these processes through the neurological system and mental models (mappings) enables varying levels of anticipatory capability. Brain actualizations represent actualized Boolean outputs or system measurements. Neuroscience research is important for these questions, but such research, focused only on Boolean actualizations and their correlations, cannot by itself solve the consciousness "problem" due to the neglect of non-Boolean landscapes of *potentiae*. The mind, with its conscious capabilities, is the real emergent complex model system that manages all inputs (both Boolean actualizations and non-Boolean *potentiae*), given environmental context and, working via complex systems modeling of enfolding inputs and unfolding responses, makes and implements decisions.[13]

13. *Problem of meaning*—What is the fundamental basis for values and meaning, which appear to lack any scientific basis?

   Response: Some experience meaning in the world as a given and an essential reality; others point to a lack of philosophical justification for such a concept, which appears to lack any scientific basis. Therefore, some scholars view any reference to meaning as epiphenomenal, something that merely supervenes on material substrate and has no separate reality. In such a view, connecting directly experienced meaning to any scientific foundation would be a "bridge too far." The *Logoi* framework provides a possible way to transform the formulation of this complex issue. Building on the reality of *potentiae* and local-global linkages, as developed in the Relational Reality model above, one can now see the multi-scale basis for discussing ultimate context for the input-output-context triad, incorporated by all complex systems. This basis includes reference and truth (viz., reliability and integrity in the representation of things and relations) and relationships between things and symbols (pointers to relations, context, and things). Indeed, the *Logoi* framework leverages multi-disciplinary elements of such context, including quantum physics, non-linear dynamics, category theory, emergence, semiotics and biosemiotics, systematic philosophy, and metaphysics. Inevitably, multiple layers of context are grounded in some ultimate context that includes reference to ultimate boundaries and other ultimates—the order of ultimacies—including the non-contingent order and the spiritual dimension (see chapter 8).

Another framing of scholarly approaches to the problem of meaning, all emergent in the past 150 years, is proposed by Kalevi Kull and colleagues in the essay *Semiotics has no Beginning*.

1. "meaning . . . as a phenomenon, as a given presence" [phenomenology: Edmund Husserl, Martin Heidegger . . .]
2. "meaning as a relation" [language based–analytic philosophy: Gottlob Frege, Bertrand Russell . . .]
3. "meaning [as a] process" [semiotics: Charles Sanders Peirce, John Deely; process philosophy: Whitehead, Hartshorne . . .] (Kalevi Kull 2005, ix).

The full meaning of "meaning" depends on these multiple layers of context (phenomenological; relational; processual) which, via landscapes of *potentiae*, via both Boolean and non-Boolean logical orders, represents relational networks of essentially unlimited complexity. Yet, because relations cannot, in principle, operate in isolation, any and all networks of relations, as argued by Shields, require some relata, some basis or grounding, to avoid incurring some infinite regress (Shields, 2016). This general constraint about possible relations indicates the need for some ultimate context that includes reference to the order of ultimacies and the spiritual dimension. These issues are finally addressed in chapter 8 through the deployment of Desmond's intimate universal (Desmond 2016) and Hartshorne's inclusive asymmetry of the contraries, necessity, and contingency (Viney and Shields 2020).

Once again, the *Logoi* framework, building on the new Relational Reality model, constitutes the magic thread which, when carefully drawn out, can effectively unravel, or make significant progress in unraveling, the Gordian knot set. This new interpretive framework yields promising proposed solutions, directly or indirectly, for the entire suite of these interrelated problems.

QUANTUM MODELS AND THE SEARCH FOR COHERENCE WITH BASIC EXPERIENCE

Based on the Relational Reality model, the fact of quantum superposition is readily understood for contemporary quantum physics as referring to superpositions of potential relations (*potentiae*). However, for those committed to actualism (i.e., denial of a distinction, within the real, of the actual and the possible), wherein superposition represents an enigma, there have been efforts to modify quantum physics to enable a realist interpretation. An example of a non-linear approach that bypasses the superposition problem is that proposed by J. R. Croca and the Portuguese group (see item #6 below).

With continued failure to resolve the quantum measurement problem and conceptual incompatibilities between quantum and relativity theory, various approaches have arisen over the past several decades that appear to celebrate high abstraction and theory. With the exception of Croca's non-linear theory, most of these proposals appear incompatible with basic human experience or intuition. Examples of such scientific exotica are "many worlds" (of the many-worlds interpretation for quantum measurement), and multiple universes (or multiverses). A few of these theory-oriented concepts are listed below along with their primary problematic features:

1. multiverse/many worlds—denies any distinction between actuality and possibility; every wave function collapse actualizes a new world, thus yielding severe ontological overflow;
2. fully time-symmetric solutions for the measurement problem solve some formal problems but, in early formulations, hold on to actualism and deny temporality. However, the Possibilist Transactional Interpretation (PTI), in Ruth Kastner's interpretive extension of John Cramer's earlier work (Kastner 2013), provides a promising alternative that avoids these limitations and affirms *potentiae*, although its current formulation does not focus on topological and phase effects. Nevertheless, PTI comprises both unitary and non-unitary evolution, the latter being the onset of a transaction, and thereby addresses both phase and topological effects. Evaluating details of the relationship of PTI and Relational Realism is a topic for future research (Ruth Kastner, private communication, 2020);
3. block universe model—denies potentiality and claims absolute determinism; inconsistent with hard-core common sense; presumes a direct entailment model for physical relationships; based exclusively on a Boolean logical model, which neglects the non-Boolean component of quantum process and the inevitable context for real physical process. An extensive critique of block universe notions is provided by Tallis (2017). Further, Kastner et al. point out that the "static block world comprising no more than a set of actual events cannot really be a dynamical ontology" (Kastner et al. 2018, 163).
4. epistemic-focused models—Bohr's Copenhagen interpretation focuses on measurement outcomes, or facts, and their correlation; within its epistemic limitations this standard model is basically correct. However, efforts to ontologize this interpretation encounter serious problems, and these problems, first highlighted by the Bohr-Einstein debates, motivate the investigation of alternatives for a realist interpretation. Another epistemic-focused approach is that of quantum Bayesian models, which take a subjectivist view of quantum probability as a measure of an individual's degree of belief. As Bunge states as part of his detailed critique,

"An alternative to the realist view of chance and probability is the sub-jectivist doctrine. This is also known as Bayesianism because of its heavy reliance on a certain interpretation of Bayes' theorem. Bayesianism is the opinion that probabilities are just opinions: that every probability value is a measure of the strength of the belief of a person in a fact or in a state-ment" (Bunge 2015, 106).

5. David Bohm's nonlocal model—uses extra dynamical variables to recover, as Virendra Singh states, "some of the desirable features of classical physics . . . The first such successful attempt was that of Bohm, who in 1952, showed that a realistic interpretation of quantum mechanics can be constructed which maintains a causal description and avoids treat-ing systems and measuring apparatus differently" (Singh 2008). Work continues on this Bohmian interpretation, especially by a community of scholars led by Bohm's colleague Basil Hiley (Bohm and Hiley 1993), but the theory does not make the Boolean/non-Boolean logical distinc-tion that Primas considers as essential. The Bohm theory is also highly nonlocal in its core variables; the "hiddenness" of these variables greatly complicates testing as well; however, at least it is, in principle, testable unlike the many-worlds interpretation. Jan Walleczek and colleagues have edited an excellent survey of contemporary work on the Bohmian approach (Walleczek et al. 2019).

6. nonlinear model—J. R. Croca and his Portuguese group have developed a non-linear theory, which attempts to unify classical physics, relativity, and quantum physics in a causal description that "contains the linear domains of physics as a particular case" (Croca 2015, 17). This nonlinear model avoids the ontological overflow of multiverse models; however, it also presumes actualism and its nonlinear theory would be very difficult to apply in practice.

Another approach, developed by Marina Cortês and Lee Smolin, less developed than any of the above, introduces energetic causal sets based on quantum information processing systems whereby only causality (and not space-time) exists at the fundamental level. The theory focuses on "real ensembles" in which, as stated by Smolin, the "brazenly non-local interac-tions between simple, causally related objects widely distributed in space explain all the probabilities, uncertainties and spooky interactions of quan-tum physics" (Smolin 2019, 37); and further, this model "explains things not in terms of objects situated in a pre-existing space, as we do now, but in terms of events and the relationships between them" (Smolin 2019, 36). This approach has some promising features such as an objective "flow" of time; however, it introduces untested new concepts and physics. In contrast, the Relational Reality model builds directly on the core quantum physics that has been multiply tested over many decades, and augments this with a robust interpretation that enables an understanding of all available experiments as discussed in chapter 2.

Although the Relational Reality model denies naive realism, it affirms a critical realism[14] that is intuitive, and maintains hard-core common sense (i.e., assumptions that we presume in our practice universally or nearly universally). For example, although there are very high levels of coherence and predictability of events (thankfully so for the safety of auto and air travel, etc.), there remains an ontologically genuine remainder of real possibility which, for human affairs, includes some amount of genuine human choice. This remainder of real possibility enables a consistent basis for ethics and supports our normal human intuition of selecting, at least at times, between real choices.

LEVERAGING WELL-ESTABLISHED
SCIENTIFIC RESULTS

It has been claimed that quantum physics provides its own interpretation and that a unique and "simple" solution to the quantum measurement problem is the many-worlds interpretation. This is incorrect: none of the proposed solutions for the quantum measurement problem arise without philosophical assumptions derived from beyond quantum physics. In particular, the many-worlds interpretation depends on the presupposed (unstated) and questionable philosophical claim of actualism, which is that the domain of the real and the actual are one and the same, thus excluding potentiality (*potentiae*) from the domain of the real.[15] Based on both an analysis of quantum physics using partial Boolean algebras (Atmanspacher and Primas 2003; Primas 2017), and via a category theory analysis of the quantum measurement problem (Epperson and Zafiris 2013), Atmanspacher, Primas, and Epperson and Zafiris, have shown that the hypothesis of actualism is not necessary, and indeed false. By conflating all non-Boolean possible systems to one Boolean system of actualizations (thus throwing all non-Boolean solutions into an inaccessible multiverse ether), such many-worlds or multiverse theories yield unimaginable ontological overflow, and neglect the powerful distinction of local Boolean systems of actualizations and global non-Boolean frameworks of *potentiae*.

The Relational Reality model leverages well-established scientific results, especially the past century of experiments and theory that form the core of modern quantum physics, a theory that is arguably the most highly developed and tested of all physical theories. The Relational Reality model enables coherent and multidisciplinary solutions for the Gordian knot of problems above and yet avoids speculative extensions beyond well-tested physics.

The power of the Relational Reality model derives from both scientific and philosophical considerations. It enables us to reframe fundamental quantum process as an exemplar of what Bradley describes as a strong theory of active existence whereby "active existence is to be analyzed independently of any notions of production or of a pregiven real. Speculative event-theory [see indented quote below] . . . refuses to refer things away from themselves to something else as their principle of actualization. Acts of existence are now to be understood as finite, groundless self-actualizations" (Bradley 1996, 235).

This feature of self-actualization arises explicitly in the Relational Reality model, as argued by Epperson and Zafiris (see chapter 2): "It is also the case in both Whiteheadian metaphysics and quantum mechanics that the local measurement context of a novel actual occasion-in-process, though not externally determined, is nevertheless internally conditioned by virtue of its internal relatedness to its dative world. In quantum mechanics, this is evinced by the fact that the presupposed global logical structure is defined by a Boolean localization scheme, where compatible local Boolean contexts overlap, and the indexical local measurement context must be part of this overlap" (Epperson and Zafiris 2013, 164–165). In this way, the self-actualization of quantum events arises from the inevitable contribution of internal relations for asymmetric, diachronic quantum process, which augments the external relations that were the focus of classical physics.

Bradley further notes a basic shift of thought in the late nineteenth century such that

> prior to the late nineteenth century, speculative metaphysics characteristically defines the active existence of things—the concept of the actualization of things—by reference to the causal or productive activity of a pregiven, grounding reality, which is understood as in some sense complete and is variously conceived as the realm of form, or as the emanation of an incomprehensible One, or as the transcendent activity of the Creator God, or as the immanent activity of the Whole or Absolute. By contrast, one central theme that characterizes the development of speculative metaphysics from the late nineteenth century onward is to be found in the work of the later Nietzsche, the later Heidegger, Bergson, and Whitehead. Here, the active existence of things can generally be said to be conceived strictly as a matter of finite, singular "acts of duration" or "events" of self-actualization. (Bradley 1996, 235)

The alternative weak theory of existence since Frege, commonly applied as a nominalist strategy and fashionable in analytic philosophy circles for the past century, as pointed out by Bradley, "is best described as treating existence in such a way that it has no independent features of its own, but is exhaustively definable as the satisfaction or exemplification of the variables of the propositional function.[16] Against such a view, speculative [systematic] metaphysics holds that existence is much more than a silent, featureless pendant of the propositional function" (Bradley 1996, 233). In contrast to this weak theory, which often resorts to a "Wittgensteinian strategy of dissolving philosophical problems" (Bradley 1996, 244), the active existence approach, applying a series-relative strategy, is capable of solving many such problems. For example, Bradley continues,

> consider that cluster of distinctions related to the contrast of "mind" and "world." In a serial analysis, mind and world, subject and object, ideal and real, are no longer treated as self-contained elements that stand in some kind of fixed contrast or opposition to one another. Instead, they are defined as distinctions of serial order, as states or stages of serial construction. Thus, the concepts of world, reality, and object refer to antecedent events or phases of events, and the concepts of mind, subjectivity,[17] and ideality refer to successor events or phases of events as they construct themselves out of their antecedents. (Bradley 1996, 234)

This series-relative strategy is part of how we have addressed many of the Gordian knot problems and builds on the fundamental succession reflected in quantum process. Recognizing the limits of his philosophical analysis, Bradley asks "How are the structures that govern the genetic-serial relations of predecessor and successor events to be elaborated?" (Bradley 1996, 243). The complexities of such elaboration are outlined by Whitehead in his seminal work *Process and Reality* (Whitehead 1929, 1978), and now a contemporary scientific and philosophical elaboration is provided by the *Logoi* framework, including its Relational Reality model, which may be helpfully augmented, at multilevel, with the quantum of explanation concept as sketched by Auxier and Herstein (2017).

NOTES

1. In contrast to nominalist "standard empiricism," Nicholas Maxwell argues persuasively for metaphysical, anti-nominalist considerations within his "aim-oriented empiricism," which is closely related to Whitehead's approach. Maxwell demonstrates the importance of metaphysical blueprints (effectively the coherence criteria), theoretical unity (viz., the rational criteria of being logical and coherent), and empirical success (effectively Whitehead's empirical criteria) (Maxwell 2017).

2. Phillip Stambovsky emphasizes the centrality of relation for the great nineteenth-century logician, Rudolph Hermann Lotze, stating "the cardinal ontological moment of *relation*–Lotze's historically influential core metaphysical principle" (Stambovsky 2009, 159).

3. Here I endeavor to avoid the improper use of Ockham's razor; see Dieter Gernert (2009).

4. The state vector approach is a powerful tool for quantitative model making in science. It can be used for both small and large-scale systems, and for both linear and nonlinear systems. Inputs are described by multidimensional vectors, and outputs are obtained by applying a system matrix to this input, then yielding an output state vector. The system matrix is usually inferred from differential equations describing the dynamics of the system. This procedure can be applied to both classical and quantum physics problems; see Mikio Nakahara (2003) and Rudolph Haag (2012).

5. Two operators (A, B) commute with each other if their commutator [A, B] = AB-BA is equal to zero. Unlike classical mechanics, key variables in quantum physics, represented by variables (not ordinary numbers), do not commute, thus yielding a fundamental asymmetry (Roland Omnès 1999).

6. In general, physical systems are dynamic, that is, they evolve in time. This is the sense of "evolution" being used here, not the biological usage of the term.

7. The projection postulate of quantum physics, due to Paul Dirac and John von Neumann, says that, upon measurement, the system of interest will be found in one of the possible eigenstates of the measured observable; see Harald Atmanspacher and Hans Primas (2003).

8. As discussed above in *Comparison of Classical Mechanics and Quantum Physics* in chapter 2, I use "classical physics" to denote classical approximations to quantum physics that, for many practical applications (such as "going to the moon"), are highly reliable provided one follows rigorous procedures for error analysis. "Classical mechanics" denotes the same physics but with an added overlay of mechanistic-materialist notions; see Čapek (1961). The form of these theories that avoids classical metaphysical assumptions is most clearly designated, in my opinion, by the terms "classical physics" and "quantum physics" because the "mechanics" term in both cases has tended to carry along classical metaphysical assumptions such as actualism and substantialism.

9. Here I use the word "response" instead of "solution" to indicate that my responses are, at best, potential routes to a solution and not a full solution as such.

10. For readability throughout this book, I will often refer to Boolean-logical outcomes as "actualizations," and to non-Boolean logic or effects and associated pre-space potential relations as *potentiae*.

11. Paradoxes of self-reference arise from the use of statements that refer to itself or its own referent. A famous example of paradox is "the *liar sentence*: 'This sentence is not true'" (Thomas Bolander 2017).

12. This lack of ultimate closure in physical systems is distinct from the important concept of relative semantic closure, enabling individuation, of complex biosystems (see Terrence Deacon and Spyridon Koutroufinis (2014).

13. Standard analytic philosophy and physicalist approaches tend to presuppose classical mechanics and causal closure with dyadic relations only; thus, neglecting input-output-context (semiotic) triads, and actual/*potentiae* or Boolean/non-Boolean logical distinctions. Within such limitations (apparently unaware of the alternative possibilities presented here), Joseph Levine concludes that "the problem of duality is

just this: how could anything like a point of view exist?" and "at least with respect to traditional attempts to understand the place of conscious experience in the natural world, we really do continue to face a genuine puzzle. The mind-body problem is still a problem" (Levine 2001, 177).

14. "Judging from his lifelong fight against subjectivism, Einstein was likely more upset by the claim that nature depends on the observer, than by the thesis that QT [quantum theory] enshrines randomness. As Wolfgang Pauli explained to Max Born, Einstein's point of departure is realistic rather than deterministic—but people, Born included, would not listen" (Bunge 2018, 236).

15. It is important to distinguish the faulty claim of actualism from the fundamental process of actualization that is an inevitable component of the causal process from given *potentiae* and actual particle and fields input to particular quantum outputs. Actualizing creativity is a major focus of Didier Debaise's excellent analysis of Whitehead's philosophy; see chapter 4 of Debaise (2017).

16. A detailed analysis and critique of analytic philosophy is provided by Robert Hanna in his works *Kant and the Foundations of Analytic Philosophy* (Hanna 2001) and *The Fate of Analysis: Analytic Philosophy from Frege to the Ash Heap of History* (Hanna 2020).

17. Bradley's more diachronic approach to understanding subjectivity avoids the typical problems encountered by a mere synchronic framing of subjectivity. As pointed out by Tallis, "We may conclude that, if subjectivity is a prison, the subject spends its entire sentence on parole. Indeed, it is essential to the very idea of a subject that it is aware of, or knows, that which it is not; that it is aware of objects" (Tallis 2018, 137).

Chapter 4

Causation, Emergence, and Complex Systems

Causation is an efficacy by which a given initial process or state (the cause) effectively guarantees the occurrence of another state or process (the effect). Substantial effort is expended in scientific experiments to minimize environmental effects and to isolate causes and effects. Such efforts are always an approximation to enable the modeling of real complex systems that involve interactions between their components and environments. Complex systems exhibit emergence wherein an entity is observed to have properties that its parts do not have on their own. The cause-effect relations of complex and emergent part-whole systems are often difficult to sort out. Here I explore the interrelationships of causation, emergence, and complex systems, and will argue that causation and emergence are interdependent processes focused, respectively, on diachronic and synchronic aspects of fundamental process.

In the history of thought, several stumbling blocks or impediments have tended to undermine a deeper understanding of causality, emergence, and complex systems. In the first six sections below, I highlight these impediments which are, in turn, substantialism, actualism, nominalism, deductivism, mechanism, determinism, and physicalism. After this analysis of stumbling blocks, I examine the implications of fundamental relations and quantum process as key pathways for an understanding of causation, emergence, functions, symmetry, and levels and thresholds of emergence. Finally, I address the emergence of physical relations (i.e., law), landscapes of *potentia*, and higher levels of emergence including consciousness.

SUBSTANTIALISM—FROM SUBSTANCE TO PROCESS

The appearance of relative permanence is encouraged by vision-dominated encounters with the world, which led the Greco-Roman world to emphasize a worldview of perceptual objects. In contrast to such substantialism, the ubiquity of change highlights the importance of process. Long time-scale processes, of course, often allow a more static interpretation (e.g., the life cycle of mountains, continents, and planets) whereas flow and dynamics is most evident with short time-scale processes. In the limit of micro-scale interactions, as Rodney Brooks concisely explains, dynamics and process are dominant as exemplified by both direct experiments and quantum field theory (Brooks 2015). Only a commitment to a problematic substance metaphysics enables the exclusive use of the adjective "particle" for quantum-level entities, which are widely recognized as being grounded in quantum fields. The importance of both continuity and change in our experience is well expressed by Elizabeth Kraus: "Being and becoming, permanence and change must claim coequal footing in any metaphysical interpretation of the real, because both are equally insistent aspects of experience" (Kraus 1998, 1). A diverse array of thinkers have added to the critique of substance thinking including, as pointed out by Timothy Mooney, the noted philosopher of de-construction, Jacques Derrida (Mooney 2002).

The substance metaphysics that so pervades Western philosophy should not be regarded as, in any way, a universal concept. Indeed, entire civilizations have instead emphasized becoming and process. In particular, as Hall and Ames have argued, an emphasis on flow and dynamics tends to dominate Chinese philosophy: "The process or field of existence viewed *in toto* and as integrated from a particular *te* [virtue] perspective is called *tao* [way]. When viewed in terms of the integrity of individual entities, however, this field is a collocation of particular foci, or *te*" (Ames 1987, 239).[1]

My own worldview includes both aspects, being and becoming, permanence and change, grounded in the organic, processual feel of my early farm experience yet adding in the usual elements of linguistic abstraction combined with formal education in physics and philosophy. During my space physics career, I was frequently reminded through practical examples that classical physics is simply an approximation to modern physics (especially quantum physics). In one project, I worked with low-light-level photoelectronic imaging systems as part of experiments in ionospheric physics; such systems were later enhanced for night vision applications. The photons of available light are converted into electrons and then multiplied using photomultipliers, and then converted back to photons for the final sensing element. The conversion of photons into electrons depends on the quantum photoelectric effect for which Albert Einstein obtained the Nobel Prize in 1921. These experiences helped me to understand, better than the abstractions of classroom study, how the default substance-oriented ontology of classical mechanics is not just misleading, but simply wrong given current understandings of field theory, and especially quantum physics and quantum field theory.[2] Quantum physics is applicable to essentially everything in the world about us even though classical physics is an excellent approximation for many real-world applications, and is often the best tool for most applications due to its relative simplicity.

We should keep in mind that the dictionary definition of *causation* ("the relationship of cause and effect") in no way requires default to the presumed ontology of classical mechanics.[3] This trend for going beyond substance-oriented ontology in science is reflected as well in the fundamentals and history of mathematics. Desmet reports that "According to Whitehead, the history of mathematics is a history of increasing 'emphasis on pattern, as distinct from the special entities involved in the pattern,' and it coincides with a transformation of mathematics into 'the intellectual analysis of types of pattern'" [imbedded quotes are Whitehead's own in *Essays in Science and Philosophy* (Whitehead 1948, 83)]. Desmet further notes that most mathematicians now agree that mathematics is the science of pattern (Desmet 2010b, 227).

ON THE FAILURE OF ACTUALISM AND NOMINALISM

Both actualizations and potential relations (*potentiae*) are genuinely part of the real, a result based on recent research outcomes in quantum physics, in addition to phenomenological and philosophical analyses of human experience along with the Relational Realism model summarized in chapter 3. This important result profoundly impacts some classic debates about "What is the real?" Proper scientific propositions about measurement results (data), and theoretical modeling of such, have sometimes been extended to buttress the metaphysical claim of actualism whereby the domain of the real is claimed to be nothing but the actual. The claim of actualism cannot be confirmed based on scientific propositions alone, however much extended; nonetheless, as we shall see, it can be readily refuted based on philosophical analysis and ordinary human experience.

Closely related to the claim of actualism is the concept of nominalism and a unifying problem that links together causation, emergence, and complex systems, namely the problem of particulars versus universals, which Ganzalo Rodriguez-Pereyra summarizes this way:

> Philosophers have often found it necessary to postulate either abstract objects or universals. And so Nominalism [being the denial of such abstractions] in one form or another has played a significant role in the metaphysical debate since

at least the Middle Ages . . . "Nominalism" carries an implication that the corresponding doctrine asserts that everything is particular or concrete . . . one kind
of Nominalism asserts that there are particular objects and that everything is particular, and the other asserts that there are concrete objects and that everything
is concrete. (Rodriguez-Pereyra 2016, 1)

In spite of the difficulties and refinements of this metaphysical debate over
the centuries, Mary MacLeod and Eric Rubenstein conclude that "a consensus does seem to be emerging though . . . that two genuine contenders are left:
Strong Realism and Trope Nominalism" (MacLeod and Rubenstein 2019,
16).[4] As will be shown below, all forms of nominalism are inadequate; thus,
we appear to be left with realism. However, such realism is most often taken
to designate Platonism, but that representation is overly restrictive as we shall
see. In addition, the particular type of realism referenced by MacLeod and
Rubenstein only makes reference to individual, quality dyads and makes no
reference to a more sophisticated theory of relations and universals as applied
in the *Logoi* framework and articulated further in this chapter and chapter 8.

Defining "metaphysics" is not simple; indeed, Ilana Moss provides thirty
definitions (Moss 2018). What appears to be an essential element of all
such definitions is that a metaphysical proposition points to some reality or
understanding that permeates all reality and is yet not immediately evident in
particular observations.[5] By this criterion, both *nominalism* (in either sense
above) and *realism* (the affirmation of abstract objects or universals) are, by
definition, metaphysical claims. Since we cannot resolve this debate by only
demonstrating the presumed scientific merits of either position, is it yet possible to make progress on this question? Indeed, we can.

A key discovery inspiring the *Logoi* framework, as seen above, is how
the real is both the actual and potential relations, or *potentiae*,[6] a result
suggested by (yet not entailed by) both human experience and the quantum
physics requirement of two fundamental kinds of logic, the Boolean logic
of actualization and the non-Boolean logic of *potentiae*. Because nominalism is basically the affirmation of actualism, which depends on the claim
that the realm of Boolean logic is all inclusive, it is now apparent why
nominalism is necessarily wrong; or, to put it more tactfully, necessarily
incomplete.[7] Paul Teel has argued that Charles Sanders Peirce, who himself had transitioned from a nominalist to a realist position, was especially
articulate in his critique of nominalism. "Peirce's debate with the nominalists is often . . . centred around the word 'mere.' Peirce has a problem not
with the statement that there are facts, but with the statement that there
are merely facts. Or again, Peirce's problem is not with the statement that
generals are thoughts, but with the statement that they are merely thoughts"
(Teel 2011, 205). Complementing Peirce's critique of the notion of mere

facts, Hartshorne's definition of *metaphysical propositions* emphasizes their generality (not their transcendence) by how any particular observation or possible observation could potentially falsify a metaphysical proposition because they must be universally exemplified. As stated by Viney and Shields, "Central to all of Hartshorne's definitions [of metaphysics] is that genuinely metaphysical propositions are unconditionally necessary and non-restrictive of existential possibilities. If metaphysical propositions are true at all, they hold true of all possible world-states or state-descriptions" (Viney and Shields 2020, 51).

Another way to put the claim of nominalism into a broader context is to outline the full range of concepts of the universal. In one formulation, Desmond itemizes five basic types of universals: Platonic (transcendent to the instances of becoming), Aristotelian (immanent in the process of becoming), nominalist (no ontological dimension), idealist (concretized in immanent becoming), and intimate universal (emphasizing, as interrelated, both immanence and transcendence) (Desmond 2016, 3–4). The nominalist form here, of course, is paradoxical because it is typically part of a metaphysical claim that no universal whatsoever has any reality! As a nominalist would claim, there is, Desmond points out, "nothing ontologically beyond, and nothing ontologically immanent, but merely a sound of the voice, a *flatus vocis*, affixed to a particular idea that tries to insinuate a more general range of reference" (Desmond 2016, 4).

As we have seen above in the analysis of fundamental quantum process, specific potential relations (*potentiae*) are an essential ingredient in such process, and no mere trope or other pseudo-concrete object can plausibly play that key explanatory role. Once again, Gonzalo Rodriguez-Pereyra notes that "according to widespread usage a universal is something that can be instantiated by different entities and an abstract object is something that is neither spatial nor temporal" (Rodriguez-Pereyra 2016). Nominalism then denies these non-particular entities. However, we have found that both the order of *potentiae* and the order of actualizations have a critical role to play in fundamental process, but neither has a specific space-time place. Recall that space-time is not pre-given; instead temporality and space-time metrics emerge from such process.[8] Fundamental quantum process, as we have seen, necessarily incorporates local-global interrelations, which are confirmed in multiple quantum experiments that test Bell's theorem and entanglement. Again, concrete objects alone cannot play the role of such local-global relations, or of specific input *potentia* from within a landscape of *potentiae*, whose ultimate relata[9] cannot be merely specific concrete objects.

Thus, fundamental quantum process and the inferred fundamental orders (of actualism; of *potentiae*), as described here, violate key claims of philosophical nominalism. Ockham's razor is a worthy principle and discourages unneeded expansion in kinds of entities. Yet, the conceptual expansion involved here is relatively minor compared to the dramatic expansion enabled (via nominalistic actualism) with the many-worlds interpretation, or multiverse hypothesis, often promoted by nominalists. Further, the emergence of general potential relations (C. S. Peirce's "generals") out of constraints and optimizations of relations among *potentiae* provide a plausible basis for physical relations generally (see section below on *"Law"—From Entailment to Constrained Processual Histories*). In contrast, nominalists are left with no such ontological explanation and implicitly rely on the God-given laws of eighteenth-century metaphysics.

DEDUCTIVISM—*POTENTIAE* AND
THE FAILURE OF ENTAILMENT

The analyses of causal relations, inspired by Newtonian science and the early modern tradition, in the shadow of highly successful deductive strategies from Euclid's *Elements* to Newton's *Principia*, have tended to emphasize strict entailment. However, in contrast to such deductivism with its necessitarian account, recent research has demonstrated the importance of distinguishing, at multiple levels, both actuality and potentiality as primary aspects of reality, including a distinction of the orders of *potentiae* and the order of actualization. There were multiple precursors for this distinction in the philosophical literature going back to Aristotle and earlier, especially Aristotle's sea-battle argument for the reality of future contingency (in *De Interpretatione*). However, as I have pointed out, within the scientific literature, simplistic determinism and actualism (the "real" as exclusively constituted by the "actual") carried over from classical Newtonian metaphysics (Eastman 2008) and tended to distract physicists from any enhanced form of realism (examples of the latter found, for example, in Peirce, Whitehead, and Heisenberg). The eventual failure of this classical option as an explanation for real *potentia*, in any ontic formulation, led many to focus on mostly epistemic solutions for the interpretation of quantum physics (e.g., Bohr's Copenhagen interpretation).

It has long been assumed that Newtonian physics provides key exemplars of deterministic equations given that specification of unique input yields, in general, unique output. Although of deterministic form, it is misleading to describe even Newtonian physics, or any physics formalism, as "deterministic" because all such equations are necessarily part of a modeling framework with varying assumptions made about initial conditions, boundary conditions, relevant scale or domains for meaningful solution, and other contexts for application. As Mathias Frisch has pointed out, such designation assumes improperly a causal symmetry view with respect to time (Frisch 2013), which presumes that symmetry alone is fundamental versus the necessity of both symmetry and asymmetry as shown by Joe Rosen (2004) and such presumption further conflates causation and necessary relation. There are strong philosophical arguments against the thesis of general determinism, which is the claim that every obtaining state of affairs is necessary and associated with an entailment relation. Uwe Meixner, in particular, argues that general determinism is an incoherent position (Meixner 2006, 88). As well, George Shields has developed a detailed nine-step modal logic argument to show that determinism is incoherent (i.e., logically disjointed) when combined with the conservative assumption that at least one possible state-description is contingent (Shields 2016, 134–135).

From the point of view of actualism and strong determinism, counterfactual conditions and possibilities represent a basic philosophical puzzle. As noted in chapter 1, a common approach has been to appeal to possible world semantics, inspired by the works of David Lewis (2001). In Lewis's account, which does not make any distinction of the actual and "spaces" of *potentiae*, such possible worlds are actualized alternative (yet entirely inaccessible) worlds, which yield dramatic ontological overflow. As Rescher states, "Semantical theorists who talk about other possible worlds have the audacity to lay claims to entities of a sort of which they are unable to provide even a single identifiable example" (Rescher 2017, 110). The conflation of *potentiae* and actuality, and of causation and necessary relation mentioned above, are highly problematic because, as Derek Malone-France states, "the world . . . must contain reference to the existence of counterfactual possibilities as a condition of factuality itself" (Malone-France 2006, 128). Indeed, what is 'fact' if not a specification out of a range of possibility? Charles Hartshorne is well known for his clear defense of real possibility, from his classic paper of 1963, quoted below, to his major work *Creative Synthesis and Philosophic Method* (Hartshorne 1970).

> [G]reat harm has been done by the timeless notion. The dogma that Truth and, hence, the divine perspective are simply above time generates antinomies. In metaphysics and theology I believe that the notion of time-independent truth is downright vicious. In science and practical life it may be largely harmless, but also in principle superfluous, and it always threatens to do harm, as when we retreat from our responsibilities by indulging in superstitious prophecies or in vain wishes that we "knew the future." What we need to know are causal laws; beyond their reach there is no definite future to know, but only real possibilities out of which countless "self-creating creatures" must decide the future. Creativity is the inclusive principle, endlessly uniting remembered or perceived actual events into new actualities. "Possibility" is creativity in its forward or

productive aspect; "actuality" is the same in its backward or preservative aspect. Logical modalities express the ways in which creatures may understand their situations as heirs of a definite past and as contributors to future creatures which are definite in advance only with respect to the contributions that will be at their disposal. (Hartshorne 1963, 605)

The famed co-founder of quantum physics, Werner Heisenberg, explicitly argued for the importance of *potentia* (Heisenberg 1958), yet this had only minor influence in the theoretical physics community, which tended to favor actualism and determinism. However, beginning with a series of experiments enabling quantitative tests of the famed EPR argument of the 1930s, the sub-field of quantum theory of measurement has witnessed a renaissance, which has led to many robust and productive debates (e.g., see the *Foundations of Physics* journal, published since 1970). The outcome of these debates remains open, but significant constraints for some form of realism have become more clearly established. In response, some realist-minded physicists have adopted variations on the many-worlds interpretation (MWI), which maintains actu-alism and refuses the actuality-*potentia* distinction but at a very high cost in plausibility due to its highly inflated ontology. Other options for a realist approach require the introduction of untested new physics; for example, those like Ghirardi-Rimini-Weber (GRW) building on the Lindblad equations, as noted by Steven Weinberg (2017). Epperson provides a substantive critique of the GRW strategy (Epperson 2009).

Without introducing any new physics, there is one approach that has argu-ably enabled a critical realist approach without highly inflated ontologies (as with multiverses) or any new untested additions to the physics. This realist approach builds on the highly successful, and widely supported decoher-ence interpretation of quantum mechanics as developed, for example, by Wojciech Zurek (2006), and simply adds to this the philosophical distinction of actuality and *potentiae* as both part of the real (thus, a denial of actualism and simple entailment), utilizing as well recent developments in mathemati-cal category theory, which are relatively uncontroversial and appropriate for this important application. As outlined in chapter 2, the first full articulation of this new Relational Realist interpretation of quantum mechanics appears in the work of philosopher Michael Epperson and mathematical-physicist Elias Zafiris (Epperson and Zafiris 2013; Epperson 2016; Elias Zafiris 2016). Independently, Ruth Kastner succeeded in a new realist interpreta-tion, also incorporating *potentia*, by adapting and enhancing John Cramer's Transactional Interpretation; as well, this approach simply uses the well-tested core of quantum physics (Kastner 2013). Of these two recent advances, the work of Epperson and Zafiris provides a focus on logic issues and yet main-tains a simple ontology, but this in turn leads to updating our understanding of the causal relation that goes beyond earlier deflations to mere logical entailment. Their approach is also highly compatible with the independent work of Hans Primas, which emphasizes the importance of partial Boolean algebras (Primas 2017). An integration of Epperson and Zafiris's relational realist program, the Transactional Interpretation (Kastner), and *Res Potentia* (Kauffman) has recently been outlined in a collaborative paper by all of these researchers within the rubric of Heisenberg's *potentia* (Kastner et al. 2018).

MECHANISM—HUMANS AND MACHINES

Embodied processes, at multiscale, with their complexity of input-output-context relations (including layers of semantic information, signs, symbols, and so on—see chapter 5), contrast with the domain of human artifacts which, by applying severe constraints and imposing dyadic input-output relations, provides for robotic and prescriptive input-output functionality to meet human needs and applications. Due to their severe constraints, such artifacts, like robots, can be relied on to accomplish their function in essentially a deterministic fashion in ways that mimic simple entailment, or deductive inference, from given inputs, constraints, and boundary conditions to well-defined outputs. I am very thankful for such highly reproducible functioning: the airplane I rode recently flew reliably. Both engines and all the complex functionality of the aircraft performed flawlessly, and such smooth functioning corresponded very well to deterministic modeling and predictions of such operations, albeit with inevitable errors and approximations that apply to any and all physical systems.

Some writers have suggested that such artifactual/robotic systems provide an adequate model for biological and even human systems, including claims that animals are nothing but complex machines. However, as stated by Stuart Kauffman, "the 'machine' thesis is wrong. Evolving life is not a machine . . . we are members of a living world of untellable creativity in its becoming" (Kauffman 2019, 1).

A concise way to express how such claims of mechanism are erroneous is to highlight how they effectively make the following false assumptions:

—*actualism;* namely the claim that the real is nothing but the actual; this is equivalent to collapsing the full Boolean/non-Boolean logics, including potential relations (*potentiae*) to only sets of actualizations (Boolean logic) (see chapter 2);
—*causal closure* of the physical, which claims that all propositions about physical systems can be ultimately mapped, without remainder, to propositions of physics, and/or propositions about measurement outcomes or facts;

in contrast, this claim has been clearly refuted by Ellis (2016) and Primas (2017) among others—see below.

Physicist Henry Stapp articulates key problems with the classical world-view, which presupposes both actualism and causal closure. (Here "theory" denotes quantum physics.)

> We live in a world where long-range, near-instantaneous transfers of information cannot be forbidden. Mainstream physicists have universally embraced a theory that explicitly exhibits such transfers yet accommodates all "empirically established" facts. This theory also violates the classical worldview by allowing our psychological acts of perceiving, *which are not determined by the atomically constituted physically described world, to influence that world.* Thus contemporary physics violates two key principles of the worldview upon which the classical metaphysical doctrine of physicalism is based. (Stapp 2015, 177)

The free will debate is substantially fueled by the erroneous assumptions of actualism and determinism, enabling problematic phrases like "man as machine." Most often such claims are dependent on assuming a limited form of physicalism, or causal closure of the physical, which may work as an approximation for local systems but ultimately fails as a broader claim due to issues of fundamental logic and physics, as shown above. Claims that some future artificial intelligence (AI) systems, being entailment devices limited to input-output logic alone, could be effectively "human" are based on the faulty metaphysical claims of causal closure, determinism, and non-contextual input-output logic. Even if these common assumptions are evaded, efforts toward "feeling" machines, even with soft robotics as proposed by Kingson Man and Antonio Damasio (2019), will fail if they do not transcend causal closure constraints and incorporate both fundamental logics, Boolean and non-Boolean. This is because loss of the latter with an entailment system, however complex, undermines any space for choice and genuine feeling. If any AI systems of the future transcend these limitations, then they are no longer, by definition, mere "machines."

ON THE FAILURE OF DETERMINISM

The above problematic claims of actualism and causal closure frequently arise in association with claims for strong determinism in which, as Daniel Dombrowski points out, there is an attempt to

> explain away temporal asymmetry by replacing it with bi-conditional necessity and an aggressive version of necessary *and sufficient* conditions for everything

that happens. Granted, a cause is a *sine qua non* that is required for a later event, but in its full actuality or concreteness an event is at least partially contingent. This is why an event depends on antecedent events [thereby "internally" related to those past events], yet is largely independent of subsequent ones [thus, "externally" related to what comes after]...It is a vain hope to think that if we discovered the "real causes" of things we could explain and predict everything. (Dombrowski 2017, 393)

The frequent effort of past philosophers to impose biconditional necessity to support the claim of determinism also led to the common notion that effects are contained in their causes. Based on apparent entailments of classical mechanics (i.e., relations of necessity), this notion was also commonly held by philosophers of science well into the past century. However, in contrast to this, as Viney and Shields point out, "for Hartshorne, it is the other way around: at the most basic metaphysical level of analysis, causes are contained in their effects" (Viney and Shields 2020, 119). As we have seen, this latter understanding is well supported by quantum physics because its fundamental data, measurement outcomes, are just that—outputs—within the input-output-context triadic. Further, such outputs arise from specific actualizations within statistical distributions (ultimately based in quantum process), which may at times represent near certainty, but never certainty per se or the God-like necessity of entailment.

Of course, the practice of science requires model making that, at times, imitates entailments and can suggest strong determinism through its deterministic form. However, this appearance is misleading because actual scientific practice, at best, embodies high levels of determination and predictability (subject to constraints of error analysis, environmental effects, complex system effects, etc.), and not absolute determinism. Such high levels of determination are sufficient to enable lunar landing and planetary exploration and certain highly precise predictions in quantum field theory, but this still remains in principle, and philosophically, distinct from strict entailment and ontological determinism. Practical success in scientific prediction, however precise, can never assure the metaphysical claim of determinism, at least not in its strong (or absolute) form. However, as a practical matter, it can be useful to distinguish certain "deterministic" systems from systems with more clearly evident statistical effects, but such casual discussion in science should never be taken to confirm metaphysical determinism. In *Minding the Modern*, Thomas Pfau drills deep into the intellectual history that underlies contemporary scientism, which typically involves a commitment to both actualism and causal closure such that all ways of knowing reduce to the way of numbers (quantification):

The ultimate objective driving deterministic reductionist accounts of human agency must be sought in a desire to establish "a tight *nexus* of cause and effect" capable of accounting for "everything there is." Yet this fixation is itself "not a result of empirical demonstration" but only exists as a utopian "postulate" of sorts. What drives the reductionist endeavor is "an interest in the continuing expansion of our mastery of nature and the possibilities of control" . . . a first premise is that all processes, mental or otherwise, are to be accounted for strictly in terms of efficient (never *final*) causation, a second premise holds that every "state" identified in such a causal chain must logically be the result of some anterior and isomorphous material cause: a third axiom holds that all causation is not only efficient but sufficient—that a cause is truly deserving of its name only if and when its exhaustive determinative power can be demonstrated. Behind this desire for total closure stands a kind of *Angst* that . . . constitutes a uniqely modern phenomenon . . . at last being diagnosed as a corollary of modernity's total commitment to method as the means by which to take control of the world. (Pfau 2015, 554–555)

In times of strife and uncertainty, it is a normal psychological and social need to seek order and control. In *Cosmopolis*, Stephen Toulmin shows that Descartes's intense focus on certainty emerged from impacts of the strife and uncertainties of his own time (Toulmin 1992). Similarly, appeals to certainty in reductive approaches over the past century have a similar correlation with the exceptional *Angst* arising from major wars of that era.

Quantum theorist Primas states that

a popular but scientifically unfounded metaphysical doctrine is the idea of the *causal closure* of the physical (i.e., non-mental) world. To say that the physical world is "causally closed" is to claim that the only causes of physical events are other physical events. Further, the *causal closure* claim entails that all predicates of physical events are fully determined by antecedent physical events. Causal closure is often defended on *a priori* grounds, claiming that it is indispensable for a scientific world view. (Primas 2017, 34)

However, such defense of causal closure is circular and question-begging when "scientific" is taken to mean "causally closed" explanations. Further, such argument effectively claims as well that effects are contained in their causes which, as shown immediately above, is an incorrect holdover from classical mechanics, and reverses our contemporary understanding from quantum physics that causes are instead contained in their effects (e.g., measurement outcomes). As Terrence Deacon states, "It takes relatively little in the way of circular architecture in physical or computational systems to produce highly complex and convoluted behaviors. The effect is quite general and is entirely a consequence of the global architecture or topology of this causal closure. Indeed, some degree of causal 'circling back,' so to speak, is inevitable in the real world because of finiteness and aggregation" (Deacon 2003, 285).

Concerning any more global application of causal closure, however, Primas points out that "such claims are without any support from physics. No serious physical theory makes the overarching claim that the physical laws uniquely determine the behavior of the whole material world . . . The first principles of physics are methodological regulative principles which refer to *strictly isolated systems*, not to the real world" (Primas 2007, 34–35). Further, Primas emphasizes in a footnote that "this and the following considerations apply to both classical and quantum physics as well as to individual and to statistical determinism" (Primas 2007, 35). One of the most clear and concise critiques of both determinism and causal closure are then laid out by Primas as follows:

> No part of the world can be faithfully represented by an isolated physical system. But under appropriate circumstances the behavior of a part of the world can be modeled mathematically by a physical system. Whether the initial state of such a model system uniquely determines the motion depends on the choice of state space of the mathematical model . . . However, there is no reason to assume that such a locally possible notional deterministic description can be extended to a global dynamical system for the whole material world. We conclude that *determinism is a property of local theoretical models, and not a feature of the world.* Therefore the prevailing opinion that the physical state of the material universe at any one time determines the state of the universe at all other times is both theoretically and empirically unfounded . . . A regulative principle does not say anything about reality . . . The idea of strict determinism is related to the principle of logical bivalence (according to which every statement is either true or false [i.e., Boolean logic]). [Jan] Lukasiewicz has shown that a bivalent system of logic is adequate for the language of the deterministic world view, but is no longer suitable for the investigation of a non-deterministic world view . . . Therefore we cannot expect the global validity of determinism for a system which requires a non-Boolean description. (Primas 2007, 35–36)

The above can be summarized in terms of the fundamental logical frameworks involved: the real, physical world requires models that incorporate both Boolean *and* non-Boolean logic, and which account for both actualizations *and* potential relations (*potentiae*). The metaphysical claims of determinism, causal closure, and actualism collapse effects down to mere causes, and also collapse these distinctions down to only the domain of actualizations (thus only Boolean logic). As Primas and others have argued, such a reduction may be scientifically applied as a useful approximation for certain modeling purposes, but is not justified as an unrestricted claim about the physical world.

The claims of strong determinism, causal closure, actualism, and Boolean-only logic are metaphysical claims, not requirements of science. However useful they may be for restricted, local modeling (as exemplified by the great success of classical mechanics for many applications such as traveling to the moon), such reductive claims are misleading for philosophy, and necessarily incomplete for modeling in its fullness the real, physical world. With respect to ontic emergence at various scales, Terrence Deacon points out that "the universe [by definition] is closed to gain or loss of mass-energy . . . but it is open to organizational constraints on formal cause and the introduction of novel forms of efficient cause. Thus, we have causal openness even in a universe that is the equivalent of a completely isolated system. New forms of work can and are constantly emerging" (Deacon 2012, 368). The Relational Realist approach to the local/global framework and part/whole relations (see chapter 2) is free from the paradoxes of self-reference (Bolander 2002) and the imposition of a classically conceived spatiotemporal continuum; no ultimate closure is available for finite systems and, even for the universe as a whole; ever new facts break such closure due to fundamental (diachronic) quantum process as discussed above. Arguably, this conclusion represents a scientific corollary for finite physical systems to Gödel's proof in logic,[10] as noted earlier.

ON THE FAILURE OF PHYSICALISM

The somewhat broader claims of physicalism, that everything can ultimately be explained by physics, are similarly impacted by the above arguments. After noting critical ambiguities in defining *physicalism*, Hans Primas states that "in any case, physics does not have the authority to tell us what exists in nature. In particular, if in a special case we can speak of causal processes, then this refers to our choice of a state space,[11] that is to a *description*, not to the ontology of the world. The claims that physics is closed and the idea of physicalism indicate a fundamental misunderstanding of physics" (Primas 2017, 158). After providing further details on observer/observed and closed versus open systems, Primas concludes that "since physics systematically leaves out human intentions, the first principles of physics are not even enough to describe physical experiments or engineering physics exhaustively. The limits of any natural science (even more so if understood in a physicalist spirit) are not the limits of human knowledge" (Primas 2017, 159). In this way, Primas is stating that the claim of physicalism is a metaphysical claim.

The close linkage between physicalism and causal closure of physics (CoP) is thoroughly analyzed by Robert Bishop and Atmanspacher (2013) with a focus on the free will issue.

The concept of efficient causation, which CoP presupposes, depends on the fact that prior causes can be distinguished from subsequent effects. As a consequence, a direction of time is necessary for implementing CoP. Therefore, time-reversal symmetry needs to be broken before it is possible to discuss CoP in any sensible way. Once time-reversal symmetry is broken, however, the domain of fundamental laws of physics has been left behind for the domain of context-dependent models.

This implies that the notions of causation and of fundamental laws of physics cannot refer to the same level of description and, hence, should not be used in the same framework. Fundamental laws can be deterministic or indeterministic, retaining all time symmetries, but efficient causation is not [in general] a concept applicable to such laws. This is a basic inconsistency in the discussion of CoP that, astonishingly, rarely has been recognized. (Bishop and Atmanspacher 2012, 103–104)

The Relational Reality approach and the recognition of both Boolean and non-Boolean logical orders, the orders of actualizations and of *potentiae*, respectively, show how the different levels of description noted in this quote are associated with our fundamental distinction of logical orders. The symmetry of fundamental laws referred to by Bishop and Atmanspacher are associated with the non-Boolean order of *potentiae* whereas the application of such laws and the notion of efficient causation depend on the Boolean order of actualizations, which in turn, because of quantum process, necessarily involves context dependence and asymmetries.[12]

ON TWO TYPES OF RELATIONS—DIACHRONIC VERSUS SYNCHRONIC FOCUS

One common problem with the conventional nominalism-universals, or anti-realism versus realism debate is that particulars and universals are both presumed to be some kind of being. In contrast to this, Whitehead, and those who follow his lead argue that the traditional focus on being (especially via substance thinking) should be replaced with a focus on the concept of relations. For example, Stephen David Ross points out that it was "Whitehead's profound insight that universals and particulars are not kinds of beings but distinct functions of eternal objects and actual entities . . . [perspectival distinctions] from a point of view" (Ross 1983, 11). Thus, the theory of relations, including functions, is a very fundamental issue.

Paul Bains has confronted the critical topic of relations in his book *The Primacy of Semiotics,* which addresses semiosis (the action of signs), and the ontology of relations. The series editors (Marcel Danesi et al.) note that he "focuses on the claim that relations are 'external' to their terms and seeks to give an ontological account of this purported externality of relations . . . [such ontology] is neither mind-dependent nor mind-independent" (Bains

2006, ix). Bains calls attention to how "Whitehead sought to develop a logic of relations in which the ultimate entities are complexes of relations or overlapping series of events . . . [Whitehead] argues in his serial pluralism that an actual occasion is internally related to its antecedents through 'prehension,' but that its completed antecedent occasions are not internally related to it" (Bains 2006, 136). However, Bains questions Whitehead's use of external relations because, in his view, they "seem to denote no relation at all," (ibid.) yet "What is nevertheless supremely relevant is that relations are a crucial problem for Whitehead (as for the history of philosophy)" (ibid.). Bains's critique of Whitehead's use of external relation is flawed in this case because it focuses on relations as merely synchronic, which is to focus on such relations at an instant of time or, equivalently, to neglect any temporal effects. In contrast, Whitehead was primarily concerned with diachronic relations, focusing on how phenomena change or evolve through time.

At the intersection of semiotics, information theory, process thought, and quantum physics lies the need to distinguish two fundamental types of relation: (1) relations with a synchronic focus as required for the analysis of emergence and semiotics, and (2) relations with a diachronic focus as required for the analysis of fundamental quantum process and causation. The former type of relation, which is the focus of Bains's analysis, fits well with the semiotic perspective and "the actions of signs, that is, how things come to stand for something other than themselves" (Bains 2006, ix) and the latter type of relation fits well with fundamental quantum process and succession. Recent developments in semiotics, information theory, complex systems, process thought, and quantum physics, which are here unified within the *Logoi* framework, help to clarify these issues; all join in the denial of nominalism. Further, as detailed below, *the diachronic focus for ontological relations is key to understanding causation, and the synchronic focus is key to understanding emergence*. This distinction in focus resolves the disagreement expressed about relations between Whitehead and Bains, and also provides a way to understand these two fundamental types of relation.

Whitehead notes that a present occasion is internally related to past events, which are given for it as data, but externally related to future events that, after all, have not yet actualized. For Whitehead, the actual-potential distinction is critical; without applying such distinction, Bains (and Deely as well) implies a different usage for external relation that is more spatialized (synchronic).[13]

The *Logoi* framework is a synthesis of four principal advances in philosophy and science over the past century; namely, (1) quantum physics, (2) process philosophy, (3) semiotics and biosemiotics (see chapter 5), and (4) modeling and complex systems studies (see last section of this chapter). The first two typically have a diachronic focus and the latter two typically have a synchronic focus. As discussed in chapter 2, the Relational Realism model provides an integration of process thought and quantum physics that incorporates advances in mathematics via category theory, which is an advanced mathematical framework for handling relations of both types, both the diachronic and the synchronic. Epperson and Zafiris point out that in diachronic aspects of this model "relations are not fundamentally metrical and continuous, as conventionally understood (e.g., requiring a point-set structure, where points are related by continuous spatiotemporal intervals); they are, rather, fundamentally topological in that the elementary relations are discrete, not continuous" (Epperson and Zafiris 2013, 65). This ultimate discreteness is exemplified by quantum process—the symmetry breaking of fundamental succession, a key feature of the *Logoi* framework. In a complementary way, the synchronic aspects of this model (e.g., the pre-space domain of *potentiae*) are continuous and exhibit substantial symmetry.

Recall that key elements of the *Logoi* framework are as follows (from chapter 2):

- *Process* → input-output succession within context (constraints/*potentiae*);
- *Logic* → logic of actualizations (two-valued Boolean logic) and a logic of potential relations, or *potentiae* (multivalued logic, non-Boolean);
- *Relations* → constitutive of process (part-whole; local-global; internal-external), including relations of relations/semiotics, extension,[14] and relations in category theory.

Once again, the *Logoi* framework incorporates two logical orders: Boolean (for actualizations) and non-Boolean (for *potentiae*), and a multilevel structure of emergence (local, local-global, and global) in which causation and emergence are complementary; both diachronic and synchronic. The background pre-space of *potentiae* and the extensive continuum are roughly like that hypothesized by Whitehead (1978). As elaborated by Jorge Nobo, "properties of space, then of time, and finally of space-time—are really properties of eternal extension . . . for physical time and physical space are, after all, only the [temporalization and] spatialization . . . of extension" (Nobo 2008, 259). Constraints on such pre-space *potentiae*, at multiple levels, give rise to general physical relationships, discoverable via minimization methods such as the principle of least action (see section *"Law"—From Entailment to Constrained Processual Histories'* later in this chapter). Conventional time and space reference (e.g., the metric in relativity theory) emerges from such fundamental quantum process and multilevel constraints.[15] In the relational-realist ontology of Kastner, Kauffman, and Epperson, based on the latest results in quantum analysis, "spacetime (the structured set of actuals) emerges from a quantum substratum, as actuals 'crystallizing' out of a more fluid domain of possibles; thus, spacetime is not all that exists" (Ruth Kastner 2018, 169).

We should be cautious, of course, with the common spatial connotations of the terms "local" and "global" because here we are working with local-global relations that reflect, in part, pre-space correlations such as quantum entanglement, which are handled with category theory, topology, and quantum physics, not metrics or direct space-time reference, which are themselves derivative, not fundamental, notions in the *Logoi* framework.[16] The derivative nature of space-time arises in contemporary research as well because, as Christian Wuthrich notes, "the emergence, and hence non-fundamentality, of spacetime is a rather generic feature of quantum gravity" (Wuthrich 2019).

CAUSATION VERSUS CAUSALITY

Menno Hulswit provides a very useful distinction between "causality" as being about facts, a relation between cause and effect as expressed by language and propositions (thus, an epistemic focus), and "causation" for "the production of an effect by a cause" (ontic focus) (Hulswit 2002, xiv). He further notes that most "contemporary discussions of the concept of 'cause' pertain to causality rather than to causation" (Hulswit 2002, 172). As an example, Judea Pearl's comprehensive treatment of causal relations focuses primarily on causality (Pearl 2000). There are some exceptions to this generalization, for example, David Fair clearly addresses causation within a physicalistic analysis as local "energy-momentum transferences" (Fair 1979). In the present work, I am focused on issues of fundamental ontology, and thus am focused on the concept of causation.

The continued failure of extant theories of causation is noted by several philosophers. For example, Michael Tooley has commented on the "failure of symmetric causal theories of time" (Tooley 1997, 283),[17] which failure the Relational Reality approach expects because symmetries pertain primarily to the order of *potentiae*, and the actualization process "breaks the symmetry of the potential" (Kastner 2013, 202). In his analysis of the causation problem, J. R. Lucas concludes that "some version of process philosophy seems therefore the only hope of understanding [causation]" (Lucas 2000, 78). Shields and Viney have provided a detailed discussion of Lucas's modal tree semantics approach to the logic of future contingents. They explain how "using the diagrammatic device of trees, Lucas' general program is to express quite precisely a metaphysics of time that is very much akin to Hartshorne's with its stress on the irreducible asymmetry of the temporal modes" (Shields and Viney 2003, 233). Scott Sehon has pointed out a key conundrum:

> The causalist account does promise to be more parsimonious, for it has one primitive [i.e., fundamental principle] (causation) as opposed to two (causation

and goal-direction) . . . That would indeed be a compelling consideration in favor of causalism, if one could actually produce a successful reductive analysis of goal-direction, and thereby show that one can get by with just the one primitive. But [Alfred] Mele acknowledges . . . that he is not offering any analysis of the fundamental notion of action, and . . . extant attempts at such an analysis fail. So, even if we do not like it, we may just have to live with both causation and goal-direction as irreducible primitives. (Sehon 2007, 156)

In contrast to the "extant attempts" referred to by Sehon, the process philosophy account imbedded in my *Logoi* framework enables the desired "more parsimonious" solution for causation[18] in part by considering, along with Hartshorne, causes as contained (via the causal process) in their effects. In part, as we have seen above, this is based on how all events are imbedded in a triadic system of input-output-context. Further, this framework incorporates, at a fundamental level, both the order of actualizations and the order of *potentiae* as comprising the full cause, the latter not included in many standard accounts. On several key points, I concur with Unger and Smolin, who state that "it is the causal connections, not the laws of nature, that are primitive and fundamental" (Smolin 2015, 37). Commenting on Unger and Smolin's work, Gare states that "their radical revision, echoing Schelling, Peirce, Bergson and Whitehead, is to take . . . creative causal process as fundamental to being" (Gare 2017, 91). The phrase "creative causal process" points to full inclusion of the order of *potentiae*. Within an extensive critique of scientism and an extended defense of systematic natural philosophy, Gare points out how "Inverting Kant's characterization of causality, Schelling argued that mechanical cause–effect relations are abstractions from the reciprocal causation of self-organizing processes. Matter is itself a self-organizing process" (Gare 2018, 104). Further, Schelling's dialectical reconstruction of nature emphasizes historical process and appears to incorporate the unending dialectic, broadly considered, of *potentiae* and actuality.

We all experience the weight of the past and the inevitability of certain effects arising from specified causes; let us call this causation in a broad sense, whether the process is bottom-up, top-down, or in-between. Similarly, as Donald Crosby emphasizes, we all experience at times a sense of openness, of novelty, that breaks the bonds of such apparent entailment or determination. "We can view the passage of time as just this interweaving of causality and novelty, these two principles need to be recognized as ultimate features of the universe" (Crosby 2005, 5). Core notions of the *Logoi* framework (process/logic/relations), by working with both logical orders (actualizations and *potentiae*), embody these features: causation, creative process, and emergence, at multiple levels.

As part of untying the Gordian knot, I have argued that causal relations arise from real relations within pre-space *potentiae*, and correlations in the passage from potentiality to actuality for each and every quantum event; physical relations (aka "laws") represent constraints on such process imbedded in correlated non-Boolean *potentiae*. In three concise essays, Anderson Weekes provides an in-depth understanding of consciousness, subject-object relations, Whitehead's unique approach, and causation (Weekes 2009a,b,c). With my insertions pointing out elements of quantum process and Whitehead's approach, Weekes explains that

> Whitehead proposes process . . . as the metaphysical basis for the synthetic necessity Kant was looking for. [During the process of actualization] Cause and effect are internally and necessarily related insofar as they are one and the same. [Upon actualization] Cause and effect are distinct and synthetically related insofar as they are not the same [i.e., distinguishable as in quantum measurement]. When the causal/experiential process is consummated, what's left are things that are now related only externally. That's why causation [genuine non-Humean connectivity[19]] will never be found among facts [as in the standard analytic philosophy focus on causality as correlations among facts]. It resides and operates only in the subjective [but, for Whitehead, non-anthropocentric] process through which new events come to pass by differentiating themselves from the facts left by still prior processes. The only direct and non-analogical access we have to this process [of causation] is in our own perception, but this becomes a basis for understanding the causal process in everything that happens. (Weekes 2009c, 452)

The *Logoi* framework's approach to the causation question, grounded in both Whitehead's analysis and the latest results of quantum physics, lends support to Weekes's summary that "the mind-body problem is simply the causation problem applied to consciousness . . . experience isn't just a paradigm case of process, but the key to its essential structure" (Weekes 2009c, 427). Such structure appears analogous to Peircean semiosis due to the application of triadic logic and such triadic structure (input-output-context) is based, at least in part, on the order of *potentiae*. Thus, as Crosby suggests, we have here a systematic naturalist way of understanding the weaving of causation and *potentiae* (yet, denying actualism), as well the ground of temporality and the asymmetry of time. Crosby uses the term "novelty" to denote non-reductive outcomes from the order of *potentiae*. Crosby states that "a selective process working on the possibilities implicit in the past...explains why temporal processes are asymmetrical and nonreversible, thus accounting for the exclusively forward direction of time" (Crosby 2005, 4). Further, "Novelty and causality work together to produce the combination of dynamically balanced stability and order . . ." (Crosby 2005, xi). In such a naturally imbedded understanding of emergent time, as Joseph Grange explains, "Each modality of time—past, present, and future—can be either thick or thin. Temporal thickness signifies the accumulation of significant value . . . A full and active sense of the value of the future is indispensable for healthy environmental growth [and yet] to lose sight of the present moment is to lose sight of reality" (Grange 1997a, 127).

Faber has pointed out "that Whitehead has, with his differentiation of modes of perception [causal efficacy and presentational immediacy], captured Derrida's insight of a metaphysics of presence and its nemesis: *différence*. Presentational immediacy, indeed, functions as the a-temporal, non-spatialized, non-differed and non-deferred "solipsism of the present moment' that constitutes metaphysics of presence" (Faber 2019, 63). In contrast to such mere correlations of externalized perception, George R. Lucas, Jr. emphasizes both modes of perception, including perception in the mode of causal efficacy, effectively a mode that involves direct experience of causation.

Unlike the approach of either predecessor [Hume/Kant], Whitehead's treatment of this problem [of primordial experience] re-establishes [causation] as the essential feature of relatedness...perception in the mode of "causal efficacy" in fact bears a close resemblance to William James' description of the "stream of consciousness" . . . and Bergson's *duree reelle* . . . If Whitehead (and James) are correct about experience, it is a trivial rather than a profound result that [causation] cannot be "observed" in Hume's sense. (Lucas 1989, 89–90)

Continuing, Lucas states that Whitehead's account of externalized perception, or

presentational immediacy . . . could be described as a projection . . . of certain highly refined and analyzed features . . . encountered . . . through causal efficacy [non-mentalistic, unanalyzed raw feels] vs. supervenient symbolic projection or attention to select percepta characteristic only of higher-order organisms . . . Whitehead's integration of these dimensions of experience into a unified theory of perception, recovering the experience of causal efficacy, ranks in my view as his chief contribution to the Western philosophic tradition. (Lucas 1989, 90–91)

Echoing this high praise of Whitehead's contribution, Pierfrancesco Basile states that "the implications of Whitehead's doctrine that the causal nexus is an object of experience cannot be overestimated" (Basile 2009). Regarding references to experience, Stephen Ross suggests that "experience in Whitehead's theory is neither anthropomorphic nor idealistic . . . perspective may be generalized such that the principle of experience is no longer needed" (Ross 1983, 13); "Whitehead's causal theory is a perspectival theory" (Ross

1983, 27).[20] However, it is likely more consistent with common usage to generalize both the concepts of experience and perspective, as do Lucas, Basile and others. Even more important is to recognize that Whitehead's order of explanation for perception, as Lisa Hedrick states it, moves "from causal efficacy to presentational immediacy instead of the reverse direction favored by much modern philosophy" (Hedrick 2019, 781). This is the same order as the ontological transition from fundamental quantum process to measurement outcome. Reversal of this order only appears in epistemological movements that focus on sense impressions. Hedrick continues, "So sense-impressions are never bare, never 'mere,' because they tell a tale of the active perceptive functioning conditioned by our own natures—natures that are what they are now because of what once was" (Hedrick 2019, 781). This move to ontological succession, instead of a focus on disconnected Humean sense impressions limited only to presentational immediacy, provides a fundamental understanding of both memory and anticipation. As Jorge Luis Nobo states, "Perception in the mode of presentational immediacy is subsequent to physical memory, for perception in the mode of causal efficacy exhibits two distinct sub-modes: (i) *physical memory*, which is the empirical subject's perception of the actual causal efficacy of its past world; and (ii) *physical anticipation*, which is the empirical subject's perception of the *potential* causal efficacy of itself in the future, and of its contemporary world in that same future" (Nobo 1986, 364) (for anticipatory systems, see *Complex Systems* section later in this chapter).

There are many precursors, East and West, for a broadened view of the causal relation. Heraclitus, Greek father of the term "philosopher," emphasized the centrality of relations in his *Logos* concept (Brann 2011); indeed, this history inspires the name for my overall approach—the *Logoi* framework. Persian philosopher Ibn Sina introduced possibility as a key logical category, thus formally creating modal logic; many Asian thinkers have emphasized active (verb-like) process over static (noun-like) substance, as reflected in both Chinese philosophy and language (Joseph Needham 1978).[21] In many ways, the concepts of contingency, necessity, and *potentia* are reflected in philosophies of the great philosophical traditions of Persia, China, and the East. Of course, the Western intellectual traditions go back at least to the ancient Greeks; here especially is Aristotle, who introduced us to *potentia*, now reflected in quantum physics as emphasized by one of its key founders, Heisenberg (1958).

CONSTRAINTS AND EMERGENCE

In a thorough and persuasive analysis of reduction, emergence, and constraints, James Blachowicz argues for a constraint interpretation of emergence in which "individuating, constitutive constraints on the common stuff and/or the physical laws that govern this stuff, because they are not derivable from this stuff or these laws themselves, qualify as emergent physical entities." (Blachowicz 2013, 28) In this approach, "neither non-individuated matter [deployed in standard reductive substantivalism] nor non-differentiated form [deployed in Platonic conceptions] actually exists" (Blachowicz 2013, 28–29). Such an emergence interpretation "that is nature-wide is a safeguard against the various dualisms that have resisted real explanation." Yet Blachowicz himself relies on two fundamental dualities "of a more basic type: that between possibility and actuality; and that between individuation and differentiation" (Blachowicz 2013, 39). Here we have a direct denial of nominalism, which would deny the reality of abstract entities; for Blachowicz, certain constitutive constraints and associated laws are themselves emergent entities even though not physical things; further, such abstract entities can have physical consequence.

The *Logoi* framework represents a generalization of this constraint interpretation; it is essentially a context-based interpretation of emergence that would include initial conditions, boundary conditions, individuation and differentiation, as well as *potentiae*, as suggested by Blachowicz in the last quote above (see Blachowicz's book *Essential Difference*, 2012). Also Robert Bishop and Harald Atmanspacher argue for a model of contextual emergence (Bishop and Atmanspacher2006). In some cases, the basic physical relations, constraints, or filters involved are not dependent on scale, and thus scale free, as with fractals within nonlinear dynamical systems and structures (such as auroral striations and coronal streamers in the field of space plasma physics). With some qualification, one can almost concur with Mariam Thalos that "the cement of the universe is its ever-evolving set of filters" (Thalos 2013, 153). However, scale freedom is not unlimited; it too is constrained, and some genuine hierarchy is maintained, through both multilevel physics and local-global constraints. Taking context (vs. constraint) as the more inclusive term, I propose that a context-based interpretation of emergence is the most inclusive, suggested as well by Carlos Gershenson in his arguments for contextuality (Gershenson 2002).

UNIFIED PROCESS APPROACH TO CAUSATION AND EMERGENCE

Causation and emergence are complementary concepts in the *Logoi* framework in that *causation represents a diachronic focus* on fundamental process (quantum actualization process from field/particle inputs and pre-space *possibiliae* to actualized particles and fields; from pre-space symmetries to broken-symmetry actualizations, including the emergence of time and temporality) whereas *emergence represents a synchronic focus* on fundamental process (hierarchical structure with local-global constraints). Although having a synchronic focus, as pointed out by Joseph Earley, emergence involves as well historical and diachronic aspects (Earley 2004). Nevertheless, descriptions of emergence in complex systems are most often focused synchronically on structural aspects, adding sequences of such state descriptions as needed for analysis. Ultimately, for both causation and emergence, fundamental process is grounded in quantum field processes that are multiscale and even partly scale free. Further, many basic processes are approximately scale free, such as those of space plasmas, which range from planetary to galactic scale and beyond in conjunction with long-range electromagnetic and gravitational field processes (the former are very strong but subject to shielding effects; the latter are very weak but not subject to shielding).[22] As Bishop and Atmanspacher state,

> Causation in the sense of efficient causation only applies to horizontal (i.e., diachronic) relations between system states at the same descriptive level. For vertical (i.e., synchronic) relations between levels of description it does not make sense to talk about a causal temporal sequence, so the type of causation involved in "mental causation" is a different story . . . [and] must be dealt with as a composition of efficient intralevel causation and a specified interlevel relation . . . contextual emergence [provides] an interlevel relation . . . in which a lower-level description (e.g., statistical mechanics) contains necessary but not sufficient conditions for features at a higher-level description (e.g., thermodynamics). (Bishop and Atmanspacher 2012, 109)

In the *Logoi* framework, consistent with such contextual emergence, causation is no longer confined to the mere dyadic correlation of facts (causality) or to deductivism, as in Newtonian physics, such that any novelty or emergence is an epiphenomenon arising from random error or chance. This classical approach to emergence tends to treat it as merely epistemological, or mind-dependent. Instead, via the *Logoi* framework, I argue that causation and emergence, the diachronic and the synchronic, respectively, are complementary realities bridged (ontologically) by fundamental quantum process and (epistemologically) by symbols and model representations that are created by the semiotic animal (humans). These complementary realities reflect as well the matter-symbol distinction (see Gordian knot #11 in chapter 3). As Howard Pattee states,

> This matter-symbol separation has been called the epistemic cut (e.g., Pauli, 1994). This is simply another statement of Newton's categorical separation of laws and initial conditions. Why is this fundamental in physics? As I stated

earlier, the laws are universal and do not depend on the state of the observer (symmetry principles) while the initial conditions apply to the state of a particular system and the state of the observer that measures them. What does calling the matter-symbol problem "epistemological" do for us? Epistemology by its very meaning presupposes a separation of the world into the knower and the known or the controller and the controlled. That is, if we can speak of knowledge about something, then the knowledge representation, the knowledge vehicle, cannot be in the same category of what it is about. (Pattee 2008, 118–119)

Continuing the theme of symbols as bridges, in the spirit of the Pauli-Jung conjecture, we could say that, as Atmanspacher and Fuchs express it, the "mental (psychological) and the material (physical) are aspects of one underlying reality, which itself is psychophysically neutral" (Atmanspacher and Fuchs 2014, 2). One could say that symbols, at their best, are pointers to a "middle way," bridging between complementary concepts such as knower and known, *possibiliae* and actuality, symmetry and asymmetry, and the diachronic and the synchronic.

One philosophical bridging concept is Whitehead's concept of prehension, which is a metaphysical (i.e., radically inclusive) claim that all physical relations have an asymmetrical internal relational structure. As a major exemplar of this hypothesis, quantum physics shows how final system states or outcome states of quantum measurement are internally related to initial states. Further, such internal relations extend beyond the system state to include the totality of system, detector, and environment, thus reflecting a prime example of our input-output-context triad. As a philosophical extension of such insights, Hartshorne argues that Whitehead's concept of prehension provides a middle way across numerous dichotomies and dualisms (Hartshorne 1979), and its dipolar character includes both the (ontological) diachronic/synchronic distinction (thus, incorporating both causation and emergence) and the (epistemological) knower/known (matter/symbol) epistemic cut. In turn, the logic of prehension is inclusive of input-output-context (thus, triadic and semiotic), Jamesian experience, and fundamental process. Inspired by the new field theory of James Clerk Maxwell, which is the basis for contemporary field theories, Whitehead innovated his concept of prehension to provide a unified approach to these aspects of fundamental reality.

The integrative power of the concept of prehension is shown by the following five key applications.

1. prehension as a philosophical embodiment of field theory, see McHenry (2015);
2. prehension as ontologizing the mathematical function, see Bradley (2003a, 2008);

3. prehension as capturing fundamental quantum process from non-Boolean pre-space (*potentiae*) to Boolean actualities reflected in topology and partial Boolean algebras; solves the epistemic cut problem via local-global constraints, see Epperson and Zafiris (2013);
4. prehension as bridging both ontological aspects (diachronic/synchronic) and epistemological aspects (knower/known); and
5. prehension as multiscale (quantum of explanation) with causation and emergence as complementary concepts (causation as diachronic versus emergence as synchronic).

Whitehead's overall scheme, with prehension as a key concept, satisfies all three key principles articulated by Bradley: (1) the principle of reason— "the principle that Nothing is without a reason" (Bradley 2010, 97); (2) the hypothesis of reality—"reality is that which has a nature of its own in the sense that it is so independently of our minds or independently of whether or not we think it to be so" (ibid.); and (3) the reality of universals. Bradley argues that the explanatorist project is to elaborate self-explanatory hypotheses out of experience, and that "this procedure of analogical generalization is neither deductive nor inductive but abductive" (Bradley 2010, 98).[23]

Michael Silberstein and John McGeever as well show how the issues of causation and emergence are closely related. Based on the reality of entanglement phenomenon in quantum physics, they argue that ontological (not just epistemological) emergence is real and not merely reducible to some micro-phenomena.

> [E]ither everything is reducible to fundamental physics or it is not. If it is reducible, if everything is quantum mechanical, then ontological emergence is ubiquitous, as we have shown. If, on the other hand, the macroscopic is not reducible to the microscopic, if quantum effects really are screened off, then the entire world of classical objects is somehow ontologically emergent. In short, ontological emergence is most probably a real feature of the world. (Silberstein and McGeever 1999, 200)

They also discuss nonlinear dynamical systems, including the so-called chaotic systems, and conclude that they, at least, exemplify epistemological emergence, but do not necessarily demonstrate ontological emergence. However, as I have shown above with the combination of the inevitable quantum process that is an integral part of any complex system, at whatever scale, combined with local-global linkages (viz., multiple levels of context) as handled in the Relational Reality model, but not addressed by Silberstein and McGeever, then a strong case can be made as well for ontological emergence being applicable to essentially all macro-systems. This argument complements arguments made above concerning the breakdown of claims for reductionism, determinism, actualism, and causal closure of the physical. Applying contemporary quantum physics with careful attention to levels of emergence, including both ontological and epistemic, William Kallfelz (2009) also affirms ontological emergence. The standard view of physics, as stated by Christopher Klinger, "constructed on an Aristotelian world view, is the imposition of an 'outside-looking-in' perspective—the exo-physical standpoint of observer divorced from that which is observed, whereby the world is reduced to an arena (spacetime) populated by material 'things' that are seen to act and interact as events are played out" (Klinger 2016, 144). Instead of such a God's eye view framing, Reginald Cahill and Klinger work out details of an endo-physical approach ("physics from within"), "which asserts a priority of *process* whereby the apparent objective material reality of modern physics . . . is an emergent feature that arises *a posteriori* rather than having been prescribed *a priori*" (Klinger 2016, 145). Through considerations of complexity, self-organization, and the limitations of logic, Cahill (2016) and Klinger (2016) utilize an information-oriented modeling of reality to demonstrate the possibility of developing a unified quantum theory of gravity.[24] As Klinger states,

The traditional approach to modelling reality employs formal, syntactical information systems. That is, physicists have always assumed that accounts of their investigations are compressible in the form of axioms and rules for the manipulation of the symbols from which their theories are constructed. The formalism has always been accompanied by meta-rules and metaphysical assertions lying outside of the mathematical language and designed to overcome the limitations of syntax by providing semantic elements that could not be formalized. Here, the distinction between the syntactical and the semantic corresponds precisely with the distinction between provable truths and the random, unprovable truths identified by [Gregory] Chaitin—the former being the product of a syntactical system and the latter being the domain of things that are true for no reason and hence algorithmically incompressible and necessarily semantic, since they cannot be condensed or encoded in the axioms of the system by which they are generated. When a meta-rule is invoked to account for a specific event (as in, for example, a single quantum measurement, which has a random characteristic that is beyond the formalism of quantum theory), it demonstrates that to fully account for quantum aspects of reality requires a bigger system than provided by the standard model of quantum theory. In other words, there is a dichotomy of syntax and semantics with what might be termed a "Gödelian boundary" separating the two domains, the existence of which provides evidence of self-referencing in that bigger system. The standard model begins with the construction of a classical spacetime geometric structure to which are attached various classical fields, with these subsequently being quantized. It is a multi-level and necessarily contrived approach with a developmental history that masks the lack of a genuinely cohesive and comprehensive theoretical underpinning. In a fully mature theory the classical features of an objective reality would be naturally emergent constructs arising from an abstract process devoid of *a priori* classical structures, while also being minimal in its assumptions and maxims. This is precisely what *Process Physics* achieves. (Klinger 2016, 162)

To assess whether Cahill and Klinger's "process physics" achieves the intended goal is beyond the scope of my present work;[25] however, the *Logoi* framework presumes that some future theoretical and interpretive framework is possible that is not only endo-physical in approach, but also addresses both syntactical and semantic dimensions. For now, however, we presume that the descriptive content of contemporary quantum physics is essentially correct based on its outstanding success in observational tests over the past century although we now apply the Relational Reality interpretation articulated by Epperson and Zafiris (2013). As noted above, this interpretive framework is supported by a confluence of several research programs as discussed in the collaborative paper by Kastner, Kauffman, and Epperson (2018). Epperson's Relational Reality interpretation and the process physics approach are broadly compatible. The key unique feature of both is that gravity physics, including temporality and metric description, is not *a priori* but is emergent.[26] Several examples of ontological emergence appear in biophysics. In particular, Stuart Kauffman emphasizes the importance of our "failure to be able to prestate the configuration space of the biosphere . . . the implications are that the number of potentially relevant properties is vastly hyperastronomical and that there is no way in the lifetime of the universe for any knower within the universe to enumerate, let alone work with, all the possible properties or categories and their causal consequences" (Kauffman 2000, 137). In his latest work, Kauffman states that "history enters when the space of the possibles is vastly larger than what can become actual. For example, the evolution of life itself is a profoundly historical process. So too may be space chemistry and the formation of complex molecules. Thus, the becoming of the universe above the level of atoms is a historical process" (Kauffman 2019, 3). All these being yet additional expressions of the unlimited vastness of real potential relations (*potentiae*). Our typical understanding of causal relations has greatly suffered from taking a highly abstracted and truncated model of physical systems as generally applicable to all causal relation. In particular, as Harry Heft points out,

our automatic and exclusive identification of the term *cause* with mechanistic antecedent-consequent relations illustrates one way that thinking from the perspective of Newtonian physics and Cartesian metaphysics has become part of the fabric of everyday discourse. With this formulation, when considering the cause of an occurrence, the tendency is to look [only] for precipitating, antecedent events. (Heft 2001, xxiv)

Heft goes into detail about how such a limited view of the causal relation has been detrimental to life studies, an argument expertly augmented by theoretical ecologist Robert Ulanowicz (2009). Similarly, there are numerous references that criticize such mechanistic causal thinking as applied to the sciences more generally; for example, Čapek (1961), Ivor Leclerc (1986), and Ellis (2016), among others. Indeed, Ellis documents multiple types of causation that go beyond the mechanistic account, the latter presuming deductivism based on a necessitarian account of causal relation (Ellis 2016, 9–11). Analytic philosopher Evan Fales states that "I believe the notion of causal relation to be more fundamental than that of natural necessity, and not, strictly used, equivalent to it . . . the ontologically and semantically fundamental notion is causation itself" (Fales 1990, 34). Indeed, Hilary Putnam responded favorably to John Haldane's summary, regarding multiple modes of causation, that there "may also be greater than six (*efficient, formal, material, final, physical,* and *creative*)" (Haldane 2015, 694). What is now needed to displace the standard, truncated (deductivist, efficient cause only) view is a fundamentally different concept of causal relation that is both more intuitively correct than the classical account and can incorporate these new developments.

Wesley Salmon has noted that "the problem of causality [causation] is still with us. It becomes especially critical for those who find an explanatory role for probabilistic causes. As my brief remarks have indicated, considerably more work is needed to clarify this concept . . . conflicting fundamental intuitions are rampant" (Salmon 1984, 186). Presently, as Salmon points out, there appears to be a vicious circularity confronting standard accounts of modalities, laws, and counterfactuals.

The most popular current approach to counterfactuals seems to be one that appeals to possible worlds . . . It has two major shortcomings in my opinion. First, the postulation of the existence of myriad possible worlds, distinct from our actual world, takes us deep into the superempirical. Second, evaluation of the similarity of possible worlds—which is essential to the analysis of counterfactuals—requires an appeal to laws. So, it has not broken us out of the circle. (Salmon 1984, 130)

Note that "possible worlds" in this quote refers to actualized possibles, not ontic *possibiliae*. The above considerations of causation and emergence have direct implications for a key philosophical argument made by Scottish philosopher David Hume. As Jessica Wilson states, "Many contemporary philosophers accept a strong generalization of Hume's denial of necessary causal connections, in the form of Hume's dictum, according to which there are no metaphysically necessary connections between distinct, intrinsically typed entities" (Wilson 2015, 138). Resisting the Humean escape route from these problems, Salmon states, contra Hume, that "I do not believe that causality resides in the mind." As for the problem of entanglement in quantum physics, Salmon continues "I have no idea what an appropriate explanation would look like; we may need to know more about the microcosm before any explanation can be forthcoming . . . to provide a satisfactory treatment of microphysical explanation constitutes a premier challenge to contemporary philosophy of science" (Salmon 1984, 279). Hume was led to his "dictum" by supposing that the distinctiveness of ideas in our mind could be mapped directly to the claims that things in the physical world have similar distinctiveness, not only as a matter of observation (epistemologically) but with their intrinsic (metaphysical) nature. We now see that Hume's dictum is based on a fundamental category error. His proper description of the distinctiveness of ideas in the mind and, comparatively, the distinctiveness of perceived objects was improperly extended from the epistemic to an ontological claim, an example of Teilhard de Chardin's analytical illusion.

Based on both scientific advances and careful philosophical analysis over the past 250 years, we now can clearly see that both diachronic perspectives [causation grounded in fundamental quantum process] and synchronic perspectives [both epistemological and ontological emergence via multilevel, local-global relations] enable us to avoid errors like Hume's dictum, and provide important new understandings of causal connections. Indeed, as shown in chapter 2, the *Logoi* framework and the Relational Reality model together provide a plausible explanation for entanglement as called for by Salmon.

As summarized in the *Fundamental Quantum Process* section of chapter 2, the Relational Reality model, whose focus is diachronic, articulates four stages of fundamental quantum process, which weave together given actualizations and *potentiae*, leading to potential states locally contextualized, then delimited to probable states upon conditionalization of *potentiae* along with restriction of the local by the global, and finally yielding an actual outcome state (fact/measurement) with its actualization of *potentiae* and extension of local to global. The unrelenting bootstrapping of such processes with multilevel weavings[27] comprises various networks of *causation* that constitute our world. With a synchronic focus on such multilevel process with local-global effects, we also have the *emergence* of various complex systems (see *Complex Systems* below). Along with many examples from the various sciences, these multilevel effects are also exemplified in the fields of cognitive and behavioral sciences, as argued by Don Ross and David Spurrett, who state that "there is indeed a deep tradition of 'causation as universal glue' . . . but that tradition has found its most sophisticated contemporary expression in analysis of causation as a special type of information-transmission or other global-structural relation" (Spurrett 2004, 623).

GENERALIZING THE FUNCTION

The *Logoi* framework, here proposed, bypasses the circularity that undermines many standard accounts of causal relations because it clearly distinguishes (for epistemology) scientific from philosophical propositions, (for logic) the Boolean from the non-Boolean, and (for ontology) the distinction between actuality and *potentiae* within the real. The needed different concept of causation, capable of avoiding the above circularity and helping to understand quantum entanglement as well, arises naturally from the fundamental notion of process, a core element of the *Logoi* framework, which refers to input-output succession within context, given *potentiae* and constraints. Structurally and functionally, this fundamental succession is very similar to the action of a mathematical function. Bradley explains:

> A mathematical function, matrix, or schema is a rule of "mapping" in which the elements from one set or "domain" are matched to elements of another set or "codomain" . . . [an example is an] infinite set of ordered pairs $<x, y>$, with x belonging to the domain and y to the codomain, where a correspondence is mapped between the member of the domain and the member of the codomain (so for $(x)^2$ we could have the ordered-pair values $<2, 4>$, $<3, 9>$, and so on). (Bradley 2003a, 233)

Noting how Whitehead characterized thought as a "generalized mathematics," Bradley explains his speculative philosophical strategy through the concept of a function and associated mapping activity: "The definition of the function as the class of many-to-one relations aligns the analysis of the function with the philosophical question as to the nature of plurality and unity . . . lifting the concept of the function to the highest level of metaphysical generality . . . defining the concept of the ultimate as the concept of *the function in general*" (Bradley 2008, 233). Fundamentally, "each occasion is triadically analyzed in terms of a given domain, its private synthetic act as a *causa sui* [cause within itself] and its public or communal role as an object of a successor occasion" (Bradley 2008, 241). In contrast to nominalist commitments of the linguistically oriented analytic philosophy tradition, Whitehead draws on his expertise in mathematical-physics and generalizes the function to a key mapping activity of fundamental, diachronic process in a way that is highly compatible with recent work in quantum physics as discussed above. Bradley continues,[28]

> Any occasion of mapping is thus intrinsically serial in nature in that it is necessarily a member of a single series of occasions, which in fact is one of a multiplicity of series which constitute its environment. These are the multiple and intrinsically complex routes of inheritance of any occasion of mapping and constitute its genealogical conditions. In consequence, all occasions necessarily have the following characters: they are asymmetrical as many-to-one constructions; they are transitive, in that the relations between them are many-to-one relations; they are connected, in that they have predecessors; they are consecutive in that their immediate predecessors are occasions; and they stand in a "cumulative" relation to their predecessors . . . The concept of series of occasions can thus be regarded as an ontological generalization and constructivist reinterpretation of the Plato-Frege theory of numbers as serial relations, for it installs serial relationality as an intrinsic feature of the nature of things by defining both an occasion and its relata as many-to-one configurations or connectives in series . . . In the iterative series, that is, occasions switch roles from being a successor mapping, or synthetic subject, to being the predecessor, object, or basis, and thus the subject or argument, of a consequent successor mapping. The result is that subject and object, as well as subject and predicate, are not here fixed ontological opposites . . . they are the basic states or sequential relations of occasions of iterative mapping. (Bradley 2008, 238–239)

Even though Lucretius's famous poem *On the Nature of Things* (mid-first century BCE) provided a useful precursor for atomic theory, the above fundamental succession of quantum process, combined with modern field theory (indeed, fields, particles, and space plasmas pervading the universe) provides a dramatic rejoinder to Lucretian "atoms and the void," which so influenced scientific thought during the Newtonian era. Indeed, the word "space" too often disables us from appreciating that there is no such thing as truly empty space anywhere in the universe even though regions of exceedingly low particle density and field energy, presumably space plasmas, are pervasive in inter-galactic "space."

At the time Whitehead was developing his systematic philosophy, quantum theory was in its early stages, and both category theory and quantum field theory were developed later. Nevertheless, working only with subsets of these, namely set theory, basic quantum physics, and field theory, respectively, Whitehead's philosophical intuitions were unusually prescient. For quantum physics and field theory, this exceptional anticipation is shown in detail by Epperson (2004) and Bettinger (2015). In mathematics, the fundamentals of succession and process were not adequately modeled by the relatively static concepts of set theory, and Whitehead's philosophy worked to overcome its limitations. Indeed, in the same decade as Whitehead's passing, category theory emerged and has since proven to be a worthy successor to set theory, and capable of representing more complex and dynamic systems. Michael Heather and Nick Rossiter state that "to apply the metaphysical methodology of mathematics to the logic and form of process in natural philosophy requires a metaphysics above modeling, a methodology more than method and a mathematics beyond the set based topics of arithmetic, algebra, geometry and topology" (Heather and Rossiter 2009, 1). From this category theory perspective Heather and Rossiter articulate a view that is highly compatible with Whitehead's metaphysical adaptation of the mathematical function:

> A top-down approach begins with the Universe as process. The highest structure in category theory is the topos which can be identified as an arrow, itself containing distinguishable identity arrows. That is distinguishable in the manner that every entity in the Universe is different but related to every other entity. This identification of the Universe as process seems really self-evident in the sense that everything is process. This concept does not view the Universe as a container where things go on. Rather the Universe is just "goings on." This does not even need the concept of entity or "thing." Following Aristotle, types can be defined as categories. This is in effect only a label for a recursive process. Within the topos, arrows are components relating other identity arrows. Each identity arrow may itself be composed of arrows that relate other identity arrows.
>
> Therefore while sets are representable as number, process is representable as the arrow. An arrow points in some ordered sense. That is it defines an ordering. At the highest level an arrow neither begins nor ends but just goes on. (Heather and Rossiter 2009, 2)

As well, Heather and Rossiter discuss Whitehead's philosophy, including the concepts of prehension and concrescence, in framing a useful summary of the implications of category theory for a fundamental framework of world process. "Category theory is not restricted by the constraints of set membership. It therefore avoids the problems of independence and atomicity of elements. It avoids too the undecidability of Gödel as well as Russell's paradox. It therefore has the property of recursion to be found in the real world" (Heather and Rossiter 2009, 4). Overall, they argue that "the universe operates as a quantum information processor" (Heather and Rossiter 2005, 375). In a closely related development, referenced by Heather and Rossiter, Cahill states that "this new physics is . . . that of a self-referential information system, where the information is semantic and active" (Cahill 2016, 216).

The above ordering of fundamental process, inspired by research in fundamental logic, category theory, quantum physics, and information theory, supports the view that, as Anderson Weekes expresses it, "Whitehead proposes that apparent continuity of becoming results . . . from a moment-by-moment becoming of continuity. Each present moment involves a subjective durational spread within which an actuality-in-the-making appropriates its predecessors before it bleeds into its successors. According to Whitehead, the evidence for such a process, indeed, its paradigm example, is consciousness itself" (Weekes 2009b, 147). The asymmetry of such fundamental process is reflected in an analysis of the concept of symmetry in fundamental physics.

SYMMETRY IN SCIENCE

The scientific process is characterized by at least eight notions: observation, reproducibility, predictability, reduction, synthesis, theory, modeling, and approximation. *Observations* or, equivalently, Boolean measurement outcomes or data, are the most basic of scientific elements. *Reproducibility* assures that experimental results can be reproduced, under the same conditions, in the same or other laboratories. *Predictability* points to how relationships and order can be found and expressed in mathematical form. Science's *reductive methodology* separates things into parts that can be individuated whereas *synthesis* puts those parts back together again in a way that approximates the initial whole (whether via modeling or in practice). *Theory* and *modeling* provide quantitative ways (most often mathematical) to express discovered relationships and order, which enable successive improvements in predictability, reproducibility, reduction, and synthesis. Last, but not least, is *approximation* wherein the apparent perfection of propositions about theory and models is sacrificed in applications to the real world wherein errors and error analysis are inevitable.

The most common three ways of segmenting nature into workable components or parts are as follows:

(1) observer-observed (i.e., ourselves vs. the remainder of nature);
(2) quasi-isolated systems vs. surroundings; "quasi" because any "isolation" is an approximation;
(3) initial state and evolution; "initial state" often being the specification of a quasi-isolated system.

Joe Rosen has stated that "what symmetry boils down to in the final analysis is that the situation possesses the possibility of a change that leaves some aspect of the situation unchanged," or, equivalently "Symmetry is immunity to a possible change" (Rosen 1995, 157). For example, "if a reduction separates out a part that can be understood individually, then that part exhibits order and law regardless of what is going on in the rest of nature. In other words, that part possesses aspects that are immune to possible changes in the rest of nature. And that is symmetry" (Rosen 1995, 172). Rosen demonstrates in a similar way how reproducibility and predictability depend on such a general notion of symmetry; likewise for the above three modes of reduction.

However, in spite of the centrality of symmetry in the methodology of science, asymmetry is fundamental to the world. Rosen's point about the symmetries of fundamental physics emerging from considering asymmetry itself bears repeating:

> For there to be symmetry, there must concomitantly be asymmetry under the same change that is involved in the symmetry. For every symmetry there is an asymmetry tucked away somewhere in the world. So symmetry implies asymmetry. That relation is not symmetric, since asymmetry does not imply symmetry. (Rosen 1995, 161)

In *Creative Synthesis and Philosophic Method*, Charles Hartshorne has a chapter on "The Prejudice in Favor of Symmetry" (Hartshorne 1970, 205–226) in which he discusses logical relations and symmetry. With specific reference to this chapter, Rosen has argued that "just as in Hartshorne's 'paradigm for metaphysics,' even in physics asymmetry is primary" (Rosen 2004, 130).

SYMMETRY AND QUANTUM STATISTICS

Quantum physics has shown that the substances and structures of our everyday world emerge from particle and field interactions at multiple levels involving, at the most basic level, "particles" or composites called fermions that have half-integer values of intrinsic angular momentum (or spin), and bosons that have integer multiples of spin.[29] All matter comprises one or both of these basic types. Benjamin Schumacher, in a clear and concise lecture for the lay audience, characterizes bosons as "gregarious particles" whose symmetric quantum states enable them to dramatically intermix, as for example, with the bath of photons that you are imbedded in now as you read this book, and many examples from low-temperature physics. For example, liquid helium becomes a superfluid at two degrees above absolute zero and, as Schumacher states, this "superfluid state represents trillions of helium atoms in a single quantum state–a macroscopic example of the quantum gregariousness of bosons" (Schumacher 2009, 41). In contrast, fermions are anti-symmetric and, as Schumacher characterizes them, "antisocial" because no two fermions can occupy the same quantum state. Just as liquid helium and the "sea" of photons that we live in every day are bosons, with their own unique logic and statistics (called Bose-Einstein statistics), there are unique statistics for fermions (called Fermi-Dirac statistics), which then substantially account for the physical and chemical properties of the elements and molecular configurations, and enable the electromagnetic bonds that make complex chemistry and life possible. In this way, the two fundamental modalities of the *Logoi* framework, symmetries that are especially characteristic of the order of *potentiae*, and asymmetries that are inevitably part of the order of actualization, become reflected in these two basic logics[30] and statistics, Bose-Einstein, and Fermi-Dirac, respectively, thus being key enablers of our quantum world.

LOGIC, MODALITY, AND EXTENSION

Modal logic[31] as a distinct subject began about a century ago as the formal study of necessity and possibility as well as temporal notions, which are neglected in standard Aristotelian logic. Within the *Logoi* framework, in treating logic, modality, and extension, we have the order of *potentiae* and the order of actualization, the former potentially characterized by something like S5 modal logic, the latter perhaps by S4 modal logic, an extension of Boolean algebra (Shields, private communication, 2019); see Patrick Blackburn's *Modal Logic* for details (Blackburn 2015). A full mereo-topological theory of extensive connectedness that can be applied both to the pre-space order of *potentiae*, and the order of actualization, has yet to be developed. For example, contemporary philosophical works in modal science appear to neglect the possibilities pointed to here concerning the implications of having real effects associated with both Boolean and non-Boolean logical domains; for example, *Modal Logic as Metaphysics* (Timothy Williamson 2013). An appropriate precursor to this distinction may be Whitehead's theory of extension in Part IV of his *Process and Reality* (Whitehead 1929) and discussed in chapter 5 of Auxier and Herstein's work (Auxier and Herstein 2017). Based on a study of quantum physics, and following an excellent survey of that topic, Karen Barad hypothesizes an "agential realist ontology" that appears to complement the *Logoi* framework. She argues for seeing causal structure in terms of intra-actions, which describe fundamental quantum process and, more generally, something like Whiteheadian prehension in which "Space, time, and matter are mutually constituted through the dynamics of iterative intra-activity" (Barad 2007, 181). Iterative intra-activity occurs at multiple levels of extension, on both spatial scales and temporal scales.

CAUSATION AND OBJECTIVATION

At the time of Whitehead's writing of *Process and Reality*, first published in 1929 (Whitehead, 1978), it was plausible to highlight consciousness as a prime exemplar of fundamental, diachronic process. Augmenting this, we now have the following fundamental considerations, among others, to support the concept of process, with asymmetry, as central to causal relation:

—category theory analysis of fundamental process, and quantum physics: Epperson and Zafiris (2013); Kastner et al. (2018); Heather and Rossiter (2018);

—asymmetry as fundamental, as with the arrow in category theory: Rosen (1995); Heather and Rossiter (2018);

—concept of the mathematical function: Bradley (2003a);

—information-theoretic analysis for quantum process: Cahill (2005, 2016); Klinger (2010, 2016);

—objectivation (object-subject): Weekes (2009c, 437–443).

Anderson Weekes[32] developed in depth the last point on object-subject relations. He proposed that if we consider "experience" in its most elemental form as simply some type of response, we may consider that such experience is "simply the obverse side of causation—what it looks like from the perspective of the effect or the person undergoing the effect. If A affects B, then B 'experiences' A, where experience can be understood minimally as a physical or chemical reaction" (Weekes 2009c, 443). Such analysis closely parallels Klinger's analysis of fundamental physics in terms of the need for both exophysics (i.e., the analysis of systems from an external viewpoint), and "endophysics—literally, 'internal physics' or 'physics from within.' Here, the observer must necessarily be part of any theory of that which is observed. Since the act of observation may become part of the dynamics, endophysics accommodates notions of self-referencing—indeed, the inevitability of self-referencing in sufficiently rich systems is intimately tied to the distinction between exophysics and endophysics" (Klinger 2016, 145). Further, the input-output-context (reflexive response) structure of endophysics reflects, as Weekes points out, "the always-useful language of Peirce, a reaction seems to display Secondness [input-output only], but not Thirdness [input-output-context]. Whitehead's proposal [i.e., that elemental 'experience' being the obverse side of causation], which doesn't seem too far from Peirce, is that this lack of reflexivity [and context] is an illusion. Pure Secondness is possible only as a kind of limiting case of Thirdness, where the difference between what a thing is for itself and what it is through and for others becomes vanishingly small" (Weekes 2009a, 443). At the same time, notes Weekes, this self-referential perspective or "endophysical view asserts a priority of *process* whereby the apparent objective material reality of modern physics (i.e. the whole 'box and dice' of container and contents) is an emergent feature that arises *a posteriori* rather than having been prescribed *a priori*" (Klinger 2016, 145). Thus, fundamental physical relations emerge from such foundational process, subject to the limitations of logic (Gödel, Chaitin, etc.), instead of arising from externally imposed law. Further, as will be discussed later, these limitations of logic forbid the meaningfulness of strict entailment (or absolute determinism), which is reflected as well in quantum indeterminacy (arising from the necessity of non-Boolean logic in quantum physics).

EMERGENCE OF PHYSICAL RELATIONSHIPS

Many excellent physicists, Stephen Hawking and others, have speculated about a possible physical Theory of Everything (TOE) (Hawking 2005). Sean Carroll proposes what is arguably the best articulation of such a theory by providing an equation that explicitly represents a claimed TOE. In his book *The Big Picture*, with his God's eye perspective, Carroll champions the "Core Theory . . . One equation that tells us the quantum amplitude for the complete set of fields to go from some starting configuration . . . to some final configuration" (Carroll 2016, 440). Although admitting that this "can't be the final story," (ibid.) Carroll confidently claims that "the Core Theory underlying our everyday lives is extremely precise, rigid, and well defined. There is no ambiguity in it, no room to introduce important new aspects that we simply haven't noticed yet . . . an accurate description of nature in its claimed domain" (Carroll 2016, 441). This core equation, presented in two lines, combines quantum mechanics, spacetime, gravity, other forces, matter, and the Higgs fields; for details, see Carroll (2016, 437).[33] It is the holy grail of reductionism; a physicalist's and deductivist's dream; one ring to "rule them all!" It reminds me of t-shirts that display the "whole shebang" in one equation.[34] The components of this one equation are arguably the best of contemporary physics, and they do represent a great achievement. However, no scientist in practice has ever combined all or even most of the terms of this equation in any practical model or simulation. Whole sub-fields of physics are consumed with continued research on aspects of each such component (e.g., high energy physics with the Higgs field term). Carroll's "core theory" is a mashup[35] of such separate components, an aggregate of results from various research fields, and is not a practical, working equation. Further, Carroll presupposes several problematic metaphysical claims without discussion, including actualism, physicalism, and causal closure.

Through its use of mainstream quantum physics, the Relational Reality approach has built into it the Feynman path-integral approach and least action principle. Similarly, Carroll does mention that several terms of his core theory have a basis in the principle of least action; for more on that important insight, see the section below on *"Law"—From Entailment to Constrained Processual Histories.* However, it is very misleading to combine these separate terms as one equation and then claim that it is an appropriate proxy for a "final and ultimate" equation as part of some ultimate TOE that will capture all reality.[36] Implicitly, Carroll is making important and questionable metaphysical claims, which are common for TOE advocates, including the deductivism that he presupposes in stating the core theory. Nicholas Maxwell argues that such metaphysical claims should be made explicit so that they can be evaluated on their own terms (Maxwell 2017). For the core theory, as expressed by Carroll, these presuppositions are, among others, that (1) ultimate reality is grounded in only physics (i.e., physicalism, including causal closure), all else is derivative; (2) deterministic entailment, dyadic input-output is ultimate (not triadic input-output-context), all other relations are derivative; (3) genuine possibility and/or emergence is implicitly excluded because all results can be derived from this one equation; and (4) one unifying equation is meaningful, only the details are yet to be filled in, and only technical, procedural limitations inhibit its ultimate application to provide unlimited predictive capability; thus renewing *fin de siècle* dreams.[37] Albeit "dreams" can be sources of great creativity, and I do not deny the importance of such unitary explanations or the value of identifying unifying trends in physical explanation. Nevertheless, I here wish to emphasize a "both-and" argument; both reduction and emergence, both unity and diversity, both the order of *potentiae* and the order of actualizations (Eastman 2003).

In contrast to this confidence in deductivist dreams and deterministic entailment "law," in considering the limitations of science, Robert Rosen states that "Mathematical rigor (i.e., 'objectivity') does not reside in finitely-based syntactic rules alone . . . Gödel's Theorem demonstrated the *complexity* of number theory—its irreducibility to simple formalizations" (Rosen 1996, 212). Here, the reference to Gödel's theorem indicates how propositions in general (here, including infinite sequences) enable the construction of further propositions that go beyond the initially presumed framework (here, finite sequences alone). Continuing, Rosen states that "from the standpoint of finite arithmetic, divergence is itself an emergent property. The dependence of a limit of an infinite sum on the way its summands are ordered and parenthesized is something without a counterpart in finite sums, and is unpredictable from them *alone*" (Rosen 1996, 214). And then, questioning some moves from the finite to the infinite, Rosen cautions us that "to replace 'arbitrary sequence' by 'convergent sequence' . . . is not mandated or entailed by anything in the content of mathematics itself. Rather, it is motivated by an intention, to retain customary habits, familiar from the finite realm, as intact as possible in the infinite one" (Rosen 1996, 210). Carroll's core equation assumes the adequacy or "finitely-based syntactic rules," number theory, and proper closure of infinite sums, but these assumptions are all questioned here by Rosen based on very fundamental grounds. (Please note as well that a thorough critique of both physicalism and causal closure of the physical has been provided above in the sections entitled *On the Failure of Determinism* and *On the Failure of Physicalism.*)

The high-level structure of a plausible formula sufficient for a TOE can help us to see why all attempts at a TOE, such as Carroll's, are set up for failure. Suppose that we somehow infer a most general mathematical function for a current event E in process of actualization that captures relationships of both finite and infinite sequences (s), both Boolean and non-Boolean logic (l), both local and global aspects of relations (r), and all aspects of more inclusive context (c). Then we would have a causal relationship as follows, resultant E = complex function $f(s, l, r, c \ldots)$. As a matter of practice, science always constrains this to at most $f(s, l, r)$ (i.e., effectively that any fully global context is presupposed and beyond science to evaluate), that is, unless we were to somehow fully incorporate recent category theory analysis of quantum process as outlined by Zafiris (2010a). However, most science does not include such, which then leaves out reference to local-global effects, leaving only $f(s, l)$. Indeed, most conventional science (primarily outside of quantum physics) leaves out the non-Boolean order of *potentiae*, thus leaving only $f(s)$. Finally, as noted above, Robert Rosen points out that much standard science avoids infinite sequences and limits one to only convergent sequences. Even with these multiple layers of constraints, much science can still be accomplished (e.g., most of classical physics). However, complex systems and life systems are now left out. To be fully inclusive, and for any TOE worthy of the claim, the full range of $f(s, l, r, c \ldots)$ needs to cover both physical systems and measurement of such, and both science and humanities, especially philosophy, due to the inclusion of ultimate initial conditions and boundary conditions arguably beyond the "way of numbers," viz., the scope of science (i.e., quantification; emphasis on context-independence). Scientism is effectively the reductive claim that $f(s, l, r, c \ldots)$ collapses to just $f(s, l, r)$ or (often) just $f(s)$.

Suppose that we map Carroll's core theory to the following representation, $W = f(QP, ST, G, F, M, H)$ where QP=quantum physics, ST=space-time, G=gravity, F=other forces; M=matter, H=Higgs field. This corresponds to $E = f(s)$ above, presuming that non-convergent infinite sequences are handled; indeed, they mostly are not incorporated, although they are to a limited extent in contemporary quantum field theory (via renormalization). Thus,

Carroll's strong claim that his core theory provides a proxy of a final theory stumbles because it excludes most of the full range of $f(s, l, r, c ...)$ as argued above. Yet, to his credit, he had the courage to at least put down a clear and quantitative form of a TOE hypothesis. Nevertheless, such scientism allows much of reality to escape the net of its equations due to not addressing some key questions of logic and philosophy. Among others, examples include limitations to Boolean actualizations only versus Boolean plus non-Boolean effects (including *potentiae*); the neglect of local-global relations; and constraints of measurement and observation involving human intention; or some more inclusive context (c) that goes beyond scientific applications as currently practiced, which treats most levels of context (especially any reference to ultimate context) as something to ignore because not efficacious given the applied approximations, which as noted above, inevitably involve essential limits.

We have earlier commented on how Verlinde views the concept of a metric[38] as emergent from more fundamental aspects of entropy and thermodynamics (Verlinde 2011). His approach also involves pre-space quantum process. With a focus on Verlinde's work, Jesse Bettinger discusses these issues in greater depth (Bettinger 2015). Using an alternative approach and gravity model, Cahill (2005, 2016) and Klinger (2010, 2016) have formulated a "process physics" approach, also based on quantum field theory, in addition to information theory, that focuses on fundamental quantum process. These new developments, each indicating a possible way to consider metric relations as derivative from fundamental quantum process, could eliminate any need for Carroll's space-time term within the core theory and effectively imbed temporal and spatial relations within quantum physics and his "other Force" terms.

Many reductionist accounts presume that higher and more complex system levels can be simply reduced to lower-level, simpler components. Along with the common hypothesis of physicalism, such accounts tend to assume that higher-level properties are in some sense merely dependent upon, or supervenient, on lower-level, physical properties (Daniel Stoljar 2010, 115). However, given substantial advances made over the past two decades in understanding examples of top-down causation (e.g., Ellis 2016), the supervenience strategy has become much less plausible. Further, as shown above, the core assumption of physicalism, which is the causal closure of the physical, can now be shown to be false. The general concept for understanding relationships across levels is "grounding," which may be understood in either reductionist or non-reductionist accounts. As Jonathan Schaffer states, "Grounding is something like metaphysical causation. Roughly speaking, just as causation links the world across time, grounding links the world across levels" (Schaffer 2012, 115). Schaffer later adds nuance to this concept when he similarly argues that "*Grounding-causation unity* is the claim that there is a single unified relation of generation called 'causation' when it drives the world through time, and 'grounding' when it drives the world up levels" (Schaffer 2016, 94). Overall, in the *Logoi* framework, the "single unified relation of generation" is effectively Whitehead's concept of prehension, the former "drive" is the diachronic aspect of prehension, and the latter "drive up levels" is the synchronic aspect or emergence.

"LAW"—FROM ENTAILMENT TO
CONSTRAINED PROCESSUAL HISTORIES

Arguments about both causation and physical "law"[39] are often limited to empirical laws to set aside any claim about the metaphysical basis of such law. Up through the eighteenth century and beyond, scholars would often appeal to God-given laws to fulfill such metaphysical requirements. Aside from that explanation, the past two centuries have yielded almost no alternative explanation at the metaphysical level, although substantial progress has been made in understanding the very deep role of symmetry principles in fundamental physics. Indeed, in addition to field theory, principles of symmetry are central to all of modern physics. Electromagnetism is based on a gauge symmetry, and it has now been established that the strong and weak forces of physics are based on symmetries that are mathematically similar to the case for electromagnetism. These discoveries are the basis for the current standard model—essentially Carroll's core theory, discussed in the last section. Nevertheless, however powerful, these are descriptive, almost circular, arguments in terms of ultimate philosophical explanation. For what is the basis for the symmetry principles themselves? For this deeper philosophical question, the Relational Reality model now enables a possible explanation, which is laid out below.

Combining the above analysis of causation and emergence with recent results in quantum physics, category theory, and philosophy, exemplified most clearly in the Relational Realist model, enables an improved understanding of contingency, necessity, and *potentiae*. The modal distinctions of past, present, and future map roughly to actuality, conditional-necessity, and possibility, respectively, as discussed by Hulswit (2002, 201). Given the diachronic nature of fundamental quantum process, events are never simply in the form of input-output dyads only (except as an approximation), but are always imbedded in some continuous sequence of events with a triadic logical structure (input-output-context). This triadic general structure or form for causation has its ultimate basis in the requirement of triads and asymmetry in fundamental logic; as Shields states, "The *most* definitive of functions, the only functions capable of defining all others in singular fashion, are the Sheffer functions, which possess a triadic asymmetry that yet *includes* dyadic symmetry…symmetry *within* an all-embracing asymmetry" (Shields 2003, 20). Summarizing the above, the contemporary affirmation of asymmetry, triadic structure, and contingency is reflected in fundamental modal logic, quantum theory of measurement, top-down causal effects (see Ellis 2016), informatics, and semiotics (see Søren Brier 2013).

Given this fundamental analysis of causation and the importance of *potentiae* for quantum process, any necessities are conditional, and contingency inevitably characterizes quantum events. Instead of being grounded in the necessities of deduction or entailment, fundamental physical relations (laws[40]) in contemporary physics and conservation principles derive primarily from variational principles, such as the Principle of Least Action (PLA)[41] or, similarly, Hamilton's Principle (HP),[42] which contingently optimize from among a full array of possible trajectories in appropriately formulated phase spaces given particular relevant histories, including initial conditions and boundary conditions (i.e., *potentiae* of input-output relations within a context).[43] Instead of using action principles for explanations of why the field equations take their given form, a common strategy is to use only symmetry and uniqueness arguments. However, for purposes of philosophical interpretation, reference to PLA or HP helps us to recognize the transition between fundamental orders (here being the transition from the order of *potentiae* to the order of actualization) as a fundamental aspect of quantum process, which inevitably goes beyond symmetry anyway because such process necessarily involves symmetry breaking.

Through the use of differential equations, much of modern physics is expressed in terms of relatively simple local properties. At the same time, research in the calculus of variations shows that there is approximate equivalence[44] between local properties of a system and global properties of an associated trajectory. As shown in detail within the classic thesis by Richard Feynman, the PLA provides a way to quantify continuous deformations of such trajectories, establishing functions that, when minimized, can be used to derive many basic physical relations of modern physics (Laurie Brown 2005). In applying this method to derive the Schrödinger equations, the basic equation of quantum physics, Gerhard Grossing has shown that "a quantum 'particle' can both be 'guided' by the surrounding context, or it can alter the latter via . . . spontaneous fluctuations. This is also why one can speak . . . of a mutual dependence, or 'circular causality,' between the particle and its environment" (Grossing 2004, 17). In the case of classical physics, it could be thought that the above equivalence of local and global properties might be treated as a simple equivalence with reduction to the local. In contrast, in quantum physics, there is an intrinsic interdependence of the local and the global as indicated by the entanglement phenomenon and supported both by Grossing's point about coupling with the "surrounding context," and represented as well by quantum local-global correlations as shown by Zafiris based on category theory analysis (Zafiris 2016).

Building on the principle of least action, Vladislav Terekhovich hypothesizes a "deep ontological connection . . . between the possible paths of the PLA and quantum possible histories of the Feynman path integral formalism (FPI[45])" (Terekhovich 2018, 190). Terekhovich evaluated connections of FPI with the metaphysical notion of "*possibilia*" and Leibniz's concept of the essences or possibles striving toward existence. Terekhovich concludes that "unfortunately, this concept has long been rejected by most philosophers; today, however, it finds an ally in quantum behavior . . . another source that inspires me is a deep relationship between the PLA and the quantum sum-over-histories model or the FPI" (Terekhovich 2018, 199). Another major alternative to the entailment model for laws is to treat them as habits, as C. S. Peirce does. Rupert Sheldrake calls this "morphic resonance" and states that "the more the repetition, the deeper the grooves of habit. When habits are very deep-seated, like the behavior of hydrogen atoms or nitrogen molecules, they look as if they are changeless, as if they are governed by eternal laws" (Sheldrake 2018, 103). A common argument for basing laws on simply habits comes from David Hume. However, the error here is to convert a reasonably defensible Humean epistemology into a nominalistic Humean metaphysics. Nora Berenstain and James Ladyman analyze how realism in science has a "*prima facie* commitment to objective modality," and conclude that "since sophisticated Humeanism cannot offer a reasonable account of special-science laws or explain the success of inductive inference, it is deeply at odds with the spirit of scientific realism. We thus conclude that the scientific realist must embrace natural necessity" (Berenstain and Ladyman 2012, 167).

The hypothesis that physical laws are simply habits is arguably a category error because, for consistency with contemporary physics and biosemiotics, as Kalevi Kull argues, "we [need to] interpret habit-taking as exclusively a feature of living or life-produced systems." (Kull 2014) The above references to habits are merely descriptive; we seek the underlying process. In pursuit of such, physicist David Finkelstein states that,

> the idea that things or happenings tend to increase their probability of happening again, we don't call it habit anymore in physics, of course, we call it Bose-Einstein statistics. That's a guess that natural law is a condensation phenomenon . . . I suspect that the things we call laws today are simply phenomenological descriptions of the quantum fine structure of the vacuum. That I guess is a condensation phenomenon. The limited number of possible laws is the result of a

limited number of possible phases. And so the apparent constancy of law arises because there are jumps between them, just as there are between the various crystalline forms of ice. You don't have a smooth variation from one to the other. It takes a real disaster. (Finkelstein 2004, 191)

I have reviewed the literature concerning both the PLA and FPI concepts and conclude that the modal interpretation of the PLA argued by Terekhovich (his "modality model") is highly compatible with our *Logoi* framework as well as with the latest research in quantum physics. An extended quote from Terekhovich provides some detail of his argument.

According to the modality model, the possible histories in the PLA have essences in the possible modality but do not actually exist. Only actualised histories have existence in the actual modality. In compliance with the Leibnizian doctrine of the striving possibles, the essence of every possible history tends towards existence in our actual world. Using an analogy with the FPI, the modality model claims that all of the physical system's possible histories are jointly in the possible realm of our world. Therefore, this approach replaces the classical representation of a system's motion along a single actual history by a representation of simultaneous motions along an infinite set of all possible histories.

The modal interpretation of the PLA changes the view of causality in this principle . . . Indeed, a system does not need to "calculate" the value of the action or anything else. The rule of the summation of the history's actions does so, since the action is merely the physical measure of every history's essence. The system merely uses or actualises the maximal number of possibilities to move in each subsequent actual event. The continuous mutual play of a system's attempts in the possible modality and the following combining of these attempts create the system's actual events and actual history. Consequently, the significance of the PLA lies not with the mystic economy of nature, but merely in the observable effect of the collision and combination of all possible movements.

Such a modal approach to the PLA does not need backward causation because, in the possible modality, the exact direction of time does not matter. It is also not contrary to the principle of locality and the relativistic limit of the speed of causal influences. In the possible realm of our world, there are not any physical restrictions. It means that all speeds of light and all time-like intervals are possible. (Terekhovich 2018, 199–200)

Within this quote, please note that when Terekhovich states that "the exact direction of time does not matter," I interpret him to be referring to pre-space *potentiae* within a non-Boolean logical order; in contrast, the output, or measurement, from quantum process (Terekhovich's "actual modality") abides with a Boolean logical order in which time sequence is ontologically real and can also be mapped to space-time description. Further, when he refers to "no physical restrictions," he means that potential relations (*potentiae*) are only constrained by whatever limitations apply in the non-Boolean logical order, which is currently unknown; in contrast, a key constraint in the Boolean order of actualizations is that of relativistic (speed-of-light) limits. It is notable that Carroll, in setting up his core theory discussed above, depends substantially on Feynman's path-integral (FPI) approach in providing unity to the various terms of his ultimate equation. Although not mentioned by Carroll, emergence of such physical relations (i.e., terms of Carroll's core theory) via PLA, may be grounded in real *potentiae* through correlations emerging in the non-Boolean logical order via alternatives paths in such possibility pre-space. Further, unlike the order of actualizations, the pre-space order of *potentiae* could be an ultimate foundation for the symmetry principles of modern physics.

A complementary description is provided by Helmut Tributsch who, for all basic processes capable of effecting change, points out that

> it is known that all changes (*C*) are originating from conversion of energy (*E*). Changes must consequently be a function of energy. Mathematically also the inverse relation must therefore hold: $C=f(E)$ and $E=f(C)$ . . . available [free] energy is fundamentally time oriented and aims at decreasing its presence per state . . . time orientation is fundamentally imposed. This explains why action is indeed minimized. It is minimized because energy has the drive [presumably without intentionality] to minimize its presence per state. Thereby waste energy in not usable form is generated and entropy increases. The second law of thermodynamics follows immediately . . . *"free energy has the tendency to decrease and minimize its presence per state, within the restraints of the system."* (Tributsch 2016, 368)

Within a more detailed assessment of the history and science of both PLA and FPI, Michael Stöltzner concludes that "an appropriate view of the path integral formulation[46] of quantum mechanics therefore contains a certain globality, not in the sense that we were forced to consider boundary terms, but that we ought to take it as representing an ensemble in the statistical sense" (Stöltzner 1994, 53). Here then is a broadened notion of "teleology following Kant as the search for systematization. This concept stands in opposition to a world void of any structure" (ibid.). Avoiding the connotation of intention is important for such a broadened naturalist teleology; here instead teleology is focused on chance, as well potential relations (*potentiae*), operating within correlations of structure and constraints. This description accords with diachronic, fundamental quantum process as discussed above within the

Relational Realism framework of Epperson and Zafiris (2013). In a complementary way, Kastner points out that "the classical wave conveys energy through its intensity . . . the quantum wave conveys possibility" (Kastner 2013, 139)[47]—the quantum wave here enables the local-global correlations of structure and constraints as noted above.[48]

Another general treatment of laws in science is provided by Giovanni Boniolo and Paolo Budinich, who discuss three levels of physical relationships that put classical laws within a broader framework. In turn, classical laws are themselves grounded in fundamental quantum process:

1) the *evolutive laws*, (they include also the phenomenological laws of the Galilean phase), which are the laws closer to the empirical world since they describe the temporal evolution of the phenomena and therefore they permit us to represent what happens in a given place and in a given time (for example, the law of motion, the wave function solution of Schrödinger's equation, etc.). Of course, these first level laws may be checked directly by experience;

2) the *frame laws* (generally discovered in the Newtonian phase), which enable the deduction of the *evolutive laws* as their solutions (for example, the equations of classical dynamics which enable the inference of the law of the falling bodies and, in general, the classical laws of motion; Maxwell's equations; the Schrödinger's equation; etc.). In this case, their empirical control is realized via theoretical *modus tollens* because of the results obtained at the level of the *evolutive laws*;

3) the *principles* which, in a certain sense, mark the boundaries of the working domain of the frame laws, and at times, also promote their construction. Here, we are thinking about principles such as that of causality which often have a *metaphysical* counterpart, but we are also thinking about *formal* principles such as those of symmetry from which, for example, owing to the powerful Noether's theorem, we can derive the frame laws of conservation. (Boniolo and Budinich 2005, 88)

The first evolutive level concerns empirical relationships and what are properly laws in my usage. As noted above, the latter two are about physical relations more broadly, not simply empirical law. One of the *principles* within item 3 is the principle of least action discussed above. Boniolo and Budinich argue for a semiotic triad of physical-mathematical signs [index-icon-symbol] with icons as fallible conjectures about representations of the physical world (models, theories, etc.). Both the independent power and limitation of scientific models and theories are usefully surveyed in this semiotic framework. Boniolo and Budinich also provide a broad discussion of minimization principles in comparison with the methods of Galileo, Newton, and

Dirac. Within a section on "Dirac's methodological revolution," they point out that,

> as Dirac wrote in the quoted passage: "it will be beyond the power of human intelligence to get the necessary new ideas by direct attempts to formulate the experiment data in mathematical terms." Therefore, whilst working within certain mathematics, at a certain point one may realize that it may be a physical-mathematical sign. In other words, one may realize that the mathematics with which [one] is working also has an indexical aspect that indicates something which exists in the world. This is what Dirac meant. In this case, it is by reflecting on the pure mathematics that we have a direct access to the level of the frame laws. In this manner, the mathematical thought assumes the role of a powerful creator of conceivably new physical-mathematical signs, and thus, as a promoter of the discovery of new phenomenic aspects of the world, derivable from those framing laws. (Boniolo and Budinich 2005, 89)

By way of "Dirac's methodological revolution," through conceptualizing possible relations (*potentiae*) at multiple levels (*evolutive, framing, principles*), physical-mathematical signs and evolving models and theories indeed now leverage far greater power of scientific knowledge than was ever possible via the base level of direct empirical-evolutive physical relations alone.

As *principles* in the above three-part framing of physical relationships, the key parts of the *Logoi* framework comprise the fundamental notions (process, relation, logic), which incorporate input-output-context (multiplied multiscale and indefinitely), part-whole relations, local-global linkages, and two logical orders. Constraints on *potentiae* enabled by these factors is partly captured by optimization principles such as the principle of least action, which enables derivations of essentially all basic physics and explains the importance of symmetries, including application of Noether's Theorem,[49] which is applicable to *potentiae* pre-space relations. Yet particular actualizations or measurements inevitably involve symmetry breaking.

In this way, physical relations, such as the Schrödinger equation of quantum physics, emerge from such relations of relations in *possibiliae*-space context. In addition, as Zafiris argues, local-global connectedness, exhibited in category theory analysis of quantum process, enables non-local connectedness of such law (Zafiris 2010a). This provides a natural explanation for the highly precise uniformity of physical relations across extragalactic scales, the principle of universality, which otherwise remains an unresolved mystery of modern physics.

That physical relationships arise from "relations of relations" (and category theory being an algebra of relations) provides a viable alternative account for physical relations that avoids simplistic entailment and deductivism. Due to the part-whole, local-global features of the fundamental notions, we expect the scale-free emergence of modular hierarchical structures, as Ellis states, "orthogonal but interacting hierarchies, physical and logical, in both computers and natural systems" (Ellis 2016, 38). Further, Noether's Theorem is a principle based in the symmetries of non-Boolean *potentiae* (functioning at a pre-space level[50]) and their associated conservation principles. Through symmetry breaking, inevitably part of diachronic, fundamental quantum process, there emerges finite actualizations and the Boolean logical correlations of facts obtained via measurement, including temporality and time-space relations.

A crowning achievement of modern science, as Carroll properly characterizes it, is the creation of quantum field theory and the core theory (Carroll 2016, 437). This robust theory developed over three principal stages: (1) electromagnetism and Maxwell's equations, introducing field theory (1830s–1857); (2) the initial development of quantum physics (1905–1928); and (3) quantum field theory (primarily 1965–1983; see Sunny Y. Auyang 1995). As discussed above, in a highly abstracted form, Carroll presents the core theory as an equation for "the quantum amplitude for undergoing a transition from one specified field configuration to another, expressed as a sum over all the paths that could possibly connect them" (Carroll 2016, 437). The theory is "perfectly reversible" and "It's only when we start observing things that quantum mechanics violates reversibility" (Carroll 2016, 220). Of course, the "perfectly reversible" feature applies only in the idealization of models, or some possibility spaces (the order of *potentiae*), not with any set of contingent actualizations, or measurements, as admitted in the last quote from Carroll.

In my classes in quantum physics, reference was often made to ongoing interpretive issues but for us, in practice, it was "learn, obey, compute." For our classwork, particles were treated as just that (particle-like entities, or substance); only later did I realize that any "particle" was essentially a localized field entity and only particle-like in approximation. Ironically, contemporary field theory was developed primarily by theorists whose basic worldview was that of a classical metaphysics, which emphasizes substance and determinism (Eastman 2008). Although the famed quantum theorist, Richard Feynman, admitted that high energy physics could be called either field physics or particle physics, the latter term was adopted, likely due to the reigning substance metaphysics. This bias is also reflected in the title of 't Hooft's survey of quantum field theory, "In search of the Ultimate Building Blocks" ('t Hooft 1996)—as well, his commitment to a deterministic foundation is reflected in his paper "Determinism beneath quantum mechanics" ('t Hooft 2005). Such an approach raises two further difficulties, however, because of a dependence on space-time description as primary (instead of being treated as possibly deducible from more fundamental quantum process) and the inevitable reference to fluctuations. As Andrei Khrennikov states, "Although in general 't Hooft's subquantum mechanics is totally deterministic, to explain the violation of Bell's inequality, vacuum fluctuations have to be involved. The latter are understood as fluctuations of space-time itself. This is an interesting question whether the total determinism on fluctuating space-time can indeed be treated as determinism" (Khrennikov 2014, 18).

When quantum physics is put into the Schrödinger wave framework,[51] the focus is on how system configurations change with changing wave functions, and this can be done with particle-wave (field) language. Equivalently, when quantum physics, or the more inclusive core theory, is put into Feynman's path-integral formulation, in which the Feynman path integral accesses, as Carroll states, "all the ways the field could evolve in between . . . we can think of a quantum system as taking every path . . . So the largest quantum probability gets associated with evolution that looks almost classical. That's why our everyday world is well modeled by classical mechanics; it's classical behavior that gives the largest contributions to the probability of quantum transitions" (Carroll 2016, 437–438). If one insists on holding on to actualism and a particle picture with the "system as taking every path," then one's scientific hypothesis can be led into many-worlds hypothesis, or multiverses, and on the philosophical side, a dependence on "possible world" narratives. Instead, and far more simply, interpreting the real in quantum physics as both ontic *potentiae* and actualities enables one to think of the phrase "taking every path" as being incorporated in samplings of a *potentiae* pre-space, which is Terekhovich's strategy as discussed above, as well as that of Kastner et al. (2018). In this conception, path integrals can be applied to this *potentiae* pre-space in combination with constraints of symmetry, and so on. Thus, physical relations emerge from this multiple sampling of *potentiae* pre-space, which is operationally handled by the principle of least action, reflecting optimization of relations of relations in this pre-space. In a way that goes beyond standard approaches to the *Laws of Nature,* as surveyed in a recent edited volume (Walter Ott and Lydia Patton 2018), the *Logoi* framework approach, and the Relational Reality model within that, is both bottom-up, due to grounding in fundamental quantum process, and top-down, with symmetry conditions and correlations in *potentiae* pre-space.

Time and space are coextensive with the inevitable, pervasive transitions from *possibiliae* pre-space to actualizations, which constitute each and every event. Groundedness of local-global connections with actualities enables nonlocal connectedness of such law, making possible an intuitive and reasonable understanding of quantum superposition and entanglement, perhaps involving global topological phase or other structure/form correlations, not some "spooky action-at-a-distance" that presumes applying only the Boolean order of actualization. In contrast to grounding physical law in constraints on pre-space *potentiae*, and utilizing the distinction of Boolean and non-Boolean logics, the conventional analytic discussion of law, dispositions, essences, powers, modality, and universals, whether Humean or non-Humean, appears limited to Boolean logic and set theory, for example, see review by José Marambio (2010). A substantive non-Humean, dispositionalist account[52] has been articulated by Barbara Vetter in her work *Potentiality: From Dispositions to Modality* (Vetter 2015), providing an analytic treatment of how to work out a metaphysics based on the reality of potentiality. This object-oriented treatment is certainly useful for handling the linguistic analysis of dispositions and modality but falls short in handling time and temporality. Such standard analyses would clearly be transformed by attention to a more general theory of relations via category theory (vs. just set theory) and the inclusion of non-Boolean logic and insights from fundamental quantum process, which enable solutions to temporality issues via the distinction of both the orders of actuality and *potentiae* (see *The Relational Reality Model* in chapter 2). One effort to reduce the basis of physical law to dispositions, with reference to the Principle of Least Action, is provided by Benjamin Smart and Karim Thébault who argue "that action is extremized is indeed no coincidence; it flows from the dispositional properties inherent to the actual world" (Smart and Thébault 2015, 391). Yet, in their analysis, dispositions are treated as primal and without further explanation; indeed, their argument appears to be circular. In contrast, I argue here that a modal analysis of *potentiae* and constraints thereof provides a yet more fundamental level of explanation utilizing both the power of PLA techniques and the basis of physical law. Of course, substantial scientific and philosophical work is yet needed to work out the details of such a modal analysis as a grounding for physical law. A limited sketch of such development is provided by Arnold Koslow in his technical treatment of natural possibilities (*potentiae* in my terminology) and "laws as a byproduct of [the] reduction of possibilities" (Koslow 2003, 182).

My approach to physical relations is sufficiently general to include both biology and physics because it incorporates both *potentiae* and context, notions often excluded from standard accounts of causal relations. Considering that each and every event is the result of fundamental quantum process, and that in turn necessarily involves input-output-context, part-whole, and local-global relations, all multiscale, we now see that the fundamental succession of events ("one darn thing after another") is like a weaving together of *potentiae* and actualizations as argued by Kastner (2015, 157–158). This weaving together, utilizing landscapes of *potentiae*, builds on causation, yet with attention to both constraints and context.

COMPLEX SYSTEMS

The *Logoi* framework achieves greater unity and coherence by framing causation and multiscale emergence as closely interrelated yet distinct in terms of their diachronic and synchronic focus, respectively. Further, there is conceptual simplicity in seeing how all events exemplify fundamental quantum process and have the triadic structure of input-output-context, combined with local-global relations. This portrayal of a fundamental theory is like a generalized field theory with speculative philosophical aspects added in. Such an event-oriented theory may be compared with Whitehead's concept of prehension (see McHenry's *The Event Universe* 2015). However, the same unity and coherence of interrelatedness that I hypothesize for the *Logoi* framework leads to practically unlimited complexity. By reducing complex problems to much more simple and manageable problems, the scientific method provides one important way of handling problems of complexity. Nevertheless, although the way of numbers (science) and the way of context (arts and humanities) are distinct in goals and emphasis (e.g., their respective emphases on quantification and context independence versus qualitative analysis and context dependence), we here treat these modes of knowledge discovery as complementary and synergistic. Both are greatly needed to address the incredible complexity of the real world.

With a focus on scientific application, in recent decades a relatively simple way of characterizing complex systems has emerged that respects the above synergy of the ways of numbers and context. This inclusive synergy is embodied in Robert Rosen's analysis of complex systems and anticipatory systems (Rosen 2000, 2012). Rosen's model of complex systems is compatible with my analysis of causation and emergence through its emphasis on alternative possible relations and, effectively, on input-output-context. As shown in figure 4.1, this model also incorporates Aristotle's four basic causes (formal, efficient, material, and final). For complex systems, Rosen explains that

> modeling relations are . . . relations between measurable properties and inferable potentials of nature. We can call the localized aspects real or realized, and we can call the non-localized aspects contextual or contextualized . . . we specify models as symbolic systems that commute with and thus describe natural systems, thus establishing an epistemological modeling relation that describes nature via information relations, specifically encoding and decoding. As we see that much of nature itself behaves like modeling relations, it becomes clear that the very practice of science recapitulates the entailment of nature; which is one explanation for why science is possible and why mathematical descriptions work. (Kineman 2011, 397–398)

The use here of the fourfold Aristotelian framework is simply heuristic for the *Logoi* framework in recognition of the limitations of Aristotelian causes (see Campbell 1992, 145–169).

Infinite hierarchies of modeling relations, with their features of encoding, decoding, and self-referential relations in context, provide a valuable basis for understanding complex systems. These modeling relations are reflected as well in fundamental limits to entailing laws (Kauffman, 2016). As John Kineman states, "A mechanistic reduction or truncation of the hierarchy indicates that a natural system is sufficiently identified with its environment causally such that a common set of laws can describe both. Complex systems thus exist between the theoretical extremes of isolation and connection; they are independently identified sub-systems and interconnected components of greater contexts" (Kineman 2011, 400). Thus, Rosen's complex systems model provides a unified way to understand both the power of science (enhanced in that limit, and truncation of context, whereby with sufficient constraints there emerge useful quantitative mappings of model to physical system) and the efficacy of humanistic knowledge (whereby context and qualitative factors are dominant and any mechanistic reduction is only a partial description, at best). The four classic causes of Aristotle fit naturally into this complex systems model; however, final cause need not be considered to be as strongly teleological as Aristotle considered it to be. Instead, consistent with my discussion of alternative possible trajectories in, for example, abstract quantum "spaces" of *potentiae* and the application of variational principles (as imbedded in contemporary quantum fields theories such as quantum physics), one can think of final causes as not goals coming from some external or future source, but instead as present anticipations of future alternatives. Thus, instead of the word *final* in Aristotle's "final cause," one could substitute anticipatory or an equivalent adjective.

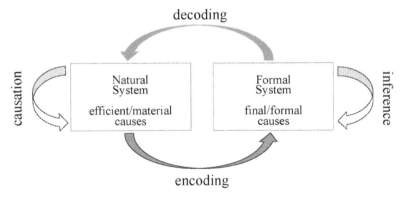

Figure 4.1   Robert Rosen used modeling relations to characterize science ideally as commuting relations between formal systems (logic, math) and natural systems. (Source: author; adapted from Kineman (2011, 396, figure 1).

Søren Brier builds on such complex systems analysis through contemporary information theory, cybernetics, and biosemiotics to generate a model for both physical and social culture using effectively the way of numbers, the way of context and, in turn, the way of signs (Brier 2013). Brier's analysis is just one among many possible extensions to Rosen's complex systems analysis, and closely related developments of biosemiotics as reviewed by Hoffmeyer (2009). Although strong conceptually, Rosen's modeling relations have lacked formal rigor. However, using the framework of category theory, which can be thought of as an algebra of relations, Zafiris has provided a rigorous mathematical formulation for relations of complex systems (Zafiris, 2012).

In developing his ideas on modeling relations, Robert Rosen was rethinking the nature of mathematics and its relation to the world. He argues that "mathematics took a disastrous wrong turn some time in the sixth century B.C." (Rosen 2000, 63), identifying effectiveness with computability. Instead, Rosen explains, mathematics should be understood as a way of modeling, and then he uses category theory to characterize this. Category theory, unlike set theory, is essentially holistic, focusing on patterns and relations, and providing the means to model one domain of mathematics by another. This enables us to understand more accurately what is involved in modeling that which is called "the world." In doing so, it highlights the way in which modeling always involves simplification of that which is modeled. Modeling is really only a special instance of analogical thinking, ubiquitous in everyday life where the study of one system is used to learn something about another that is judged to be congruent with it. Compatible with these new understandings of modeling in science, with a special focus on analogical inference schema, Ann Plamondon has analyzed and favorably articulated Whitehead's unique approach (Plamondon 1979). As Peirce argued, mathematical modeling is essentially diagrammatic reasoning in which mathematical diagrams are studied to learn about what is modeled. Modeling, Rosen argues, "is the art of bringing entailment structures into congruence . . . It is indeed an art, just as surely as poetry, music, and painting, are. Indeed, the essence of art is that, at root, it rests on the unentailed, on the intuitive leap" (Rosen 1991, 152).

These recent developments in both the way of numbers and the way of context demonstrate that any simplistic reduction to just one (most often some mechanistic or physicalist reduction to the former) is entirely inadequate to accommodate contemporary research in biosemiotics, complex systems, and quantum physics, among other key research fields; in turn, the consequence of this result for these fields and for essentially all fields of science and humanities is that our basic language, our basic narrative, our common concepts have often yielded a problematic truncation of real complex systems (with *potentiae*) to some inadequately modeled "actualized" subset. Modeling is important for introducing anticipatory systems; however, Vasilov Petrov highlights a distinction introduced by Daniel Dubois:

> Dubois refers to Rosen's concept of an anticipatory system (a system evolving by using future state values and/or environmental values as predicted by an associated model to determine the future behavior of the system) as having a weak anticipation (the anticipation is model-based) as opposed to self referential systems which he termed as having a strong anticipation (the anticipation is system-based)... Weak anticipation for Dubois occurs when systems use a model of themselves for computing future states, and a strong anticipation takes place when the system uses itself as a model for the construction of its future states. (Petrov 2010, 42)

The *Logoi* framework and Rosen's systems theory, suitably generalized, converge in the way that anticipatory systems help us to understand constraint approaches to both emergence and complex systems functioning, including the full range of anticipatory systems, from weak model-based examples to strong anticipation. Petrov further argues that system complexity and dynamics correlate in a dynamic ontology such that "the ontology of anticipatory systems is a kind of dynamic ontology . . . a process ontology" (Petrov 2010, 38). Of course, not every dynamic system is an anticipatory one. In addition, working with multiple potential states, Dubois states that "the brain may be considered as an anticipatory hyperincursive neural net which generates multiple potential future states which collapse to actual states by learning: the selection process of states to be actualized amongst the multiple potential states is independent of the fundamental dynamics of the brain, independent of initial conditions and so completely unpredictable and computable" (Dubois 1999, 28). He further argues, in a way fully compatible with the *Logoi* framework's emphasis on the reality of *potentiae*, that this constitutes a "basic theory of free will" (ibid.). Finally, Dubois points out that "any anticipatory system obeys, as any physical system, the Maupertuis Least Action Principle" (Dubois 1999, 29), which correlates with our argument for a foundational linkage between the principle of least action and physical law (see previous section within this chapter on *"Law"—From Entailment to Constrained Processual Histories*).

That real, complex systems go beyond any context-independent, physicalist description is illustrated by the mismatch between our standard exercises in modeling and the deep implications of quantum physics. Finkelstein framed the problem in this way:

> Exercises in physics often give a complete mathematical model of the system.
>   This does not prepare the student for quantum physics. No one has ever encountered anything near a complete description of any physical system, classical or quantum. If quantum theory is right, there are none . . . Physics is

a performing art, and physicists are the performers, not the spectators; experi-
menters, not observers. The relation of a physical theory to physics is that of
a menu to a meal. It is natural but naive to think that anything in nature has a
complete objective description; naive in the sense that throwing a bottle at a
villain on a movie screen is naive. (Finkelstein 2013, 8)

Recognizing the essential incompleteness of physicalist models, which
presume that all reality is "reducible to simple physical-chemical process,"
Terrence Deacon and Tyrone Cashman (2016) argue for a "metaphysics of
incompleteness" in which "the apparent incompatibility between teleological
and mechanical causality reflects a default tendency to consider only tangible
substance to be real and to ignore the necessary complementary reality of its
now absent attributes or future potentials" (Deacon and Cashman 2016, 401).
The suggestion of final cause implied by "teleological causality" [causation]
is side-stepped by the contrast between moral causality (with choice and
responsibility) and natural causality in neo-Confucianism (see chapter 7).
Concerning problematic substance thinking, Finkelstein shares the following:

Heisenberg formulated the quantum theory in the same city and decade in which
Kandinsky coined the phrase non-objective art. I assume that Heisenberg bor-
rowed from Kandinsky when he called quantum theory "non-objective physics"
. . . Heisenberg set up an algebra of observables in which the fundamental elements are operations, and could just as well be called "processes." They represent what we do, not what "is." (Finkelstein 2004, 182)

Bradley explains how, for Heidegger, Henri Bergson, and Whitehead, "the
active existence of things can generally be said to be conceived strictly as a
matter of finite, singular 'acts of duration' or 'events' of self-actualization"
(Bradley 1996, 235–236). This is in contrast to the speculative metaphysics
dominant prior to the late nineteenth century whereby the concept of actualization is "referenced to the causal or productive activity of a pre-given, grounding reality, which is understood as in some sense complete and is variously
conceived as the realm of form, or as the emanation of an incomprehensible
One, or as the transcendent activity of the Creator God, or as the immanent
activity of the Whole or Absolute" (Bradley 1996, 235). Arguably, a holdover of such speculative metaphysics is the continuing strong commitment to
absolute determinism (e.g., Weinberg, t'Hooft), strong Platonism (Tegmark),
and various forms of strong reductionism and deductivism (much of analytic philosophy; scientism); the opposing position is often taken as simply
Humean skepticism, which reduces all to epistemological claims and linguistic
reductionism and denies any basis for realism. In contrast, Bradley calls for a
third way that overcomes such false dualities by hypothesizing a concept of

the event in which "active existence is to be analyzed independently of any notions of production or of a pregiven real . . . Acts of existence are now to be understood as finite, groundless self-actualizations" (Bradley 1996, 235).

LANDSCAPES OF *POTENTIAE*

In an integrative work on complex systems, dynamical systems and causal relation, Alicia Juarrero highlights systems theory.

> General systems theory was first articulated by organismic biologist Ludwig von Bertalanffy (1981) as a counterpoint to classical science's mechanistic understanding of human beings and nature. Its fundamental claim is that when living things are embedded in a orderly context, properties emerge that are not present when the things exist as isolated individuals. Picking up where Darwin left off, systems theory continued the revival of relational or secondary properties by reminding us that context matters. But it does so very differently than behaviorism. (Juarrero 1999)

Following a detailed review of nonlinear, far-from-equilibrium science, and self-organizing dynamical systems, all topics important for the emergence of complex systems, Juarrero explains that "self-organizing structures are not concrete things. Dissipative structures and autocatalytic webs are meta-stable networks of transformations, nested, hierarchical arrangements of *organizational* patterns: 'structures of process'" (Juarrero 1999, 124). As one among other examples that go beyond reductive description, she notes that "as a dynamic system, therefore, an autopoietic system's identity is given by the coordinated organization of the processes that make it up, not the primary material of its components" (Juarrero 1999, 125). Here, *autopoiesis* refers to how living organisms can enable the production of their own components in a purposeful manner with their members working in interdependent fashion to enhance persistence, against entropic forces, of the whole system. Further, self-organized dynamical systems demonstrate that "by coordinating previously independent parts, context-dependent constraints enable a more complex organization to emerge, with novel properties that the isolated parts lacked. Self-organization enlarges a system's phase space by adding degrees of freedom" (Juarrero 1999, 142–143). Finally, as a segue into recognizing the importance of top-down causal effects, Juarrero continues as follows:

> Paradoxically and simultaneously, that is, self-organization also constitutes the appearance of the remarkable and unpredictable properties of the global level: the cauterizing ability of the laser beam, the enzymatic capabilities of

a protein—or, I speculate, consciousness and self-consciousness—and their attendant states. These emergent properties of the higher level are the phenomenological manifestation of those dynamic relationships. But I emphasize that they are emphatically not epiphenomenal. Although not in a push-pull, forceful manner, the higher level of organization is causally effective: as a second-order, top-down constraint. (Juarrero 1999, 144)

More recently, Ellis has provided numerous examples of top-down constraints and causal effects, and distinguishes six different types: deterministic top-down processes; nonadaptive feedback control systems; adaptive selection; feedback control with adaptive goals; and adaptive selection of adaptive goals; and "goals and learning in relation to these kinds of causation" (Ellis 2016, 53). In contrast to the standard account that reduces all causal relation down to efficient cause alone, Juarrero states that "context-sensitive constraints are thus a causal (but not efficiently causal) engine that drives creative evolution, not through forceful impact, but by making things interdependent" (Juarrero 1999, 150).

To represent such interdependence, contemporary research in complex dynamical systems often constructs landscapes in some parameter space, effectively landscapes of *potentiae*. Thus, Juarrero points out "one way in which distributed wholes contextually constrain their parts top-down—is by modifying their prior probability in real time. That is what second-order contextual constraints do—or are. In the laser . . . faster, lower-level processes relax and allow themselves to be driven (entrained) by the slower, higher-dimensional attractor (the coherent laser beam), which functions as their virtual governor. Gene regulation works that way too" (Juarrero 1999, 162). As noted by Jeremy Butterfield, the concept of landscapes has also been important in articulating the concepts of reduction, supervenience, and emergence (Butterfield, 2011).

Although powerful and practical for many modeling applications of complex systems, the landscapes concept is limited because it tends to spatialize processes, sometimes in ways incompatible with the basic dynamics. As Spyridon Koutroufinis points out for the example of biological organisms,

Only we as outside observers are able to draw a "map" containing all possible trajectories . . . living occasions cannot have such a "map" at their disposal as they are not endowed with consciousness . . . The organism corrects its embryogenesis by means of its inner perspective or self-experience, its inwardness, which it possesses even as an embryo. Every multicellular organism has an embryogenetic and an immunological memory. The latter is mainly individual as it results from experiences encountered during ontogeny which only occurs once; the former is supra-individual as embryogenesis is rooted in the species. (Koutroufinis 2014, 125)

Treating organisms as dynamical systems solely in terms of physics and chemistry cannot explain their full autonomy. Koutroufinis continues,

> Organisms viewed in this limited way would succumb to the serious problem of instability: The organism's dynamics would permanently enter phases in which the trajectories of its development would diverge strongly; furthermore, most of them would derail the organism's development into fatal disorganization . . . The essence of each living occasion is a [anticipatory] decision which has an anti-entropic effect, since it strives to prevent the organism from increasing its entropy . . . Bio-systemic thinking can in principle describe the possible developments of an organism, while the organism's actual development, consisting in the decision between real possibilities, is accessible to Whiteheadian process philosophy. (Koutroufinis 2014, 129)

It is sometimes argued that process thought is incompatible with emergence, especially among those who (mistakenly) presume that process thought is committed simply to pan-psychism (versus, say, a broader framework of pan-experientialism argued, for example, by Griffin (2007)). Through the *Logoi* framework, we see that ontic causation of diachronic quantum process is complemented by synchronic relations of multilevel emergence. Weaving such an understanding of emergence with Whiteheadian process thought, Auxier and Herstein apply a multiscale, yet scale-free approach[53] to understanding the concept of actual entities (Auxier and Herstein 2017). The scale-free character of such, and of key scientific areas (nonlinear dynamics, space plasmas), further supports an emergence concept.

Physicists who have written clearly about the concept of emergence include Robert Laughlin (2008) and Ellis (2016) among others. Indeed, as noted by Clayton, Harold Morowitz identifies "no fewer than 28 distinct levels of emergence in natural history" (Clayton 2005, 5). We have discussed above a constraint interpretation for the origin of physical relationships via the principle of least action, among other constraints. Similarly, emergence has multiple constraints, both at larger and smaller scale. Blachowicz has argued persuasively for a constraint interpretation of emergence, with specific reference to Polanyi's work, including attention to both constitutive and non-constitutive constraints, and how constraints individuate and differentiate (Blachowicz 2012).

LEVELS OF EMERGENCE

My summary of fundamental quantum process emphasizes diachronic characteristics as noted above (i.e., "processes through time"). In a complementary way, the same process can be viewed synchronically ("at a given 'time'"). From such a perspective, the multilevel whole-part relations of emergence can be understood as effectively a synchronic hierarchy. Here I call attention to five levels of emergence, which are based especially on the work of Terrence Deacon (2012) and Joseph Earley (2016).

Below, building first on Earley's work, I indicate the scholars whose work is to be correlated with the given level of emergence. Such correlations often serve as pointers to a middle way, bridges between complementary concepts such as knower and known, domains of actualizations and *potentiae*, asymmetry and symmetry, and the diachronic and the synchronic. Each level of emergence is only semi-autonomous, subject to only partial closure because each level has its own context that transcends any strict closure.

[1] first-order emergence:
     closure Louis de Broglie—coherence of hadrons/leptons to produce atoms; nuclear, atomic and molecular physics;
[2] second-order emergence: supervenience—aggregates with cancellation effects at micro-level;
     closure Henri Poincaré—new kinds of relationships (novel topologies) via cooperative interactions;
[3] third-order emergence: chaotic and self-organized systems; autopoietic systems;
     closure Ilya Prigogine—large-scale coherences from open system dynamics;
[4] fourth-order emergence: evolutionary emergence with information/memory; individuation; self-referential self-organization (life);
     closure Robert Rosen—biosemiosis (oriented to present givens; functioning enhanced through modeling-response (MR) systems, constrained by evolved habits (Rosen, 1991);
[5] fifth-order emergence: consciousness
     closure Peirce-Whitehead—present givens vis-à-vis future; prehension (*à la* Whitehead), semiosis (*à la* Peirce), anticipatory function (*à la* Rosen), local-global relations (*à la* Zafiris).

These five levels have been most useful for scholarly work to date and provide a rather comprehensive (synchronic) framing of physical and biological systems. However, added levels may yet be needed to provide a fully comprehensive emergence framework; for example, a zero-level pointing to a pre-space level of fundamental process.

At each level of relative closure there is approximate symmetry in the basic applicable parameters, but such symmetry is inevitably broken, which leads to a higher level of context-dependent model. As Roland Omnès has pointed out, ultimate symmetry breaking arises at the quantum level in quantum field theory and the canonical commutation relation of quantum physics (Omnès 1999, 27). The symmetry of fundamental physical relations ("fundamental laws") is a symmetry within non-Boolean possibility pre-space (*potentiae*), and not a symmetry that is broadly applicable to all reality (as presumed in claims of actualism and claims of causal closure of the physical). Symmetry breaking is an inevitable part of fundamental quantum process, which then requires context-dependent models to handle; only such models with their inevitable asymmetry can encompass the full range of reality, both non-Boolean and Boolean, both *potentiae* and actuality. This perspective is reflected as well by Kastner, who shows how "basic physical laws are symmetrical with respect to both space and time but describe only potentialities, and that actual events and processes arise because of symmetry breaking . . . [via boundary conditions, etc., giving] the 'arrow of time . . . the actual breaks the symmetry of the potential'" (Kastner 2013, 201–202).

Each case of distinct, synchronic-level emergence reflects a unique pattern and implementation of the general triadic relation input-output-context, yet with increasing complexity at successive hierarchical levels. *The Self-Organizing Universe* by Erich Jantsch, a classic in evolutionary theory, articulates such multiscale emergence (Jantsch 1992). Such truly embodied process with local-global linkages occurs at all levels, from fundamental quantum process, to human scale and beyond. At the most complex level currently known to *Homo sapiens*, that of consciousness, there emerges a self-awareness that leverages anticipatory modeling, dynamically comparing present givens vis-à-vis possibilities for the future, including the active comparison of possible outcomes among alternative choices (thus, a basis for free will). Over the next three sections, I will build up to even more complex systems, including consciousness (also see *On the Emergence of Consciousness and Mind* in chapter 7).

As we consider key stepping stones to more complex problems such as that of consciousness, I here briefly review the stumbling blocks covered early in this chapter. Nominalism asserts that everything is particular without remainder and denies the reality of abstract entities such as potential relations. This view is often converted into actualism, which is the claim that the only real things are concrete actualities. These views partner with substance thinking to reduce everything to nothing but nominalistic particulars. Such ontological reductionism often links up with a presumption of mechanistic materialism that derives from the metaphysics of classical mechanics. Even though the above metaphysical claims have weakened beginning in the late twentieth century, as I have argued in an earlier paper, interpretations of contemporary scientific results are often filtered through a presupposed classical metaphysics (Eastman 2008). This is illustrated through continued commitments to physicalism and causal closure of the physical which, as we have seen, are both denied by the *Logoi* framework with its attention to the orders of both actuality and *potentiae*, as well as multilevel processes of causation and emergence (both top-down and bottom-up), including local-global effects. By recognizing and going beyond the above stumbling blocks, it should now be possible to make substantial progress on much more complex issues that strongly resist simplistic reductions, like the problem of consciousness itself.

EPISTEMIC CUTS AND ONTOLOGICAL THRESHOLDS

Multilevel process with constraints associated with active causation, having both bottom-up and top-down components, combined with local-global relations, enables multi-scale emergence. The Relational Reality model for quantum process proposes that there are asymmetrical relational structures extending beyond the system state, which includes the full world as given (system, detector, environment); consequently, the local (state) is internally related to the global (context) (see Epperson 2016). This result of local-global relations, a key aspect of quantum physics, was demonstrated by Zafiris using category theory analysis (Zafiris 2010b).

Spatialized descriptions of system hierarchy typically classify systems into four basic levels: micro-, meso-, and macro-system level, and astronomical. The particular scale lengths involved depend on the particular system in question. For common macro-systems, one might treat the micro-level as that of quantum process from nuclear to atomic scale; the meso-level as that of chemical and polymeric bonding; and the macro-level as being that of chairs and mountains. For space plasmas, for example, one will likely focus on electron and proton gyroradii (<1 km to >100 km); the meso-level as that of shock fronts and plasma boundary layers (~10 to >1,000 km); and the macro-level as being the full space plasma system (>10,000 km up to full solar system scale, and beyond). As noted in chapter 2, both microscopic and astronomical levels are, in general, not directly accessible and require special tools for observation; in contrast, mesoscopic and macroscopic systems are, in principle, directly accessible to human perception (of course, in some cases, special radioactive or chemical markers may be required for such "observation").The most relevant frameworks for a focus on the concept of emergence are as follows:

1. quantum process, always with fundamental local-global connection;
2. complex systems and self-organizing dynamical systems;
3. teleodynamic systems with self/other/world (*umwelt*) (see chapter 5 on semiotics).

Evolution considered most fully involves both emergence, cooperation, and selection although the focus of most evolutionary research since the time of Darwin has been on the relatively simple issue of selection, not on the more complex emergence and cooperation issues. The selection process, although crucially important, acts as a filter to weed out nonadaptive yet newly emergent complex systems. The deep question for evolution, not addressed by natural selection alone, concerns how to explain the emergence of genuinely new self-organizing dynamical systems that can compete for resources in various environments. Such emergence must involve active causation with the weaving together of past fields, "particles" and *potentiae*, and enhanced tapping of *potentiae* by associated complex systems as discussed by Robert Rosen in his seminal work *Anticipatory Systems* (Rosen 2012), and not just "blind chance" which would require, for most biological settings, statistically impossible conditions. As Ellis states "this can only occur because of adaptation to the environment: hence data must flow from the environment into the living entity and alter its structure and behavior. Thus this is based on top-down causation . . . not the same as a bottom-up process of self-assembly" (Ellis 2016, 402). Then, "repeated thousands of times over geological timescales, it is this relentless repetition of the top-down process of adaptive selection that gives Darwinian evolution its enormous power" (Ellis 2016, 404). Yet the sampling of *potentiae* cannot be simply blind; such alone would leave evolution powerless—some type of anticipatory capability is required for complex adaptive systems to viably provide input for the competitive natural selection process; suggestions for such anticipatory capability will be addressed in chapter 6 on the complex whole.

An important application of anticipatory capabilities is how that capacity provides a means of leveraging natural processes such that one can go significantly beyond mere chance, which is presumed in standard neo-Darwinian accounts, and regarded by many scholars as being inadequate to explain many complex evolved systems. For example, Cobb and colleagues emphasize the need for *both* competition *and* cooperation in *Back to Darwin* (Cobb 2008). By working with both Boolean and non-Boolean logical orders, and multilevel evolution within a local-global correlated framework, it becomes possible to develop models (as yet undeveloped) of strong emergence up to consciousness and beyond (see end of this chapter, and chapters 7 and 8). Koutroufinis argues that, without such constraints, both top-down as well as bottom-up, nonlinear dynamical effects would make it essentially impossible for biological systems to avoid "*derailments* into areas of disorder" (Koutroufinis 2013, 326).

One starting point for analyzing the required weaving of the biological web is to consider the fundamental bases of complexity as discussed, for example, by Ellis, especially his chapter on "The Basis of Complexity," which incorporates an emphasis on environmental context (Ellis 2016, 100). In addition, a critical part of environmental context is the overall consistency and coherence enabled by local-global constraints; clearly such contextual emergence denies, as Ellis shows, the possibility of strong reductionism or exclusive bottom-up causation (Ellis 2016, 373). Ellis points out as well that "there are no constraints from below on the actual logical operations that higher levels can perform. This is the essential understanding Turing gave us when he discovered the nature of universal symbolic computation . . . Logical Independence: The underlying physics does not restrict what logical operations are possible in emergent structures" (Ellis 2016, 127).

In *A World Beyond Physics: The Emergence and Evolution of Life*, Kauffman (2019) clearly shows how propagating work and constraint construction can achieve closure in certain nonequilibrium systems. Indeed, as a holistic property of protocells, such constraint closure may play a key role in the origin of life, and yet such closure is focused on the order of actuality. Kauffman's book is a concise and very readable introduction to contemporary origin of life research, which is outside my current scope.[54]

Another fundamental threshold is the so-called epistemic cut of subject-object (Gordian knot #11, see chapter 3) which, as Howard Pattee emphasizes, is at the core of epistemology: that is, problems of knowledge (Pattee 2008). Indeed, such an essential subject-object framework appears fundamental to quantum physics when one applies Bohr's orthodox interpretation. In this approach to the quantum theory of measurement, whatever the object, there is necessarily a subject doing the measurement. An epistemic cut problem arises, however, in considering at what scale the cut (subject/object distinction) applies—at the microscopic level?—at the human experimenter level? Within this framework, Stapp has argued that there is necessarily some basis for posing the question. The questions posed are not constrained directly by nature (a mode of freedom within standard quantum physics), but upon measurement, nature always provides specific yes/no answers. "The essential point here is that quantum theory has a lacuna that can very naturally be filled in such a way as to allow our thoughts to exercise real, though not absolute, control over the mechanical aspects of mind-brain dynamics" (Stapp 2004, 99). The counterpart to this in the Relational Reality model is that, given constraints specific to any quantum experiment, there is necessarily some open range of values of the associated parameter space, which is itself indeterminate (non-Boolean logic of *possibiliae*), but that upon measurement there is necessarily a determinate result of such measurement (Boolean logic of actualization). Stapp's "posing the question" is part of pre-measurement constraints and preparation of experiment. Combining common elements of three basic quantum interpretations, all consistent with the basic physics that Bohr and von Neumann built on, Kastner, Epperson, and Kauffman demonstrate the need for the fundamental distinction of actuality and *possibiliae* within the real (Kastner et al. 2018).

There have been many advances in neuroscience in the past few decades, but it is also important to recognize its basic limitations. Such research can substantially advance our understanding of brain and brain states, and on neurological connections and correlations, and constraints on such correlations. However, measurements and data related to such research are limited to the Boolean domain whereas the active "mind" denotes fundamental mental (in part, quantum) process that bridges the Boolean (actualizations) and non-Boolean *potentiae*. Typical physicalistic discussions of mind-brain relations reduce to just brain states on the (incorrect) presupposition that all is Boolean, thus effectively making the metaphysical claim of actualism.

PAN-EXPERIENTIALISM AND EMERGING CONSCIOUSNESS

The clear failure of causal closure and physicalism (reductive or not) to explain human intentions and consciousness has, in recent years, substantially enhanced prospects for the hypothesis of pan-experientialism,[55] and for improved explanations of emergent high-level mentality and consciousness as documented in edited volumes by Edward Kelly, Adam Crabtree, and Paul Marshall (2015); Godehard Brüntrup and Ludwig Jaskolla (2017); and William Seager (2019).

Although recent scholarship has provided highly nuanced approaches in applying pan-experientialism (e.g., see George Shields, 2012), including moderate approaches such as naturalistic pan-experientialism, a key difficulty has continued to be the combination problem.[56] This problem was initially articulated by William James as the question of how can qualitative occasions be properly ordered into macro-level experiences? Chalmers states the problem as follows: "How can proto-phenomenal properties combine to yield macro-phenomenal properties?" After a thorough analysis of this classic combination problem, Chalmers concludes that the constraints imposed by this problem are so strong that they may "point someone toward the correct form for a fundamental theory of consciousness" (Chalmers 2017, 211). If one stays limited to the order of actualizations, then pan-experientialism deserves special attention and, under such restriction, is clearly a better option than reductive physicalism given the above severe problems that arise for that position, especially as articulated by both Primas (2017) and Bishop and Atmanspacher (2012). The reductive aspects of simple forms of pan-psychism share many problems with other forms of reductionism, as Auxier and Herstein (2917) have pointed out, in contrast to emergentist strategies, for example, context-driven approaches such as Atmanspacher's contextual emergence (Atmanspacher, 2007). For example, Eric Weiss illustrates a Whitehead-inspired understanding of mind by stating that consciousness is "*the fundamental agency of actualization* . . . Nothing becomes actual and definite without the decisive participation of mind" (Weiss 2015, 467).

In contrast to such mentalistic reduction and despite common assumptions about his work, Alfred North Whitehead himself lets prehension[57] do the job and never refers directly to pan-psychism, whether in his published works as documented by Leemon McHenry (1995), or in the recently published notes of his lectures, and he generally avoided presuppositions that would generate a combination problem. As for the core principle of Boolean logic, according to Winfred P. Bell's notes, in his lecture of October 25, 1924, Whitehead explicitly discussed possible denial of the principle of excluded middle: "Instead of Subject-Predicate you began to talk about Matter and Form. (More elastic—not so worried by 'Excluded Middle' law. —That law's what's in the way of Transition). Finally . . . we pluck up courage and use Potentiality" (Bell 2017, 48; underline used by author). This quote shows how, in 1924, Whitehead already anticipated the reality of *potentiae*, which he makes fully explicit in his 1929 major work, *Process and Reality* (Whitehead, 1978). However, Whitehead never gave up on the Law of Excluded Middle (LEM) as applied to actualized states—a "satisfied" occasion is what it is and not something else.

Emergent effects arise within the *Logoi* framework by working with both the orders of actualizations and *potentiae* in combination with local to local-global correlations. This combination enables input-output-context responsiveness to environments at any level, effectively pan-experiential, although responsiveness can certainly be minimal depending on many factors. A basic response of an entity can also be a response to another entity's response. In a somewhat more pan-psychist context, Charles Hartshorne emphasized the importance of "feeling of feelings" (Viney and Shields 2020, 48). Regarding a minimal level, with their Free Will Theorem, John Conway and Simon Kochen state that "if indeed we humans have free will then elementary particles already have their own small share of this valuable commodity" (Conway and Kochen 2006). That is, the basic quantum physics provides no clear divide for levels of context-dependence, responsiveness to a given environment, or threshold of "experience," however rudimentary. The term *psyche* has the connotation of more integrated or evolved responsiveness to experience; thus, I prefer the term pan-experiential to pan-psychism.[58] Further, the pan-experiential aspect of entities at multiple levels can function in combination with emergence. In this dual manner, William James's combination problem may finally be resolved. By leveraging such multilevel relations, higher-level responsiveness to environments can gradually emerge and evolve, up to the successive synchronic levels 1–5; namely (1) first-order emergence; (2) second-order emergence/supervenience; (3) third-order emergence/self-organizing systems; (4) fourth-order emergence/evolutionary emergence; and (5) fifth-order emergence/consciousness. Such emergence operates in part by tapping non-Boolean *potentiae*, as both Rosen (2012) and Bettinger and Eastman (2017) argue, through anticipatory systems (see section below on *Complex Systems*).

One promising framework, forwarded by Giulio Tononi and Christof Koch, is that of Integrated Information Theory (IIT), which "holds that consciousness is graded, is common among biological organisms and can occur in some very simple systems . . . [yet] digital computers, even if their behavior were to be functionally equivalent to ours, and even if they were to run faithful simulations of the human brain, would experience next to nothing" (Tononi and Koch 2015). They carried out simulations based on optimizing a parameter that is a proxy for conceptual structure, and includes a logic to handle the "space of possibilities." From their simulations, Tononi and Koch conclude that (1) consciousness is a fundamental property, (2) consciousness is graded and comes in various qualities, (3) consciousness is adaptive and evolving, (4) mere aggregates are not conscious, and (5) complicated systems can be unconscious (i.e., zombies). These results suggest that a viable route to understanding consciousness needs an interplay of pan-experientialism and emergence to handle the combination problem and other issues.

CONSCIOUSNESS AND HIGHER
LEVELS OF EMERGENCE

Clearly, certain conscious states and capabilities are achieved by humans, including the recognition of *qualia*,[59] but many may be attained to varying degrees by higher apes as well.[60] The topic of consciousness warrants continued and careful analysis, both scientific and humanistic. There are many kinds of consciousness and, as Bunge has pointed out, "given that the literature on consciousness, though bulky, is quite inconclusive, one suspects that the ideas on the subject are confused. It may be that the problem of consciousness is like that of the Holy Grail: Because there is no consensus on what it is, some knights doubt its existence while others wander hither and thither" (Bunge 2013, 209). Bunge follows this with a listing of at least five kinds of consciousness: (1) reactivity or sensitivity, (2) awareness or phenomenal consciousness, (3) self-awareness, (4) consciousness, as perceiving, feeling, or thinking, and (5) self-consciousness.

Given this complexity, my suggestions for approaching this issue are admittedly speculative; however, a presumption of actualism or determinism (assuming classical metaphysics) is common in this arena and, based on the

Logoi framework, recognition of a distinction between actualizations and *potentiae* would be critically important for rethinking the premises on which much consciousness research is based.

The complexity of high-level mental functioning and consciousness is concisely summarized by Ralph Pred. "Accordingly, there is no sudden emergence of mental phenomena from the merely physical; rather, in keeping with the categorical obligations, in more and more complex organisms, with presiding occasions capable of more and more complex concrescences, the mental or conceptual figures in more and more complex contrasts until propositional feelings and then the affirmation-negation contrast (and so consciousness) are reached" (Pred 2005, 309). Continuing, with a focus on consciousness itself, Pred proposes that "consciousness as a term then does not refer to an entity, but to a process or function—that of contrasting what is and what might be, of uniting a lure for feeling and the immanence of the past in a novel concrescence" (Pred 2005, 219). Cobb has concisely explained concrescence as "the process of becoming 'concrete'" (Cobb 2008a, 59). However, the complexity multiplies at yet higher levels. As Weekes points out, "The most spectacular pyrotechnics in *Syntax and Solidarity* [unpublished manuscript] were to occur in Pred's application of these insights to society and social intentionality" (Weekes 2017, 76). Unfortunately, Pred died before these insights could be published.

As argued by Pred, the mind and consciousness are clearly more than merely the brain or combinations of brain states. This non-reductive conception of mind is affirmed by recent research that focuses on emergence in multilevel complex systems. After explaining that "skull and skin are not limiting boundaries of energy and information flow," Daniel Siegel proposes that the "self-organizing aspect of the mind can be briefly defined as *an embodied and relational process that regulates the flow of energy and information*" (Siegel 2017, 37). Emergent from such relational process that constitutes the mind is "consciousness and its felt texture of subjectivity" (ibid. 38); further, that the mind is "happening within you and between you, in your body, and in your connections with others and the world in which you live" (ibid. 50). The inner and outer aspects of mind and consciousness have both physical and multilevel relational aspects, including information and semiotics (see chapter 5).

We have just begun to understand possibilities for the hierarchy of emergent phenomena. Deacon emphasizes the multilevel, recursive, and ultimately unbounded possibilities with a semiotic dimension of the higher levels of biological emergence, as follows:

> Third-order (evolutionary) emergence contains second-order (self-organizing) emergence as a limiting case, which in turn contains first-order (supervenient)

emergence as a limiting case . . . This hierarchic categorization does not exhaust the possibilities of increasingly more complex forms of emergent phenomena. Evolutionary emergent systems can further interact to form multilayer systems of exceeding complexity. Indeed, this is the nature of complex organisms that is exemplified in the ascending levels of "self" that proceed from gene to cell to organism to lineage to species, and so on, in the living world. But this logic does not lead to what might have been called fourth-order emergence. Instead, I think we must rather analyze these more complex processes as first-, second-, and third-order emergent elaborations of third-order emergence, and so on, in recursive series. This is because third-order emergence includes the capacity to evolve new forms of emergence itself. This is implicit in its inherently representational or semiotic character. The introduction of referential relationship as the defining feature of third-order emergence creates a spatial and temporal boundedness that is able to encompass any physical system, and represent any system with respect to its correspondences with another. So there is no upper, outer, past, or future bound to what can constitute a third-order emergent phenomenon. Representational capacity is ultimately unbounded. (Deacon 2003, 301–302)

We have already seen that dyads (input-output) are always superseded by triads (input-output-context), and how such triads have many manifestations, including fundamental logic and quantum physics. Here above, Deacon has shown how a third-order emergence in biological systems enables a recursion, which means that higher-order elaborations can always be mapped to the triadic form; see Koutroufinis's paper on semiotic evolution (2013). Broadly relevant to the emergence issues, Deacon and Koutroufinis fruitfully apply the concept of dynamical depth, a quantitative measure of nonlinear dynamical organization, to multiple levels of living systems. With a focus on constraints, they show how this new measure of complexity demonstrates relevance to living systems in ways that are largely absent from standard thermodynamics or information-based methods.

The brain's capacity to produce level-upon-level of increasing dynamical depth is a consequence of the potential for massively non-linear recurrent signal processing within a highly interconnected web of billions of incessantly active neurons. Paying attention to this substantial increase in dynamical depth may help explain many of the striking differences distinguishing biological cognition from computation. (Deacon and Koutroufinis 2014b, 421)

My final section on mind and consciousness is *On the Emergence of Consciousness and Mind* in chapter 7. For now, in chapter 5, I proceed to the study of semiosis, sign process, which is not only pervasive but also triadic and cyclic.

NOTES

1. The earlier Wade-Giles romanization of the concepts "tao" and "te" is no longer used in China, which romanizes these terms as "dao" and "de." (Carolyn Brown, private communication, October, 2019).

2. An accessible treatment of quantum physics is provided by Tony Hey and Patrick Walters in *The New Quantum Unive*rse (2003). James Cushing, in his book *Philosophical Concepts in Physics,* also addresses the field's historical and philosophical dimensions (Cushing 1998).

3. As discussed in a *Comparison of Classical Mechanics and Quantum Physics*, chapter 2, within this paragraph I am here using "classical physics" to designate the proper classical approximation that it represents, relative to quantum physics; in turn "classical mechanics" here denotes the same physics but added to that are some common presuppositions based on an overlay of mechanistic-materialist metaphysics.

4. Trope theory makes properties into particulars. For the term "nominalism," a concise summary is provided by Ghislain Guigon (2019).

5. Charles Hartshorne defined metaphysical propositions as being "unconditionally necessary and non-restrictive of existential possibilities . . . they are propositions which are illustrated or exemplified by any *conceivable* observations or experiences" (Viney and Shields 2020, 51).

6. References here to *potentiae* are intended to exclude Lewisian "possible worlds," which are typically discussed nominalistically within a presumption of actualism in contrast to ontic *potentiae* within the *Logoi* framework.

7. In this critique of nominalism, I am effectively arguing for the falsification, based on current scholarly research, of nominalism, treated as a metaphysical claim. Charles Hartshorne has argued that proper metaphysical propositions, being nonrestrictive existential affirmations, such as the statement something exists, are necessarily true and will always fail to be falsified; see Hartshorne (1958).

8. The very existence of viable temporal logics that are not simply coordinate divisions or spatialized mappings also argues for a focus on fundamental process versus taking as ontologically basic some abstracted or projected time and space metrics; for example, see Robert Brumbaugh, chapter 4 "Logic and Time" (1982, 49–60).

9. Relata are the objects between which a relation is proposed to hold.

10. Gödel's incompleteness theorems of mathematical logic show the inherent limitations of every axiomatic system capable of modeling basic arithmetic. Published by Kurt Gödel in 1931, these theorems are widely interpreted as showing, as Peter Smith states, that "any nicely axiomatized and sound theory of basic arithmetic must remain incomplete, however many new true axioms we give it" and set theory is similarly limited (Smith, 2013, 4–5).

11. Vectors in physical space are mathematical objects that have both magnitude and direction. The mathematical language of quantum physics is built on abstract vectors that have nothing to do with position in space, but whose properties are analogous. Generalizations of such abstract vector spaces can work with complex numbers and any number of "dimensions." The state of a quantum system can always be represented using such vector spaces, and such a state is sometimes referred to as a "state space."

12. Works in analytic metaphysics, which focus on careful linguistic and logical analysis, can lead to results supporting law statements as either metaphysically necessary or, in a Humean account, entirely contingent. Such analyses illustrate important and useful philosophical tools, but such should be based on the best scientific accounts and interpretations. Currently, however, many analytic philosophers simply presuppose classical metaphysics and/or Boolean-only description; thus, many such accounts mistakenly presume that physics forces one to accept physicalism, actualism and causal closure. As pointed out by Dennis Bielfeldt, "Since the 1960s considerable doubt has been cast on the reductive physicalist project" (Bielfeldt 2003). Such doubt is very much amplified by the logical, philosophical, and scientific arguments brought out within the *Logoi* framework.

13. Fraser MacBride explains that "a relation is internal if its holding between things is somehow fixed by the things themselves or how those things are; external relations are relations whose holding between things isn't fixed this way" (MacBride 2016).

14. Physical time and space are ultimately based on the temporalization or spatialization of extension as argued both by Nobo (2008, 259) and Whitehead (see footnote 55 of chapter 2).

15. Erik Verlinde hypothesizes that gravity itself, as well as the associated metric, emerges from quantum field theory. In this approach, both the concepts of metric and of gravity are derivative notions, and not really fundamental as presumed in nearly all theories of gravity, including Einstein's; see Verlinde (2011). Another approach to understanding the emergence of gravity and associated metric from a more fundamental physics of quantum process, based on information-theoretic modeling and also grounded in quantum field theory, is argued by both Cahill (2016) and Klinger (2016).

16. The derivative nature of metrics (along with many other scientific concerns) suggests how speculative, and problematic for philosophical synthesis, are various fashionable claims about the Big Bang, multiverses, dark matter, dark energy, and so on. For the present work, I entirely avoid such speculations because they are generally not helpful for pursuing our fundamental philosophical and metaphysical questions.

17. As Charles Hartshorne points out, "classical determinism is the symmetrical version of causality" (Hartshorne, 2011, 119). The collapse of two logical orders in actualism (Boolean and non-Boolean logics) results from symmetric-only, deterministic models, which precludes any deep understanding of temporality and causation. Mathias Frisch as well provides a detailed critique of the causal symmetry view; see Frisch (2013, 288–289).

18. Charles Hartshorne has argued that Whitehead's generalized theory of perception and concept of prehension provides a much better solution for understanding time than any symmetric causal theory. "Looked at from the past to the present, memory and perception are both examples of the cause-effect relation, which is always a temporal relation, from past to present . . . Through Whitehead's category of prehension . . . we are able to reduce several apparently very different types of relations [memory, perception, temporality, space, causality, enduring individuality, mind-body relation, subject-object relation, God-world relation] to one fundamental type of relation . . . No fewer than nine relations, all apparently quite different from each other, have been reduced to one!—the most powerful metaphysical generalization ever accomplished"

(David Ray Griffin 1989, 13); also see Hartshorne's classic essay on "Whitehead's revolutionary concept of prehension" (Hartshorne 1979). For the present work, I do not actively use Whitehead's concept of prehension although such includes many points of contact with my approach to untying the Gordian knot.

19. David Hume was a famed Scottish philosopher of the mid-eighteenth century. and a "thoroughgoing exponent of philosophical naturalism" who located "the source of the idea of necessary connection in us, not in the objects themselves or even in our ideas of those objects we regard as causes and effects" (William Morris and Charlotte Brown 2020).

20. Whitehead always maintains a realist orientation to the concepts of temporality and causation; this contrasts with Immanuel Kant, who focused on the formal conditions of possibility and, as Roland Faber states, "merely transfers the structure of causal efficacy from the world to the subject apprehending the world" (Faber 2011, 36).

21. Arguments for a very different cultural and media context for Chinese versus Western language users are given by Robert Logan in his work *The Alphabet Effect* (2004).

22. Scale free effects over the range of 10^{-5} cm to 10^{23} cm are discussed by Alexander Kukushkin and Valentin Rantsev-Kartinov (2004), and by Anthony Peratt (2015), as exhibited in the self-similarity of skeletal structures, striations and other features in laboratory and space plasmas.

23. The abductive procedure is to infer explanatory hypotheses that can best explain currently observed conditions.

24. As shown by both Cahill (2005; 2016) and Klinger (2010; 2016), a process physics approach provides a possible grounding for both gravity physics and quantum field theory itself from an underlying information-theoretic framework.

25. A substantial paper on "Process Physics, Time, and Consciousness," forwarding Cahill's process physics, has been published by Jeroen B. J. van Dijk (2017).

26. Such emergence would apply also to two other alternative interpretations of quantum physics, both of which build on a subquantum medium; among others, these alternatives are that of de Broglie-Bohm theory (Goldsein 2017) and J. R. Croca's nonlinear approach (Croca 2015). Both of these approaches appear to presume actualism and only the Boolean logical order. In contrast, the Relational Reality interpretation affirms both actuality and *potentiae*, takes the Boolean-non-Boolean distinction as critical, and proceeds to show, as discussed above, that this enables a simple and powerful interpretation based on core quantum physics without the added complications of these hidden-variable approaches.

27. The weaving metaphor for quantum process is made explicit by Ruth Kastner in her analysis of a possibilist transactional interpretation (Kastner 2015, 158).

28. Near the end of this quote, Bradley uses the word "argument" in the mathematical sense as "one of the independent variables upon whose values that of a function depends" (Merriam-Webster dictionary online).

29. Fermions and bosons (such as a helium atom) have an intrinsic angular momentum or spin. For example, an electron is a fermion with $+1/2$ spin, but it does not have a surface that can be physically rotating like a wooden toy top. Quantum spin

is not like classical spin. For its important role in quantum physics, see Roger Penrose (2005).

30. "Many natural notions in language and science have a 'modal' character, in that they talk about possibility and necessity in some space of relevant situations" (Blackburn et al. 2007, ix). We hypothesize that the orders of *potentiae* and actualization, respectively, may be characterized roughly by the so-called S5 and S4 systems of modal logic which are systems richer than standard Aristotelian logic. I leave it to experts in modal logic as to how best to apply such modal logic systems to the *Logoi* framework.

31. See Johan van Benthem (2016) for a concise treatment of modal logic.

32. See the three essays by Anderson Weekes in the volume edited by Michel Weber and Anderson Weekes (2009; Weekes 2009a, b, c).

33. Sean Carroll's *The Big Picture: On the Origins of Life, Meaning, and the Universe Itself* (2016) is a highly ambitious work covering conventional understandings in contemporary physics. It includes a summary equation, a "core" theory, which represents, through its multiple terms, effectively a "theory of everything."

34. Dan Falk uses this theme for his book *Universe on a T-Shirt: The Quest for the Theory of Everything* (2013).

35. In computer science, a data "mashup" is the integration of two or more datasets into one user interface.

36. In *The Question of Reality*, Milton Munitz provides a Kantian analysis that leads him to affirm only an "indefinitely prolonged course of inquiry" (Munitz 1992, 191) for considering the universe as a whole. Indeed, this is held to the limitations of Wittgensteinian world pictures with any metaphysical account as a futile project. Instead, I support both science and metaphysics, as needed, via a coherence approach, including theoretical unity and empirical success. The metaphysical component is both constrained by potential falsification (as emphasized by Charles Hartshorne), and checked indirectly by constraints of *possibiliae*; thus, such is more than mere worldview choice. Munitz also discusses a "Boundless Existence" as the "something more" than the "observable universe," but he assumes that such transcendence is, by definition, unintelligible. In contrast, within the *Logoi* framework, both the actual and potential relations (*potentiae*) are intelligible even if, at times, inaccessible for all practical purposes; nevertheless, such will have both direct and indirect, intelligible constraints.

37. In the 1890s Lord Kelvin dreamed of a time when classical physics could deductively explain everything; a century later, in the 1990s, Stephen Hawking had very similar *fin de siècle* [end of a century] dreams when modern physics appeared to be leading us to a final "Theory of Everything" and then *The End of Science* (John Horgan 2015). From the perspective of the *Logoi* framework, such dreams will always remain just that—dreams.

38. The commonly presumed Einsteinian gravity model, which presupposes some form of space-time metric as fundamental, may be incorrect and eventually displaced with a gravity model deriving from either fundamental quantum field theory or other approaches associated with constraints on *possibiliae*. My argument in this current work generally avoids reference to contemporary physical cosmology because of (1)

its highly speculative nature with limited alternative models, which have not been adequately tested; (2) model dependence of available observational parameters; and (3) clear falsification of certain predictions of the extant standard model; see Eastman (2010), and *A Cosmology Group* < http://www.cosmology.info>.

39. For details about laws of science or empirical laws, see Friedel Weinert (2011).

40. For physical science, the designation "laws" is often a misnomer because the judicial metaphor is not applicable as initially presumed under a now outdated Newtonian metaphysics. Further, as stated by John Henry, "the evidence suggests that laws of nature developed in the sixteenth and seventeenth centuries as part of the process of working out just how abstract mathematics could be said to relate to the physical world" (Henry 2004, 94).

41. A classic derivation of the basic equations of quantum physics and classical physics is in Feynman's thesis "The Principle of Least Action in Quantum Mechanics" (Laurie Brown 2005, 1–69).

42. Chris Gray point out that "there are two major versions of the action, due to Hamilton and Maupertuis, and two corresponding action principles. The Hamilton principle is nowadays the most used . . . [Hamilton's principle is set up to] emphasize a particular constraint on the varied trajectories" (Gray 2009).

43. With respect to grounding the concept of the Principle of Least Action, Desmond points out that "Kant connects aesthetic ideas with initiating a kind of striving after a maximum" (Desmond 2016, 95). Perhaps this connection coheres with Whitehead's emphasis on the aesthetic dimension in his later writings; see Steven Shaviro (2012) and Isabelle Stengers (2014).

44. This equivalence is quantified by the Euler-Lagrange equations.

45. Vladislav Terekhovich explains that "the FPI calculates probabilities by summing over classical configurations of variables and assigning a phase to each configuration, which equals the action of that configuration. It is assumed that a quantum system simultaneously takes an infinite set of all possible alternative paths or histories, which correspond to the boundary conditions. In our classical world, these possible paths or histories are mutually exclusive even though at the quantum level these possible histories coexist. We can state these possible histories as being in quantum superposition" (Terekhovich 2018, 191).

46. The path integral formulation of quantum physics generalizes the action principle of classical physics, replacing single, unique classical trajectories with a sum or functional integral over an infinity of possible trajectories to compute the quantum amplitude.

47. Ruth Kastner's approach using Possibilist Transactional Interpretation (PTI), with its offer/accept waves, appears to spatially project the pre-space potential relations (*potentiae*) whereas a non-Boolean logic treatment transcends such spatialization. Further research is needed to evaluate details of comparing PTI with the Relational Realism interpretation. To date, they appear to be very complementary (see Kastner, Kauffman, and Epperson 2018).

48. The logical empiricists attempted to avoid the ontic implications of the Principle of Least Action by simply assuming, as pointed out by Michael Stöltzner, that "the PLA was nothing but an equivalent mode of mathematical description" for existing physical laws. (Stöltzner 2003, 290).

49. John Baez explains how "Noether's theorem is an amazing result, which lets physicists get conserved quantities from symmetries of the laws of nature. Time translation symmetry gives conservation of energy; space translation symmetry gives conservation of momentum; rotation symmetry gives conservation of angular momentum, and so on. This result, proved in 1915 by Emmy Noether shortly after she first arrived in Göttingen, was praised by Einstein as a piece of 'penetrating mathematical thinking.' It's now a standard workhorse in theoretical physics" (Baez 2020).

50. This fundamental pre-space level incorporates extension; for a detailed philosophical analysis about extension; see Randall Auxier and Gary Herstein (2017).

51. There are two basic frameworks of quantum physics, recognized as equivalent. The wave perspective of the Schrödinger equation, first formulated in 1926, and the matrix representation introduced by Heisenberg in 1925; see Steven Holzner (2012).

52. "Realism about dispositions, or dispositionalism, argues that dispositions are causally efficacious properties inherent to objects that are sufficient to produce change" (Sungho Choi and Michael Fara 2018).

53. The scale-free approach is one in which basic concepts or parameters find application at micro-, meso- and macro-scale. One example is space plasma physics, as I have pointed out, whereby key plasma parameter ratios and physical relations can be applied at multiple scales: boundary layer scale, planetary scale, stellar scale, and beyond (Eastman 1993).

54. For an up-to-date perspective on origins of life research, see Athel Cornish-Bowden and María Luz Cárdenas' paper "Contrasting theories of life: Historical context, current theories" (2020).

55. Panexperientialism is the view that a mental-like component is fundamental and permeates the natural world. Many scholars in contemporary process thought apply either a highly nuanced form of this concept or utilize "pan-experientialism," as I do here, to emphasize that the real focus is on the ubiquitous nature of context, potential responsiveness, and experience, broadly understood, and not psychic phenomena *per se*; see David Ray Griffin (1997b).

56. The combination problem, as Philip Goff explains, is that "subjects of experience, i.e. things which have consciousness . . . don't seem to be the kind of things that can 'sum together' to make other subjects of experience" (Goff 2009, 130).

57. Using "experiencing" in a broad, non-anthropomorphic manner, Hartshorne explains that Whitehead's concept of prehension points to "the experiencing of past events, these being necessary conditions of the experience" and such input incorporates constraints and *potentia* as well (Hartshorne 1979, 256).

58. I also avoid the "panpsychism" term because of the common misconception that such a position is "positing tiny minds everywhere in nature" (Joseph Levine 2001, 177). Scholarly work on this topic overall is best represented by the "pan-experiential" term.

59. "In philosophy and certain models of psychology, *qualia* are defined as individual instances of subjective, conscious experience" (Michael Tye 2018).

60. For an example involving large apes, see Carla Krachun, "Are Apes Conscious? An Overview of Inconclusive Evidence" (Krachun 2002).

Chapter 5

Information and Semiotics

Here I explore various connections between causation, emergence, physical relations, and complex systems, all discussed in previous chapters, with information and semiotics—the theory of signs. In addition, I summarize as well the intellectual history that ties together information and semiotics with process thought and speculative [systematic] naturalisms.

In the *Logoi* framework, consistent with the contextual emergence approach of Atmanspacher (2007), we have seen in chapter 4 how causation is no longer confined to the mere dyadic correlation of facts (simply "causality" in Hulswit's terminology) or to deductivism, as in Newtonian physics, such that any novelty or emergence is necessarily some mere epiphenomena arising from random error or chance. Instead, full causation and emergence, respectively, the diachronic and the synchronic aspects of fundamental process, are complementary realities bridged (ontologically) by quantum process and (epistemologically) by symbols and model representations created by the semiotic animal (humans). Key elements of such bridging are the linkages enabled through information, broadly construed and, at multiple levels, both dyadic and triadic relations (including semiosis). Building on landscapes of *potentiae* as discussed in chapter 4, multiple levels of reality are emergent, of which the four most relevant frameworks are given below, including teleodynamic systems based on the work of Terrence Deacon.

1. quantum process, always with fundamental local-global connection;
2. complex systems;
3. self-organizing dynamical systems;
4. teleodynamic systems with self/other/world.

As discussed in chapters 2-4, the Relational Reality model is focused on fundamental quantum process, which is both pervasive of all reality and a bridge between the two fundamental logical orders, the order of actualizations and the order of *potentiae* (based, respectively, on Boolean and non-Boolean logics). This model also points a way toward a bridge between such diachronic pre-space process (from which even time and space are emergent) and synchronic multilevel emergence.

A key to understanding complex systems, and beyond, as discussed in chapter 4, is the work of Robert Rosen on complexity theory and anticipatory systems (Rosen 2000, 2012). In addition to being important to emergence, a focus on Rosen's work provides a useful segue into information and semiotics. Kineman summarizes Rosen's contribution as follows:

> Rosen's very thorough development of the mathematical and philosophical foundation for relational theory thus allows a new science to be articulated that is compatible with both Western and Eastern thought, and that vastly improves our ability to understand complex phenomena.
>
> In simple language the idea of relational theory is to describe nature in terms of material systems that represent (model) each other and that are themselves expressions of such models. The result of this approach is to relax the mechanistic constraints on what we think nature can do. Less constrained systems in nature may then exhibit self and universally creative phenomena because of causal loops (self-entailments, or "impredicativities") that are not otherwise allowed in mechanism. These are information feedback loops that are considered to be responsible for all behaviour and complexity, generating system dynamics and structure. When fully constrained, or reduced to equivalence between model and system, these relations account for classical existence and behaviour. That has been the primary subject of Western science for centuries. When unconstrained, i.e., unreduced, they account for complex existence and behaviour, which is now obvious in quantum, cosmological, and dissipative systems phenomena (such as whirlpools or other energy vortices). In a sense, these systems "buy" various forms of self-causation by dissipating energy. When they are more organized, unconstrained modelling relations may then account for living systems and their phenomena. (Kineman 2008, 3–4)

Just as the *Logoi* framework, as discussed in chapter 4, adopts a constraint interpretation for the emergence of physical relations, constraints within the landscape of *potentiae* enable the full range of evolved systems at multiscale, both nonliving (with its contextual emergence) and living (contextual emergence augmented with biosemiotics, including information and meaning); arguably this corresponds to Koutroufinis's understanding of Deacon's concept of teleodynamics (Koutroufinis 2013). Such evolution is reflected in language for which, as summarized by Robert Logan, there are

> distinct modes of language, which form an evolutionary chain of development
> . . . [speech, writing, mathematics, science, computing and the Internet repre-
> sent] languages in their own right because of their unique semantics and syntax
> . . . New modes of language evolved to represent increasingly more complex
> phenomena, and hence . . . required a richer vocabulary and more complex
> structures to function . . . language is defined by both its informatics and com-
> munication capacity [meaning and grammatical patterning]. (Logan 2014, 63)

INFORMATION AND MEASURES OF COMPLEXITY

For a deeper understanding of emergence, we need to briefly review the relatively recent history of the concept of information. Technically, as initially formulated in 1948 by Claude Shannon, the information contained in any communications channel can be evaluated in terms of the degree of unpredictability of any potential message. Over the past seven decades, information theorists, building on Shannon's work, have developed various additional ways to define and measure the complexity of sequences of symbols. These various approaches, generally compatible, can be referred to as models of algorithmic complexity, which normally focus on quantification and computer utilization. Such measures of algorithmic complexity "only characterize *descriptions* of physical systems, not how they came about or how they are causally organized. In this sense they refer to the 'map' and not to the 'territory'" (Deacon and Koutroufinis 2014, 407) and thus constitute a syntactic approach. However, "any assessment of the complexity of physical phenomena needs to also consider any semantic (referential) and pragmatic (functionally relevant) aspects of these descriptions, especially since these aspects are critically relevant to biological and cognitive systems" (ibid.). Thus, once again we encounter the importance of context—Logan expertly demolishes the false idols arising from the neglect of context.

> Each generation makes a god of their latest technological or scientific achieve-
> ment or breakthrough. For the Hebrews it was the written word and the law
> "written with the finger of God." For the Greeks it was their deductive logic and
> rational thought disembodied from practical experience and empirical evidence
> of the physical world. For the Enlightenment it was Newtonian mechanics and
> God, the clock maker, where things were explained in terms of mechanical

models. In the Information Age the god is disembodied information, information without context where everything is explained in terms of the transfer of information, and some times it is information without meaning. (Logan 2014, 48)

To get a sense of an information map relevant to complex systems generally, figure 5.1 provides a visual representation of the progression in complexity of real systems as increasing from the limit of extreme order (left-hand square), which can be characterized by a small amount of information, through intermediate zones of mixed order and disorder (requiring substantial information to describe), and on to the limit of complete randomness (right-hand square), which requires very little information to describe because such can be mapped to simple probability distributions.

Standard syntactic treatments of algorithmic complexity only handle one dimension of organization (i.e., how simply to infer structure of one discrete element from that of adjoining discrete elements). As a result, they paradoxically attribute higher complexity to entirely chaotic phenomenon because, within such a one-dimensional treatment, the amount of information required scales with the number of such discrete elements such that any complex system is "its own simplest description." In contrast, Deacon and Koutroufinis explain, "real physical systems may involve multiple dimensions, including their generative history and functional attributes" (Deacon and Koutroufinis

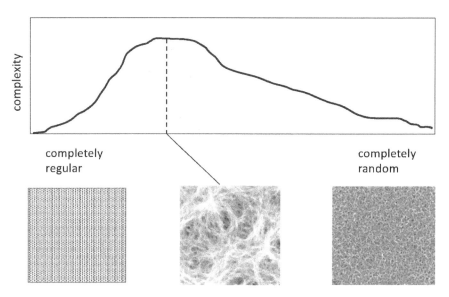

Figure 5.1 An optimal measure of complexity is situated between completely ordered and entirely random distributions (Source: author, adapted from Deacon and Koutroufinis (2014, 406, figure 1.1)).

2014, 407). Standard approaches are "well-suited for analyzing the complexity of descriptions that can be rendered in abstract sequences of symbols, numbers, or computational steps, but will not be able to account for features that are not distinguishable and countable in the immediately present physical object of analysis. Thus they often lead to counterintuitive results when applied to [real] dynamical systems" (Deacon and Koutroufinis 2014, 408).

Building on approaches that incorporate the fact of numerous possible trajectories within a multivariable "space" (i.e., landscapes of *potentiae*), Deacon and Koutroufinis utilize "dynamical depth" as a multidimensional measure of complexity for self-organized dynamical systems. This approach as well incorporates the multiple ways in which systems can handle constraints and context. In summary, they conclude that

> Living (teleodynamic) processes limit the variety of possible *forms* of constraint-generating processes, rather than any specific physico-chemical process. In this respect they are like descriptive compressions or representations. This is, of course, characteristic of the role of DNA in living organisms and is what warrants describing DNA structures as containing information contributing to the functional design of the organism. This implicit incorporation of a compressed self-representation explains why assessing the complexity of organisms requires a subtler concept of complexity than is required for assessing the complexity of non-living processes. Organisms decompress (re-expand) this information during their development by virtue of the way this information constrains the organization of morphodynamic epigenetic processes. So to ignore this dynamical infrastructure is to ignore the complexity of life's complexity-generating process. (Deacon and Koutroufinis 2014, 419)

In properly characterizing information in association with algorithmic complexity, we once again encounter the importance of constraints and context, and of the interaction of system components with the system as a whole. As Deacon and Koutroufinis state, "a formal analysis of living and mental phenomena is fundamentally incomplete unless it captures this semiotic-physical interwovenness created by life's dynamical depth" (Deacon and Koutroufinis 2014, 421). Kauffman and colleagues point out that "the definition of information is relative and depends on the context in which it is to be considered. There appears to be no such thing as absolute information that is an invariant that applies to all circumstances" and, further "information is not an invariant but rather a quantity that is relative to the environment in which it operates" (Kauffman et al. 2008, 37). Here is yet another example reflecting the fundamental input-output-context triadic of the *Logoi* framework. Such context dependence, either on history and/or environment, is illustrated in three distinct types of information such that "instructional or biotic information is a useful definition for biotic systems just as Shannon information was useful for telecommunication channel engineering, and Kolmogorov . . . information was useful for the study of information compression with respect to Turing machines" (ibid.). What is common to these perspectives on information is how they afford "a direct union of matter, energy, and information as constraint or boundary condition" (Kauffman et al. 2008, 43). Another way of phrasing these linkages is "that we take information to be constraint or its physical equivalent, boundary conditions that partially cause events, where the coming into existence of the constraint is itself part of propagating organization" (Kauffman et al. 2008, 42). The "propagating organization" here is a logical causality as featured in the Relational Reality model (see chapter 2); such may or may not be subject to relativistic limitations.

THRESHOLDS OF INNOVATION

Marcello Barbieri (2009, 239), as noted in chapter 2, calls attention to three thresholds of innovation (semiotic, hermeneutic, cultural) with the evolution of the theory of signs, or semiosis. By adding information to Barbieri's set, we have four basic thresholds, corresponding to distinct levels of nonlinear dynamical organization that can be understood within our *Logoi* framework, building on the concepts of process, *potentiae*, local-global, and triadic relation (input-output-context), as follows:

1. *information threshold*—operating at the quantum process level and upward; fundamental input-output-context relations; *relata*-relation combinations for which information theory of multiple dimensions can apply;
2. *semiotic threshold*—the origin of organic semiosis; sign-meaning-code; complex systems within the domain of biosemiotics;
3. *epistemic threshold*—the origin of interpretive semiosis, the hermeneutic threshold; involving matter-referent-interpreter; also sign-signified-interpretation—also see Barbieri (2007, x);
4. *cultural threshold*—the origin of linguistic semiosis.

None of these thresholds are simply bottom-up emergent. As Ellis states, "there are some higher level variables that are not emergent. Though they are realized in various lower level physical substrates, they are determined by higher level logic, and so are intrinsically of a higher level nature" (Ellis 2016, 108). Ellis describes four examples in this context (algorithms, laws of physics, social agreements, conceptual plans), which are analogous to the thresholds above in terms of involving a higher-level context, or logic.[1]

HISTORICAL PERSPECTIVES ON
SEMIOTICS AND PROCESS THOUGHT

The *Logoi* framework builds on scholarly work over the centuries in semiotics (the theory of signs), philosophy, and science. My conclusions about the importance of context (indeed, that even for fundamental quantum process the essential structure is that of the triad input-output-context, not just the input-output dyad) are complemented by an affirmation of the importance of contextual analysis and expressions for all forms of art, humanities, music, etc. Thomas Pfau defends such an affirmation in depth with his major work *Minding the Modern* (Pfau 2015). An even weightier *magnum opus* (literally so at 4.2 pounds and 928 pages) is that of John Deely in his great work *Four Ages of Understanding* (Deely 2001). According to Kenneth Schmitz's review, Deely's exposition on the Latin age contains "a vein of pure gold: for it tells the story of the emerging doctrine of signs and its postmodern systematization as semiotic . . . [Deely's] text picks up speculative energy as it dismantles the Nominalists on the path of war against the 'way of ideas' that is characteristic of modern philosophy. To this modern development, the author counterposits 'the road not taken,' i.e., 'the way of signs'" (Schmitz 2010, 120).

Complementing Pfau's thorough analysis of trends in the modern era, including trends toward reductionism and nominalism, Deely grounds such critique in a detailed intellectual history, from the Greeks to modern times, with a focus on linkages from John Poinsot's *Tractatus de Signis* of 1632, in the Latin age, to Charles Sanders Peirce's rediscovery of semiosis in the late nineteenth century.

Deely's four ages are as follows:

Age 1: *ancient*, realist; ancient philosophers speculated about simple forms of monism and pluralism but "perhaps the most seminal and enduring scheme to emerge from these ancient mists was rather the idea that a binary logic suffices to explain the physical world" (Deely 2001, 29) [i.e., dualism];

Age 2: *Latin age*, "the origin of semiotics and triadic schemes, from Augustine to Poinsot, and finally C. S. Peirce; an intellectual tradition affirming that being and intelligibility are coextensive" (Deely 2000, 4);

Age 3: *modern period*, Descartes, Kant, and so on, with the denial that being and intelligibility are coextensive combined with a neglect of semiosis and a tendency to support dualisms—primary example being the dualism of René Descartes;

Age 4: *post-modern period*, semiotics, process, critical realist, and so on; once again to affirm realism and, without Platonism, to deny nominalism.

In Deely's time, C. S. Peirce's rediscovery of semiotics with works of Poinsot's intellectual milieu in Iberia marks the beginning of a "post-modern" period.

> This contemporary notion of sign, thus, understands that what it signifies as properly consisting in an irreducibly triadic relation...In modern times, after Descartes (1596–1650), the hard-won Latin notion of sign [John Poinsot, *Tractatus de Signis*, 1632] in general disappears, to be replaced by the notion of ideas as self-representing objects, until the Latin notion is taken up again in the writings of Charles Sanders Peirce (1839–1914) under the banner of "semiotics." Peirce brings an end to the notion of idea as objects being the fundamental presupposition of philosophy and initiates a new way of philosophizing, "pragmaticism," or the way of signs. (Deely 2001, 740)

In my diverse readings of semiotics, process thought and speculative (systematic) philosophy, including many natural philosophers and scientists, I find many overlaps and complementary arguments. Gare, in particular, brings these perspectives together in his latest work *The Philosophical Foundations of Ecological Civilization.*

> The goal of speculative philosophy is to take into account the whole range of human experience—scientific, social, ethical, aesthetic and religious, and to develop a coherent conception of reality that does justice to all of these. In contrast to the naturalism of analytic philosophers, speculative naturalism not only affirms the ambitions of philosophy in the grand manner against any tendency to dissolve philosophy into apologetics for mainstream science; it has provided the basis for overcoming the deficiencies of mainstream science, and along with it, the Hobbesian conception of humans. Schelling's work exemplified this quest. (Gare 2017, 161)

In another section focused on speculative naturalism and the Schellingian tradition, Gare correlates that tradition with recent advances in biosemiotics:

> Combining Peirce's semiotics with Jacob von Uexküll's biology to explain how all organisms, including plants, define their environments as meaningful surrounding worlds (*Umwelten*) and then the sequence of more complex worlds . . . leading up to and including humans' with-worlds (*Mitwelten*) and self-worlds (*Eigenwelten*), biosemioticians have effectively overcome Cartesian dualism and shown what is involved in the development of human culture and reflective consciousness very much in accordance with the insights of Schelling. (Gare 2017, 131)

In addition to semiotics, another closely related, unifying discipline is, according to Gare, ecology. "Ecology, the study of 'households' in biotic communities, where emergence, hierarchical order, semiosis, symbiosis, and anticipatory systems are central, is pre-eminently an anti-reductionist science exemplifying, and further developing process-relational thinking" (Gare 2017, 177). Such process-oriented, ecological thinking, indeed a "process ecology" (see chapter 6 in Ulanowicz (2009)), accords well with speculative naturalism such that, Gare continues, "the ultimate existents of the universe will have to be seen as creative processes, or durational self-constraining patterns of activity, and configurations of such processes at multiple scale in dynamics interaction, rather than objects or things, which are taken to have only a derivative status" (Gare 2017, 178). Although the mechanistic metaphysics dominant in the nineteenth century contributed to some important advances in physics such as the kinetic theory of gases, Val Dusek argues that Schelling's nature philosophy had an important role in enabling several key advances including, among others, Johann Ritter's discovery of ultraviolet radiation, Ørsted's discovery of electromagnetism, and Faraday's discovery of diamagnetism and other features of electromagnetism (Dusek 1999, 254–278; also see Gare's survey of Schelling's influence (2019)). These nineteenth-century advances formed the core of a new field theory, which remains a core component of modern physics and field theory in general.

Whereas Deely focuses his "Age 4: post-modern period" on semiotics, Gare expands the scope of this period by adding process thought and a new naturalism. These additional fields are convergent as well with the latest scientific work in complexity theory, information theory, ecology, biology, and physics. There is a distinct irony in how the so-called realism of Deely's "Age 3: modern period," with its substance thinking and actualism, ended up with a denial of realism, even leading to nihilism, as Gare (1994) has argued. In contrast, Deely's Age 2, Latin tradition, with a focus on theological and ethical issues, led ultimately (via John Poinsot[2] to C. S. Peirce) to the affirmation of realism, as evidenced in contemporary semiotics, biosemiotics, and speculative (naturalistic) philosophy. These developments show how taking modernism to its extremes contributed in part to the deconstructive "post-modernism" of the French school, which is effectively a type of anti-realist hyper-modernism. A more authentic post-modern framework, yet allowing for useful critique of power structures is, as Griffin argues, ultimately constructive, not destructive (Griffin 1988).

In summary, the monad-dyad-triad sequence can be framed within conceptual phases of philosophy as illustrated in table 5.1.

Table 5.1   Monad-dyad-triad Sequence in the History of Philosophy

1. monad	Aristotle	subject-predicate form
2. dyad	modern (*à la* Descartes)	simple modeling
	nominalism	Cartesian, modernist rationality
		(*ent rationis*)
3. triad	post-modern	complex systems modeling (Rosen)
	relational reality	semiotics, *ent reale* + *ent rationis*
		(Poinsot/Deely)
		(both cognition-independent
		and cognition-dependent)

A PROCESS PHILOSOPHY OF SEMIOTICS

Semiotics has roots both with the works of Ferdinand de Saussure and Charles Sanders Peirce. Whereas de Saussure's work, and his semiology, focused on linguistics and the social sciences, and used dyadic constructions, Peirce's work emphasized triadic logical structure, thus a full semiosis. Contemporary biosemiotics primarily builds on Peirce's triadic conception.

Whereas de Saussure focused on dialectics in his semiology, James Williams fleshes out a process philosophy of signs that goes beyond all prior forms of semiology. His process approach always constitutes an asymmetrical transformation and, using a triadic structure for the definition of sign, Williams states that "the sign as multiplicity and process replaces all versions of the sign as duality" (Williams 2016, 116–117). He notes that Gilles Deleuze affirms both the realms of the "actual and the possible" (Williams 2016, 135) and provides analyses of paradox and good sense supporting that distinction. After his treatment of Deleuze, Williams moves on to a discussion of Whitehead's philosophy in which "Individual unity is always about process, rather than identity and stasis. The philosophy of organism is always about the combination of the processes of an extended individual unity of experience . . . The sign must be an indivisible multiplicity of processes extending through the whole of the world but it must also have its determining givenness, its close matter of fact" (Williams 2016, 147). This framing comports with the possible/actual distinction noted above, and he further emphasizes that "I have argued for the life of signs independent from human forms of life and meaning" (Williams 2016, 172). While Williams's analysis goes beyond the dualities and symmetries of standard semiology and structuralism, his book neglects Peirce because, he argues, Peirce "skews process in the sign towards human use, meaning and experience" (Williams 2016, 184). This contrasts with some other scholars, such as John Deely, who argue that Peircean semiotics goes beyond any such simple anthropocentrism—see

Deely's *Introducing Semiotic* (1982, 196). Indeed, Williams's process philosophy of semiotics appears to blend quite well with the very inclusive, triadic and asymmetric Peircean approach that is highlighted for the *Logoi* framework.

This approach is reinforced by Jeroen B. J. van Dijk in his process-information approach whereby

> our universe is an experiential psychophysical natural world in which self-organizing reciprocal dynamics continuously develop within and between coupled process-structures, thus "*in*-forming" each other on all levels of organization . . . nature forms one huge processual whole of synergetically evolving and complexly interconnected dissipative structures . . . our higher-order conscious experience follows from nature's process-based reflexive informativeness—as a highly evolved confluent extension of it. (van Dijk 2011, 82)

Thus, such process-information approaches go well beyond standard syntactic signs to include "semantic information relating to meaning and truth of these signs, and pragmatic information dealing with the effects and impact of these meaningful signs on those who use them" (Dijk 2011, 78), and all this within a triadic relational structure. Information theories to handle such higher levels of meaning and context have just begun to be developed.

BIOSEMIOTICS AND ANTICIPATORY SYSTEMS

The fields of biology, philosophy, and semiotics are integrated in the burgeoning discipline of biosemiotics which, according to an Oxford dictionary, is "the study of signs, of communication, and of information in living organisms" (Cammack et al. 2006, 72), an international scholarly activity (biosemiotics.org). As noted above, the triadic logic of fundamental process can be simply expressed as "input-output-context"; in quantum physics, the triadic form can be expressed as "input-output-environment." Immediate human experience, quantum physics, ecology, and current complex systems studies all build on such fundamental triadic logic although, for certain applications, approximations based on dyadic logic can be efficient and practical, yet not philosophically fundamental. Søren Brier points out that "no facts are absolutely free of context. The important thing is to discuss them, to compare them, to calibrate them according to standards determined by our dealings with other facts, while consciously reflecting on the significance of the context" (Brier 2013, 8–9). Such triadic logic is a key part of the *Logoi* framework along with process, *potentiae*, and local-global relations. Brier emphasizes the observer's role as follows:

> The information processing paradigm will never succeed in describing the central problems of mediating the semantic content of a message from producer to user because it does not address the social and phenomenological aspects of cognition. Furthermore, it will fail because it is built on a rationalistic epistemology and a mechanistic world view with an unrealistic "world formula" attitude towards science. Science can deal only with the decidable [i.e., facts or Boolean actualizations], and as Gödel has shown, there are undecidables even within mathematics. The problem for the now-classical functionalistic information processing paradigm is its inability to encompass the role of the observer. (Brier 2013, 83)

The information processing paradigm, as here characterized, is limited to syntactic input-output dyads, and cannot handle semantic (semiotic) triads. As Brier states, such limitation is evident in comparing human and computer languages: "When we look at language as a means of information, it seems clear that a word's metaphorical meaning depends on the organization of the living system (its body) and its context of living. Contrast this with computer language, which is free of context" (Brier 2013, 87). This relative lack of context (obviously no natural language is completely free of context) contrasts with Peirce's triadic framework which, even for complex systems studies and information science, as Brier points out, provides a basis for addressing both syntactics and semantics, both dyads and triads, both discrete information and meaning.

> In Peirce's triadic philosophy, feelings, *qualia*, habit formation, and signification are basic ontological constituents of reality. This suggests that the semiotic paradigm should be able to penetrate beyond chemistry and physics to "the bottom of nature." This amounts to a clash with basic beliefs in sizable parts of information science, which seems to want to construct meaning as a bottom-up procedure from a thermodynamically based information science. (Brier 2013, 42)

Given such limitations of standard approaches, Brier works on developing a Peircean-based pan-semiotics. Key ways to build up such a pan-semiotic framework include, among others, utilizing hierarchical frameworks and, as Howard Pattee recommends, to fully build on the power of symbols.

> The amazing property of symbols is their ability to control the lawful behavior of matter, while the laws, on the other hand, do not exert control over the symbols or their coded references. It is just for this reason that evolution can

construct endless varieties of species and the brain can learn and create endless varieties of models of the world.

That is why organisms and symbol systems in some sense locally appear to escape the global behavior of physical laws, yet without ever disobeying them. Fully understanding this power of symbols over matter at *all* evolutionary levels is what I call "the symbol–matter problem" [always triadic because imbedded in Peirce's "system of interpretance"].

The four most notorious symbol–matter levels are the genetic code in biology, pattern recognition and sensorimotor control in nervous systems, the measurement and control problem in physics, and the mind–body problem in philosophy. (Pattee 2011, 222)

The multiple levels of the symbol-matter problem, here noted by Pattee, is featured in chapter 7 where, based on the *Logoi* framework, I point a way to a solution. The symbol-matter duality is just one among many related dualities without dualism that were analyzed by Jesper Hoffmeyer when he introduced the concept of a symbolic semiosphere (Hoffmeyer 1997a), updated to "symbolosphere" by John Schumann, who emphasizes that "since the ideas that emerge from interaction among brains only exist within (and because of) a powerful symbolic system (i.e., language) that represents them, ideas are essentially free from the body/brain while, at the same time having downwardly causal influence on brains, minds, and behavior" (Schumann 2012). Such later emphasis on the importance of the symbolic was notably anticipated by Whitehead in his work *Symbolism* (1927) which, as Roland Faber points at, argued that "the evolution of the world of organisms is a process of 'mutual symbolic reference' and, in the best case, of the mutually intensifying interactions they support" (Faber 2019, 69).

The open-ended possibilities enabled with the symbolosphere are illustrated very effectively by Donald Favareau in his treatment of Peirce's process ontology of possibility, actuality, and lawfulness, corresponding roughly to Peirce's "firstness, secondness, thirdness" (see chapter 2).

Thus, while all action in the universe is both current-context dependent and next-context creating, the emergence of ever-more complex semiotic capabilities in organisms has expanded the possibility space of immediate-next action in the world exponentially, and has brought into being not a pre-given, singly end-directed ordered world, but an emergent, many ends-directed world of promiscuous, unforeseeable possibility and interacting *telos*. The goal of Biosemiotics is to understand and to explore this world. (Favareau 2015, 600)

Robert Poli documents how the study of anticipatory systems has emerged from recent studies in complex systems. "Anticipation concerns the capacity exhibited by some systems to tune their behaviour according to a model of the future evolution of the environment in which they are embedded. Generally speaking, the thesis is defended that [quoting Robert Rosen] 'An anticipatory system is a system containing a predictive model of itself and/or its environment, which allows it to change state at an instant in accord with the model's predictions pertaining to a later instant'" (Poli 2010, 769). Robert Rosens's most extensive development of this concept is within his major work *Anticipatory Systems* (2012). Kineman, Bela Banathy, and Judith Rosen explain Rosen's perspective this way: "Especially in systems we call living . . . nature models itself and is causally entailed in this way, both interactively and contextually . . . mappings in this model, which correspond to category-theoretic mapping, are informational in nature . . . implicating a holarchy of contexts providing information influences. Accordingly, information (as a process of encoding or decoding) is the 'glue' that holds nature together" (Kineman et al. 2007, 4). Another perspective, as Bettinger and Eastman state, is that "in contrast to classical causality that approaches the future directly, anticipatory systems approach the future indirectly through generative models. To embrace such systems reflects an expansion of causal logic to include an anticipatory, or predictive process that enables complex systems with sources of free energy to counteract the second-law of thermodynamics and maintain order through the minimization of outstanding parameters" (Bettinger and Eastman 2017, 109).

Recent works in neuroscience and artificial intelligence attempt to quantify complex systems and anticipatory systems for, as Karl Friston states, the purpose of "optimizing the parameters of a generative model to maximize the accuracy of predictions, under complexity constraints" (Friston 2010, 132). For many global theories of brain function, Friston continues, "the brain optimizes a (free-energy) bound on surprise or its complement, value. This manifests as perception (so as to change predictions) or action (so as to change the sensations that are predicted)" (Friston 2010, 135–136). Given this description of predictive models, Bettinger and Eastman state, "Clearly, there are substantial overlaps of Rosen's analysis of models in complex systems, of predictive models in neuroscience, and of the analysis of *Umwelts* (models) in biosemiotics" (Bettinger and Eastman 2017, 116).

FROM TRIADS TO ENHANCED
INFORMATION AND SEMIOTICS

Several stages of semiosis bridge the logic of actualizations and the logic of *potentiae*—triads in the following, at multiple levels.

—fundamental logic
—science (input-measurement-environment; input-output-context)

—biosemiotics
—human activities—the semiotic animal
— language and high-level interpretation
— symbolic semiosis (symbolosphere)

The requirement of context at various levels, thus a universality of the input-output-context triad, is fundamental to scientific measurement and the ontic description of individual systems. On this point, Atmanspacher and Primas affirm that

> distinguishing epistemic and ontic descriptions of quantum systems is a key to avoid the category mistake of confounding concepts of observation-dependent and observation-independent quantum realities. Epistemic descriptions refer to a statistical description of ensembles of experimental outcomes. By contrast, ontic descriptions refer to individual systems without any respect to their observation or measurement. Epistemic and ontic descriptions require different mathematical codifications.
>
> Although all applications of quantum theory are based on epistemic formulations, this does not imply that ontic descriptions are altogether pointless. Since they are free from particular contexts required for particular applications, ontic descriptions necessarily feature a higher degree of symmetry than epistemic descriptions. It is possible to derive epistemic descriptions from ontic descriptions, if the particular contexts can be implemented precisely enough. An ontic description of a system can give rise to many different epistemic descriptions mutually excluding each other.
>
> An ultimately context-free ontic description or, equivalently, a universal context would be of perfect symmetry and cannot be formulated. Hence, any ontic description presupposes an "ontological commitment," an agreement about a fundamental domain of discourse based on some context which is as general as possible or reasonable. This entails a relativity of onticity which is crucial for the coherent discussion of emergent behavior and can be formalized by contextual symmetry breakings. (Atmanspacher and Primas 2003, 319)

The "contextual symmetry breaking" that occurs upon each and every fundamental quantum process bridges the order of *potentiae* (the landscape of symmetric, ontic quantum process) and the order of actualization (the domain of epistemic descriptions) and, as argued in chapter 2, concurrently ties in local-global linkages at multiple scale. Feedback effects of triadic complex systems process, at multiple levels, lead to a succession of thresholds as discussed above (information, semiotic, epistemic, cultural). Although very powerful for many standard statistical purposes, disembodied syntactic information (without context) is not adequate to explain such complex processes that require, as illustrated in figure 5.1, a means to infer maximum complexity for systems intermediate between low information content cases of either very high order or complete randomness.

New tools are needed to capture semantic information, such as the concept of "dynamical depth" introduced by Deacon and Koutroufinis as a multi-dimensional measure of complexity for self-organized dynamical systems (Deacon and Koutroufinis 2014). Studies in such enhanced information theory and semiotics are leading to progress in understanding complex systems and anticipatory systems that go beyond standard reductive evolutionary accounts. The *Logoi* framework points to a universality of the input-output-context triad, in combination with the reality of *potentiae*, that addresses both the distinction of epistemic and ontic descriptions in quantum physics and the multilevel balancing of information and semiotic description needed to understand emerging complex systems from molecules to biological systems to human consciousness.

The multilevel universality of input-output-context triads and triads in general suggest a generalization to multilevel information, both syntactic and semantic, in addition to fundamental communicative capacities in the world. As stated by Matthew Segall, "Whitehead's organic cosmology invites us to recognize that the transmission and transformation of experience is the very basis of causal connection throughout the universe. Human language is just a further elaboration upon this cosmic capacity for communicative transaction . . . a living God at the heart of our human perception and symbolism . . . a *logos* of the *cosmos*" (Segall 2019, 245–246). How such communicative capabilities are imbedded in Whitehead's framework is examined via his concept of prehension within the *Unified Process Approach to Causation and Emergence* section of chapter 6. As documented by Matthew Segall, a number of information theorists have turned to

> Whitehead's metaphysical scheme in search of a more cosmological media ecology. Recognizing that humans represent only one of the cosmos' many forms of communicative being, and that the storage, transmission, and transformation of meaning occur at every scale—from the quantum to the geological to the galactic—new theoretical perspectives on and practical interventions into the study of media as environment and environments as media open up. Becoming conscious of a communicative cosmos has profound technological, ecological, and theological implications. (Segall 2019, 240)

Such attention to communicative transaction, at multiple levels of prehensive integration, contextual emergence, and semiosis is just the beginning to transform the many possibilities of understanding information and communicative action, from the individual level to the cosmos (via local-global effects as discussed in chapter 2).

NOTES

1. Concerning another type of inference to higher-level context, Joe Rosen points out that "the *anthropic principle* states . . . that the existence of *Homo sapiens* may, within the framework of science, serve as an explanation" (Rosen 2010, 123). Some scholars have proposed that the anthropic principle can be usefully applied for inferences about fundamental origins and cosmology. However, physicist Joe Rosen argues that, besides having a tendency for circularity, such explanations have both subjective and objective difficulties (ibid. 126).

2. Based on extensive research into scholarship during the Latin age and the origin of semiotics, John Deely concluded that "the decisive development in this regard was the privileged achievement of John Poinsot, a student with the Conimbricenses [referring here to the *Collegium Conimbricenses*, Jesuits of the University of Coimbra in Portugal], and the successor, after a century, to Soto's own teaching position at the University of Alcalá de Henares. With a single stroke of genius resolving the controversies, since Boethius, over the interpretation of relative being in the categorial scheme of Aristotle, Poinsot (1632 . . .) [in *Tractatus de Signis*—Treatise on Signs] was able to provide semiotics with a unified object conveying the action of signs both in nature virtually and in experience actually" (Deely 1990, 112).

Chapter 6

Complex Whole

MY VISION AND THE *LOGOI* FRAMEWORK

My vision builds on the central elements of the *Logoi* framework (process, logic, relations), combined with local-global relations and the actuality-*potentiae* distinction (corresponding to Boolean and non-Boolean logics, respectively). I have built on this framework (developed in chapters 1–3) to address various aspects of causation, emergence, and complex systems (chapter 4) and information and semiotics (chapter 5). In this chapter on the "Complex Whole," I apply the *Logoi* framework to a set of topics and concepts that are pointers to a fully integrative scheme.

Beginning in a rather human-centric manner, I set up story lines that are both personal, broadly human, and cosmic. I briefly survey the current geologic transition from the Holocene era to the anthropocene era, of which the latter is partly driven by the global impacts of *Homo sapiens*. By some accounts, such as standard materialism and epiphenomenalism, humans have no responsibility because the very concepts of meaning and ethics lack a substantive basis. In contrast, I argue in a section on transformative thinking and ethics that the *Logoi* framework can provide the needed substantive basis. However, the underlying context for such discourse requires a grounding; for this, I address the need for a systematic philosophical framework (whether the *Logoi* framework or some other equivalent framework), and an unrestricted universe of discourse. Key elements (both ontological and epistemological factors) of such a systematic framework are summarized. Scales and hierarchies of the natural world are then surveyed, both synchronic and diachronic. Standard "big histories" (or equivalent) typically presume some form of particularism (or substance philosophy). Here we focus on how process-oriented ontologies can provide realistic interpretations without particularism. This is followed by a section on a theory of relations based on category theory, which is an algebra of relations.

The *Logoi* framework is based on recent scientific and philosophic developments, primarily since the turn of the millennium, but has exceptional resonances with key insights articulated by Alfred North Whitehead almost a century ago. Many books that attempt to cover the "whole shebang" often focus on physical cosmology and/or "particle" physics. After summarizing the measurement problem at extremes of scale, I conclude that available scientific knowledge of the universe as a whole is not sufficiently mature for philosophical work. Furthermore, all objectives of the current work can be achieved without confronting unsettled questions of physical cosmology. After that, I note some open questions in contemporary biology and evolutionary theory, and call attention to recent progress toward a new semiotic biology, followed by a brief review of complex systems and anticipatory systems. I end the chapter by reviewing multiple perspectives on the whole and address limitations of standard approaches to Big History or the Universe Story. In short, my survey of the complex whole begins with a very human perspective on our everyday world, then scales up via geological epochs, and finally scales out indefinitely through space plasmas; further details on scales and hierarchies will be addressed later in this chapter.

SCALING UP FROM OUR EVERYDAY WORLD

We have seen in chapter 5 how research in biosemiotics, complex dynamical systems, and anticipatory systems substantially add to evolutionary resources in helping to understand human evolution. The processes of evolution are overall not random, and the slow step-by-step emergence of new structures enables evolution to achieve great complexity in the long term. As shown by David Bailey, creationist probability arguments that assume single-step structural creation (as with the alpha-globin molecules needed for oxygen transfer) are incorrect because they neglect the power of gradual step-by-step emergence (Bailey 2019). At the same time, standard evolutionary arguments about probabilities of complex evolution still fall far short of what is needed if they do not take into consideration new results in complex and anticipatory systems.

Although the evolution of an intelligent bipedal mammal might be considered likely overall given evolutionary resources since the dinosaur extinction event 66 million years ago, the likelihood of the emergence of our particular species, *Homo sapiens*, is exceedingly small, and the likelihood of any particular person being born at any time is astronomically small. Such a statement is entirely compatible with evolution; here I am simply focusing on the radical contingence of any given individual. Any very small fragment of a near infinite set of past contingencies demonstrates this point. I would not be here writing this book if I had hit my car break one second later some twenty years ago, if one of my parents had become ill the day of my conception, if my tenth great-grandmother had married someone else, if my fiftieth great-grandfather died in his youth instead of having children; the list goes on indefinitely. In spite of such highly improbable facts and radical contingency, we humans nevertheless enjoy life, are intelligent and can read challenging books like this one—what a miracle—and yet we scarcely notice.

We have a hard time conceiving in any visceral way the scale of anything that is out of the range of direct experience. Thus, for example, relative to a fixed position between the Earth and moon, the Earth's surface is moving at about 28 kilometer/second (or 1,037 miles/hour), the Earth overall revolves around the Sun at a speed of about 30 kilometers/second, and relative to the rest frame[1] of the microwave background radiation, we are zipping along at 370 kilometers/second; compare these speeds to a typical airliner's cruising speed of only 15 kilometers/second or the typical 45 kilometers/second speed of a bullet. Yet in a given vehicle, without new acceleration, we are stable within our new frame of reference. In truth, we are able to witness and experience a rather limited range of speeds and accelerations. The speed of light at 299,792 kilometers/second is truly an abstract concept, beyond our direct experience, however well we can enjoy the warmth of sunlight. Our direct experience of different scales is similarly very limited. The scales of humans and their artifacts are typically less than 1 kilometer, Earth's circumference is 40,000 kilometers, and the distance to the moon is 382,500 kilometers on average. Solar system distances begin to be only abstract notions with the distance to the Sun being about 150 million kilometers. Such scales are calculable but, arguably, not available for direct experience. The human impulse to understand global realities of various kinds is hardly new. In Europe, the printing press has spread knowledge via the written word for more than 550 years. For approximately 150 of those years, the Plantin-Moretus printers of Antwerp[2] grew prosperous by holding the printing contract for the Spanish crown, publishing information about the Spanish empire's "discoveries" of Central and South America. Unfortunately, beyond the immediate confines of family, village, and local culture, people have a hard time grappling with encounters with radically different cultures. Seeking and distributing printed information was a limited attempt to handle that need. Arguably, frequent failures to properly understand and meet the challenges posed by more expansive contacts with other peoples, along with colonization, and more broadly human greed and lust for power, have been major drivers toward continuing strife and wars over the centuries.

Our limited ability to grasp or directly experience speeds and scales correlates with our inability to fully appreciate any physical process that functions primarily beyond the scale or scope of our immediate experience such as, for example, the long-term impacts of climate change. To some degree, scientific models and simulations play an essential role in helping us overcome the above conceptual gaps in perceiving speed, scale, long-range planning, etc. Such research work is never perfect and always involves modeling, testing, and approximation, and the recognition of error. Working to offset such limitations is an important part of what enables science and technology to be so successful in its applications. Yet humans sometimes strain to accept the insights that science enables. Our inadvertent initiation of the anthropocene era[3] is a dramatic and dangerous case in point.

FROM THE HOLOCENE ERA TO
THE ANTHROPOCENE ERA

The geological epoch that began with the last glacial period about 10,000 BCE is called the Holocene era. Unknowing, I experienced its direct effects when, year after year, I helped my father remove rocks, rocks, and yet more rocks from fields on our western Minnesota farm, which were initially part of the shoreline of ancient glacial lake Agassiz. Indeed, those rocks were signs of such glaciation! As I grew up, I became increasingly aware of a wider world with its ever-expanding webs of relations. Only gradually did I also become self-aware of the human impact on that wider world. Similarly, human civilization is only now beginning to gain cultural and physical self-awareness of its global influence, both culturally and physically.

In *Earth in Human Hands*, David Grinspoon lays out the broader historical and scientific context of this emerging anthropocene era (Grinspoon 2016). An important way to understand planet Earth is through systematic comparison of different planetary systems. With such tools in hand, Grinspoon's focus is on the emerging new field of astrobiology, which is fueled by groundbreaking discoveries about extraterrestrial planets (e.g., geysers on Jovian moons; water on Mars, etc.), which enable him to place our precious planet in context of other planets and their environments. For our particular planet Earth, many scientists agree that a new era has begun. As stated by Will Steffen and colleagues, "The human imprint on the global environment has now become so large and active that it rivals some of the great forces of Nature in its impact on the functioning of the Earth system" (Steffen et al. 2011, 842). In addition to gradual geological impacts, *Homo sapiens* have collectively impacted Earth's climate in ways that are increasingly irreversible; such is already indicated in the accelerating frequency, worldwide, of extreme weather events as have been documented by Spencer Weart (2008) and Gary Braasch (2007) among others.

Now that a human presence has been fully global for the last few centuries, and that more recently we are acutely feeling the limits of planet Earth, some have looked increasingly outward. Since the beginning of the space age over sixty years ago, humans have ventured out, primarily via robotic spacecraft, to explore the solar system. While Earthly frontiers have largely vanished, the frontiers of space are effectively infinite. Space exploration now actively includes the study of extraterrestrial biological systems, and this research has confirmed the presence of complex organic molecules in space that can serve as building blocks for life. Historian Steven Dick, in *The Biological Universe* (1999), reviews the twentieth-century extraterrestrial life debate and features the new field of astrobiology and its implications.

FROM FLUIDS TO PLASMAS

The "space age" began with the first orbiting satellites, Sputnik in October 1957 and then Explorer I in January 1958. James Van Allen of the University of Iowa designed and built the only scientific instrument for Explorer I, which became the first satellite carrying a scientific instrument. (Sputnik only contained a transmitter.) As data first arrived, Van Allen's colleague exclaimed "My God, space is radioactive!" This discovery of Earth's radiation belts (often called Van Allen belts) soon led to several discoveries of space plasmas: the solar wind with its complex dynamical effects and structures, various planetary magnetospheres, including Earth's magnetosphere with its complex structure (upper ionosphere, thermosphere, plasma sheet, plasma boundary layers, etc.). In turn, in a synergistic combination of remote sensing observations and direct in situ observations, made newly possible by unmanned satellites sent throughout the solar system, the past sixty-plus research years have revolutionized our understanding of space plasmas and space environments, which in turn impacts our understanding of all stellar and galactic systems, thus impacting all of astronomy. Modern astronomy comprises three main fields: planetary science, astrophysics, and space physics, the last focused for now on solar system studies where *in situ* observations are currently possible, such direct observations thus far limited to its heliophysics subset.

Setting aside speculations about dark energy and dark matter, which (if they exist) are not directly visible, plasmas comprise more than 99 percent of visible matter in the universe, primarily stars, stellar, and galactic environments. Additionally, plasmas permeate intergalactic space, although these regions are generally not directly visible and only inferred. Here I define *plasmas* as an interactive combination of electromagnetic fields, neutral and charged particles that can carry a current and exhibit collective effects.[4] Other than neutral solids, the primary dominantly occurring natural systems (setting aside more than thirty special "states of matter") are fluid systems and electromagnetic/plasma systems, the former modeled by Navier-Stokes formalism, the latter modeled by Maxwell-Boltzmann formalism. The common reference only to the three states of matter as solids-liquid-gas is highly misleading because it drops out the fourth state of matter—plasmas. The standard reference to plasmas in astronomy as simply "gas" is similarly misleading because it drops out reference to electrodynamics and plasma processes that can lead to results very different from the conventional fluid approximation in which plasmas are simply treated as electrified gas. Only in recent years has the sub-field of astrophysical plasmas just begun to overcome this problematic simplification.[5] Arguably, such misleading reductions have their origin, in part, with substance metaphysics and the subsequent neglect of fields, non-linear effects, and multiscale interactions. Working out the consequences and possibilities of these complexities for many areas of science is only just beginning. For example, the implications of nonlinear dynamics for many applications only began after the advent of supercomputers in the 1970s. The vast majority of scientific discoveries to be made in this first millennia of applying the scientific method (with its rudimentary sixteenth-century beginnings) are almost certainly in the future, not the past.

ON CHOICE AND DECISION MAKING

Based on the Relational Reality model, I have discussed in chapter 2 how both specific actualizations and individuation arise from fundamental quantum process, which is grounded in both physical causal and logical causal orders as well as *potentiae*. Multiple levels and scales of hierarchies emerge and provide a vast array of emergent possibilities (see *Scales and Hierarchies* below). Although rudimentary selection occurs at the quantum level, anything resembling basic self-reflective choice only occurs at high levels of biological complexity. In chapter 5, we summarized four basic thresholds that, in the *Logoi* framework, build on the concepts of process, *potentiae*, local-global, and triadic relations (input-output-context): (1) information threshold; (2) semiotic threshold; (3) epistemic threshold; and (4) cultural threshold.

I hypothesize that meaningful basic choice can emerge above the semiotic threshold in a way that is consistent with contemporary biosemiotics research. At the most basic level, choice here denotes self-reflective capability for selections among alternative possibilities in response to some basic problem of evolutionary survival. Such basic choice goes beyond mere chance and habitual stimulus-response dyadic logic by including the triadic of input-output-environment along with some capacity for antici-patory action (see *Biosemiotics and Anticipatory Systems* in chapter 5). Clearly any object can be part of some value proposition (e.g., the value of trees in the forest as part of my affirmation of a park's value); however, only high-level biological creatures, having passed the semiotic threshold, can participate in meaningful semiotic choices (sign-meaning-code). For example, dogs and many other animals share information, through signed behaviors, about impending danger. In most cases, what we mean by human choice goes beyond the epistemic threshold, which includes interpretive semiosis. Reference to psyche (mind) typically indicates a capability that goes beyond the semiotic threshold if not also the epistemic threshold. For this reason, the *Logoi* framework is not a pan-psychism in that it does not require reference to lower-level mind-like capabilities although the *Logoi* framework is arguably pan-experiential in that it affirms some elemental selective processes as pervasive.

ON TRANSFORMATIVE THINKING AND ETHICAL DECISION MAKING

Our *Logoi* framework affirms a basis for meaning and values in a way con-sistent with a fundamental triadic structure of relation highlighted by environ-mental ethicist Brian Henning.

> Every entity is self-important *and* important to the universe . . . everything that in any sense exists has intrinsic value...which includes having instrumental value, and religious value. This axiological triad of self, other, and whole cap-tures the essence of Whitehead's unique sense of intrinsic value. To have intrin-sic value is (1) to have incorporated the values of others (concrescence), (2) to subsequently become a (instrumental) value for others (principle of relativity), and (3) thereby to contribute to the value experience of the whole, that is, for God. (Henning 2005, 63)

This fundamental triadic structure of relation correlates with the funda-mental triadic structures of our *Logoi* framework, viz., input-output-context, among others, at multiple levels, without limit, from local context to ultimate context. This contrasts with the nihilism of standard materialist views.

> The very concept of something with intrinsic value is unintelligible for the mate-rialist . . . without an objective ground for value, questions of axiology become a matter of social and political convention; that is to say, the locus and scope of value is completely relative . . . a function of particular agents' interests . . . For

Hume, how something *is* tells us nothing about how it *ought* to be. (Henning 2005, 18–19)

G. E. Moore has called this dictum of Hume the "naturalistic fallacy," which has become a straitjacket for ethical theory over the past century. However, Henning continues,

Moore's very notion of a purely nonrelational property is unintelligible . . . According to the organic model being defended, since there are [considered ultimately] no independent, substantial individuals, there can be no properties that could inhere in these substances, whether relational or nonrelational. This also entails the repudiation of Moore's so-called naturalistic fallacy. For, as we have seen, at the heart of the philosophy of organism is the rejection of the view that there is such a thing as a mere fact or a vacuous actuality. (Henning 2005, 59)

There are many possible routes to the needed transformative thinking: political, religious, psychological, social; although many aspects of these are part of the problem, all of these facets of human affairs need to be part of the solution. Many standard worldviews that contribute to our current problems presuppose substance thinking, strong determinism, mechanistic materialism, reductionism, and various forms of false dualities. The *Logoi* framework provides a way (or at least opens a way) to better articulate foundational concepts and understandings that can aid such transformative thinking.

There is always hopefulness in possibility and a sense of meaning—aspects of reality that go beyond any and all scientific frameworks (see chapter 8). As noted by John Haught, some hopeful and anticipatory readings of the book of nature are both realistic and pragmatic.

The way of anticipation, consistently informed by the discoveries of science, trusts that a full encounter with what is really real can happen only through an unflagging expectation of what is not-yet. Anticipation reads the universe as having always had the prospect of becoming more than it is or has been . . . The deepest happiness humans can experience here and now in an unfinished universe, therefore, is anticipation itself. (Haught 2017, 185)

In contrast to this way of anticipation—of hope, hopelessness creates a self-fulfilling prophecy, which could undermine human survival during the coming global climate crisis which, as highlighted by Griffin, is being made increasingly worse by human ignorance, greed, war, and inaction (Griffin 2015).

As humankind embarks on this new anthropocene era, with something like the *Logoi* framework in mind, we need to evaluate the full range of history and context, both local and global, and then decide collaboratively on the best possibilities (given the full range of given facts and constraints) for responsible action toward the common good. Because such choices and action are imbedded in reality, both the actual and the possible, they are not just epiphenomena, but have a certain reality. Insofar as such choices and action reflect ethical considerations and options, then ethics itself is "real," not just some disembodied universal (as claimed by nominalists—see beginning of chapter 4), but as a framework of specific *potentia*—relations concerning real alternatives in ethical choice and action.

THEMATIZING AN UNRESTRICTED UNIVERSE OF DISCOURSE

By envisioning various levels of the complex whole, in no way do I claim to achieve some God's eye view from outside that complex whole;[6] after all, in that case the whole would fail to be inclusive because it would not include the hypothetical observer. In a very fundamental way, this problem cannot be addressed by science alone (being the way of numbers, context-independent models, and actualized (Boolean) measurement results) and is, at least in significant measure, a philosophical problem, or even a metaphysics problem involving ultimate context. As an example of the type of philosophical analysis required for this fundamental question, and other deep metaphysical problems, see the two major works by Lorenz Puntel, *Structure and Being* (2008) and *Being and God* (2012) including an integrative summary by Alan White (2014).

Nathan Strunk's review of White and Puntel's work captures some essential points as follows:

The structural-systematic philosophy is a [philosophical] theory of everything because it thematizes the unrestricted universe of discourse, not a restricted universe of discourse (as does for example physics). Rejecting theoretical frameworks that relate their semantics and ontologies solely to subject-predicate sentences, it takes its semantic and ontological bearings instead from sentences of the form "It's such-and-suching"—the structure found in, for example, "It's raining" and "It's morning"—which [White and Puntel denote as] "sentencings." This forms the basis of White's theory of truth. Alluding to Tarski's 1933 definition, "a true sentence is one that says that the state of affairs is so and so, and the state of affairs indeed is so and so," White argues against deflationist accounts of truth in favor of a significantly revised—or better stated, a significantly reframed—version of correspondence theory . . . Not only does the confluence of "propositionings" and "factings" in White's theory of truth avoid problems arising from subject/predicate frameworks of correspondence theory, but it relies on an ontology that departs from what White calls "thing or substance ontologies." (Strunk 2014, 346)

In addition to the problems with substance frameworks, the so-called Theories of Everything, promoted by certain scientists based on scientific tools alone, are doomed to failure because they are working with a restricted universe of discourse (sometimes limited further to that subset of discourse called scientism)—indeed, besides often presuming a substance framework, these more limited frameworks are often working with only the actualist hypothesis, which fails to acknowledge the non-Boolean order and landscapes of *potentiae*, and thus are incomplete even as science; for added critique, see *Science and Myth* by Wolfgang Smith (2012).

In summary, there are both fundamental ontological and epistemological factors within an unrestricted universe of discourse, as follows:

Fundamental ontological factors:
- Mode of being/becoming—contingent and non-contingent;
- Logical orders—non-Boolean and Boolean; *potentiae* and actualizations;
- Extensive connection (prior to metrical relations[7])—local-global, category theory;
- Quantum process—diachronic focus—prehension, succession, symmetry breaking, causation/actualization;
- Emergence—synchronic focus—multiple levels with grounding, semiosis/triadicity;

Fundamental epistemological factors:
- Modes of perception—presentational immediacy/causal efficacy; physics/semiotics;
- Ways of Knowing—numbers/science, context/semiosis, ultimate context/spirit.

Arguably, the most fundamental ontological orders are that of the contingent and the non-contingent; many standard accounts simply presuppose only the former, but systematic philosophical argument indicates that claim to be false. For this issue, see chapters 5 and 8 of Puntel's *Structure and Being* (2008) as well as arguments based on Hartshorne's work by Dombrowski (2017), and Viney and Shields (2020), all discussed further in chapter 8. Consequently, I hypothesize, as part of the *Logoi* framework, that there is necessarily a non-contingent dimension of being/becoming that encompasses the above fundamental ontological factors; that is, the fact of these ontological factors as such are aspects of non-contingent being/becoming and are aspects of reality that could not be fully non-existent. Further, this argument is necessarily a philosophical argument and transcends any particular set of scientific propositions. Logician George Shields has noted that this contingent/non-contingent argument is arguably one of the most rigorous examples of an argument that is necessarily a philosophical one that is not reducible to a scientific argument—an exemplar of the failure of scientism (George Shields, personal communication, 2016).

A more Peircean way to conceive of the above fundamental factors is to incorporate both the contingent and non-contingent, and the Boolean and non-Boolean orders, with three levels of reality, vis-à-vis the Peircean triad. For examples, levels tentatively deployed for the *Logoi* framework are as follows: (1) (non-Boolean) order of *potentiae* (modally "present in process, and future")—Peirce's first; (2) (Boolean) order of actualization (modally past and actualized present)—Peirce's second; (3) ordering principles—Peirce's third—fundamental relationships; some contingent, some non-contingent.[8] With this framing, meaning is enabled through multiple levels of context, and the interrelated combination of three basic questions framed by Bradley: the nature of origin, difference, and order. These questions and their answers, respectively, are associated primarily with (1) the concepts of *potentiae*, the non-contingent and ultimates; (2) succession, quantum process, and *actualization* (diachronic) along with extension and multilevel emergence (synchronic); and (3) multilevel constraints on *potentiae* to yield physical relations (law), including local-global relations, and ultimate context. As Nicholas Rescher states, "To achieve a synoptically ultimate explanation of the domain of contingent existence/reality, we thus have to shift to another domain of deliberation altogether—and move outside of the evidential *realm of what is* to the normative *realm of what ought to be*, that is from actuality to value . . . from actuality to possibility" (Rescher 2017, 16). Given that, as Rescher states it, "context determines meaning" (Rescher 2017, 37), the above linkages of meaning and value fit well with the passages above from Brian Henning about the importance of questions of axiology. Further discussion of the concept of "meaning" is taken up in chapter 8.

It is within the scope of my integrative efforts, but unfortunately beyond my current means, to carry out a careful inter-comparison of the *Logoi* framework with other fully integrative frameworks such as that of perennial philosophy, Ken Wilber's *Integral Theory*, or Roy Bhaskar's new axial vision. For such inter-comparison, I recommend *A Complex Integral Realist Perspective* by Paul Marshall (2016). Another major effort toward an unrestricted domain of discourse is that provided by White (2014) and Puntel (2008), yet even these impressive works are just a beginning to the awesome challenge posed to such integral theories. I offer the *Logoi* framework as yet another candidate of grand schema, but in a way that provides more scientific grounding than most other frameworks like those above that do not presuppose physicalism. In any case, in the unending process of conceiving such integrative schema, I submit that something like the above fundamental ontological and episte-mological factors need to be clearly identified and applied with the ultimate goal, as articulated by Alfred North Whitehead: "Speculative Philosophy is the endeavor to frame a coherent, logical, necessary system of general ideas in terms of which every element of our experience can be interpreted" (Whitehead 1978, 3).

One important function of an integrative framework is to articulate a new narrative, an improved world view, well grounded in both science and humanistic scholarship, that can overcome the disenchantment of our secu-lar age as detailed by Charles Taylor (2007). In contrast with the prevailing inauthenticity of contemporary politics, Taylor argues that if we can succeed in being truly authentic, as people and as cultures, we may yet be able to enable a higher level of genuine fulfillment than that apparently achieved by a few in the pre-1500 age of enchantment. With similar scholarly depth to Taylor's, Thomas Pfau articulates numerous details on the "*de facto* loss of a differentiated and historically informed moral conception, and that the result has been a growing inarticulacy within humanistic inquiry and indeed the public sphere broadly speaking, which has rendered modern theories of agency and practical reason increasingly marginal and often incoher-ent" (Pfau 2015, 72). A deep intellectual backdrop for these problems of modernity is detailed in *Four Ages of Understanding* (Deely 2001), which outlines key developments with a focus on the *way of signs*—the semiotic perspective. Additional historical background for both successes and failures of modernity and the secular age are documented by Stephen Gaukroger in three volumes spanning 1210 to 1841 (Gaukroger 2006, 2010, 2016). Gare is less sanguine about possibilities for overcoming the failures of modern-ism. He paints a realistic, yet despairing portrait of the effects of modernity which, combined with unsustainable growth models, consumerism, and mili-tarism, steadily worsens the problems that so critically need to be addressed. As he concludes, Gare hails the heroes and heroines of the worldwide envi-ronmental movement who are

rising to the ultimate challenge of the age, and to the greatest challenge in human history. There is reason for hope that the future belongs to these people; but there is always the possibility of total failure, either of a World War which will obliterate all their efforts or the successful entrenchment of a global ruling class committed to augmenting their levels of consumption come what may. In taking up the challenge, in taking the courage to risk their careers, their security, and in some cases, their lives, environmentalists are proving that life is more than satisfying appetites, petty vanities and a grubby struggle for money and status. They are revealing through their own lives the significance of all life. In doing so they are creating a community transcending national boundaries, transcending the confrontation between East and West and between North and South, a community of all those who strive to live for what is highest in life. The gathering strength of this community will, hopefully, transform the world, creating the conditions for all life, human and non-human, to flourish. (Gare 1993, 431)

Gare further documents the struggle against nihilism in his more recent work *Philosophical Foundations of Ecological Civilization* (Gare, 2016), which highlights a speculative naturalism in its evolution from late Friedrich Schelling to contemporary process philosophy. I propose that the *Logoi* framework can be thought of as a possible way to further Gare's systematic project of speculative naturalism.

A fundamental choice in ontology is whether to adopt a unimodal or polymodal ontology—that is, are all "true" propositions about reality mappable to only one form of ultimate being/becoming (e.g., matter—or the "physical"— in a materialist (physicalist) vision), or are there two or more fundamental modes of being/becoming (e.g., Descartes's dualism of mind and matter; body and spirit as in many religious frameworks, etc.). After setting aside all past problematic dualisms, and failed reductionisms, we are still left with this difficult choice. As Iain Thomson argues, there is a continuing need to avoid traditional onto-theological ideologies (Thomson 2000) in contrast to evolving understandings of ultimate context/ground. In part, this is a requirement of good scholarship in which one considers any properly articulated problem or goal, evaluates possible hypotheses and approaches to solution, applies appropriate criteria and methods for testing between hypotheses, and then formulates a solution or conclusion, yet always as tentative in the unending efforts of scholarship. Such scholarly process (of which scientific methodology is a sub-set) does not directly deny propositions made in the affected disciplines, whether fundamental physics, cosmology, or theology, but such process does discourage claims to finality and the certainty of dogmatic claims, whether arising from atheism, scientism, or religion. Indeed, perhaps the Christian first commandment of "Thou shalt have no other gods before me" is a reminder of the need for humility before the radically inclusive non-contingent, the need to be cautious of claiming a God's eye view or any form of ultimate act (e.g., killing) in the name of some abstracted dogma. Within this perspective, decisions and acts of killing and war are arguably, by definition, anti-religious acts.

The issue of community is central to an essay by Grange who argues that our understanding of community needs a systematic metaphysics and semiotics. Inspired by Charles S. Peirce, he states that we need a "triadic semiotics that envisions an ever-deepening relation to reality through the pragmatic efficacy of the symbols used to understand the world of experience, natural and human. The difference that these signs are supposed to make can be seen as growth in intensity, integrity, wholeness, and depth. Each of these normative measures can be used to estimate the value of the level of communication that undergirds an actual human community" (Grange 1997b, 199). In contrast to movements toward nihilism, which lack a value dimension, Grange affirms the importance of values and here suggests ways to provide measures for healthy communities.

There are a number of integrative efforts that are, overall, set within a major school of thought. One example of special note is Søren Briers's *Cybersemiotics* (Brier 2013), which builds on Peircean semiotics and contemporary information theory to infer an inclusive integral framework in which human beings are:

1. Embodied and biologically situated—our body is the principal system for the manifestation of life and cognition;
2. Conscious and intentionally situated—consciousness is the source of an inner life of cognition, volition, feeling, and perceptual qualities (*qualia*);
3. Meaning-situated in cultural practice—that is, through language in a social and cultural activity with a network of other living, linguistic, conscious systems; and
4. Environmentally situated—in a nature or a universe that is partly independent of our perception and being (Brier 2013, 361–362).

Within the scholarly literature of process-relational thought, arising especially from the works of Alfred North Whitehead and Charles Hartshorne, there are many exemplary integrative efforts such as, for example, Auxier and Herstein's analysis of Whitehead's work. At the outset, they state that "our central idea is that *concrete existence explains the abstract aspects of experience* and not vice-versa" (Auxier and Herstein 2017, 2). Given the intrinsic limitations to attempts at generalization, Auxier and Herstein argue that "Whitehead found a way to secure our norm of self-limitation, while yet asking the profoundest question: given that there is no single method of generalizing from the unique event to its world, is there not, accessible to our imaginations and reasonings, a basic *unit* of explanation? . . .Whitehead answers in the affirmative. *That unit is the actual entity.* That is what we mean by calling it 'the quantum of explanation'" (Auxier and Herstein 2017, 6). For such systematic philosophy (at a metaphysical level of description), generalizing "actual entity" (or "dynamic particular" in Hartshorne's work) to a "quantum of explanation," instead of some exemplar of microphysical events, results in a productive reinterpretation of Whitehead's works that is compatible with our *Logoi* framework. This is because it explicitly builds on a theory of relations grounded in a mereotopological framework (in contemporary scientific parlance, "category theory"—an algebra of relations) that highlights both fundamental quantum process (via the Whiteheadian concepts of prehension, concrescence, and transition) and extensive connection, and which incorporates pre-space local-global connections (see section below on *A Theory of Relations for Modeling and Process—Category Theory*).

Overall, my *Logoi* framework, at this stage, simply calls attention to such integrative works as briefly mentioned above—very much more such scholarly work is needed. The integrative works that appear to be most helpful for the *Logoi* framework, in addition to scientific inputs, arise primarily from process philosophy, semiotics, phenomenology, pragmatism, and systematic philosophy, especially in the tradition of Schelling-Peirce-Whitehead.

In summary, any proposed grand synthesis requires a highly multidisciplinary approach. The *ways of knowing* to be incorporated need to go beyond just the way of numbers (focus on context-independence, and quantitative representation) as with some claimed theories of everything (most often presuming a science-only approach). A more inclusive framing would be to include the way of context that, in turn, includes the way of signs (semiotics). Finally, to truly incorporate an unrestricted domain of discourse, the way of spirit is needed to incorporate the reality of ultimate boundaries, ultimacies, and spiritual experience (see chapter 8).

SCALES AND HIERARCHIES

A very engaging short video is "Powers of 10" by Charles and Ray Eames (1977) that dramatically evokes the relative size of things in the universe.[9] It depicts a multiscale snapshot of things from sub-microscopic realms to extra-galactic scales. Although based on many good science findings, this 9-minute video has some serious limitations, both scientific and philosophical. The video leaves out any indication of space plasmas, which are known to permeate all space environments from planetary and stellar scale to galactic scale and beyond. Vast domains of "empty" space are depicted even though contemporary space physics research falsifies such a claim, however common such may be implicit in astronomy educational materials. Even more problematic, however, is the subtle suggestion made concerning the meaningfulness of some unlimited God's eye view, a snapshot freeze of process, deploying a substance-only description. This dramatic video, however, remains as merely a snapshot like the treasured one of my daughter leaving for her first day of school. It is a special snapshot for me because of all that it reminds me about. It's an icon—a semiotic carrier, dramatically limited compared to the history and process of the real person.

The Eames's video, however dramatic, simply spatializes the world, leaving out vast domains of the between (space plasmas and more), and reinforces our tendency toward spatializing processes, and focuses attention on mere descriptions of actualized things versus the more difficult, indeed more scientific, effort of understanding multiscale processes and evolution, including both the actual and *potentiae*.

Combining the results of modern science with Peircean biosemiotics, Søren Brier has shown how a combined information and semiotic (cybersemiotic) framework operates with five levels of reality, which are adapted here for the *Logoi* framework.

1. *potentia—non-Boolean*: "A primary chaotic level of continuity, quality and potentiality with a tendency to take habits (Firstness). This goes beyond the physical conception of vacuum fields that are still purely materialistic, but may be included as an aspect."
2. *actualizations*—Boolean: "A 'causal' level of matter, energy and causality by natural forces. This is Secondness that has, as its inner aspect, will and mental force."
3. "An *informational cybernetic system level* [italics added] of informational signals, which encompasses the goal-oriented mechanical systems described by first order classical cybernetics."
4. "The *semiotic level* [italics added] belonging to all living systems (biosemiotics), which are so far the only systems capable of true triadic semiosis (producing signification spheres in sign games)."
5. "The *level of conscious languaging systems* [italics added] (language games, arguments), to our knowledge so far only occupied by humans.

Sign-making is thus immanent in nature, but only manifest in full triadic semiosis in living systems." Quoted passages are from Brier (2010, 715–716).

The Eames's video captures only a snapshot component of the causal level number 2; however, it is important to recognize the limitations of such eye-catching snapshots. More substantial portions of level 2, and materialistic aspects of levels 3 to 5, are retained in many standard ontologies that treat the world as being sufficiently characterized via the way of numbers. Although these ontologies are often highly practical and scientifically based, all too frequently such approaches encourage a hegemony of the way of numbers, thus inadvertently promoting a simplistic scientism. Examples of this include, among others, works by Edward O. Wilson (1998), Mario Bunge (1977), and Roger Penrose (2005). As well, many works of "Big History" fall into this category. These works can be excellent and helpful, but when framed as representing the entirety of reality, such frameworks can become problematic distortions by neglecting triads versus dyads, by neglecting the semiotic dimension, or by neglecting ways beyond that of numbers, and so on.

As an example of what can be dropped out, consider *The Road to Reality: A Complete Guide to the Laws of the Universe* (Penrose 2005) which, instead of being "complete," omits direct reference to middle scales. A critique of such a standard view is provided, with technical details, by Hans Goedbloed and Stefaan Poedts (2004, 23–24). Most standard approaches all tend to presume a space-time monadism. For example, Einstein's general theory of relativity is often laid out as sheets of space-time substance[10] with discrete properties at each space-time grid point, which then constitute a convenient basis for mapping to computer simulations. However, although very useful for modeling purposes, such simple mereological (part-whole) linear causal frameworks are inevitably incomplete, simply objectual approaches to levels of reality. Roberto Poli shows how such an approach to levels of reality, often based on a structurally reductionist account, is entirely inadequate for philosophical purposes due to the neglect of multilevel relations and categorical overlaps, and thus, instead, a categorical approach is needed (Poli 2001). Basarab Nicolescu also addresses levels of reality in a non-reductive manner (Nicolescu 2011). A simple categorical approach is exemplified by the extensive schema created by Nicolai Hartmann, one of the most ambitious to date (Hartmann 2013). Extending and properly updating Hartmann's ontological and categorical schema, or some comparable schema for levels of reality, is a future task. For now, the most extensive, effective schema that we currently have available is epistemological framings that enable contemporary online library catalogs and database search algorithms. Fully handling the semiosphere (the spheres of mind, language, and culture) with contemporary information systems is yet a work in progress, as Logan points out, especially due to the requirements of semantic (meaningful) information (Logan 2014).Various descriptive efforts have been carried out to capture the whole, from the "universe story" as portrayed by Brian Swimme (1994), along with Mary Evelyn Tucker (2014), to David Christian's Big History (Christian, 2019). Although much of these descriptive efforts have just epistemological import; nevertheless, as indicated by Poli, the very fact of levels of reality does have ontological significance (Poli 2001). Certainly there are distinct hierarchical levels in the universe, such as the sequence provided by Ellis, who lists ten levels each for ordinary matter and life, respectively (Ellis 2016, 88).

TWO BASIC TYPES OF HIERARCHICAL STRUCTURES, COMPOSITIONAL (SYNCHRONIC) AND SUBSUMPTIVE (DIACHRONIC)

Stanley Salthe provides a methodology for representing hierarchies that is completely general and utilizes standard set theory part-whole notation, as follows [whole[part]]. The two hierarchy sequences below arise by applying Salthe's part-whole notation to the hierarchies outlined by Ellis.

> *ordinary matter hierarchy*:
> [cosmology[astronomy[space science[Earth science[materials science[physical chemistry[atomic physics[nuclear physics[particle physics[fundamental theory][11]]]]]]]]]];

> *matter/life hierarchy*:
> [sociology[psychology[physiology[cell biology[biochemistry[chemistry[atomic physics[nuclear physics[particle physics[fundamental theory]]]]]]]]]]

Complementary to such scalar hierarchies is a *temporal hierarchy*:
[time since "Big Bang" ($\sim 10^{17}$s) [human lifetime ($\sim 10^9$s) [human consciousness ($\sim 10^0$s)
[period of atom ($\sim 10^{-15}$s) [elementary particle (10^{-25}s) [fundamental pre-events ($\sim 10^{-43}$s)]]]]]]
This temporal hierarchy is adapted from Geoffrey Chew (2004, 87).

In addition to clear linkages and overlaps between such levels, there is a minimum set of levels. For example, for life systems, as Ellis explains,

> emergence of complexity such as life requires a reverse of flow of information, from bottom-up only to also including a flow from the environment down . . . This reverse flow is needed because adaptive selection causes adaptations of the organism to the environment: but this cannot happen unless information flows down from the environment into the organism, where it alters both structure and behavior . . . it is clear that the selection mechanisms in operation can only be of a multilevel kind, because there simply is no direct link from the adaptive environment to either neurons or genes. (Ellis 2016, 181)

Ellis points out as well that for the hierarchy [ecosystem [group [individual [organ [cell [genotype [gene]]]]]]], there are top-down environmental effects affecting the first four levels, and individual-induced effects affecting the last four levels (Ellis 2016, 182).

In evaluating possibilities for a broader framing of the problem of ontology and of universals, Michael Loux has described more than ten different possible positions for understanding "familiar concrete particulars" (Loux 2017, 29). Nicolai Hartmann developed a very comprehensive ontology that filled out a four-volume series, the second volume of which is *Possibility and Actuality*.

> This ground-breaking work traces the historical development of philosophical concepts of possibility and necessity, discussing differences between

the real and ideal spheres . . . Hartmann described the logical relations . . . between the modes of possibility, actuality, and necessity, defining the intermodal laws that govern these relations. (Hartmann 2013, 4; from the translater's preface)

Nicolescu is one of the few scholars to properly appreciate Hartmann's great achievement, and he builds on it, along with a 1942 manuscript of Heisenberg's, in developing an integrated approach to a unified theory of levels, which he terms "transdisciplinarity." As part of his realist ontology, Nicolescu highlights the role of a third between subject and object.

The role of the Hidden Third and of the included middle in the transdisciplinary approach to Reality is, after all, not so surprising. The words three and the prefix trans have the same etymological root: "three" means "the transgression of two, what goes beyond two." Transdisciplinarity means transgression of duality, opposing binary pairs: subject-object, subjectivity-objectivity, matter-consciousness, nature-divinity, simplicity-complexity, reductionism-holism, diversity-unity. This duality is transcended by the open unity that encompasses both the universe and the human being. (Nicolescu 2015, 209)

The importance of incorporating triads instead of just dyads has been brought out above in chapter 5 on *Information and Semiotics*. While Nicolescu documents the importance of Peirce's semiotics (Nicolescu 2015, 114–118), he especially highlights the work of Stéphane Lupasco with respect to issues of logic and the included third (Nicolescu 2015, 125–127). For our purposes, however, we look principally to the earlier sources of this advance laid out by Deely, who traces the genesis of triadic thinking and semiosis from the medieval period (especially John Poinsot's work of 1632) to Charles S. Peirce's 1867 rediscovery of this tradition (Deely 2001).

In chapter 4, we covered various aspects of causation and emergence, and their complementary relationship. A concise summary could be, as Jonathan Schaffer expresses it, that "grounding is something like metaphysical causation. Roughly speaking, just as causation links the world across time, grounding links the world across levels" (Schaffer 2012, 122). This quote effectively says, as argued here, that causation is basically diachronic whereas grounding, and emergence, are synchronic in focus. Both causation and grounding here necessarily involve a triadic relation—again, that for any input-output dyad there is always some associated triad of input-output-context. Scott Kelso and David Engstrom provide many examples of dyads in their work *The Complementary Nature* (Kelso and Engstrom 2006) and, in my view, for each example they provide, there is always an appropriate triad; if nothing else, context represents the third component.

As for the fields of physics, biology, and semiotics, which weave together dyads, triads, causation, and levels of reality, Kalevi Kull notes that it is useful to consider how "biosemiotics means the study of living systems that interprets these as sign systems, or communicative structures, and involves the description and analysis of various organic codes (e.g., epigenetic, genetic, behavioural codes, including intracellular, intercellular, and interorganismic codes)" (Kull 2007, 175). With this in mind, as Hoffmeyer frames it, "Rather than understanding biology as a separate layer 'between' physics and semiotics, we should then see biology as a science of the interface in which these two sciences meets, an interface in which we study the origin and evolution of sign processes, semiosis" (Hoffmeyer 1997b, 362).

The scale-free characteristic of some basic physical processes (e.g., interactions at multiple scales in space plasma physics) and multilevel fundamental process reflected in Whitehead's process, as characterized by Auxier and Herstein in *The Quantum of Explanation*(Auxier and Herstein 2017), are both reflected in arguments made for a flat ontology (without hierarchy) by Justus Buchler in his *Metaphysics of Natural Complexes* (Buchler 1989), Stephen David Ross in *Transition to an Ordinal Metaphysics* (Ross 1980), William Wimsatt in *Re-Engineering Philosophy for Limited Beings* (Wimsatt 2007), and Lawrence Cahoone in *The Orders of Nature* (Cahoone 2014), or even a one category ontology as suggested by L. A. Paul (2013). Nevertheless, our given world exhibits a hierarchical framework in both temporal and spatial scales as detailed especially by Salthe in his hierarchy theory (Salthe 1985). The primary difference in the above two perspectives is that of a focus on diachronic process, which enables univocity in the quanta of explanation (*à la* Auxier and Herstein), thus a reduction in ontology, versus a focus on synchronic process whereby multiple temporal and spatial scales are considered as basic, thus a hierarchy. The *Logoi* framework works with both of these perspectives, involving both monistic and pluralistic framings, which can be both unitary in fundamental quantum process (diachronic, including linkage to highly interrelated non-Boolean *potentiae*) and radically plural in the realms of Boolean actualizations, indeed plural in both specific actualizations and unbounded hierarchies of such.

As another perspective on this issue, Salthe argues for two hierarchical frameworks for complexity generation in natural systems: "(a) a synchronic system, extensional complexity, of wholes and parts, with the levels having dynamics separated by about an order of magnitude, and (b) a diachronic system, intensional complexity, with each higher level entraining all lower ones" (Salthe 2006, 99). I infer from this quote that Salthe's use of "diachronic system" is part of his hierarchical frameworks of natural systems, focused on the logic of Boolean actualizations, and is distinct from the more fundamental diachronic quantum process that I have discussed above in association with the *Logoi* framework. Salthe continues

(a) The *extensional complexity* framework, modeled by the scale hierarchy . . . as in the nested hierarchy: [biome [population [organism [cell [macromolecule]]]]], which is interpreted as [higher level [lower level]]. Note as well, [rare event [uncommon events [common events]]]. So square brackets, [ ], signify both physical enclosure and differences in rates of change, with slower rates entraining faster ones.

Dynamical rates at the different levels in a scale hierarchy are separated by about an order of magnitude . . . thereby preventing direct dynamical interaction between levels in favor of indirect constraint imposition across levels. This essentially synchronic structure, modeling a situation at a given moment, has been viewed as the most stable configuration for the simultaneous co-occurrence of systems of many different sizes . . . and one that maximizes overall entropy production as well . . . A triadic structure: [contextual boundary conditions [focal dynamics [initiating possibilities]]] is canonical and primordial for this system, which cannot be derived from unconstrained bottom-up processes. New levels are interpolated between preexisting ones. (Salthe 2006, 99)

A comprehensive hierarchy for both structure and causation is summarized in ten levels by Ellis, expressible as follows in Salthe's bracket convention (Ellis 2016, 88):

[cosmology [astronomy [space science [Earth science [materials science [physical chemistry [atomic physics [nuclear physics [high-energy physics [fundamental theory]]]]]]]]]]

Although hierarchies of order are discussed in essentially all works about the universe at large, Salthe's emphasis on the fact of both extensional and intensional hierarchies is critical because it shows how all such frameworks (when fully fleshed out) necessarily incorporate both bottom-up and top-down causation, as argued by Ellis, due to the inevitable entry of initial conditions, boundary conditions, and context or environment.

A network of causal influences and constraints interact to produce an outcome . . . a web of influences and multiple causations is in action all the time . . . the dynamics in complex systems involves the combination of bottom-up and top-down action in the hierarchy of structure. The higher and lower levels are related to each other because the higher levels are based on the lower levels. But the higher levels set constraints on lower level dynamics in a top-down manner and this influences them in many ways. It enables the activation of interlevel feedback loops which can then facilitate genuine complexity. Boundary conditions shape lower level outcomes, but these in turn influence the environment. (Ellis 2016, 95)

REALISTIC INTERPRETATIONS
WITHOUT PARTICULARISM

At the bottom of the ordinary matter hierarchy, the field of high energy physics is often labeled "particle" physics (as done, for example, by Ellis in his summary of a ten-level hierarchy), which appears to be a remnant of metaphysical "thing" language.[12] In the past, ontology has often been framed as a question of realism (focus on particulars) versus idealism (including the affirmation of abstract objects and universals). Guided by long-standing nominalistic commitments, many interpreters of quantum field theory (QFT) have introduced trope theory where *tropes* refer to particular occurrence of some property, as encouraged by the particularist tradition, versus repeatables, or universals; thus maintaining a nominalism (i.e., the denial of universals).

Richard Campbell, in *The Metaphysics of Emergence* (Campbell 2015), discusses these questions in detail, especially applying the sophisticated analysis carried out by Johanna Seibt in her research on a formal process ontology (Seibt 2003). Instead of maintaining the standard nominalist collapse of the distinction between particularity and individuality, Seibt affirms and demonstrates the importance of this distinction. In an approach fully consistent with the *Logoi* framework, Seibt and Campbell show how "the logic of stuffs, activities, and processes offers a plausible ontological interpretation of QFT" (Campbell 2015, 64). Meinard Kuhlmann critiques Seibt's approach and defends trope theory but, as argued by Campbell (2015, 61–68), Seibt's analysis is notably superior in handling the subtleties of QFT; see papers by Seibt (2002) and Kuhlmann (2002). In particular, Kuhlmann's comments regarding the apparent limitations of Seibt's approach to questions with the QFT application are readily overcome when applying considerations from our *Logoi* framework. This is because Seibt's account of free processes can flexibly handle both particular actualizations (Boolean outcomes of quantum process) and specific potential relations, which need not be fully determinate (thus, as well accommodating non-Boolean constraints). Kuhlmann's preference for trope theory appears to be based on a nominalist commitment, if not actualism, which is rejected in the *Logoi* framework. As Campbell points out,

The logic of discourse about stuffs, activities, and processes has rarely been investigated systematically. Despite this neglect, Seibt has shown that they sustain a coherent ontology which departs more fundamentally from the entity paradigm which has dominated Western philosophy ever since Aristotle, even when Aristotelian metaphysics has been rejected. For more than two decades she has been developing an ontological theory which abandons the assumption that what is referred to in language are necessarily particulars . . . Her suggestion is that the logic of stuffs, activities, and processes offers a variety of aspects which could make it attractive to those searching for a plausible ontological interpretation of QFT. (Campbell 2015, 64)

Seibt's free process theory and this ontological framing of both QFT and core quantum physics are readily accommodated by the *Logoi* framework, which incorporates both Relational Realism and Primas's realist interpretation of quantum physics (Primas 2017). Although these realist approaches reject nominalism and actualism, they nevertheless avoid a simple hold to universals characteristic of many idealisms. Campbell continues with how Seibt

insists that a minimal requirement on any ontology is that its basic concepts, even though they might be axiomatically defined, are *founded* in people's everyday experience. An ontological description is something which we have to be able to understand "in the pragmatic Heideggerian sense in which we do not 'understand' infinite vector spaces or the imaginary parts of complex numbers" (Seibt 2002, 59). Understanding, in this sense, is not just having an appropriate theoretical formulation; it involves the ability to do something, to enact possibilities, as constitutive of our way of being (Heidegger 1927/1996, 134) [Heidegger 1996]. In the latter sense, we have no trouble understanding our being already engaged with stuffs, activities, and processes, unlike talk about tropes and Whiteheadean actual occasions. They are concepts founded in everyday experience. (Campbell 2015, 65–66)

Campbell's reference here to Whiteheadian actual occasions appears to reflect a particularist interpretation of such; for example, that such actual occasions could map one-to-one to the "particles" of QFT. In contrast, Auxier and Herstein argue persuasively that Whitehead's intent was not just particularist, but metaphysically general as a relational "quantum of explanation" (Auxier and Herstein, 2017). Another approach to fundamental ontology has been proposed by Randall Dipert (1997) based on asymmetric graph theory in which he points out that

if one is an anti-relationalist, that is, a monadist, then one must believe—if one believes there are many distinct entities in the world—that they are ultimately distinguished by the different combination of monadic properties each has. Far from being a minimal, Ockhamite assumption, this entails a commitment to a very large number of irreducible, exemplified, monadic properties. Reduction of arity[13] (from 2 or higher to 1) of basic predicates in the world is thus possible only if one tolerates an explosion of the number of basic monadic predicates. This is artfully hidden from us by the casual assumption in materialist metaphysics, for example that entities are ultimately and simply distinguished by their locations in space, time, or space-time. For this account not to turn out to be disguised relationalism, however, we would require a commitment to a view of space (and time) as being constituted by unique one-place spatial properties: absolute locations and a sufficient number of them to distinguish all basic material entities. While it is possible that some such view is palatable, it seems wrongheaded to have such a view unwittingly forced on us by a commitment to a monadistic metaphysics without conscious regard to this commitment's far-reaching implications for other kinds of metaphysical inflation. (Dipert 1997, 351)

Dipert then proceeds to show how asymmetric graph theory provides a basis for far less complex mathematical models of the world. Further, as shown by Joe Rosen, asymmetry is more fundamental than symmetry; see *Symmetry in Science*, chapter 4. The emphasis on the power of a fundamentally relational account is an important step toward enabling more adequate world models.

Dipert's asymmetric dyadic relations based on graph theory need to be put in context of full triadic relations as discussed in chapter 5 on semiotics. In particular, the arrow in category theory provides such an asymmetric dyadic relation, which is boosted to triadic form through fundamental quantum process in the form of input-output-context.[14]

A THEORY OF RELATIONS FOR MODELING AND PROCESS—CATEGORY THEORY

A relatively simple yet powerful theory of relations is set theory and constitutes a formal foundation for mathematics. An even more inclusive algebra of relations is category theory, which is still in development but promises to provide enhanced foundations for logic, mathematics, and physics. Jean-Pierre Marquis summarizes category theory as follows,

Categorical tools in logic offer considerable flexibility, as is illustrated by the fact that almost all the surprising results of constructive and intuitionistic mathematics can be modeled in a proper categorical setting. At the same time, the standard set-theoretic notions, e.g., Tarski's semantics, have found natural generalizations in categories. Thus, categorical logic has roots in logic as it was developed in the twentieth century, while at the same time providing a powerful and novel framework with numerous links to other parts of mathematics. Category theory also bears on more general philosophical questions [with] impact on almost all issues arising in philosophy of logic: from the nature of identity criteria to the question of alternative logics, category theory always sheds a new light on these topics. Similar remarks can be made when we turn to ontology, in particular formal ontology: the part/whole relation, boundaries of systems, ideas of space, etc. (Marquis 2014, 15)

As discussed in chapter 2, the Relational Reality model demonstrates the power of applying category theory to quantum physics in a way that articulates the distinction of two logical orders, the Boolean and the non-Boolean, a key foundation of the *Logoi* framework. This distinction, along with the corresponding distinction of both the actual and *potentiae* within the "real," is also demonstrated in a complementary way in algebraic quantum theory as shown by Primas (2007). Applying category theory to fundamental process, and just after pointing out that Whitehead, in his time, only had set theory to work with, Heather and Rossiter argue that "a top-down approach begins with the Universe as process. The highest structure in category theory is the topos which can be identified as an arrow, itself containing distinguishable identity arrows . . . while sets are representable as number, process is representable as the arrow" (Heather and Rossiter 2009, 2). In turn, the fundamental ordering that arises from such arrow representation provides a useful model for conceiving of fundamental process in terms of succession—as "one darn thing after another." This new way of understanding fundamental process, and Whitehead's concept of prehension, is made explicit by Heather and Rossiter when applying these concepts to Whitehead's *Process and Reality* (Heather and Rossiter 2018)—see chapter 4 section *Generalizing the Function*. The formal properties of the concept of prehension, including asymmetry and other elements, are presented by Leemon McHenry in a paper that highlights the ways in which Bertrand Russell's metaphysics was deeply influenced by Whitehead's early work (McHenry 2017, 326).

WHITEHEAD'S HARVARD LECTURES OF 1924–1925

Inspiration for the *Logoi* framework derives in part from my readings of the works of Alfred North Whitehead. Precursors for many concepts featured in his later works appear in the Harvard lectures of 1924–1925 (Paul Bogaard and Jason Bell 2017), a treasure trove of philosophical insights. The highlights below are adapted from Desmet's paper on the Harvard lectures; these highlights correlate with many aspects of the *Logoi* framework; as well they provide useful pointers to important elements of the complex whole (Desmet, 2020a).

- the methodology of his systematic philosophy through imaginative generalization;
- the organic metaphor of his new ecological vision;
- philosophy as the critique of abstraction, and the avoidance of scientism;
- goal of an inclusive and realist philosophy that comports with common sense;
- transition from continuous to discrete becomings as interdependent processes of realization;
- the first presupposition of science is the essential togetherness of things;
- focus on inferences from field theory and the internally relatedness of events;
- multiterm relations instead of subject-predicate dyads;
- fallacy of misplaced concreteness (error of taking abstract things to be more concrete than they really are);
- phenomenalist restriction to avoid anything that cannot in principle be observed;
- new concepts should pass not only the narrow gauge of empirical testing, but also the broad gauge of consonance with the general character of experience;
- affirmation of real causation;
- avoidance of performative contradictions (whereby one's actions, in practice, are inconsistent with one's theoretical claims);
- early speculations on quantum physics, broadly compatible with recent developments;
- alternative theory of gravitation that avoids Einstein's measurement problem (see below).

The last two items are featured in Desmet's companion paper from the same volume focusing on Whitehead's lectures on quantum theory (Desmet 2020b). Finally, relevant to the Relational Realist interpretation of quantum physics, within the section *Pan-experientialism and Emerging Consciousness* of chapter 4, we address how Whitehead, in 1924–1925, had considered a modal logic that could include violations of the excluded middle (i.e., non-Boolean logic).

This set of key points from Whitehead's Harvard lectures of 1924–1925 (incorporated in his major work *Process and Reality*, and other works) are close to key points of our *Logoi* framework. Similar prescience by Whitehead applies to quantum physics whereby his schema, inspired by field theory and the early quantum physics, correlates reasonably well with contemporary realist interpretations as argued above in chapters 2 and 3. Finally, in addition to affirming the reality of possibility, Whitehead emphasized that *Mathematics is the study of possibilities* (Lucien Price 1954, 252) as well as patterns of relatedness, and "essentially a study of types of order" (Price 1954, 175).

A complementary systematic philosophy and theory of relations was formulated by the Charles S. Peirce, which emphasized semiotics but overlaps Whiteheadian process thought in many ways (Jaime Nubiola 2008). I envision the *Logoi* framework as being a synthesis of Whiteheadian process thought, Peircean semiotics (see chapter 5), Hartshorne's neoclassical metaphysics (see chapter 8), quantum field theory, ecological and systems analysis, and several other strands of contemporary scholarship in science and philosophy. Such synthesis was a common goal for both Whitehead and Peirce—as Bradley points out, "the significance of Peirce and Whitehead resides in their defense of speculative reason against its critique by continental and analytical philosophers alike" (Bradley 2004). Another significance for basic metaphysics is that, with his new theory of events inspired by the emerging field theories in physics, and within the early analytic tradition exemplified by George Moore, Bertrand Russell, and Frank Ramsey, "Whitehead had already taken the decisive step away from categorial dualism towards categorial pluralism" (MacBride 2018, 128).

MEASUREMENT PROBLEMS AT EXTREMES OF SCALE

As a particular example and application of Whitehead's thought, in his summary of the Harvard Lectures, Desmet notes that Whitehead had early demonstrated a critical problem with Einstein's General Theory of Relativity (GTR).

> Whitehead highlights the most devastating performative contradiction that is entailed by Einstein's Kantian interpretation of GTR: GTR holds that the space-time structure is contingently contorted, but its measurement practices tacitly rely on our recognition of congruence, and hence, on a necessarily uniform space-time structure . . . In general, we simply cannot resist from believing in what the common world of sense prompts us to believe. (Desmet 2020a, 140)

This same point has been developed in detail by Gary Herstein (2013) based, in part, on an analysis of Whitehead's *Principles of Relativity* (Whitehead, 1922). Auxier and Herstein summarize this as follows,

> While we must have a standard unit of spatial comparison for *conjugacy*, we must also have standard(s) of spatial *projection* such as will allow that unit of comparison to be uniformly brought into comparison with—i.e., meaningfully

projected onto—those things we mean to measure. The conjugate relation must be formally possible.

It is this second step which GR denies us. The requirement of uniform geometrical relations that make such projectively conjugate comparisons possible are rendered dubious if not impossible by the fundamental assumptions of GR. These assumptions include the idea that the necessary and uniform relations of geometry are collapsed into the contingent and heterogeneous physical relations of matter, energy, and gravity. Thus, the very geometry of space is dependent upon the varying physical effects of matter and energy at each "point" of space. Einstein's move of collapsing the formal and *logical* structures of geometry into the contingent and variable relations of physical interactions, has long been viewed by physicists as one of Einstein's most brilliant postulates. Einstein himself viewed this conceptual collapse as an act of essential insight, and looked with disdain upon such alternatives as that formulated by Nathan Rosen. By eliminating the distinction between geometry as a purely mathematical discipline and physical space (as it is studied in empirical cosmology), Einstein also compromised the relational structures that make a coherent theory of measurement possible. (Auxier and Herstein 2017, 102–103)

As a space physicist (albeit in a different field from physical cosmology), I take this conclusion seriously and have not, to date, seen any adequate response. Some alternative cosmological frameworks have addressed this problem by maintaining the necessary level of uniformity to avoid this measurement problem. However, Herstein continues, arguing that mainstream "gravitational cosmology has outrun the empirical content of the available observational evidence in its rush to justify its adored standard model. Rather than evidence-driven science, gravitational cosmology has become model-driven speculative mathematics" (Auxier and Herstein 2017, 108). Despite these problems, much of modern astrophysics, at less than cosmological scale (i.e., low or moderate red shift[15]), has made major advances over the past century and is generally based on reliable research. For my own readings in space physics and astrophysics, I depend on works that build on evidence-based research that complements any model-driven speculations with independent observations, both remote sensing and in situ observations (e.g., *Astrophysics: A New Approach* by Wolfgang Kundt (2004); *Principles of Magnetohydrodynamics* by Hans Goedbloed and Stefaan Poedts (2004); *Physics of the Plasma Universe* by Anthony Peratt (2015); *Astrophysics for Physicists* by Arnab Rai Choudhuri (2010)). In general, such works avoid reference to the results of "model-driven speculative mathematics," such as dark energy. Unlike space physics with its capabilities, within the solar system, for in situ observation, the fields of astrophysics and cosmology are entirely dependent on remote sensing observation in addition to some theoretical techniques to indirectly extend proxies for "observation" to ever greater distances. At low red shift, such techniques can be reasonably reliable. However, at ever greater scales, basic assumptions can be increasingly unreliable, especially at large red shift. My own limited evaluation of research in cosmology extends these skeptical concerns (Eastman 2010).

Inferences concerning extremes in scale are a basic problem. Astrophysicist Wolfgang Kundt states that

> frontline physics is not as unique and reliable as the multiply tested physics of every-day life. The further the frontline advances towards unreachably large, or unresolvably small separations, or timescales . . . [the more] plausible assumptions have to replace redundant experience, and hasty interpretations can lead astray . . . Our politically organized society then takes care of suppressing minority opinion. (Kundt 2001, 611)

Many popular books emphasize the great importance of recent "discoveries" in physical cosmology for our worldview as noted by Neil deGrasse Tyson (2017). Nevertheless, however seemingly adequate our descriptions of the physical universe at cosmological scale, one cannot argue from mere descriptions to any deep worldview issues without interpretive claims that go beyond the scientific propositions themselves. In addition to the measurement problem and other limitations mentioned above, some recent research results cast serious doubt on several claims of "standard" cosmology (e.g., detailed implementation of a surface brightness test by Eric Lerner (2018); Christopher Fulton and Halton Arp's in-depth analysis of the physical association of quasars (Fulton and Arp, 2012); and Hilton Ratcliffe's concise summary of various skeptical conclusions (Ratcliffe, 2010a)). Another consideration concerns the assumed gravity model for cosmology. Standard cosmology assumes Einstein's particular general relativity theory whereas there are more than forty extant alternative theories,[16] and at least a quarter of these are considered viable candidates by some researchers. For example, some of these alternatives avoid singularities and thus do not lead to black holes or a "big bang." I conclude that the current state of knowledge in physical cosmology is not adequately mature to provide a reliable basis for philosophical speculation. Further, for essentially all objectives of the current work, including inferences needed for the *Logoi* framework, we can set aside questions about physical cosmology.

TOWARD A NEW SEMIOTIC BIOLOGY

Philosopher Thomas Nagel argues that "The modern materialist approach to life has conspicuously failed to explain such central mind-related features of our world as consciousness, intentionality, meaning, and value [indicating that] the standard materialist version of evolutionary biology is fundamentally incomplete" (Nagel 2012). In his call for "A New Biology for a New Century," after extended discussions about the problems of mechanistic reductionism and the implications of non-linear systems and biocomplexity, Carl Woese states that

> society cannot tolerate a biology whose metaphysical base is outmoded and misleading: the society desperately needs to live in harmony with the rest of the living world, not with a biology that is a distorted and incomplete reflection of that world. Because it has been taught to accept the above hierarchy of the sciences [physics $\longrightarrow$ chemistry $\longrightarrow$ biology], society today perceives biology as here to solve its problems, to change the living world. Society needs to appreciate that the real relationship between biology and the physical sciences is not hierarchical, but reciprocal: physics $\Leftrightarrow$ biology. Both physics and biology are primary windows on the world; they see the same gem but different facets thereof (and so inform one another). Knowing this, society will come to see that biology is here to understand the world, not primarily to change it. Biology's primary job is to teach us. In that realization lies our hope of learning to live in harmony with our planet. (Woese 2004, 185)

As a way to articulate such needed harmony, Koutroufinis weaves together Uexküll, Whitehead, and Peirce. As for Uexküll's concept of *Umwelt*, he explains that "those relevant features of the physical surroundings that are represented in the organism with respect to its self-preservation and reproduction constitute its *Umwelt*. In other words '*Umwelt*' refers to those features of a living being's surroundings which are meaningful to it . . . An organism implicitly incorporates within its organization information about many, even if not all, aspects of its surroundings that are specifically relevant to its self-preservation" (Koutroufinis 2019, 1–2). Koutroufinis further points out that

> Uexküll's distinction between Umwelt und Umgebung (surroundings) characterizes an essential difference between biology and physics that a biological theory of semiotic processes must deal with: *Whereas organisms have Umwelts, systems studied in physics are considered to have only surroundings.* Inanimate macroscopic physical systems react to forces from their surroundings. Organisms additionally act on their Umwelts and thereby can modify these extrinsic influences with respect to intrinsic factors. All systems studied in physics react only to a specific part of their surroundings—their so called "boundary conditions." In contrast, organisms do not simply react to boundary conditions. They rather generate boundary conditions supportive to their organization through purposeful teleological actions directed to their Umwelt. That an organism continuously

creates its Umwelt means that it continuously creates a "sphere" of *potentiality* on which the organism may act and generate its boundary conditions. An animal that feeds itself actively imposes on itself an input of energy which is a boundary condition that it has created through purposive teleological actions directed to its Umwelt. (Koutroufinis 2019, 13–14)

The potentiality in question here is ultimately grounded in the *potentiae* of fundamental quantum process, and thus in all systems, at multiple levels. Yet there are multiple constraints on such *potentiae*, most fundamentally the general constraints that enable physical relations. Further, at multiple levels, there are constraints and context that delimit possible trajectories in the associated phase space[17]—a key procedure for representing system dynamics in self-organization and complexity theory. Standard approaches to such systems theory focus on only basic driving forces and constraints of external parameters. In contrast, there can arise autogenic processes comprising, as Koutroufinis describes it, "an autonomous molecular system consisting of two coupled non-linear self-organizing processes—*autocatalysis and self-assembly*—which *mutually constrain each other*" (Koutroufinis 2013, 328). Such autogens can avoid depleting the environmental conditions upon which they depend in the way that ordinary self-organizing systems do (i.e., minimizing entropy production versus maximizing entropy production). Deacon has called the specific organization of autogenic dynamics "teleodynamics" because it enables "end-directedness and consequence-organized features" (Deacon 2012, 552). Consistent with Deacon's work, Koutroufinis states that "teleodynamics is always constituted by the mutual constraint and reciprocal synergy of two or more strongly coupled self-organized processes" (Koutroufinis 2013, 330). Continuing, he states that the "highly constraining effect of the teleodynamical level on the lower level self-organized processes enormously reduces the number of possible physicochemical trajectories" (Koutroufinis 2013, 331). In this way, Deacon's autogen model "*merges the logic of organismic causality with its physics*. This clearly goes beyond cybernetics and informatics." (Koutroufinis 2013, 334) In the *Logoi* framework, autogenic processes provide a specific way to tap non-Boolean *potentiae* to optimize system dynamics toward enhanced self-preservation—such is the beginning of a viable nonmechanistic theory of life.

What clearly discriminates the theory of teleodynamics, along with other new biological ideas presented in this volume, from physicalistic approaches to organism, like self-organization and systems-biology, is that they include semiotic concepts in biological explanation. Instead of introducing ad hoc semiotic terms, Deacon's thought experiment about the evolution of autogens provides a way to bridge the gap between the conceptions of causality in physics and biosemiotics. It shows how a specific physical organization (i.e., teleodynamics) gives rise to the emergence of phenomena like representation, sentience, interpretation, anticipation etc . . . , which Deacon summarizes under the term "ententional phenomena." (Koutroufinis 2013, 336)

With this in mind "biological neo-naturalism" could be defined, as Koutroufinis explains, as "the generic term referring to all kinds of biological thinking emphasizing the explanatory power of ententional phenomena in the understanding of organismic causality. It would be the attempt to re-invent semiotic biology a hundred years after its first introduction by Jacob von Uexküll. Biological neo-naturalism, as proposed here, is a scientific biophilosophy" (Koutroufinis 2013, 336).

Such a new semiotic biology would build on the best of biological and biosemiotics research and move to a new stage of development by shedding any dependence on the mechanistic reductionism of classical metaphysics, thus opening up new approaches in understanding complex systems, anticipatory system models, and *Life Itself* (Robert Rosen 1991).

POTENTIAE AND ANTICIPATORY SYSTEMS

Anticipatory systems are complex systems with predictive models that enable them to rapidly respond to inputs within appropriate predictive ranges and, further, enable them to modify such models upon encountering surprises to improve the efficacy of future responses. Such complex systems were discussed above in the second to last section of chapter 5. The Relational Reality interpretation of quantum physics, part of the *Logoi* framework (see chapter 2), provides a systematic and scientific account, employing contemporary category theory (an algebra of relations) and quantum physics, of how the domain of the real comprises both non-Boolean (potentiality "pre-space"—*potentiae*) and Boolean actualities; actualities now past remain real (indirectly via fields propagating into the future, and as data—observations, records, etc.), whereas future events, although real *potentiae*, can only become actualized upon participating in a present actualization. With this minimal environment of a diachronic mix of the order of actualizations and the order of *potentiae*, in conjunction with synchronic multilevel emergent relations, relations inclusively are necessarily triadic because of the input-output-context framework. In the fullness of this framework, there is always, and necessarily, a relevant and significant context, or environment, for any given process of actualization, at whatever scale. This contrasts with common presuppositions of a God's eye view, simplistic dualisms, spatializing things (as with both time and space), monadism (as with isolated, windowless Leibnizian monads), and actualism.

When focused previously on the topic of emergence (chapter 4), we have seen how some type of anticipatory capability is essential for complex adaptive systems to viably contribute to the natural competitive selection process. The alternative is to consider only blind chance as the sole driver of evolutionary improvement; however, without some (potentially indirect) incorporation of fitness or context such blind searches involve astronomically improbable chance coincidences as argued by William Dembski and Robert Marks II (2010).[18] Some form of anticipatory capability and possible tapping of *potentiae* are likely needed to overcome this limitation of standard evolutionary systems theory. Indeed, recent research is moving beyond the standard exclusive dependence on chance coincidences alone. Eugene Koonin states that "the exclusive focus of Modern Synthesis on natural selection acting on random genetic variation has been replaced with a plurality of complementary, fundamental evolutionary processes and patterns" (Koonin 2011, 400).

A comprehensive review of anticipatory system studies carried out by Jesse Bettinger and myself indicates their importance for contemporary research in physics and biology.

Ultimately, physics and biology represent two pillars of an even more general discipline: the theory of complex systems . . . As we continue to explore the earmarks of anticipatory (predictive) processes, we are drawn closer to complex many-bodied systems operating in a platform of dynamic instability . . . and criticality. At the epistemic core, there is a fundamental shift from a reductive bias to multi-level complex systems that is only just beginning with the renewed recognition that fundamental logic is actually triadic, not dyadic (*à la* Peirce); that contemporary number systems and mathematics are a small subset of what will be available to us within a few decades; and that recognition of the real richness of complex systems, bio-systems, biosemiotics, nonlinear dynamics has only just begun. (Bettinger and Eastman 2017, 118)

There are numerous examples of anticipatory capabilities, some of which go beyond any hypothesis that is based only on the Boolean logic of actualization, which was largely the focus of the Bettinger and Eastman study quoted above. Many exceptional examples of anticipatory capabilities that go beyond our usual notions of cause-effect relations arise from studies of psychic abilities as documented, for example, by Edward Kelly and colleagues (Kelly et al. 2007) and by Griffin (1997a). Some researchers make strong claims about overall research results in terms of statistics; for example, Dean Radin states that "after a century of increasingly sophisticated investigations and more than a thousand controlled studies . . . there is now strong evidence that some psi phenomena exists" (Radin 2009, 275). Physicist Russell

Targ has concluded that "we live in a nonlocal world" (Targ 2012, 250). Nevertheless, the voices of qualified skeptics, such as James Alcock (1990) should be kept fully in mind.

Edwin May and Sonali Marwaha have provided a compilation of research that suggests mixed results, and they document several key challenges for this research area: (1) lack of funding for qualified research projects, (2) lack of consensus within the scholarly community, and (3) difficulty in replicating results (May and Marwaha 2014). My interpretation is that some of these phenomena are associated with the logic of *potentiae*, which are nonlocal, but this conclusion does not require us to maintain actualism and suppose that the actualized world is itself fully non-local; again, within the *Logoi* framework, we maintain that the domain of the real is both the actual and the possible. Relevant to this topic, William James, in his classic work *The Varieties of Religious Experience*, concludes that "the existence of mystical states absolutely overthrows the pretension of non-mystical states to be the sole and ultimate dictators of what we may believe . . . It must always remain an open question whether mystical states may not possibly be . . . windows through which the mind looks out upon a more extensive and inclusive world . . . indispensable stages in our approach to the final fullness of the truth" (James 2004). I will return to this topic in chapter 8.

MULTIPLE PERSPECTIVES ON THE WHOLE

I have focused thus far on the limitations of standard philosophical and scientific accounts in terms of their tendency toward substance-thinking, deductivism, determinism, causal closure, and actualism, all of which, as we have seen, involve philosophical or metaphysical claims that are problematic or simply false. As an example of what Goedbloed and Poedts characterize as the "standard view of nature, as developed in the twentieth century and widely held to provide the correct scientific representation of the Universe" (Poedts 2004, 23–24), I return to Penrose's *Road to Reality* (Penrose 2005). This book provides an excellent survey of standard accounts at the level of nuclear forces and electrostatic forces up to the atomic level, and also usefully summarizes astrophysical systems from stars to galaxies and beyond with a focus on gravitational forces. However, such standard accounts have substantial limitations as Goedbloed and Poedts point out in their book on plasma astrophysics. They state that such an account

> jumps the eighteen order of magnitude from atoms to stars . . . under the assumption that nothing of fundamental interest happens there. One could remark that we just happen to live on the least interesting level of the physical

Universe, or one could dwell on the disproportion of man between the infinities of the small and the large (Pascal), or one could join the recent chorus of holistic criticism on the reductionism of physics. So much appears to be correct in the latter viewpoint that the given picture does not have any place for the complexities of solid state physics, fluid dynamics or biological systems, to name just a few. It should come as a big disappointment that nature would hang together from elementary particles to cosmology without really involving the intermediate stages . . . however, another misrepresentation is implicit . . . more than 90% of [visible] matter in the Universe is plasma so that *the Universe does not consist of ordinary matter (in the usual sense) but most of it is plasma*! It is true that plasma is usually also almost electrically neutral, like atoms and molecules, but the important difference is that the ions and electrons are not tied together in atoms but *move about freely as fluids*. The large scale result of this dynamics is the formation of *magnetic fields* which in turn determine the plasma dynamics: a highly nonlinear situation. These magnetic fields not only bridge the gap between microscopic and macroscopic physics, but they also reach far into the astrophysical realm at all scales. The subject of plasma-astrophysics is of basic importance for understanding phenomena occurring everywhere in the Universe. (Goedbloed and Poedts 2004, 22–23)

Most notably, the word "plasma" is entirely absent in Penrose's book, and yet its subtitle claims that it provides a "complete guide!" Unfortunately, the same critique applies to a significant number of contemporary books on the fashionable topic of physical cosmology, especially those for the lay audience. If instead, we combine Penrose's book (which actually is excellent on high energy physics) along with some coverage of space plasma systems from stellar to galactic scale and beyond, in addition to some good texts on complex systems and biological systems, then we would just begin to provide a more complete narrative. However, this would still be incomplete in the sense that most such treatments presuppose one or more problematic metaphysical notions such as substance-thinking, deductivism, determinism, causal closure, and actualism, among others. The lesson here is that we all, myself included, need a hearty dose of humility. The end of science is nowhere near, and that just covers the way of numbers (with its focus on domains of actualizations and data thereof), setting aside the way of context or signs (semiotics), and the way of ultimate context (see chapter 8).

Of course, there are a few examples of science-based narratives, striving to be fully inclusive of current understandings of the universe at large, that do better at covering the "eighteen orders of magnitude from atoms to stars" that were dropped out of Penrose's "complete guide." Examples of such include several recent efforts at the so-called Big History (Christian 2016) and attempts at covering fully the "Universe Story" (Swimme and Berry 1994).

However, even these accounts most often appear to simply presuppose some combination of causal closure and actualism. The *Logoi* framework is very much undeveloped as a comprehensive narrative, but it strives to be explicit about handling fundamental philosophical and metaphysical issues before constructing some complex edifice.

Given the need for humility, and also for the practical purpose of promoting a more realistic grand narrative, I recommend that we remain skeptical of the entire genre of monological narratives and, with Arran Gare, encourage a "dialogic grand narrative."

> A dialogic grand narrative is required, allowing for the diverse voices of participants, situated in diverse and complexly related communities, organizations and economic, social and cultural fields with diverse histories, to question and participate in revising, reformulating and developing the narratives they are living out, from the local to the global level, preserving the autonomy of their communities, institutions and fields as the condition for such participation. (Gare 2017, 145)

There is a very practical aspect to the above distinction between a monological narrative and a dialogic (multivoiced) approach. Gare continues, "The most underestimated dialectic in the modern world is the dialectic of recognition associated, as [a student of Habermas] Axel Honneth . . . argued, with love (which includes friendship), rights, and solidarity (through which each individual's unique contribution to the community is acknowledged). It is through this dialectic that people gain and accord significant identities and a sense of their own and each other's significance" (Gare 2017, 148). We might suppose, as Philip Rose states, that "the only form of knowledge that we are denied is what Putnam calls a God's eye point-of-view. While the finite is clearly within our grasp, the infinity of creative advance transcends the finitude of all actualized and actualizing points of view" (Rose 2005, 14). Thus, our radical finiteness, however enhanced by scientific means, will forever remain outstripped by the limitless depths of both the contingent and the non-contingent, both actualizations and *potentiae*.

Laying out the needs and implications of a dialogic grand narrative, Gare summarizes his call as follows:

> This manifesto for speculative naturalism and ecological civilization is a quest to revive philosophy, and more generally, the humanities, forging a new direction for them and for humanity. It is a call to carry through and further advance the project begun by Herder, Goethe and Schelling to replace the Cartesian/Newtonian conception of the world, including the conception of physical existence, of life and of humans, and thereby of the place of humanity in nature,

opening up new possibilities for what humanity and nature can become, and to rethink ethics and political philosophy accordingly. (Gare 2017, 7)

Efforts toward a dialogic (multivoice, inclusive) grand narrative are clearly important, at both individual and social levels, to offset several human tendencies toward hubris and control. Such narratives also need to be grounded in ever wider contexts and human meaning, which is the focus of my concluding chapter.

NOTES

1. In relativity theory, the rest frame is that coordinate system in which a particle or field structure is at rest.

2. Plantin-Moretus Museum, Antwerp, Belgium <https://www.museumplant inmoretus.be/en>

3. The term "anthropocene" has been proposed but is not yet officially adopted, thus not herein capitalized. An excellent summary is provided by Will Steffen et al. (2011).

4. Some basic science about plasmas is provided in my "Perspectives on Plasmas" Web site

<http://www.plasmas.org> (accessed August 1, 2020).

5. For details on astrophysical plasmas, see references by Anthony Peratt (2015), Hans Goedbloed and Stefaan Poedts (2004), and Carolus Schrijver and George Siscoe (2009).

6. On the issue of any "God's eye view," please note the importance of perspective and fundamental limits to any "view from no-where"—see Weekes (2009b); also the analysis on perspective presented by Philip Rose (2005). Throughout this book, I add to skepticism about God's eye view perspectives and cosmologies (*à la* the "whole shebang"), analogous to Heidegger's critique of onto-theologies.

7. Space-Time metrics are basic parameters for relativity theory, but are not fundamental concepts as often assumed. For the *Logoi* framework, although extension is a fundamental concept (see Auxier and Herstein, 2017), space-time metrics can be considered as emergent from fundamental process. Indeed, such a possibility is exemplified by recent research results in quantum field theory; see Erik Verlinde (2011), also Cahill (2016), and Klinger (2016). Further constraints on this question arise from the assumptions of isotropy and homogeneity of space; see Paul White (2019).

8. For an analysis of Peirce's basic categories (Firstness, Secondness, Thirdness), see Søren Brier (2014).

9. Eames' video was based on the book *Powers of Ten* by Philip and Phylis Morrison (1982).

10. Čapek provides an extensive critique of the common space-time substance view and argues for a dynamic "time-space" rather than "space-time" (Čapek, 1991, 324).

11. The term "particle physics" is a vestige of eighteenth-century substance metaphysics and the field is more properly termed "high-energy physics" or "fundamental physics." Kenneth Schmitz addresses this issue by arguing how, "against the background of nominalism, and in the spheres of physics, astronomy, and various technologies, sixteenth-century mechanics launched scientific inquiry and technique upon a search for ultimate and elementary particles—at first called *minima*, corpuscules, and more rarely, atoms. It is a search that continues to this day, though it is presently yielding pride of place among some theorists to more holistic approaches. According to its own terms, the search for absolutely ultimate and simple particles has been in vain" (Kenneth Schmitz 2007, 225).

12. The famed quantum theorist Richard Feynman commented on how high-energy physics could equally well be called "particle" physics or "wave" physics. This ambiguity goes along with the prolonged and ultimately failed quest for an ultimate "thing" or "particle" in the spirit of traditional atomism (i.e., irreducible, external relations only).

13. The "arity" of a function or operation is the number of arguments needed to employ the function; binary functions are of "arity 2" and called "dyadic"; functions with three arguments are called "triadic"; see MacBride (2016).

14. A quantitative formalization of the arrow can be implemented with John Lango's concept of "synonty" as argued by George Shields (2019). Another logical framework, focused on quantifying Whitehead's system and his concept of prehension, has been laid out by mathematician Granville Henry (1993).

15. "Red shift" refers to an increase in wavelength for electromagnetic radiation; the term is most often applied in astrophysical settings where it is used as a proxy for measuring extra-galactic distances. Whereas local red shifts, especially those due to the Doppler effect, are well understood, the basic cause of such cosmic-scale red shifts remains disputed; see Hilton Ratcliffe (2010b).

16. Alternatives for a gravitational theory include several types: scalar field, tensor, scalar-tensor, vector-tensor, quasilinear, and non-metric, as any search for alternatives to general relativity will reveal.

17. In dynamical systems theory, a phase space is a representation of all possible states of a system (presuming the given model), with each possible state corresponding to a unique location in the phase space. The system's evolving state over time creates a path, or trajectory, through the high-dimensional space.

18. Dembski and Marks provide some substantive information theory arguments against exclusive dependence on "blind search" or standard "searches for a search"; however, in other works they appeal, problematically, to intelligent design arguments. The *Logoi* framework suggests a third way, compatible with a deeper appreciation of Darwin's original work; see Cobb (2008).

Chapter 7

Peirce's Triads and Whitehead's Process

Fundamental Triads and Schemas

The essential triadic logic that permeates our fundamental notions was deployed as a centerpiece for the topic of semiotics in chapter 5. Again, our logic of the world, and our experience of the world, is fundamentally triadic; briefly, in the form of input-output-context suggesting a fundamental semiosis in the world. Understanding this fundamental semiosis was the goal of Charles Sanders Peirce in his Grand Vision, as Deely describes it, of his "deep conviction of the coextensiveness of semiosis with nature" (Deely 1994, 374). From the *Logoi* framework we expect that such triadic structure, evidenced in fundamental logic and quantum physics, should be reflected as well in immediate human experience.[1]

Using a phenomenological analysis of our experience of time, Wolfgang Achtner, Stefan Kunz, and Thomas Walter explain how to distinguish a triadic structure of endogenous, exogenous, and transcendent time. By endogenous time, they mean "the forms of time that are accessible to human beings through immediate, inner experience" and, by exogenous time, they mean "all the forms of time in which human beings walk in relationship to the environment," both natural and social. Finally, by transcendent time, they point to "all those phenomena that can be interpreted in the widest sense as a religious experience of time." They further distinguish, within endogenous time, three modes of experiencing time, the "mythic-cyclic, rational-linear, and mystic-holistic" (Achtner et al. 2002, 8–10).

Understanding such triadic structures is likely an important bridge between philosophical approaches across cultures. At a meta-level, one tripartite schema is that of neo-Confucian Chu Hsi's form, dynamics, and unification that Berthrong argues provides a bridge between Western and East Asian philosophical frameworks, from Chu Hsi (Zhu Xi 1130–1200) to Whitehead and Neville (Berthrong 1998).

A complementary view that Kineman finds in Vedic philosophy is that "nothing exists that is not whole in some extent" and "both actual and contextual must be considered 'real,' as complements of each other. Thus we would speak of 'actualization' of a model . . . and 'contextualization' of events" (Kineman 2017, 413, fn19).

In chapter 2, we introduced James Bradley's argument about the fundamental questions of origin, difference and order, a tripartite schema that appears to be similar to Chu Hsi's neo-Confucian framework. There are numerous such three-way schemes that often correlate with a semiotic perspective. Table 7.1 summarizes some prominent examples that focus on fundamental issues. This includes as well Arran Gare's triad of activity, order and potentiality, discussed in detail by Glenn McLaren (2004, 85) based on Gare's original analysis published in his work *Nihilism* (Gare, 1993).

Within table 7.1, one can think of the second column (origin/form/creativity) as associated with possibility space (*potentiae*) and the non-Boolean logical order. The third column (dynamics/difference/world) correlates with measurement outcomes, facts, actualizations, and the Boolean logical order. Finally, the fourth column (order/unification/primordial relations) associates with context, law-like relations, and ultimacies.[2] As well, the holism of Vedic philosophy which, in Kineman's reading, is not a reductive holism but incorporates a unification that permeates all parts, is perhaps analogous to how the *Logoi* framework incorporates non-Boolean *potentiae* as an inevitable component of quantum process.[3]

Deely argues for a concept of physiosemiosis, which he lays out as follows:

> . . . already at the level of their fundaments, signs are virtually present and operative in the dyadic interactions of brute force [due to inevitable triads of input-output-context], and weave together in a single fabric of virtual relations the future and the past of such interactions.
>
> This is semiosis, but semiosis of a specific dimension or kind. I have proposed that we call it . . . *physiosemiosis*, so as to bring out by the very name the fact that it is a question here of a process as broad as the physical universe itself. For this process is at work in all parts of nature as the foundation of those higher, more distinctive levels of the same process that come into existence as

Table 7.1   Examples of Fundamental Triads in Philosophy

Source	*Fundamental Triads*		
James Bradley	origin	difference	order
Arran Gare	potentiality	activity	order
Neo-Confucian	form/creativity	dynamics	unification
Whitehead	creativity	world	primordial relations

the conditions of physical being themselves make possible the successively higher levels first of life, and then of cognitive life. Thus, the definition of semiosis is not just coextensive with the definition of life but broader than it. (Deely 1994, 389)

Here Deely points to a fully inclusive semiosis similar to Peirce's Grand Vision. The embodiment of such a vision may be enabled by the multilevel, relational and semiotic grounds of the Relational Reality interpretation of quantum process that, as we have seen, provides both a framework for fundamental quantum process incorporating both Boolean and non-Boolean logical orders (i.e., the order of actualizations, and *potentiae*, respectively), both local and local-global process, and both diachronic quantum process and multilevel synchronic emergence (see *The Relational Reality Model* in chapter 2).

WAYS OF KNOWING

Recall that we have three fundamental ways of knowing,[4] all helpfully augmented via phenomenology: the way of context (relation/semiosis[5]), the way of numbers, and the way of spirit, arising from a focus on context dependence, context independence, and ultimate context, respectively, as summarized in table 7.2.

Table 7.2   Ways of Knowing Correlated with Scope of Context

Scope of Context	Ways of Knowing	
Independent	way of numbers	science
Dependent	way of context	arts and humanities
Ultimate context	way of spirit	ultimacies; meaning

One can further distinguish within the first two ways between a synchronic focus (semiosis, relations, semiotic emergence), and a diachronic focus (succession, causation, quantum events).

In our *Logoi* framework, one can think of anticipatory systems as those capable of enhanced tapping of pre-space *potentiae*, and certain (arguably real) cases of spiritual or psychic experience as suggesting deep acts of such tapping (see chapter 8).

COMPARISON OF FRAMEWORKS

In table 7.3, with comparison to classical metaphysics, there is a concise summary of *Logoi* framework interpretive elements, which incorporates both

Table 7.3   Mapping of Major *Logoi* Framework Elements to Major Theoretical Models

Frameworks	Logic	Physics	Scope	Semiosis?	Consciousness possible?
Logoi Framework	B + nB	Q (ontic), RT	Q + QFT	yes	yes
Epistemic focus	B only	Q (Bohr), RT	Bohr	yes	no
CP with nB	B + nB	CP, RT	CP	yes	yes
Classical Metaphysics	B only	CM, RT, GTR	CM	no	no

Notes: B = Boolean, nB = non-Boolean, Q = quantum physics, QFT = quantum field theory, RT = special relativity, CP = classical physics, CM = classical mechanics, GTR = general theory of relativity.

fundamental logical orders, Boolean (B) and non-Boolean (nB), with mappings to major theoretical models as follows: quantum physics, epistemic only (Q Bohr); quantum physics, ontic (Q ontic); quantum field theory, ontic (QFT); relativity theory (RT); classical physics, ontic (CP); gravity model of Einstein's General Theory of Relativity (GTR); and classical mechanics, ontic (CM).

Table 7.3 indicates how the *Logoi* framework provides an interpretative overlay for major theoretical approaches that include, explicitly or implicitly, reference to the non-Boolean logical order (of *possibiliae*). One major exception is Bohr's Copenhagen interpretation, which is focused on epistemic considerations, and limited to Boolean measurement outcomes—basically correct within its epistemic scope. The other major exception is classical mechanics, and its commonly associated classical metaphysics, which makes the Boolean-only claim of actualism. Special relativity theory (RT) is accepted for all physics theories, setting aside differences in ontological claims, and Einstein's general theory of relativity (GTR) is added to the last row for classical metaphysics. I have assigned GTR in this way because it, like CM and RT, is a continuum-based, Boolean-only theory, which presupposes the principle of excluded middle (Boolean logic). Options for a general relativity theory (GR) that are not restricted by Boolean-logic arise when one considers emergence of such from quantum field theory (QFT) (e.g., Cahill 2016; Verlinde 2011). In such approaches, both the generalized logic and fundamental quantum basis would be embedded in QFT instead of being treated as a separate continuum-based theory.

For classical physics, I here apply both a narrow and a broad interpretation. The latter case ("CP with nB" in table 7.3) applies when that theory is not burdened with the presuppositions of classical metaphysics such as Boolean-only logic. The commonly held narrow interpretation of classical physics (Boolean-only logic) is here termed "classical mechanics" (CM). Classical physics (CP), the broader interpretation, is treated as a very precise, yet imperfect approximation to quantum physics for a wide range of applications (not including topics such as quantum electronics or low-temperature physics where quantum effects are most clearly evident). In contrast, while CM works with the same physics as CP, CM is linked to metaphysical claims such as absolute determinism whereas CP can be productively applied without such metaphysical assumptions. Arguably, both CM and GTR are tied to Boolean-only logic due, in part, to such metaphysical claims, whether made implicitly or explicitly.

ON THE EMERGENCE OF
CONSCIOUSNESS AND MIND

In application to the mind-body problem, a common practice is to presuppose and then apply classical physics in only its narrow CM version (presuming Boolean-only logic), which has led some researchers to avoid the limitations of classical physics and pursue uniquely quantum explanations for brain functionality. Although there may be such uniquely quantum effects, as both Henry Stapp (2017) and Mae Wan Ho (2008) have argued, a broader interpretation of classical physics (CP) as an approximation to full quantum physics provides an opening to treating the brain as primarily a CP system and yet allowing for the denial of absolute determinism and certain non-Boolean logical effects without necessarily appealing to quantum effects per se. This broader understanding of CP, however, does not deny the possible relevance of quantum effects for free will, as Stapp has argued persuasively. Nevertheless, it is important to recognize that the "wet chemistry" brain, for which the basic relevant physics is primarily CP, may importantly underlie mind-brain and free will phenomena without necessarily appealing to quantum effects as such because, after all, CP is an approximation to quantum physics (not a separate theory; such separation requires interpretation). In particular, as I have argued before, the claims of Boolean-only logic or absolute determinism are, at least in part, metaphysical claims, not claims of physics (Eastman 2008).

As for the issue of consciousness and its emergence, the fact of consciousness (given the realist assumption that we are not always functioning as zombies) is widely recognized as impossible given standard CM assumptions, which presume strict entailments and materialist reductionism, combined with the fact that a wet chemistry brain will be dominated by classical physics processes. Yet, at best, quantum theorists have only been able to show the possibility of consciousness being, in part, associated with uniquely quantum processes (e.g., Stapp's discussion of quantum Zeno effects and Ho's hypothesis of quantum coherence). From the perspective of the *Logoi* framework, this discussion needs to be reversed. The fact of consciousness is a basic observation and a basic experience for all of us who have sufficient self-awareness to be part of the dialogue addressing this question. Quantum physics, and its derivative CP (without a Boolean-only metaphysical claim) and associated basic theoretical frameworks (chemistry, thermodynamics, complex systems theory, information theory, etc.), are arguably primary scientific tools to be applied for studying the emergence of consciousness. In addition, due to the inherent complexity of the consciousness issue, this study necessarily requires, in addition, a large array of interdisciplinary fields such as neuroscience, psychology, and philosophy, among others. Claims that because the brain is only wet chemistry, and thus presumed to be dominantly a classical mechanics (CM) system, inevitably leading to claims that consciousness must be merely an epiphenomena, are incorrect because they presuppose CM and its associated classical metaphysics claims (e.g., the denial of non-Boolean logic, affirmation of absolute determinism, etc.). This is not only a scientific issue, as claimed by those who advocate scientism, which I have shown to be false; it is necessarily a multidisciplinary issue that includes science, psychology, philosophy, and much more.

A more productive way to think about consciousness is as an emergent capability of the mind. From this perspective, mind is distinct from brain actualizations (Boolean outputs), has the capacity to reflexively contrast "that which is" with "that which could be" and make decisions among alternative possibilities, and these capacities derive from non-Boolean *potentiae* associated with fundamental quantum process. From this perspective, self-conscious awareness and its subjective feeling arise from non-linear feedback between such contrasts and active selection, quantum process *potentiae* to actualizations, and channeling of these processes through the neurological system and mental models (mappings) enabling varying levels of anticipatory capability as discussed above in chapter 6 (note: *Brain* actualizations or brain states represent Boolean outputs or effective system measurements). Neuroscience research is important for these questions but such research approaches, when focused solely on the order of actualizations and their correlations, cannot by themselves, in principle, "solve" the consciousness issue due to the neglect of landscapes of *potentiae*. Rather, the *mind* can be thought of as the real emergent complex system that manages inputs (both the order of actualizations and the order of *potentiae*), given both environmental context and interoception, and working via complex systems modeling of enfolding inputs and unfolding responses, makes and implements decisions. Neuropsychiatrist Daniel Siegel provides useful detail about the relation of an expanded mind concept, arising from information and energy flows, along with emergent consciousness within that in addition to an emphasis on the transition from possibility to actuality. Such transition can be modulated not only during states of normal consciousness but also in practices of focused meditation practice (Siegel 2017). As shown by Jason

Brown, a similar complexity applies to creativity and its underlying mental processes (Brown 2017). From a *Logoi* framework perspective, creativity would correlate with enhanced tapping of the order of *potentiae*.

Several contemporary thinkers have argued from different perspectives that consciousness cannot be simply synonymous with brain states or brain functioning,[6] and these broader perspectives are often compatible with the *Logoi* framework. Further, the *Logoi* framework comports with Weekes's summary that "the mind-body problem is simply the causation problem applied to consciousness . . . experience isn't just a paradigm case of process, but the key to its essential structure" (Weekes 2009c, 427). Such structure appears similar to Peircean semiosis due to the application of triadic logic and Peircean thirds as, at least in part, based on non-Boolean *possibiliae*. Thus, as suggested by Crosby, we have here a systematic naturalist way of understanding the weaving of causation and novelty (yet, denying "actualism"), as well the ground of temporality and the asymmetry of time. Novelty, as Crosby expresses it, is "a selective process working on the possibilities implicit in the past . . . it explains why temporal processes are asymmetrical and nonreversible, thus accounting for the exclusively forward direction of time" (Crosby 2005, 4). Further, "Novelty and causality [causation] work together to produce the combination of dynamically balanced stability and order" (Crosby 2005, xi).

A very promising advance has recently been made by Stuart Hameroff and Roger Penrose in bridging the gap between localized brain states and overall brain functioning and consciousness. They summarize their own research results as follows:

> *Consciousness results from discrete physical events; such events have always existed in the universe as non-cognitive, proto-conscious events, these acting as part of precise physical laws not yet fully understood.* Biology evolved a mechanism to orchestrate such events and to couple them to neuronal activity, resulting in meaningful, cognitive, conscious moments and thence also to causal control of behavior. These events are proposed specifically to be moments of quantum state reduction (intrinsic quantum "self-measurement"). Such events need not necessarily be taken as part of current theories of the laws of the universe, but should ultimately be scientifically describable. This is basically the type of view put forward, in very general terms, by the philosopher A.N. Whitehead and also fleshed out in a scientific framework in the Penrose–Hameroff theory of "orchestrated objective reduction" ("Orch OR"). In the Orch OR theory, these conscious events are terminations of quantum computations in brain microtubules reducing by Diósi–Penrose "objective reduction" ("OR"), and having experiential qualities. In this view consciousness is an intrinsic feature of the action of the universe. (Hameroff and Penrose 2014, 40)

Given that normal physical processes (the order of actualizations) and entanglement (enabled via the order of *potentiae*) are both essential parts of quantum physics, the above Hameroff-Penrose model appears to be overall consistent with the *Logoi* framework. A yet more speculative suggestion is that provided by Ervin Laszlo who is drawn to "suggest that brain and mind do not exist on the same plane of reality . . . The brain is a part of the material plane of reality: the manifest M-dimension. Mind and consciousness, on the other hand, participate in, and essentially belong to, the deep Akasha dimension" (Laszlo 2014, 44). In the *Logoi* framework, the manifest M-dimension is the order of actualizations, and the Akasha A-dimension is the order of *potentiae*. Laszlo further argues that the brain

> translates the information carried in [the Akasha A-dimension] in a holographically distributed form into linear signals that affect the functioning of the brain's neural networks. This—nonlocal—information first reaches the subneural networks of the right hemisphere, and then, if it penetrates to the level of consciousness, also reaches the neuroaxonal networks of the left hemisphere . . . Thus our brain is imbued with the totality of the information that pervades the cosmos. (Laszlo 2014, 49)

Along with this right and left hemisphere difference is another less-known feature. Laszlo calls attention to evidence that

> we have two distinct systems in the brain that process information: the classical neuroaxonal network and the quantum-level microtubular network . . . The neuroaxonal network gives us the "perceptual-cognitive-symbolic" mode of perceiving the world, and the microtubular network offers a "direct-intuitive-nonlocal" mode. The perceptual-cognitive-symbolic mode dominates consciousness in the modern world; information processed in the direct-intuitive-nonlocal mode is mostly filtered out. (Laszlo 2014, 53)

These findings of brain physiology suggest that humans may have specialized neuronal systems for optimal access to both the order of actualization (normal perception; basically Whitehead's "perception in the mode of presentational immediacy") and the order of *potentiae* (non-local perceptual mode; perhaps aspects of Whitehead's prehension and "perception in the mode of causal efficacy"[7]).

Over 2,500 years ago, Hippocrates realized that the brain is the primary source of the mind—a rare offering of ancient science that remains supported. Indeed, for many researchers, the mind is simply treated as only brain activity and such a reductive perspective has been productive for many advances in neuroscience. However, as argued thoroughly by Siegel, the mind "is both embodied and relational"—a complex system with "social and neural connections that are both the source of and the shaper of energy and information flow" (Siegel 2017, 47). For human awareness, a critically important aspect of mind is conscious experience, which is "the experience we have of being aware of this felt sense of life, the experience of knowing within awareness" (Siegel 2017, 1). With such an expanded concept of mind in hand, Siegel continues,

> we've suggested that consciousness may arise from a sea of potential, a plan of infinite possibility. Mental processes, such as intention and mood, arise as this energy curve moves toward higher degrees of certainty that we are calling plateaus of probability. Mental activities, such as emoting and emotion, thinking and thought, remembering and memory, are viewed as elevated positions on the curve, sub-peak values preceding the emergence of the peak value of an actualized possibility. This is how the mind can be viewed as an ever emergent unfolding of potential into actual. We've also proposed that beyond consciousness and the subjective feeling of lived life, and perhaps beyond information processing, one aspect of mind can be defined as an emergent, self-organizing, embodied and relational process that arises from and regulates energy and information flow, within and between. Offering this definition of one facet of the mind as a self-organizing process empowers us to define a healthy mind and ways to cultivate mental well-being. (Siegel 2017, 257)

In emphasizing complex systems, emergence, multilevel processes within both individual and social context, Siegel's triadic framework of mind-embodied brain-relationships is entirely compatible with the *Logoi* framework. Although Siegel does not specifically discuss the similarities, his framework is also compatible with contemporary research on information and biosemiotics (see chapter 5).

Human experience throughout the ages attests to evidence that the mind is more than the brain. Most of us have had the sense of being stared at without directly knowing the sources of the starring (Radin 2009, 125–130). This common phenomenon could arise from a non-local mode of perception. More dramatic psychic phenomena such as direct viewing and spiritual experiences are less common. The quantity of research is limited due to materialist presumptions, and the quality of research is mixed as noted by Sheldrake (2012). However, let me call attention to the class of phenomena known as near-death experiences (NDEs), which have been described consistently since antiquity, yet only studied scientifically within the past few decades. As shown in a paper by Bruce Greyson, such NDEs have many features (peace, joy, cosmic unity, out-of-body experience) that overlap with reports of spiritual experience (Greyson 1983); also see the study by Cassandra

Musgrave, who provides more detail on such overlap (Musgrave 1997). One dramatic, personally experienced NDE case is documented by neurosurgeon Eben Alexander, who reports that during his NDE "the part of the brain that controls thought and emotion . . . shut down completely. For seven days he lay in a coma" (Alexander 2012, back cover). David Griffin summarizes six cases of veridical out-of-body experiences (including the NDE as just one type) in which the subject reports on episodes in which the physical body was not present yet corroborated by others; in turn, Griffin quotes another source stating that nonphysical "perceptions" under such conditions are "remarkably accurate" (Griffin 2019, 356). All standard physicalist explanations continue to be unable to explain these experiences. An excellent and rigorous compilation of such psychic phenomena (also termed "subliminal phenomena") is provided in the 800-page encyclopedic work *Irreducible Mind,* edited by Kelly et al. (2007).

My hypothesis, given the *Logoi* framework, is that Alexander's coma was a period in which the quantum-level microtubular network still functioned (enabling the above nonlocal mode of perception), while the standard cognitive mode, depending on the neuroaxonal network, was shut down. To test this hypothesis, observational techniques will need to be developed to assess the microtubular network without dependence on the neuroaxonal network. Perhaps during his coma, Alexander's nonlocal perception was tapping into the realm of non-Boolean *potentiae*, and newly freed up to provide vivid NDE experiences without the usual efficient filtering out by standard consciousness. Even if we set aside NDE cases, the repertoire of well-attested cases of anomalous cognition (or parapsychological phenomena) is voluminous. Griffin has provided one concise summary that argues clearly for the reality of such phenomena (Griffin 1997a). Also, May and Marwaha have organized an impressive set of research results on anomalous cognition (May and Marwaha 2014). While some attempt to simply explain away such phenomena, I regard it as more consistent with the spirit of empirical science to consider such experiences and associated documentation as valuable data for future explanation. Arguably, the *Logoi* framework opens a new way to think about these anomalous phenomena that leverage both science and philosophy, and incorporate both the order of actualizations and the order of *potentiae*.

Anticipatory capabilities that are part of the order of *potentiae*, and associated constraints on future events, may help to understand reports of precognition such as discussed by Russell Targ (2010). Targ and other researchers evaluating anomalous cognition often treat future events as roughly equivalent to past events, except for disallowing any future event from directly changing a past event which, as Targ points out, would result in an intervention paradox (Targ 2010, 79). In contrast, the *Logoi* framework denies actualism and affirms the distinction of an order of actualization and an order of *potentiae*; correspondingly, it affirms that there is a succession of fundamental process (sequencing of metaphysical "presents") such that past events are actualized, settled and definite, whereas future events have varying levels of possibility but are never per se actualized until they become part of the metaphysical past. This affirmation of temporal modality does not conflict with modern physics and relativity theory because, as discussed in chapter 4, measured time and space metrics are emergent from fundamental process; thus, time travel literally into the future (except indirectly via anticipation) is impossible. In a detailed scholarly study of Hartshorne's work, Viney and Shields state that

> Hartshorne . . . is affirming that reality is a *growing totality*, an idea that is also prominent in Peirce's evolutionary cosmology. The growth of reality, moreover, is thoroughly temporal—*time itself is the process of creation.* The past is determinate, the future is a field of relatively indeterminate *possibilia*, and the present is the process of determination. Finally, Hartshorne argues that what comes to be, once it has become fully determinate, is a permanent fixture of all subsequent becoming, guaranteed in the final analysis by God's memory of it. This is why Hartshorne speaks of creation as a *cumulative process.* (Viney and Shields 2015, 17)

My understanding of the available literature about precognition and the so-called time travel is that all known cases can be explained as anticipations or constraints on future events based on current reality, including possible tapping of realms of *potentiae*. Arguments based on relativity theory that argue for a lack of succession in space-like separated domains are, to the best of my knowledge, based solely on epistemic claims about sets of Boolean propositions and the order of actualization. It is a future task for scholars to work out such relativistic arguments with explicit inclusion of both the orders of actualization and *potentiae*.

We will return to Laszlo's concept of the deep Akasha dimension, as well as the emergence of spiritual experience, in chapter 8. For now, my primary reservation concerning the theories of Laszlo, as well as Hameroff and Penrose, is that they often appear to assume actualism, which does not distinguish the order of actualization and the order of *potentiae*. For Laszlo, both the M-dimension and the A-dimension appear to be characterized as "actual," and the deep A-dimension is simply hidden. Such actualism characterizes the work of most physicists and philosophers, even the work of some researchers who totally affirm the reality of anomalous cognition (e.g., see papers edited by May and Marwaha 2014).

THE SYMBOL-MATTER PROBLEM

"Knowing about" is key to what is meant by knowledge; epistemology inevitably sets up the knower/known duality. As Howard Pattee has stated, and summarized in chapter 3 for one of the Gordian knot items, "the knowledge vehicle cannot be in the same category as what it is about . . . the epistemic cut" (Pattee 2010, 164). The knower-known relation always maps to some form of input-output, and this in turn always involves, ontologically, both an input-output-context triadic and fundamental quantum process, which bridge the logic of *potentiae* and the logic of actualization. The epistemic cut and symbol-matter issue emerge from standard input-output logics, and they are overcome through the interplay of triadic forms and fundamental processes featured in the *Logoi* framework. Pattee continues,

> Fully understanding this power of symbols over matter at *all* evolutionary levels is what I call "the symbol–matter problem." The four most notorious symbol–matter levels are the genetic code in biology, pattern recognition and sensorimotor control in nervous systems, the measurement and control problem in physics, and the mind–body problem in philosophy. (Pattee 2011, 222)

The multiple levels of the symbol-matter problem, here noted by Pattee, can be readily understood via the *Logoi* framework. The multiple synchronic levels of the symbol-matter problem reflect a duality without dualism (e.g., system cut, epistemic cut, etc.) that arises from the two logical orders (Boolean and non-Boolean) that underlie fundamental quantum process, and these phenomena are expected at multiple levels just as much as Auxier and Herstein's "quanta of explanation" function at multiple levels, as do the associated processes of multilevel emergence as discussed in chapter 4. As Robert Logan points out, such symbol-real dualities at multiple levels can be compared with Ulanowicz's Logan-Schumann neo-duality of emergence of mind, and the symbolosphere, which incorporate the mind and all of its symbolic products, and which extend the semiosphere concept as mentioned in the latter half of chapter 5. Using symbolosphere to denote Hoffmeyer's concept of a symbolic semiosphere,[8] Logan argues

> that verbal symbolic language led directly to human co-operation, altruism and spirituality and these uniquely human qualities are products of our minds.
>
> Contrary to a commonly held notion that the brain and the mind are the same, neo-duality entails the notion that the brain and the mind are distinct and that they belong respectively to the physiosphere and the symbolosphere...the brain is a thing, quite a complex thing but a thing nevertheless and the mind is a process. I would also argue that the mind is basically an emergent phenomenon

possessing properties not possessed by its two main components, namely the brain and verbal language. (Logan 2013, 424)

Based on the *Logoi* framework, with its orders of *potentiae* and actualization, symbol-matter relations arise from linkage of these two orders. Similarly, the neo-duality concept places the brain (as a "thing") within the order of actualization and the mind (as a "process") as including active linkages with the order of *potentiae*. The symbolosphere and semiosphere are also incorporated in the order of *potentiae*. A symbol-matter problem is reinforced by staying only within the order of actualization (e.g., via actualism) and applying only standard input-output dualism. Deploying the neo-duality distinction of both orders, along with the triad of input-output-context, enables an understanding of the brain-mind distinction, and provides a basis for the symbolosphere and semiosphere. Further, as we have seen, these concepts aid in advancing the understanding of human consciousness (see chapter 4).

SUMMARY OF INTELLECTUAL DEVELOPMENTS

Through an intercomparison of intellectual developments, ancient to modern, science and philosophy, albeit primarily via the Western philosophic tradition, I conclude that there really have been key humanistic/philosophical and scientific advances on several key issues over the past century. The full impact of these important developments on many applications is just beginning. The *Logoi* framework, with its distinction of both the orders of actualization and *potentiae*, and its triad of logic, process, and relations, provides a unified way to thinking anew and productively about every one of these conceptual developments.

1. from reductionism only to both reduction and emergence (required for complex systems and biology);
2. from particulars only (nominalism) to both particulars and universals (see Blachowicz, *Essential Difference* (2012, 278); also Campbell (2015) and Seibt (2004);
3. from substance only to both substance and process (both *relata* and relations);
4. for fundamental relations, from dyads to triads (emergence of semiosis, biosemiotics, etc.);
5. for possible relations (*potentiae*), from epistemic only to both epistemic and ontic (real);
6. from dualism and dualistic-thinking, to dualities without dualism (third way);

7. from homogeneous systems to non-homogeneous (former as common approximation);

8. from Boolean-only logic, to both Boolean and non-Boolean (required for quantum physics), or from actualizations only (actualism) to both actual and *potentiae* as part of the real;

9. from strict entailment and formal completeness in mathematics and theory, set theory, classical (Boolean) logic only, to fundamental limits (Gödel), non-Boolean logic, para-consistent logics, and category theory;

10. from parts-aggregates simplistic part-whole mereology to category theory mereotopology, including composites, multiscale emergence, and hierarchies;

11. from linear dynamics of context-independent components, to non-linear dynamics of multiscale, interdependent processes;

12. from classical mechanics of substances within pre-given three-space structures (metric) to complex systems and modern physics (whether via quantum physics or its classical physics approximation), incorporating dynamical processes (process, extension (pre-space)) with temporality and specific metric as emergent.

Some implications of the above conceptual developments, all integrated with the *Logoi* framework, are as follows:

physicalism—the claim that the actuality domain is all inclusive—incorrect;
causal closure—the claim that the Boolean logical order is all inclusive—incorrect;
scientism—the claim that its domain of discourse is all inclusive—incorrect;
atheism—depends on the metaphysical claim that all is contingent—incorrect;[9]
many-worlds interpretation of quantum physics (as with physicalism)—makes
metaphysical claim of actualism, that the domain of the "real" is nothing but the
actual—incorrect.

These implications, among others, are testimony to why the kind of scholarship that enables the *Logoi* framework, or equivalent systematic philosophical frameworks, are profoundly important. Arguably, speculative philosophical work, like that carried out here, can help bolster critiques of nihilist worldviews and some common presuppositions that contribute to ethical and economic failures arising from laissez-faire capitalism, or all-too-common presumptions of some zero-sum game, us-versus-them, or security-at-all-cost and pro-war mentality. Relevant to these themes, see the critiques by Gare (2017), Weber (2016), and Griffin (2018).

We inevitably hold to a kind of inclusive framing of things, most often implicit and presupposed. Explicitly formulating and testing an inclusive framework, such as the *Logoi* framework or a metatheory framework like critical realism or integral theory, enables us to become more self-aware and enhances valuable critiques of incoherent or internally inconsistent world-view notions. Such critique is best served by radically multidisciplinary studies involving science, philosophy, logic, semiotics, and so on. We now have new resources available for a renaissance in philosophy and science, making possible a new approach to problems that have puzzled thinkers for centuries, and opening the way for further progress in a range of fields. My hope is that new integrative approaches like the *Logoi* framework can free people from ideas that have kept them stuck because of faulty presuppositions, and thereby open the way toward intellectual liberation and, hopefully, developing new strategies for gaining enhanced self-awareness, other awareness, and genuine freedom for everyone.

NOTES

1. Details on the argument for the primacy of triadic structures are provided in the paper "Triads as Fundamental: Triadic Asymmetry as Primal in Logic, Mathematics, and Physics," by George Shields and Timothy Eastman (2020).

2. Ken Wilber has introduced an analogous triad: "*the eye of the flesh*, which informs us about the world of our senses; *the eye of the mind*, which allows us access to mathematics, ideas, and logic; and *the eye of contemplation*, which is our window to the world of spiritual experience" (Jane Katra and Russell Targ 1999, 7).

3. Not all Vedic philosophy avoids a reductive holism; for example, Advaita Vedanta commits one to an eternalist ontology of a block universe including a strict monism in which there is only one Being for whom there is no time in the standard sense of past, present and future; see Chakravarthi Ram-Prasad (2002).

4. "Ways of knowing" were discussed long ago by William Monague's (1925). However, his "ways" (authoritarianism, mysticism, rationalism, empiricism, pragmatism, skepticism) are epistemic or pragmatic in focus whereas my focus is ontological.

5. Instead of using just the word "sign," semiosis is used here to denote general forms of semiotic relation (general "sign" process; pointers to a "third") because the connotation of "sign" is often simply epistemic, whereas my current focus is ontological.

6. Our work complements that of Pierfrancesco Basile, who points out that "it seems preposterous to pretend, as eliminative philosophers do, that mental states are not genuine realities . . . As a matter of fact, what may be called the Leibniz-Whitehead argument against materialism is a very strong one—as good as any of the best proofs in philosophy" (Basile 2018, 7–8).

7. Whitehead's concept of prehension and theory of perception is developed in most major treatments of process philosophy; for example, John Lango (1972) and Nicholas Rescher (1996).

8. The term symbolosphere is a hybrid concept in that it combines epistemological features (i.e., the symbolic) with an ontic feature of the world (the semiosphere).

Within the last line of the quote, "verbal language" is also a hybrid feature, being not only a component of mind, but also an emergent feature of the symbolosphere.

9. Atheism (i.e., a-theism) is often presumed to be the denial of classical theism, which neglects major alternative interpretations of religious frameworks (see chapter 8).

Chapter 8

Contextuality—From Experience to Meaning

THE GENESIS OF MEANING

In our shared journey of speculative philosophy, struggling with a Gordian knot of problems, I have suggested some tentative routes to solutions by way of an integrative framework, the *Logoi* framework, which leverages developments within the past century in quantum physics, semiotics, complex systems, philosophy, among other scholarly fields. Further, with respect to addressing the most fundamental of philosophical problems, I have attempted to avoid the high abstractions and exotic concepts favored by some, instead focusing on concepts compatible with basic human experience. Building on the most fundamental of notions (process/logic/relations), the fundamental ontological factors that we have revealed are as follows: (1) mode of being/ becoming (contingent vs. non-contingent); (2) logical orders (Boolean vs. non-Boolean; actualizations vs. *potentiae*); (3) pre-space extensive connection (local-global); (4) quantum process (diachronic; fundamental succession); and (5) emergence (synchronic; multilevel; triadicity and semiosis). In conjunction with these ontological factors, I have focused on two fundamental epistemological factors: (1) modes of perception (presentational immediacy versus causal efficacy, based on Whitehead's analysis), and (2) three basic ways of knowing: the way of context independence (science, the quantitative, mathematical, and physical relationships); the way of context (humanities and the arts, the qualitative, the way of signs or semiosis); and finally, the way of ultimate context (way of spirit; for example, the contemplative traditions, theology, and religion). By deploying the *Logoi* framework, a unified approach is enabled that takes us beyond discrete substances, mechanism, and separateness to fundamental events, processes, and interconnectedness; instead of a simple reductionism of all things to discreet, separable "things,"

237

we have both reduction and emergence, both analysis and creative synthesis. Rethinking the relational web and working through multiple levels of context and synthesis, we have arrived at a vision of transformative thinking, ultimacies and meaning, human and more.

The *Logoi* framework offers a new way to think about the issue of how meaning might be embedded in the universe without invoking ad hoc some divine entity. This is in contrast to how the meaning of "meaning" has often been presumed to be based simply on psychological projections or limited to epistemological issues. Instead, I highlight a set of stepping stones toward meaning—a convergence of arguments from fundamental process, fundamental philosophical results, and human experience that points to an ontological ground for meaning. As we have seen in chapters 2–4, fundamental process yields multiple levels of (diachronic) ontic causation and (synchronic) emergent context. Analysis of the former enables explanatory models for science; analysis of the latter comprises both general systems theory and multiple levels of context to partially ground "meaning." Fundamental philosophic analysis, including arguments from philosophical logic, demonstrates that triadic structures are primal (viz., that triadic relations in the relational web of fundamental process and input-output-context structure are radically pervasive and unlimited). As stated by Shields and Eastman, "building on the pervasive presence of triadic forms in logic, mathematics, field physics and fundamental quantum process, we abductively infer from this radical ubiquity of triads that triadic structures are metaphysically primal" (Shields and Eastman 2020). Such unlimited triadic form and input-output-context structure enable the relational web of the real, the fundamental processual weavings of both the orders of actuality and *potentiae*, that can fully ground ontological meaning.

Physical constraint closure, critically important for complex biological systems as argued by Kauffman (2019), does not by itself enable a full ground for meaning because of their limitation to the order of actuality, and because the metaphysical primal triadic forms, discussed above, inevitably link the orders of actuality and *potentiae*, which then point to a needed ground for the latter. As we have seen, the order of *potentiae* is central to the basis for physical law (see *"Law"—From Entailment to Constrained Processual Histories* in chapter 4), the principle of universality (see *Logoi Framework in a Nutshell* in chapter 2), and a basis for fundamental quantum process and temporality (see *The Relational Reality Model* in chapter 2). Finally, both human experience and philosophic argument, considered inclusively, point to three ways of knowing, including ultimate context, which suggests that such affirmation of ontological meaning has an ultimate ground. Within the *Logoi* framework, such ultimate ground is not invoked ad hoc but arises naturally from a confluence of arguments, experiential, philosophic, and scientific.

MEANING, ETHICS, AND HISTORICAL CONTEXT

We have seen how deepening our lived experience and enabling enhanced understanding of ourselves and the world around us requires three fundamental ways of knowing as noted above. John Battista and Richard Almond argue that the search for some form of intrinsic meaning derives from self-transcendent models, humanistic models, notions of Being, or from the spiritual dimension (religious models) (Battista and Almond 1973). Whereas these are attempts to best characterize the concept of meaning, I offer some speculative hypotheses on the ontological ground of meaning.

Harry Heft argues for the reality of meaning by noting that "one essential quality of human experience that has received scant attention in experimental psychology is *meaningfulness.* Unlike the world described by the physical sciences, the world-as-lived is meaningful; and clearly, much of human action is characterized by 'efforts toward meaning'." He then goes on to provide us with a clue to its more fundamental ground by stating that "At its most basic level, meaning is a relational or contextual property of human experience" (Heft 2001, xxvii). The *Logoi* framework provides a unified framework to systematically correlate such relational or contextual properties so as to point to an ontological ground for meaning.

The *Logoi* framework builds on the reality of *potentiae* and local-global linkages, as developed in the Relational Reality model and argued above in chapter 3, to enable a ground for intrinsic meaning, referenced in the last Gordian knot. Working with the input-output-context triad, incorporated by all physical systems at multiple scales, we can formulate a multiscale basis for ultimate context. This basis includes truth and reference, and relationships between things and symbols (pointers to relations, context, and things). Indeed, the *Logoi* framework leverages multidisciplinary elements of such context, including quantum physics, nonlinear dynamics, category theory, emergence, semiotics and biosemiotics, systematic philosophy, and metaphysics. With such leveraging and fundamental principles, the *Logoi* framework indicates that multiple layers of context are inevitably grounded in some ultimate context that includes reference to ultimate boundaries and other ultimates—the order of ultimacies—including non-contingent order and the spiritual dimension (see *Systematic Philosophy and Ultimacies* section below).

Arguably, some form of an affirmation of meaning is hardcore common sense, as Griffin defines it, a notion that is "presupposed in practice" (Griffin 2013, 266), the denial of which constitutes a performative contradiction. Paradoxically, there are people who expend great effort to demonstrate the meaninglessness of the world, but inevitably do so within a context that presupposes the meaningfulness of such anti-meaning activity. Many years ago,

I read a philosophical pamphlet on the topic of meaning that basically concluded, on philosophical grounds, that reference to meaning is meaningless. Indeed, arguably in violation of hardcore common sense, such an argument may appear convincing under the assumptions of actualism and Boolean-only propositions upon measurement outcomes, or isolated, bare facts separated from context. However, as argued above, ours is not a Boolean-only world, actualism is false, and some form of context is inevitably relevant; instead, we have both the actual and *potentiae* as part of the real, along with context at multiple levels, without limit. Such multiple levels of context are the ground of meaning (see chapter 3, *Untying the Gordian Knot 13. Problem of meaning*); without that, the world really is meaningless.[1]

Our direct experience is always local but our immediate inferences of the world always include global aspects. In our daily living we presuppose some measure of meaning, however limited, which is associated with multiple levels of context, reaching conceptually outward to the global. Further, one form of global connectedness that everyone has experienced is witnessing the night sky, the viewing of photons associated with stellar sources at astronomical distance. Via long-range electromagnetic fields, which enable such long-range photons, this is a real and practical link to a global connectedness. Scientific counterparts to such connectedness are the local-global relations treated by Zafiris by applying category theory analysis to quantum physics (Zafiris 2010); another related example is the entanglement phenomenon that we infer to be associated with correlations among non-Boolean potential relations, or *potentiae*.

Bradley's results, discussed in chapter 3, can be fruitfully compared to our *Logoi* framework. In his analysis, meaning is enabled through both multiple levels of context and through the interrelated combination of his three basic questions: the nature of origin, difference, and order (Bradley 2009). These questions and their answers correspond closely, for "origin," to the concepts of *potentiae*, the non-contingent and ultimates; for "difference," succession, quantum process and *actualization* (diachronic) along with extension and multilevel emergence (synchronic); and, for "order," multilevel constraints on *potentiae* (enabling Peircean generals or physical relations, viz., laws).

Along with meaning, from the above argument for an intrinsic ground for meaning based on input-output-context triads at multilevel, finally to ultimate context, there follows as well a basis for ethics. A classic work in understanding human happiness is Aristotle's *Eudemian Ethics* where happiness is framed in a comprehensive view as involving, as Nagel expresses it, "the interaction of reason, emotion, perception, and action in an ensouled body" (Nagel 1972, 252). Inspired by Aristotle's concept of *eudaimonia*, combined with a thorough analysis of ethical theories over the centuries, Robert Spitzer has distilled the basic elements of ethical theory down to a concise four-level framework for happiness, desire, and purpose in life.

> The purpose of education from the days of the Greek Academy to the present has been to help students to move from the immediately gratifying to the enduring, from the apparent and superficial to the deep, from the narrow and intensive to the pervasive. This is why these four levels of happiness have found their way into so many philosophies, psychologies, sociologies, and anthropologies. They are not simply part of our inner makeup. They are really a culmination of many cultures' reflections on the common good and the purpose of education. (Spitzer 2000, 64)

The four levels are then provided by Spitzer in a concise diagram containing the following elements:

Level 1: immediate gratification, hedonistic, obligation to self alone;
Level 2: personal achievement/ego, short-term gratification, promotion of self as primary, focus on coercive power and control;
Level 3: good beyond self, long-term gratification, focus on justice, love and community, greater good; focus on relational power (vs. coercive power) and cooperation (vs. control);
Level 4: ultimate good, participate in giving and receiving ultimate meaning, goodness, and love. [adapted from Spitzer's diagram 2]. (ibid. 65)

Ken Wilber has summarized a similar four-level schema as, respectively, ego-centric, ethnocentric, world-centric (universal), and integral consciousness (ultimate meaning) (Wilber 2011). Spitzer elaborates on how transitions between these levels occur as we seek higher levels of psychological and emotional integration.

> Interestingly, both Eastern and Western ancient systems of ranking levels of happiness and crises coincide closely with our modern understanding of human psychological development. Further, it seems that the crises actually serve an important developmental function: just as each of the lower levels of happiness generates a specific crisis, so each crisis opens the way to the next higher level of happiness. (Spitzer 2000, 66)

After childhood and its level 1 focus, most of us get beyond the level 1–2 struggle, and then wrestle with the transition from level 2 to level 3. On rare occasion, a fellow human goes beyond that to level 4.

In addition to the above levels of psychological and emotional integration, Wilber also distinguishes structures of psychological maturity or "growing up," based on research in developmental psychology, and states of spiritual awakening or "waking up" which, he points out, are generally neglected in contemporary worldviews (Wilber 2017, 8–16). As with any complex worldview, applying Wilber's framework has its limits—as noted by Daryl Paulson:

> An integral philosophy, such as that promoted by Ken Wilber, can be very useful in providing an individual with a wide-scope theory to serve as an orienting worldview and container enabling them to develop their spiritual practices. Wilber's view is particularly useful in that it covers objective, intersubjective, and subjective world spaces at once. Used too rigidly, it can become an overly mechanical process of merely downloading a canned integral program into one's internal operating system. (Paulson 2008, 364)

With regard to the field of ethics, the works of Rem Edwards (2014) and Brian Henning (2005) are consistent with the *Logoi* framework, and especially promising because they frame an ecological vision that is very compatible with some works in the philosophy of nature; for example, Joseph Grange (1997a) and Frederic Ferré (1996); see also the Ferré festschrift (George Allan and Merle Allshouse 2005). Another ecological perspective that is focused on pedagogy, grounded in people and the land, was the emerging understanding, beginning in the late eighteenth century, as stated by Lene Andersen and Tomas Bjorkman, that all "people must be able to control their emotions, internalize the norms of society and take individual moral responsibility. In German, this kind of personal ego-development goes under the name *Bildung*" (Andersen and Bjorkman 2017, 9). A path toward developing everyone's potential, which came to be known as "folk-*Bildung*," was sketched out in a "farmhouse on the small Danish island of Funen in 1851" (ibid.). Andersen and Bjorkman argue, in *The Nordic Secret*, that an enhanced form of folk-*Bildung* has been central to how, over the century following that farmhouse gathering, "the Nordics were transformed peacefully from dirt-poor farming countries to some of the richest industrialized countries in the world" (ibid.), and who also rank year after year as among the happiest people in the world. Their folk-*Bildung* concept employs levels of personal and social development that are closely related to contemporary research results in developmental psychology and social science. Andersen and Bjorkman also provide extensive discussion of the intellectual background for folk-*Bildung* and associated changes in worldview, going beyond the standard modernist worldview, and ultimately to an ecological vision. One player in their story is Friedrich Schelling, an early nineteenth-century philosopher of process, whom Gare highlights in his recent work *The Philosophical Foundations of Ecological Civilization* (Gare 2017). Andersen and Bjorkman argue persuasively that attention to both education and worldview, with emphasis on wisdom, ethics, and reason, can make important and practical differences in the world.

Our *Logoi* framework had its debut in chapter 2 with acknowledgment of several translations of *Logos*, as summarized by Tallis (2018) and Brann (2011). Tallis, for example, summarizes various meanings of the word *Logos*, including, among others, "ratio, proportion, principle, standard; reasoning power; hypothesis, ground for belief or action . . . to gather together, to arrange, and to put in order . . . that which results in a world picture" (Tallis 2018, 32). Setting aside specifically religious connotations, the Greek word *Logos* provides linkages to all of our fundamental notions: process, logic, relations, and points beyond these as well with special emphasis on experience and context. Attending to multiple levels of context, which contribute to both human meaning and ethics, we inferred the three ways of knowing reviewed at the beginning of this chapter.

In discussing Heraclitus's views, Tallis states that "in the mind of the philosopher, the microscopic human *Logos* was united with the macroscopic *Logos* of the *Cosmos*. Specifically, *Logos*, in the sense of The Word, provided the link between rational discourse and the world's rational structure, the universal reason governing and permeating the world" (ibid. 34). A similar micro-macro bridge of *Logos* undoubtedly motivated efforts by Swimme and Thomas Berry toward articulating *The Universe Story* (1994), which attempts to open space for a spiritual dimension. However, most such "Big History" efforts are more limited in scope (e.g., often neglecting the way of ultimate context), however excellent in what they may accomplish.

In a classic philosophical work on *Truth and Historicity*, Campbell states that

> it was the metaphysical theories of Parmenides and Plato which reified being as the Real, and from there the tendency to think ahistorically flowed into the Western metaphysical tradition. The narrative traced in this book is the story of a massive intellectual struggle lasting more than two millenniums to find more dynamic ways of thinking. (Campbell 1992, 436)

In contrast to ahistorical approaches, our systematic philosophy efforts and the *Logoi* framework are all within the context of what Campbell calls "the trans-historical notion of truth [recognizing] that everything in this world is transitory, that even the most reliable is only relatively so. We are all too fallible, and so is everything else in the world. The sense of truth invoked in this notion is of the utterly faithful and ultimately reliable." As well, Campbell adds a future orientation to his argument as follows, "Truth as an eschatological ultimate stands to the future as a limit stands to a mathematical series . . . [and] retains a reference to futurity" (ibid. 438).

To emphasize our embeddedness in history and context at multiple levels, Campbell continues,

> To be faithful in this way—to act with integrity and insight towards others and the reality in which we are situated—is a challenge confronting us in all our life-activity. The truth, therefore, is not to be found by renouncing our historicity, nor in trying to construct an impersonal and timeless account of reality which flies in the face of our own humanity. It is rather to be achieved in the quality and authenticity of our faithful life-activities. (Campbell 1992, 438)

Such life-activity for myself is that always incomplete struggle with understanding the world, with meaning and values, with both the past and the future—efforts at philosophizing grounded in experience, truth-seeking, context, and historicity.

George Ellis states that "our system of values and ethics shapes what we regard as desirable or undesirable actions, and what we see as meaningful or not. The brain is searching all the time for meaning, and our concept of what is meaningful changes our life choices" (Ellis 2016, 296). Within a multidisciplinary argument for both top-down and bottom-up influences, Ellis continues,

> we need values to guide our rational decision; ethics, aesthetics, and meaning are crucial to deciding what kind of life we will live. They are the highest level in our goals hierarchy, shaping all the other goal decisions by setting the direction and purpose that underlies them: they define the *telos* (purpose) which guides our life. They do not directly determine what the lower level decisions will be, but set the framework within which choices involving conflicting criteria will be made and guide the kinds of decisions which will be made, particularly by setting constraints on what is acceptable behavior and guiding as to what is desirable...The search for meaning is not an optional extra: as made so clear by Victor Frankl, it is a basic need, and a core driver of mental life. (Ellis 2016, 313–314)

Recently, Ellis has made an even stronger case for moral realism, and how one cannot, as David Hume famously argued, simply derive "ought" from "is."

> This nature of morality . . . greatly strengthens arguments against any purely materialistic attempts to derive the nature of ethics or morality. Scientific explanations of morality try to reduce it to self interest. And that is precisely what it is not. Kenotic morality is based in love for the other: that is its underlying deep value. My view is that moral realism points to meaning and purpose underlying

physical existence. How can such a kenotic morality come to be? It must reflect the forces or intentions that created the universe, because it is part of the deep structure of the cosmos. This strongly suggests a Creator whose central value is love. How else can you explain it? (Ellis 2020, 13)

Such attention to values and meaning by a prominent physicist is refreshing, and is augmented by philosopher Robert Neville, who highlights philosophy's recent tendency to be seduced by the power of reductive scientific strategies.

Given the enormous damage to human civilization in the loss of value-reference and realistic valuation in modern Western science, the price of failure to recognize the difference between knowledge of the physical world as such and knowledge of the physical world as reduced to the terms of non-valuational mathematics has been extraordinarily high. (Neville 2013, 53)

Not only were many early modern philosophers, such as Descartes, blind to this distinction but, unfortunately, similar blindness afflicts more recent advocates of scientism. Thus, Neville continues, "one of philosophy's major difficulties: to maintain sufficient connection with reductive inquiries so as to understand them without being seduced into forgetting that they exclude all aspects of their real subject matters that do not fit their reductive analyses" (ibid.). It is the intent of my present work and its *Logoi* framework to help articulate those aspects of the "physical world as such" and of our daily experience that drop out of simple reductive analyses. Numerous scientists have attempted to overcome such simplistic reductionism; for example, Charles Birch, prominent biologist and ecologist, wrote clearly about the importance of meaning and purpose (Birch, 1990), and theoretical biologist and complex systems theorist Stuart Kauffman argues that creativity and meaning and purposeful action are real properties of the universe that can be the subject of scholarly investigations (Kauffman 2008). If we excise such critical data of human experience, our theories set themselves up to inevitably be incomplete.

INTEGRATIVE FRAMEWORKS AND METHODOLOGY

My struggles for understanding have led me through a wide diversity of world views,[2] philosophical frameworks, patterns in the history of thought, varieties of scientific conceptions and frameworks, and various "-isms" (skepticism, empiricism, rationalism, Platonism, idealism, pluralism, pragmatism, scientism). Even the sophisticated and wide-ranging "radical empiricism" of Whitehead, which framed much of my earlier philosophical thinking, now appears incomplete, in part due to numerous scholarly advances made over the past century. There have been some worthy recent efforts at fully integrative frameworks of understanding, such as those formulated by Roy Bhaskar (critical realism), Edgar Morin (complex thought), and Ken Wilber (integral theory); these have been thoughtfully surveyed by Paul Marshall (2016). Another broad and inclusive framework centers around Thomas Berry and *The Great Work* (1999), which builds on the works of Pierre Teilhard de Chardin, and is concisely summarized by Herman Greene (2018). These works provide a useful segue into *The Universe Story* articulated by Brian Swimme and Thomas Berry (1994), which weaves together science and the humanities; also see the video documentary by Swimme (2011), and *The New Cosmic Story* by John Haught (2017). Collectively, the de Chardin-Berry-Swimme works constitute a fourth integrative framework. Another integrative effort worthy of mention is that created by Joseph Bracken as surveyed by Marc Pugliese and Gloria Schaab (2012). Finally, the highly integrative framework of Basarab Nicolescu, called "transdisciplinarity," specifically incorporates multiple levels of reality, the logic of the included middle (here referred to as non-Boolean logic), and complexity. Details are laid out in Nicolescu's most recent work, *From Modernity to Cosmodernity* (Nicolescu 2015). The transdisciplinary framework, in addition, emphasizes meaning and ethics.[3]

Maintaining a skepticism toward "-isms," the *Logoi* framework is my attempt at an integrative framework of systematic philosophy which, although less developed, appears more comprehensive than most of the integrative philosophies listed here. The strength of the *Logoi* framework lies in the useful contributions it could make to an improved integrative framework because its scope is broader, taking into account, among other features, (1) its compact set of fundamental notions (process, logic, relations, context) yet incorporating both reduction and emergence; (2) its focus on two aspects of the real (both the actual and *potentiae*) and, correspondingly two logical orders within the real (the Boolean order of actualizations, and non-Boolean order of *potentiae*); (3) distinguishing diachronic and synchronic focus as key ways to characterize, respectively, causation and emergence; and (4) attention to multiple ways of knowing and associated levels of context; namely, context independence (science); context dependence (arts and humanities; semiotics); and ultimate context (dimensions of spirit). The combination of all four of the above features is unique to the *Logoi* framework.[4]

In comparison to the fully integrative frameworks that Marshall discusses, however broad and inclusive they are, and admirable in attempting to address issues of both spirit and physical systems, the *Logoi* framework is set within a yet broader context that includes the structural-systematic philosophy of White and Puntel (White 2014), American philosophy and process philosophy, including the process theory of Johanna Seibt (2004, 359), semiotics (Deely

1990) and biosemiotics (Hoffmeyer 2009), evolutionary studies (Henning and Scarfe 2013), physics, mathematics, and logic (Epperson and Zafiris 2013; Primas 2017), information theory (Logan 2014), complex systems and anticipatory systems (Rosen 2012), and the humanities (Epstein 2012). This integrative metatheory attempts to synthesize basic concepts and presuppositions in all possible dimensions. In addition to the integrative metatheories noted above, there are several others that are complementary to my efforts. Exemplary embodiments of such integrative approaches are summarized in *What is Ecological Civilization?* by Philip Clayton and Wm. Andrew Schwartz, who call attention to "some of the main concepts that are being used: 'integral ecology,' the 'new story,' 'unity in diversity,' constructive postmodernism,' the 'ecozoic era,' the Japanese notion of 'Yoko civilization,' 'organic Marxism,' 'process philosophy,' an 'open and relational worldview,' and the 'philosophy of organism'" (Clayton and Schwartz 2019, 72). The unifying feature of multiple movements engendering these concepts, they continue, is a "vision for a radically different future in which the systems of society—economics and politics, systems of production, consumption and agriculture—are redesigned in light of planetary limits. The vision emerges from the death of the modern *expand, conquer, and consume* mentality and tells a new story of harmony with a living Earth: *contract, cooperate, and cultivate*" (ibid. 92).

Methodologically, I try to remain grounded in common sense, broadly construed, within endless cycles of experience/model-making/testing. The scientific method is a special case of such evidence-based methodology, which contrasts sharply with the advocacy-based thinking (often with confirmation bias) that appears so common in the *polis*. It is commonly argued, as noted by Anton Lawson, that the scientific process is adequately characterized by the hypothetico-deductive framework (Lawson 2015). In contrast, in scientific work that I have both practiced and witnessed, there are innumerable examples of both data-driven and model-driven endeavors, both deductive and inductive approaches, both bottom-up and top-down perspectives; such diversity of method is not easily captured by any one single methodological scheme. As Ilkka Niiniluoto and Raimo Tuomela have argued, one framework that explicitly handles the importance of induction is the hypothetico-inductive approach (Niiniluoto and Tuomela 2012). In addition, Farzad Mahootian and I have argued that an observational-inductive (abductive) framework provides an important supplement to the model-centric hypothetico-deductive framework to better represent the full range of actual scientific practice (Mahootian and Eastman 2009). Concerning scientific practice with even more inclusive terms, Ann Plamondon has inferred from Whitehead's corpus some important added perspectives on the use of metaphor and analogical inference schema (Plamondon 1979). A concise summary of scientific methodology and the influence of metaphysical presuppositions is given by Dusek (1999, 282–291).

The scholarly methodologies described above are especially appropriate to the way of numbers (science) and the way of context (arts and humanities). However, the way of spirit requires a further methodology. For example, Fr. Richard Rohr has argued for a critical augmentation that arises from an open and deep listening process, which he summarizes with the word "contemplation." Such contemplative practice is key to enabling awareness of the way of spirit, but is also important for all other ways of knowing because it enables a grounding for meaning, and in turn awareness of the ground of being/becoming.[5]

Campbell calls for truth and historicity in order to overcome what he describes as two millennia of a "tendency to think ahistorically" (Campbell 1992). In response, I now see, in a number of recent scientific and philosophical developments, albeit not yet dominant (even, in many respects, marginalized),[6] some clear and hopeful signs of convergence toward more experiential and context-oriented, evidence-based frameworks of understanding. This characterization, in my view, is most evident in certain areas of process-oriented science (ecology, ecological developmental biology (eco-devo), astrobiology, biosemiotics, quantum physics, plasma physics, dynamical systems, semantic information theory), and philosophy (process philosophy, semiotics, pragmatism, phenomenology, philosophy of quantum physics, philosophy of chemistry). These integrative developments and frameworks may also serve to enhance the culture of communities in their total environment, such as Paul Schafer has promoted, not only with social levels of culture but also dimensions of culture that are artistic, folk, media recreational, environmental, scientific, educational, religious, political, and economic (Schafer 2014, 197–198).

LIMITATIONS OF THE *LOGOI* FRAMEWORK, OR ANY INTEGRATIVE FRAMEWORK

Although intended to be unlimited in scope, my *Logoi* framework remains necessarily limited, being a highly fallible product of human speculation (as with any other attempted systematic framework or worldview). In particular, using the Greek word *Logos* itself points to one basic limitation, linked to a central purpose of religious scriptures, which is transformation. Keeping in mind the possibilities of deep transformation, or second-order change, we must seek guidance for full understanding of ourselves and the world through both *Logos* and *Mythos*, through both rational discourse and stories providing multilevel access to *possibiliae*, including second-order change, or *change of change*.

Based on an argument grounded in group theory and the theory of logical types, Paul Watzlawick, John Weakland, and Richard Fisch describe

> two different types of change: one that occurs within a given system which itself remains unchanged, and one whose occurrence changes the system itself. To exemplify this distinction in more behavioral terms: a person having a nightmare can do many things *in* his dream-run, hide, fight, scream jump off a cliff, etc.—but no change from any of these behaviors to another would ever terminate the nightmare. *We shall henceforth refer to this kind of change as first-order change.* The one way out of a dream involves a change from dreaming to waking. Waking, obviously is no longer a part of the dream, but a change to an altogether different state. *This kind of change will from now on be referred to as second-order change* . . . Second-order change is thus *change of change.* (Watzlawick et al. 2011, 10–11)

A basic point of religious scripture, common to many of the world's contemplative traditions, is transformation, effectively a call to second-order change. As stated by Rohr,

> when we stopped understanding myth, we stopped understanding how to read—and profit from—sacred story. Art, myth, and poetry invite us into the transformative world of sacred story. This kind of knowing has the power to change us at the level of the subconscious and intuition because it can open mind, heart, and body simultaneously. (Rohr 2018)

Our *Logoi* framework, however inclusive, is necessarily set within our two fundamental logics, the logic of actualizations and the logic of *possibiliae*. Both are multilevel in their infinite variety, but our conceptual horizons transcend the limits of first-order change. Recognizing finiteness and fallibility, our frameworks are always fallible inferences and approximations, not perfections (as well, this applies to all sciences). The logic of *possibiliae* is especially open to creativity in the world (Whitehead's category of the ultimate[7]), and to second-order change, indeed possibilities for transformation in our encounters with the world—extending at times to encounters with ultimate context, marked by sacred story—the way of spirit.

In such transformation then arises a new sense of meaning, reality in its fullness, beyond all dualistic thinking, but then to a new commitment, a call to re-enter the world in a new way, beyond mere advocacy to evidence, reason, and understanding, beyond divisiveness and hate to forgiveness and love. I will return to these practical concepts again later in this chapter.[8]

Using examples from only a couple of highly quantitative and theory-oriented research fields, John Horgan concluded that, coming into view, was the end of science (Horgan 2015). In contrast to such premature closure, it is clear to me that both science and philosophy confront endless frontiers; in science, this is partly due to the unlimited plethora of contingent beings, process and relations to observe and understand at multiple scales. Horgan's "end of science" presumes a deductive account of science in which, when the ultimate equation is identified and confirmed (*à la* Carroll's core equation), then everything is, in principle, deducible. Such speculations presuppose a Boolean-only logical framework, actualism (i.e., denial of the distinction of the actual and *potentiae*), and causal closure of the physical—as argued above, all these notions are false. Methodologically, effective and productive science requires all aspects of the human quest for understanding: systematic thought and creativity, abduction, deduction and induction, reason and intuition, observation and theory, modeling and simulation, epistemology and ontology, physics and philosophy, science, humanities, religion, institutions, publications, and (lest we forget) people.

In this quest for understanding, a classic integrative work in the genre of speculative philosophy is Whitehead's *Process and Reality* (1929), which has played a key role in inspiring the present-day worldwide scholarly activity in process thought. However, as stated by Clinton Combs, even the many advances achieved by Whitehead have their limits as admitted by the master himself. Combs highlights Faber's insight on such limitations:

> Roland Faber observes an interesting paradox in Whitehead's speculative endeavor: Whitehead both goes to great lengths to develop a systematic scheme (or schemes) and simultaneously warns us to mistrust such schemes due to their oversimplification of reality. While many would try to resolve such a paradox by arguing for one side over the other, Faber argues that Whitehead chose to preserve this paradox as a series of deconstructions of his own metaphysical claims. Far from showing the futility of metaphysics, such a deconstruction moves one "beyond metaphysics" in the sense that a metaphysical scheme can never be the final word. (Combs 2010, xiii)

Combs cites, as an example of this evolution of thinking, how mathematician and philosopher of mathematics Robert Valenza "takes us back to Whitehead's surprising mathematics of objects and *their* relations. He points to a major shift that occurs between *Universal Algebra* and *Process and Reality*. Valenza then argues that Whitehead later shifted from having a metaphysics that relied upon having near static eternal objects (in *Process and Reality* [1929]) . . . to a later metaphysics that dispensed with eternal objects in favor of a "reciprocity" between actuality and form in which both are understood organically" (Combs 2010, xiii). Combs further explains how Valenza observes that "the plain irony here is, of course, that the philosopher who would so much celebrate the primacy of relations in his metaphysics, would so neglect it in his mathematics" (Valenza 2010, 114). After continuing his survey of Whitehead's evolution in thinking about eternal objects in his philosophy of organism, from static forms to the later dynamic concept, which comports with our use of *potentiae*, Valenza states that we need

> to allow some significant reciprocity between the abstract and the particular, or objects and relations. At the heart of this is a simple acknowledgement that one cannot speak of reality without simultaneously invoking both poles symmetrically . . . [within his later works] in dropping the language of eternal objects, he restores the symmetry and reciprocity in less technical language. (Valenza 2010, 119)

Because potential relations (*potentiae*) are dynamic, not static, such reciprocity accords well with the *Logoi* framework and its key element of Relational Reality, as based on the work of Epperson and Zafiris in their category theory analysis of fundamental quantum process (Epperson and Zafiris, 2013). Setting aside the fundamental asymmetry, previously discussed, that generates temporality from pre-space process, along with emergent metric forms (not pre-given as with GTR whereby is generated the measurement problem of cosmology—see chapter 6, section titled *Measurement Problems at Extremes of Scale*), such process clearly goes both ways with respect to input and response—input particles, fields, and *potentiae*, enabling new actualizations—in turn, actualizations persistently changing the possibility space, texture, and landscapes of *potentiae*. In this process, once again, there is both asymmetry and symmetry, symmetry in *potentiae* and asymmetry in actualizations; that is, the fundamental asymmetries (context, etc.) that encompass all partial reductions and symmetries—see chapter 4 section on *Symmetry in Science*. Fields and multilevel relations, concepts central to the *Logoi* framework and to other integrative frameworks noted above, are concepts emphasized as well by physicist Lawrence Fagg (1999) and philosopher Joseph Bracken (2001).

Differences between Whitehead's non-protean theory of possibilities, utilizing the concept of eternal objects, versus the Peirce-Hartshorne protean theory of possibilities are most clearly brought out in a special *Process Studies* journal issue on "Eternal Objects and Future Contingents" (Malone-France 2010). In that journal issue, George Shields argues that Hartshorne's final position involves both a General Modal Realism, which affirms the existential character and reality of possibilities, and a Peircean Realism affirming the real modal distinction between possibility and actuality. Correspondingly, these features are central elements of the *Logoi* framework with its distinction of Boolean logical constraints on actualized outcomes, and the reality of possibility and of non-Boolean constraints on *potentiae*. Further, efforts to save the earlier Whiteheadian approach by introducing a dense infinity of eternal objects inevitably fail. As summarized by Shields, "the internal incoherence of this ensemble of notions and systemic requirements is relieved only by postulating the *emergence* of specific forms from a more general continuous background such as found in the Hartshorne-Peirce doctrine" (Shields 2010, 161).

AESTHETICS AND VALUES

Deploying the *Logoi* framework, the human experience of the aesthetic can be rethought in terms of fundamental relations enabled through *potentiae* and linkages provided by local-global relations and the intimate universal (see below). Hedrick points out that "the test of truth, while pragmatic, requires an aesthetic ontology . . . the pragmatic test of truth is ultimately narrower than the broader test of beauty: because the new fact is ultimately subject to appraisal for its ability to facilitate enjoyment of a new harmony" (Hedrick 2019, 780). This appeal to harmony, incorporating as well *mythos* (nonrational apprehension), is brought out by Whitehead in his unique definition of *beauty* whereby "Beauty is the mutual adaption of the several factors in an occasion of experience" (Whitehead 1933, 324). As a way to describe such mutual adaptation of factors, Charles Hartshorne created a graphic called the aesthetic circle that displays the continua of possibilities between the four poles of unity, diversity, complexity, and simplicity. As discussed in detail by Henning, the notion of harmony points to a dynamic balance of these multiple factors (Henning 2005, 99–121). The term intensity, the focus of Judith Jones's work *Intensity*, has been used to characterize the relative effectiveness of such harmony (Jones, 1998).

These considerations of balance and harmony within an aesthetic ontology require us to move beyond the confines of Boolean actualizations and survey the landscapes of *potentiae* that enclose the aesthetic circle. Along with the broader test of beauty noted above in chapter 6, Rescher states that we need to "move outside of the evidential *realm of what is* to the normative *realm of what ought to be*, that is, from actuality to value" (Rescher 2017, 16). This conclusion of an inevitable value dimension resonates with Henning's effort to "bring the ethics of creativity into dialogue with established moral and environmental theories" (Henning 2005, 7).

Another way to frame the issue of aesthetics and values is to build on Friedrich Schleiermacher's analysis of three domains of consciousness in terms of three basic forms of intuition or feeling. Two of these are sensate and affect intuition, correlated with external versus internal stimuli, respectively, and the third is an integrative domain of consciousness arising from an over-lap or co-occurrence of the perceptual and affective levels of human experi-ence, a unification that enables not only a sense of self but also a sense of value and meaning. In her work *Love and Belief,* Thandeka shows how these three domains, as developed by Schleiermacher, correlate well with contem-porary neuroscientific research and how, with higher aspects of this integra-tive function, "the interior and exterior domains get linked together into a unitive experience of cosmic consciousness . . . Religion, by definition, is a cultural creation. But the human experience to which it originally refers is not a cultural creation. It's a feeling of being aligned with and supported by life itself. The dancing priest called this feeling 'God'" (Thandeka 2018).[9] Such linking together is also a basis for the many modes of the "between" analyzed in detail by Desmond in his work *Being and the Between* and involving many aspects of aesthetics and values (Desmond 1995).

CONTEMPLATING THE INTIMATE UNIVERSAL

Is it possible that the *Logoi* framework can open a way to rethinking the Western philosophical notion of universals and new ideas about non-con-tingent reality? With the *Logoi* framework, including its Relational Reality interpretation of fundamental quantum process, we have found that the world is permeated by triadicities and a duality of logical orders, the order of actu-alization and the order of *potentiae*, reflected in quantum complementarity and in multiple dualities in our experience; see Eastman (2004) and Nicolescu (2015). Our direct experience is dominated by actualized outcomes of the Boolean order, yet both complex modeling and our consciousness link "that which is" to "that which may be," or actuality and *potentiae*; thus, as Primas argues, a weaving of both the Boolean and non-Boolean orders similar to what occurs in fundamental quantum process (Primas 2017). Such intimate, diachronic connection of these logical orders, of actuality and *potentiae*, permeates all things and all living beings. Yet only life with highly advanced neurological systems can take advantage of this interplay through anticipa-tory system dynamics. However, as noted by Aloisius Louie, the modeling of such complex systems remains rather limited (Louie 2009). From the perspective of the *Logoi* framework, we have only just begun to avail our-selves of possibilities that could be enabled through the systematic tapping of *potentiae*. At present, we most often either simply deny such a notion, or refer vaguely to chance or the seemingly ungrounded mysteries of creativity.

Desmond has proposed a fruitful approach to reconceiving the relationship between universals and particulars with profound implications for metaphysi-cal analysis. He begins his inquiry by reviewing the prominent senses of the term "universal" in the philosophical tradition, beginning with the dominant Platonic universal, which is "the Idea as transcendent to the instances in becoming" (Desmond 2016, 4); the Aristotelian universal implies that "the universal is immanent in the process of becoming"; (ibid.) and finally the idealist universal "concretizes itself in immanent becoming" (ibid.). Desmond brings these notions together philosophically into what he terms a unified "intimate universal."

As part of the *Logoi* framework, I envision that, at multiple levels of relation, the order of *potentiae* would comprise real complexes of relations, multiple levels and structures of interrelatedness, that would be transcendent with respect to any particular, thus functioning all together as a universal. Nevertheless, such a transcendent relational complex would be inevitably linked to one or more particulars, thus the designation intimate universal *à la* Desmond. In this way, as expressed by Nathan Strunk in his review of Desmond's major work, the order of potential relations (*potentiae*) represents an embodiment of the particular-transcendent contrast, a universal that transcends any and all particulars and yet is intimately involved with such, the intimate universal.

> The intimate universal is a metaxological concept between universality and particularity, balancing between indeterminacy and determinacy, the abstract and the concrete, and transcendence and immanence. These contrasting categories set forth the parameters of the problem of the universality that has preoccupied philosophy since its beginnings . . . Desmond's intimate universal navigates the Scylla and Charybdis of these Platonic and Aristotelian caricatures of the universal by proffering a metaxological metaphysics—a metaphysics determined by the "doubleness of the meta," which in ancient Greek means both "in the midst" and "beyond." The intimate universal, then, is immanently "in the midst as intimate, yet beyond as pointing to what is not reducible to immanence alone." Desmond describes this irreducibility variously as "porosity" when it concerns the openness of being, as "overdetermined" or "surplus" when it concerns the givenness (the "that it is") of being, and as "agapeic" when it concerns excessive generosity, shared community, of universal being. (Strunk 2017, 138)

Based on human experiences and deep philosophical reflection, Desmond explores the multiple facets of the intimate universal, which "makes one think of a rotating diamond that allows the light to be multiply refracted. We sometimes think that we can rotate the diamond such that only a certain kind of light is broken up by it, and that only a certain color is allowed to filter through" (Desmond 2016, 108). Such apparent control is inevitably frustrated. "Art, as speaking to the depths of the intimate, awakens the feel for the universal, but this feel can also be used, misused, abused, by propaganda, for instance, or by advertising" (ibid.).

The intimate universal, in Desmond's telling, emerges in each dimension and domain through contrasts, reflections of the fundamental universal-particular extremes relevant to each, an irreducible tension between transcendence and immanence. Along with these contrasts stands a pivotal role for otherness; again, reviewer Strunk states,

> Desmond's intimate universal names the fecundity of otherness across the spectrum of human experience, but to be appreciated one must be equally open (porous) to its numerous and often equivocal instances, whether mundane (immanent) or sacred (transcendent). If Raphael's School of Athens illustrates the human condition between these two dimensions, it is his Madonna and Child with Book that best portrays the otherness constitutive of intimate universality by depicting a face-to-face encounter between mother and child, God and humanity. (Strunk 2017, 139–140)

Building on his prior work in articulating multiple ramifications of "between" (*metaxu* in Greek) (especially *Being and the Between*, Desmond 1995), Desmond forwards his metaxological philosophy, which "holds that to be is to be between. Nothing is defined purely through itself alone; all that is is in relation; this relatedness encompasses being in relation to other things, as well as self-relation. Metaxology refers us to a logos of the between" (Desmond 2016, 423); see also *The William Desmond Reader* (Christopher Simpson, ed. 2012).

We have reviewed above several arguments for ultimacies, a concept surveyed in detail by Robert Neville (2013). With the intimate universal, we now have a wider bridge (than quantum process alone), via *potentiae* and its relational complex, from our radically finite, contingent Boolean world to the complementary non-Boolean logical order. Further, the ground of *potentiae* is arguably non-contingent for how could possibility as such be merely contingent? The nature of such ground of being/becoming is beyond the scope of this work and is best left to scholars in the field of theology and philosophical theology.[10] With respect to belief, I consider that such is best left to personal experience, reflection, and decision, yet hopefully with better appreciation of the many complex considerations involved and not just from preestablished assumptions.

Within the *Logoi* framework, my discussion of fundamental quantum process indicates how both actuality (fields and "particle" input) and potential relations (*potentiae*), upon any particular actualization, are jointly input to such diachronic process, thus requiring a distinction of both actuality and *potentia* as part of the real because both have a real impact on such process. Further, fundamental quantum process provides the key bridge between *potentiae* and actuality. What then, in asking the central query of philosophy, is the ground of *potentiae*? As Kit Fine states, "For philosophy is often interested in questions of explanation—of what accounts for what—and it is largely through the employment of the notion of ontological ground that such questions are to be pursued. Ground . . . stands to philosophy as cause stands to science" (Fine 2012, 40). William Desmond's intimate universal, as discussed above, provides a key systematic bridge from particular actualizations to the domain of potential relations (*potentiae*), with its multiple levels and complexes of relationality. But what about the ground of *potentiae*?

In the case of finite, contingent actualizations, operating within a Boolean logical order, we observe a multivarious, hierarchical natural world. A concise summary of our contingent orders is provided by Cahoone in *The Orders of Nature* (2014)[11] in which, based on multilevel options for quanta of explanation, as discussed by Auxier and Herstein (2017), one can envision, synchronically, relations all the way down (and up), with potential "actual entities" or "dynamic particulars," at multiple scale, and one can even imagine a viewpoint (for the domain of *potentiae*) of rough ontological equivalence as argued by Justus Buchler (1989) and Ross (1980). This contrasts with what Schaffer describes as

> an ontological attitude according to which the entities of the fundamental level are *primarily* real, while any remaining contingent entities are at best derivative, if real at all. Thus the *physicalist* claims that microphysical theory (or some future extension thereof) describes the fundamental level of reality on which all else supervenes; the *Humean* claims that all supervenes on the distribution of local, fundamental qualities in spacetime; the *epiphenomenalist* claims that all causal powers inhere at the fundamental level; and the *atomist* claims that there are no macroentities at all but only fundamental entities in various arrangements. (Schaffer 2003, 498)

Schaffer points out that "the proposition that there is a fundamental level is widely accepted but seldom defended" (Schaffer 2003, 499). After extensive critique of the fundamentalist assumption, he concludes: "To see that there is no evidence for fundamentality is already to regain the macroworld" (Schaffer 2003, 513), which then affirms the reality of our thoughts and experience; that is, they are not simply epiphenomena with genuine "realities" only in the microworld.

SYSTEMATIC PHILOSOPHY AND ULTIMACIES

Up to this point, I have emphasized systems of context independence (science) and context dependence (humanities), but now I raise the question of ultimate context. This inevitably leads to concerns regarding the spiritual dimension and ultimate grounds for meaning. As Neville argues,

> The real demands of the ontological ultimates push toward greater and greater transcendence while the real demands of anthropological ultimates push toward great intimacy and perhaps anthropomorphism.
>
> The push toward transcendence has to do with finding the ground or context in which things can be genuinely other than one another while also being so connected as to define one another, at least in part. Another way to put this is that what is ontologically ultimate is the . . . classical philosophical problem of the one and the many. Coupled with these metaphysical considerations is the ubiquitous dialectic countering what the West Asian traditions call idolatry, that is, taking something that itself would have to be grounded in a "higher power" to be itself the highest power. (Neville 2013, 85)

Considerations of such dialectics, the "one and the many," and ultimacy are the most speculative of my current venture in speculative philosophy, and thus the most speculative component of the *Logoi* framework. The appropriateness of such questions and their metaphysical character are addressed by Nicholas Rescher, in his book *Metaphysical Perspectives*, within which he states that "any ultimate theory of explanation that can adequately account for contingent existence-at-large must be holistic: it must address the entirety of a collective whole" (Rescher 2017, 10). I enter this arena with some trepidation because it is highly speculative, but to not do so would undermine our central long-term goal of achieving a deep understanding of reality.[12] Signatures of ultimacy that we have encountered so far include the following:

—basic human experience—spiritual dimension, personal experience, other;
—enhanced anticipatory capabilities—psychic phenomena, parapsychology, etc.;
—semiosis of the world (input-output-context), apparently unbounded (see chapter 5);
—William Desmond's "intimate universal" (see *Contemplating the Intimate Universal* above);
—fundamental process (process-logic-relations-context, including *potentiae*);
—needed ultimate grounding, with consistency and coherence, via *potentiae*;
—two dimensions of being/becoming (contingent and non-contingent, see below).

Here we need to remain mindful of the distinction between metaphysical and religious ultimates as expressed by Thomas Padiyath whereby "modern absolutized ultimates were characterized by non-transcendence, while the religious ultimate distinguished itself with transcendence" (Padiyath 2014, 348).[13] With a focus on the core metaphysical issue, Rescher states that

> to account for the being of contingent existence at large, one has to impose the burden of explanation on something that is itself entirely outside the realm of contingent existence and of existential fact. But where can one possibly look for explanatory resources if the realm of actuality, of "what there is" is not available? The answer is clear: we must look to the realm of possibility, of what *can possibly be*. For if reality is to have a basis, then *possibility* is the only available prospect. (Rescher 2017, 15)

Similarly, for Whitehead, the metaphysical ultimate is creativity which, for the *Logoi* framework, correlates with *potentiae* and some ultimate ground for the coherence and consistency of such *potentiae*. For Whitehead, such a locus of ultimacy (viz., God) has two natures that enable a symmetry between the contingent and the non-contingent: God not only (indirectly) influences any and all fundamental diachronic process via coordination of *potentiae*, but is also (in a consequent nature) affected by contingent beings (see further discussion below about the symmetry issue). In contrast, as Padiyath states, "the classical theistic conception...equates God and the metaphysical ultimate" based on a "'marriage' between Aristotelian philosophy and the Judeo-Christian understanding of creation (creation *ex nihilo*)" (Padiyath 2014, 347). For the most part, Western Christianity has been stuck with this heritage. As noted by David Schindler, this move has been broadly criticized by Heidegger and others as the ontotheology error, which "replaces the godly God . . . with a conceptual idol" (Schindler 2009, 104) based on presumptions of reason. Faber points out that this error is closely linked as well with the dilemmas of access and naming (Faber 2018, 220–228).

Clearly, we should avoid reducing all ultimacies to some macro-entity with inaccessible transcendence just as much as we should avoid the complementary extreme of non-contextualized, value-denying reductionisms, with mappings strictly to disconnected micro-entities. Instead, we recognize aspects of both with a focus on relations and context, including relations of relations (meta-level) and including the unbounded semiosis of input-output-context. As well, there can be meaningful discourse about such ultimate being/becoming provided, as Alan White argues, that one attends to reframing discourse within verb-like discourse versus substantivalism and substance-predicate forms (White 2014).

Whitehead's ontological principle is that any reality underlying an abstraction must have a basis in actuality, briefly "there is nothing which floats into the world from nowhere" (Whitehead 1978, 244). According to this principle, only *actual* things can *act*; thus, *potentiae*, although demonstrably "real," can only *act* via some embodiment in actual thing(s). From this we infer that there must be some ground for *potentiae*; concurrently this provides a basis for both logical truths, mathematical forms and ethical norms, potentially solving fine-tuning problems as well as both the Platonic and the Benacerraf problems (i.e., that abstract entities can exert causal agency); see Griffin (2007, 156–162). More recently, Griffin has concisely summarized the profound implications of the fine-tuning discovery.

> The scientific discovery that the universe was fine-tuned for life is arguably science's most important discovery for understanding the place of humans in the universe . . . human beings have a universe that was ready for them—a universe that provides the conditions for mathematical as well as moral and religious truths. (Griffin 2019, 95)

This summary is reinforced by some of the most detailed scientific analyses available on the fine-tuning issue. After an in-depth technical debunking of arguments made against certain fine-tuning claims, astrophysicist Luke Barnes concludes that "the universe is fine-tuned for the existence of life. Of all the ways that the laws of nature, constants of physics and initial conditions of the universe could have been, only a very small subset permits the existence of intelligent life" (Barnes 2012).

Lorenz Puntel has made an extensive argument for how the most fundamental ontological orders are that of the contingent and the non-contingent. After a discussion of background philosophical arguments in his major work, *Structure and Being*, Puntel summarizes the core of the logical proof as follows.

> "—If absolutely everything and therewith the dimension of being itself were contingent, one would have to accept the possibility of absolute nothingness.
> —Absolute nothingness is not possible.
> —Therefore, not everything (i.e., not the entire dimension of being itself) is contingent" (Puntel 2008, 446).

The first proposition basically derives from the meaning of contingency. However, the second premise warrants some background, provided by Puntel as follows, "the thought of even a possible emergence of beings from the unthinkable 'dimension' of absolute nothingness, or of a transition from the 'dimension' of absolute nothingness to the dimension being, is a simply senseless, impossible pseudo-thought: no being of any sort whatsoever could come from absolute nothingness" (Puntel 2008, 445). By the way, this critique of the notion of absolute nothingness is entirely compatible with contemporary physics and quantum field theory in which the quantum "vacuum" (out of which, some claim, the universe emerged with the Big Bang) is actually full of fundamental pre-space processes and is clearly not nothing. The notion of absolute nothingness has no functional presence in current physics, which is based on field theory. Puntel's proof is an indirect one, a *reductio ad absurdum* of the logical form *modus tollens* (Latin for the "mode that denies by denying"), a valid deductive argument form based on denying the consequent. The outcome of this argument is that there must necessarily be two dimensions of being/becoming, the contingent and the non-contingent.

The denial of absolute nothingness is further enhanced by multiple arguments supporting Hartshorne's Principle Zero. As summarized by Shields,

1) "'Something exists' is a necessary, or, as Whitehead puts it, 'eternal' truth. This is Hartshorne's 'Principle Zero' (P-Zero). This truth is a pre-condition for all coherent thinking, a position corroborated by the doctrine of *Principia Mathematica* that the universe of discourse cannot be empty.

2) Because P-Zero is a pre-condition of all coherent thinking, it follows that ontology precedes epistemology, not vice versa . . . Philosophy begins, for Whitehead, with the ontological, with the encounter with something given.

3) However, any adequate ontology must coherently 'make room' for a plausible epistemology. In the Harvard Lectures, Whitehead develops this motif by suggesting the main theme of his work on *Symbolism*, namely, the important distinction between prehension in the mode of causal efficacy and in the mode of presentational immediacy" (Shields 2019, 228–229).

Shields argues that Whitehead and Hartshorne share an ontological approach to fundamental questions of philosophy, which is illustrated by Whitehead's statement that "the general potentiality of the universe must be somewhere" (Whitehead 1978, 46). Correspondingly, for Hartshorne, "if possibility is meaningless without existence, then it cannot be that all existents are contingent; for this is to say that the being of *possibility* is also contingent, that it might have been that nothing was possible . . . The conclusion of this argument is that there is a primordial power whose nonexistence is not a possibility, since possibility presupposes its existence" (Hartshorne 1972, 80).

Input-output asymmetry (Boolean + non-Boolean input to Boolean-only output), and essential triadic semiotic relation (input-output-context), can bootstrap without limit in the hierarchy of actualization and, via fundamental quantum processes, *potentiae* is imbedded in such bootstrapping. In turn, the pre-space *potentiae* require grounding. This is Whitehead's ontological principle that explanation (grounding) necessarily requires reference to an actuality. For the coherence and coordination of *potentiae* this cannot be any local, finite contingent actuality, but must be grounded in a non-contingent actuality, grounding the order of *potentiae*, a unique, singular actuality, a ground of being/becoming.

Complementary arguments concerning these two dimensions, focused on their constant interplay and the necessity of contingency, are provided by Faber.

> In Whitehead's process understanding, as in the view of the *Laozi* . . . wholes and parts are spread among the oscillations of becoming (present) and being (past) of events, the life and character of societies of events, the coordinate (of the extension of the actualized) and genetic analysis (of becoming actualized), such that *any universal whole is bound back into new particular events of becoming*, avoiding any fixed stratification. (Faber 2018, 475)

Consistent with such arguments, the *Logoi* framework incorporates a non-contingent dimension of being/becoming that encompasses the above fundamental ontological factors, which are aspects of reality that could not be radically nonexistent. Further, this argument is necessarily a philosophical argument and transcends any particular set of scientific propositions. One metaphysical alternative is to argue, as does Tyler Tritten, based on the later writings of Schelling, that "the event or decision of being could not possibly be known apart from its factical occurrence, apart from its actual revelation . . . necessity only exists factically, hence contingently" (Tritten 2017, 161). The importance of such facticity is clearly part of Hartshorne's Principle Zero discussed above. However, in wanting to avoid the traditional emphasis on God's essence as prior, which many have used to argue for a classical theist God concept in which absolute determinism reigns, Tritten moves on to argue for the contingency of necessity. Currently, I am more persuaded by the arguments provided above by Puntel and Shields concerning the importance of retaining a contingent/non-contingent distinction, but implemented in a way that both grounds *potentiae* and avoids the rigidities of absolute entailments and determinism.

Another approach to understanding the relationship of individual experience and the universe, considered inclusively (both the orders of actualization and *potentiae*), which emphasizes intersubjectivity, is forwarded by Joseph Bracken for whom "God in my scheme is . . . both universal ground of being and a personal being at the same time" (Bracken 2001, 126–127). Along with taking creativity to be coexistent (not ontological prior), Bracken's project is "the creation of a metaphysics of universal intersubjectivity in which all realities, even the reality of God, are intrinsically social, that is, ontological wholes made up of interacting parts or members" (Bracken 2001, 205), ultimately yielding the understanding that God is love. Complementing this is Jorge Nobo's analysis of how eternal creativity (viz., the order of *potentiae*) "is an ontological presupposition of the primordial nature" of God, which yet allows for the full contingency of the actualized, temporal order. As Nobo states, "The metaphysical cosmology of creative solidarity infers, from the existence and nature of the temporal world, that the primordial activity freely constituted itself into that actuality by reason of whom there is a temporal world of other actualities exhibiting an evolving history of extensive and aesthetic order" (Nobo 1997, 198). My *Logoi* framework aspires to be a philosophy of creative solidarity consistent with Nobo's vision, which focuses on constructing a consistent and coherent metaphysics based on Whitehead's philosophy of organism, whereas my effort is a complementary synthesis of contemporary research in physics, semiotics, and philosophy. I recommend Jorge Nobo's master work *Whitehead's Metaphysics of Extension and Solidarity* for details on his philosophy of creative solidarity (Nobo, 1986).

REASON AND FAITH

In a practical way, one can recognize the value of ethical and spiritual practice without insisting on a particular belief about the ground of being/becoming (*aka* God). Such belief inevitably involves certain metaphysical claims, whether stated or not, and this applies whether the belief is for, or against, a particular concept of God. Griffin has surveyed arguments for and against two primary concepts, "Gawd" (roughly the classical theistic notion with emphasis on transcendence and unilateral power) and "God" (involving both immanence and transcendence, and relational power, the God of love) (Griffin 2016). With these designations, as noted by Griffin, it is interesting to note that almost all extant denials of divine reality are denials of "Gawd" and, as Griffin has shown, many of these are based on unsuccessful attempts to resolve the classic problem of evil (Griffin 2017). Examples of these denials are the six forms of atheism surveyed by John Gray (2018).

Given the *Logoi* framework and the cumulative arguments provided above for *potentiae* and a need for its ultimate grounding, my hypothesis at this time is to affirm a divine reality (Griffin's "God," not "Gawd").[14] This deeply reflective choice is based on a complex set of considerations, including philosophical and personal ones. Such insight can never be certain and confirmation of a God hypothesis (for or against) certainly cannot be resolved by any set of propositions based on science alone. On the other hand, Charles Hartshorne has argued that such hypotheses can be resolved based on a combination of logic and philosophic (metaphysical) arguments (Hartshorne 1970). Given the difficulty of these speculative issues, it may be better to trust in one's own intuitive knowledge and experience, considered most inclusively with attention to human experience across all times and cultures, and informed by the best philosophical and scientific knowledge. Reason can partner with faith.

Although discussions of philosophical theology are beyond the scope of the present work, here are two passages that are especially consonant with the *Logoi* framework. First, Catherine Keller points out that

> [Whitehead] is at pains to distinguish his ultimate from his God, who mediates creativity to every becoming creature. The process God is not process itself, which, if named God, might again take command of all the becomings in process. God is in process *with* them. Negating divine ultimacy, Whitehead is resisting the imaginary of a changeless Lord omnipotently presiding [*à la* "Gawd"] . . . And God thus provides a primordial locus of all possibilities, which begin to lose their sheer abstraction already by being housed, tabernacle. The nonlocal possibilities thus become available for local actualization. They become its lures. (Keller 2014, 188)

Keller properly notes that "God is not process itself," yet God for Whitehead is the aboriginal embodiment of process and possibility. In a way that echoes Valenza's analysis of the late Whitehead, moving from thinking of eternal objects (suggesting a more static mode) as static forms to the later dynamic concept (as with dynamic *potentiae*), Marjorie Suchocki states that "there can be no static pattern of divine harmony, since the pattern changes with every prehension" (Suchocki 1988, 143). Remembering that God (not Gawd) is intended, Suchocki goes on to say that

> God reaches toward the world both as it is and as it can be. The creativity of the world is accepted by God into the divine nature in a mutual enrichment of God and world. The world, which in its creativity is novel even to God, is made one with God through the truly responsive consequent nature. To the world, God as such an actual entity [(or Hartshornian "dynamic particular") and the ground of *potentiae*] is truly "God for us"—and yet the world is equally for God. In the rhythmic responsiveness, which is integral to the concept of God as an actual entity, the world moves toward its redemptive completion in God, adding thereby to the completion of God. And the reality in heaven passes back into the world in everlasting process. (Suchocki 1988, 152)

Relevant to creativity and the divine nature, with a focus on *potentiae*, Malone-France states that "on the view I am defending, the realm of possibility is identical to the conceptual content of the divine mind" (Malone-France 2006, 190).

THE METAPHYSICAL PRESENT

A very general result of mathematical physics, often deployed for string theory, as pointed out by Ervin Laszlo, is that "the information of any 3D volume in space is equivalent to 2D information at the periphery of that space" (Laszlo 2016, 23). Here note that "D" refers to "dimension" and "2D" and "3D" denote two and three dimensions, respectively. Currently unknown is whether this result applies one dimension higher (from 2D/3D to 3D/4D). If so, in the context of the *Logoi* framework, I conjecture that encodings of fundamental process occurring at micro-scale (yet coordinated via local-global linkages), operating in 3D normal space volumes, map on to the associated periphery of that space, which would be a pre-space eternal present.[15] Such a metaphysical "present" is possible via correlations of non-Boolean *potentiae*, which operate at a pre-space level via global topological phase information, and so on, whereas relativistic constraints (such as speed of light limitation) refer to correlations of actualized outcomes of the Boolean order. The above may be eventually understood based on the existing framework of quantum field theories, although an adequate model may require an additional field such as Laszlo's Akashic field (Laszlo 2014, 27–29). Successions of such metaphysical presents would constitute a fundamental physical memory of the universe. Details of a metaphysics of extension and solidarity that corresponds to such a vision are laid out by Jorge Luis Nobo (1986).

In conjunction with a metaphysical present, as discussed above, there would be systematic advances (Whiteheadian creative advance) through a fundamental succession of metaphysical presents, as Jorge Nobo has discussed (2004), combined with retention of information for each, bootstrapped successively without limit—"one darn thing after another." Such imbeddings, plus active topological local-global process, constitute specific context for ontological causation (input-output-context); ontological emergence then arising from non-reductive components of local-global correlations in conjunction with active selections (as reflected in quantum process) among *potentiae*. Indeed, this would comprise a Whiteheadian creative advance, as Judith Jones has discussed, with the fullness of subjective, aesthetic, and objective components (Jones, 1998). Any tapping into the metaphysical present, via linkage to pre-space and such information, would enable spiritual experiences and parapsychological phenomena, but such information would (for finite Boolean creatures like ourselves) be immediately subject to normal physical processes, including relativistic limitations and dissipative processes of our actualized world. Perhaps this process involves both a non-local mode of brain information access via a quantum-level microtubular network, and our standard perceptual mode, which would most often filter out such access to the order of *potentiae*. However, at times of special creative insight or spiritual experience, such non-local awareness may break through our filters of habit (see chapter 6; also chapter 8 of Laszlo 2014).

CHINESE THOUGHT, YIN-YANG, AND ORGANIC UNITY

Neo-Confucian scholar Chu Hsi was mentioned in chapter 7 in the context of discussing the concept of creativity and triadic forms. When I first looked at the *I Ching* or *The Book of Changes* (about 1000 BCE), the oldest text of Chinese philosophy, I had difficulty finding relevance to my research project except for the obvious duality (within a unity) of the yin-yang concept (see figure 8.1). I have since changed my perspective. Haipeng Guo describes the yin-yang Taiji diagram as follows,

> *The Book of Changes* . . . was an ancient divination text and a source book for all subsequent Chinese thought. It is highly esteemed by both Confucianism and Taoism. Taiji, or the Supreme Ultimate, also called Tao or the Way, is the most ultimate notion in *The Book of Changes*. It is also the ultimate principle that governs the cosmos in Chinese thought . . . the yin-yang Taiji diagram . . . can be seen as the most important diagram representing Chinese culture. (Guo 2018, 132)

Figure 8.1   The classsic Yin-Yang Taiji diagram (Source: Wikimedia Commons).

Manifestations of yin and yang, commonly referenced, are particle/wave, body/mind, static/dynamic, and dark/light, among others. Building on the work of Chung-Ying Cheng (1979), Guo calls attention to evidence that the eight trigrams of the *I Ching* can be correlated with Whitehead's eight categories of existence in *Process and Reality* (Whitehead, 1978). This may be just accidental, numerical coincidence. But then Guo argues that "Yin and Yang are two inseparable aspects of the Taiji, just as many and one are two inseparable aspects of creativity. Many become one and one becomes many, just like the constant movement of Yin and Yang" (Guo 2018, 135).

This classic yin-yang dynamic, as interpreted by Guo, correlates closely with the way Whitehead deploys creativity as the ultimate principle within which "many become one and are increased by one" (Whitehead 1978, 21). Within the *Logoi* framework, I hypothesize that the *I Ching*'s ultimate principle, Whitehead's creativity, and Desmond's intimate universal (see section *Contemplating the Intimate Universal* above) are closely analogous concepts, the unity amid the diversity, also the ultimate triad (creativity-yin-yang). The ultimate/creativity generates the two modes (yin/yang), which correlate with the logic of *potentiae* and the logic of actuality, respectively (a becoming-being complementarity; see Bo Mou, 2003), resulting in an interplay of complementary logics within a unity. Then the input-output framework of fundamental quantum process (diachronic/fundamental causation) generates the (2x2) four forms {"old Yin, new Yang, new Yin, old Yang" (Guo 2018, 133)}.[16] Finally, the local-Global[17] duality of the *Logoi* framework (incorporating synchronic emergence) could generate the (2x4) eight. "The Eight Trigrams contain an organic cosmology . . . a 'coherent' model in which all Eight Trigrams are interrelated and presuppose each other . . . an organic whole" (Guo 2018, 134).[18] Finally, in consideration of my generic framing of input-output-context, grounded in fundamental quantum process, and the above triads of creativity-yin-yang (from the *I Ching*), and Whitehead's creativity-many-one, we may have reached the core of Peirce's speculative extension of the ultimacy of triadic form in his Grand Vision as highlighted by Deely (1994, 389); see chapter 7. Without reference to triads, it is notable that Gottfried Leibniz, in his later work, as noted by Dusek, "develops a philosophy that greatly resembles the Chinese philosophy of nature . . . [using especially] Chu Hsi" (Dusek 1999, 202).

THE SPIRITUAL DIMENSION
AMONG WORLD CULTURES

Numerous reports of spiritual experience gathered from around the world appear to affirm a pervasive human witness to a spiritual dimension. The

Logoi framework opens a way to think of enhanced anticipatory systems as those capable of enhanced openness to pre-space *potentiae* and thus, at times, to genuine spiritual or psychic experience. This subsection sketches examples of spiritual phenomena and practices reported from several continents and hypothesizes that such phenomena are signatures of possible access to potential relations (*potentiae*) of the non-Boolean logical order. To date, commitment to actualism and conventional materialist presuppositions have impeded research on such phenomena. Evaluating such possibilities may require new tools that are yet to be developed.

In my *Logoi* framework, one can think of enhanced anticipatory systems[19] as those capable of enhanced openness to pre-space *potentia* and, at times, real cases of spiritual or psychic experience. Possibilities for what I have described above as enhanced tapping of pre-space *potentia*, as expected within the *Logoi* framework, deserve careful scholarly investigation. Such studies have been relatively rare. If real, we expect that such a process should be practically universal among *Homo sapiens*, independent of language and cultures. Indeed, spiritual phenomena and practices are as pervasive as language itself, as F. W. H. Myers, William James, Carl Jung, Joseph Campbell, W. T. Stace, and many others have highlighted. Extensive documentation of such subliminal phenomena, primarily within Western cultures, is provided in the encyclopedic work *Irreducible Mind*, edited by Edward and Emily Kelly (2007). At the same time, it turns out that an emphasis on relationality and connectedness, whether among humans or with nature, is a common, cross-cultural theme. Such emphasis may seem unusual to those of us steeped in standard secularism, substance thinking, actualism, and determinism. Here I provide just a few brief samples of a vast, often untapped, literature, which points to a richness of relational worldviews, and of spiritual phenomena and practices that we mostly neglect.

There are four concepts of the *Logoi* framework that appear to be pervasive when compared with the world's spiritual traditions: (1) recognition of deep interdependence; (2) processual features (not substance or mechanism) as fundamental; (3) non-duality (denial of substance-object split), and (4) experience of a co-present spiritual "dimension," both immanent and transcendent, even though such immediate experiences are radically contingent. Notwithstanding the tremendous diversity displayed by the world's religions and cultures, I here sketch some examples of the above features as they occur in China, India, Africa, and indigenous cultures worldwide. Although this is the most cursory sample of human experience across time and space, and largely mediated through Western eyes, it does give a hint of the ubiquity of these experiences.

In an analysis of Hindu Vedanta, Mahayana Buddhism, and Taoism, David Loy concludes with a non-dualist interpretation. "Nondual experience is not characterized by the delusive dualism between self and other, between mind and substance and modes, between things and their attributes, for all phenomena are sunya, empty, with a dreamlike maya quality, except for the One which can never be experienced as a One" (Loy 1988, 293). With relevance to the first three of the above four concepts, and complementing Loy's focus on non-duality, John Kineman discusses ancient Vedic philosophy, with its cyclic causality and holism, and compares this with contemporary complex systems theory (Kineman 2017). With a focus on the concept of creativity in neo-Confucian thought, Berthrong argues that "both Chu's and Whitehead's philosophies are relational, organic, and processive in nature . . . and inherently dialogical in nature" (Berthrong 1998, 10).

There are many relevant discussions available for African philosophy although, as pointed out by Barry Hallen, most are affected by the question of its authentic, de-colonized form (Hallen 2002). Omaku Ehusani characterizes the relational and participative character of African philosophy in these terms (with focus presumably on non-Mediterranean Africa).

> No item of the universe is a chance collocation of atoms or molecules, but that there inheres in the universe some natural, spiritual and mystical order . . . This overwhelming consciousness of the sacred, perfused and diffused in the life and environment of the African, is what the early missionaries and ethnologists could not relate to, and as a result, they called the African religion *Animism*. What the early explorers could not comprehend is the fact that the traditional African does not experience God in terms of concepts and theories. He or she experiences God as an awesome *Presence*. (Ehusani 1991, 208)

Importantly, Ehusani follows this up, noting that "the dichotomy between the sacred and the profane, matter and spirit, the supernatural and the natural, which is so characteristic of the Western world view, is strikingly absent in Africa" (ibid. 220). As an example of the processual character of African thought, Ifeanyi Menkiti states that "a crucial distinction thus exists between the African view of man and the view of man found in Western thought: in the African view it is the community which defines the person as person, not some isolated static quality of rationality, will, or memory . . . the *processual* nature of being in African thought . . . persons become persons only after a process of incorporation . . . into this or that community" (Menkiti 1984, 4).

The interconnectedness of African spirituality is similarly strong in indigenous cultures and first nations peoples of the Americas. As Sylvia Marcos explains,

> at the core [of pervasive spiritual references]: the interconnectedness of everyone and everything in the universe. The intersubjective nature of men and

women is interconnected with earth, sky, plants, and planets. This is how we must understand the defense of the earth "that gives us life, that is the nature that we are." (Marcos 2015, 44)

Then, jumping across yet another ocean, the Pacific, Vicki Grieves documents the strong affirmation of interconnectedness among Australian aborigines:

Aboriginal Spirituality derives from a philosophy that establishes the wholistic notion of the interconnectedness of the elements of the earth and the universe, animate and inanimate, whereby people, the plants and animals, landforms and celestial bodies are interrelated. These relations and the knowledge of how they are interconnected are expressed, and why it is important to keep all things in healthy interdependence is encoded, in sacred stories or *myths*. (Grieves 2009, 7)

Very similar indigenous spirituality is evident with the Sami peoples of northern Scandinavia. In this era of renewed awareness of global climate change, Trude Fonneland and colleagues have proposed that such indigenous peoples have become "a voice of Wisdom, a way of life in tune with nature, a culture in harmony, a *gemeinshaft*, that we [in the West] have all but lost" (Fonneland et al. 2013).

The above examples of spiritual phenomena, especially indigenous spirituality, encountered in every culture and continent, suggest a real phenomenon at its core. Unfortunately, these phenomena are not only difficult to study scientifically but scientists have largely not attempted to study them because they seem to violate widely accepted presuppositions of the scientific worldview.[20] Even setting aside cases of anomalous cognition, a prime example is the notion of consciousness itself, the nature of which is a major unsolved problem. As noted by Radin, "Some neurophilosophers don't even believe awareness exists. They think consciousness is a brain-centric illusion" (Radin 2018, 12). We have discussed above (chapters 3 and 4) a way of understanding consciousness within the *Logoi* framework, which involves a weaving together of science, semiotics, and philosophy; Radin expresses it similarly:

Philosophers analyze the concepts, logic, and assumptions used to describe consciousness. Scientists study consciousness from the outside in, typically by measuring the activity of the brain and body . . . Meditators study consciousness from the inside out, by introspection. [Lastly, parapsychology investigates] phenomena that challenge commonly held assumptions about the brain-mind relationship . . . by investigating psychic phenomena, often abbreviated as *psi*. (Radin 2018, 12)

Based on the *Logoi* framework, my hypothesis is that psychic phenomena, at least in part, are signatures of the possibility of tapping into potential relations (*potentiae*) of the non-Boolean logical order; equivalently, this would enable openness to what Desmond terms the "intimate universal."[21] From this perspective, certain psychic phenomena may have as firm a basis in the real world as entanglement phenomena in quantum physics, the latter being (in our Relational Reality interpretation of quantum physics) as real as electrons. However, evaluating this possibility appropriately depends on forefront scholarship, both scientific and humanistic. Yet such scholarship has been severely impeded by conventional materialist presuppositions. Radin summarizes the result: "The upshot of the social taboo is that most academic scientists avoid parapsychology as though it's a virulent strain of a zombie plague...This is a pity, because parapsychology involves the application of orthodox scientific and scholarly methods to a class of commonly reported but as yet poorly understood human experiences" (ibid. 14).

As for myself, I rely on personal experience, inclusively considered, taking into consideration various scholarly accounts. As a skeptical participant in a spiritual workshop several years ago, I witnessed such tapping of *potentiae* firsthand. A workshop partner (a perfect stranger whom I had never met before or seen since) had a vision of me in a uniform, which she (the stranger) described in detail, including an insignia and an eight-digit number. Indeed, the symbol she described accurately matched my Army uniform's specific logo and the number she reported in her vision was exactly (except for one digit) my Regular Army (RA) number, which I had long forgotten but then confirmed upon immediately checking my discharge document. Such experiences of anomalous cognition have been rare for me although I now recognize them as sometimes real. For the leader of this workshop, such psychic phenomena are relatively common. Clearly, we all vary immensely in such psychic abilities, which may be effectively the ability to tap *potentiae* that could enable several features characterizing parapsychological phenomena (clairvoyance, telepathy, out-of-body experiences, precognition), which have been surveyed by Kelly and colleagues (Kelly et al., 2007), Griffin (1997a), and Radin (2018). Based on likely flawed metaphysical claims, many researchers have ignored the possibility of psychic phenomena and thus have systematically ignored relevant data. As a scientist (PhD physicist), I regard it as a violation of our common scientific ethos to systematically ignore such data; by itself, lack of a viable theory does not excuse such neglect. In spite of the difficulties associated with such data (reproducibility, etc.), I think that it is important to carry out scholarly investigations (both scientific and philosophical) of psychic phenomena and related spiritual experiences.

A possible outcome of enhanced scholarly investigations, as suggested here, is to identify common traits of spiritual development and practice that are endemic to humans worldwide and thus, arguably, foundational for *Homo sapiens* generally. Research today into the multiple modes of human intelligence—spiritual, moral, emotional, logical—appears to show some commonality of stages and structures of human development, intelligences, and spiritual awareness. Continued research is needed, particularly in phenomena that tend toward the spiritual; very preliminary results appear to have some overall compatibility with the *Logoi* framework. One such example is the work of Carl Jung, founder of analytical psychology, with respect to synchronicity, that is meaningful "coincidences" in which there seems to be an "acausal connecting principle" (Cambray 2009, 1). As Joseph Cambray has noted, Jung in his clinical work in analytical psychology and in dialogue with physicist Wolfgang Pauli hypothesized the concept of synchronicity, which he regarded as pervasive. If synchronicity and other such seemingly "acausal" phenomenon derive from tapping into pre-space *potentiae* in ways that transcend the particular sentient species in question, then signatures of such phenomena should be not only worldwide but also common across all sentient organisms, wherever their galactic residence. In physical location, *Homo sapiens* are bound by standard limits of time and space and limited to just one stellar system within a remote corner of the Milky Way galaxy, one among a unified galactic cluster and one among millions of galaxies. And yet, with quantum entanglement and correlations among non-Boolean *potentiae*, there may be a substantive basis for synchronicity and boundless spiritual phenomena in human experience.

DAKOTA SPIRITUALITY

In concluding my inquiry, I return to my childhood spiritual experience and offer the *Logoi* framework as a response, from relatively late in life, to my childhood quest. The Dakota people had lived in the region of our farm and much of the spiritual knowledge and practices embedded in their cultures have been lost. Yet what remains may still provide clues to accessing the spiritual dimension of human life. Study of and engagement with that deep indigenous knowledge may reveal insights into the spiritual dimension and paths for accessing it that are less encumbered by the presuppositions of post-Enlightenment religious frameworks. In proposing this path toward addressing the Gordian knot of problems, I have argued that reconceiving fundamental philosophical presuppositions and their implications will substantially advance progress toward resolving these problems. Even if some of my proposed solutions ultimately are not successful, I believe that rethinking the foundations of what is real will open conceptual space for us human beings to rethink our relationship to reality and to rewrite new universe stories that are more ethical, deeply human, and perhaps even more sacred than those in which the mainstream Western world is living today. That child who I was so long ago, on the brink of adulthood, indeed sensed a connection between the natural world and a more inclusive context, indeed felt an inchoate link to something beyond my own small purview, some spiritual something beyond my senses. At the time I knew I was standing on indigenous land. Still, I had not yet embraced my current commitment and sense of obligation to understand and honor the Dakota peoples and their spiritual wisdom because I had not absorbed the implications of the fact that my family was a recipient (via federal land grant) of their stolen land and thus a beneficiary of their loss.

For millennia in this same region, perhaps even in that very place where I stood,[22] Dakota peoples[23] lived sustainably with the land and all living things, humbly recognized their radical finiteness, sustaining a deep connectedness to nature and to spirituality. According to Victor Douville, the triad of their tipis both connected with the land and represented, in its three-point outline, a star. Further, he noted, the "tripod of the tipi divides the secular world from the spiritual world" (Douville 2007, 19). As a key component of essentially all ceremonies, the pipe ritual provides a "bridge between the spiritual world and the natural world via the smoke" (ibid. 55).

Words of wisdom from native peoples themselves, provided by the educational site firstpeople.us, speak to the multilevel interrelatedness and sacred dimensions of world:

> The first peace, which is the most important, is that which comes within the souls of people when they realize their relationship, their oneness, with the universe and all its powers, and when they realize that at the center of the universe dwells Wakan-Taka (the Great Spirit), and that this center is really everywhere, it is within each of us. (Black Elk—Oglala Sioux)

> The character of the Indian's emotion left little room in his heart for antagonism toward his fellow creatures . . . . For the Lakota (one of the three branches of the Sioux Nation), mountains, lakes, rivers, springs, valleys, and the woods were all in finished beauty. Winds, rain, snow, sunshine, day, night, and change of seasons were endlessly fascinating . . . The Lakota was a true naturalist—a lover of Nature. He loved the earth and all things of the earth . . . Their tipis were built upon the earth and their alters were made of earth. (Chief Luther Standing Bear—Oglala Sioux)

> I would much more glory in this birthplace, with the broad canopy of heaven above me, and the giant arms of the forest trees for my shelter, than to be born in palaces of marble, studded with pillars of gold! Nature will be Nature still, while

palaces shall decay and fall in ruins. (George Copway (Kahgegagahbowh)—Ojibwe) (First People 2020)

David Martinez affirms that the Dakota/Lakota version of the vision quest tradition embodies openness to receiving spiritual wisdom and is fully consonant with the first people's own words.

> For the Lakota, the fact that one cannot always choose one's vision is evidence for the hypothesis that the needs of the people, even the cosmos, and not simply those of the individual, settle one's fate. One does have control over the decision to embark on a vision quest, to see it through to its end, and to accept whatever is revealed . . . Because of the significance of learning one's purpose, the Lakota maintain that visions are not acquired by an ambitious ego, but rather are *given to* a humbled soul. (Martinez 2004, 83–84)

The indigenous peoples of the United States and indeed worldwide have suffered the devastating losses of their land, their languages,[24] and the integrity of their cultures. This is also an enormous but largely unrecognized loss to the world community because of the deep interconnectedness of human life, experience, and wisdom. A United Nations report documents that the remaining indigenous peoples around the world number only something over "370 million in some 90 countries" (United Nations, 2009). From the perspective of the *Logoi* framework, many of these peoples may still carry clues to understanding and accessing the spiritual dimension of human life, which appears to be pervasive among *Homo sapiens* and which might broaden our perceptions of reality. In particular, indigenous peoples may still hold capacities for tapping the order of *potentiae* not easily available to people immersed in post-Enlightenment cultures, and thus offer all of us a special window into Desmond's intimate universal (Desmond, 2016) and signatures of ultimacy as discussed by Neville (2013). A systematic, scholarly engagement with indigenous spirituality has the potential to reveal key insights into the spiritual dimension that would be comparatively less encumbered by the overlay of centuries of organized, Western religious frameworks. Of course, properly distinguishing the overlay of Christian influences involves substantial difficulty,[25] as the life of the Lakota elder Black Elk so clearly illustrates. According to Clyde Holler, although this Lakota "'medicine man," that is, spiritual leader and healer, converted to Catholicism later in life, nevertheless, his "life and work embodies the best that was in his people and justifies his position as the greatest religious thinker yet produced by native North America" (Holler 1995, 221).

Keeping in mind the grief and trauma sustained by indigenous peoples around the world, Thomas Berry in *The Great Work* put substantial emphasis on indigenous spirituality. Mary Evelyn Tucker, John Grim, and Andrew Angyal, in their biography of Thomas Berry, state that

> as Thomas developed his thinking about cosmology and ecology, he increasingly understood that Indigenous peoples had come to profound spiritual insights regarding the interdependent, or ecological, nature of reality. It became clear to him that Indigeonous myths described ecological realities not only in their place-based homelands, but also in relation to living beings on the land. These relationships that were developed in oral traditions often extended out to spiritual beings in the stars and deep space, not as distant realities but as close kin. (Tucker, Grim, and Angyal 2019, 244)

OUR SHARED JOURNEY

Living within a context, worldview, and history different from our own, in their deepest mode of inquiry the Dakotas undertook the vision quest to encounter, perhaps, another dimension of reality. My own quest to understand this great unknown propelled me into a lifetime of scholarship, in science and philosophy, and into deep reflection about the given world at its multiple levels. David Martinez expresses a view that I hope represents not just the Dakota perspective but also my own. "At the root of the vision . . . is humility. It is not a matter of gaining power for its own sake, but of needing power[26] and using it responsibly because one is ultimately powerless" (Martinez 2004, 79). In confronting the psychological challenges of nihilism, denialism, and assorted despairs of contemporary life, in facing up to the physical threats of war, pandemics, human suffering, and in newly realizing the deterioration of earth's climate, ecology, and habitability, can we somehow embrace what we have learned through science and philosophy and what we may yet draw on from indigenous and other spiritualities so as to bring into being a world in which we humans can live and flourish over the long term?

NOTES

1. There is also Jean-Paul Sartre's existentialist gambit of giving up on meaning by living practically in a world of presumed meaninglessness or, as with Søren Kierkegaard, regenerating meaning through sheer assertiveness.

2. As articulated by Nicholas Rescher, "World views provide us with a conceptual framework—a coordinated manifold of basic categories and concepts—for portraying the world and its ways" (Rescher 2017, 22).

3. Founded by Basarab Nicolescu, an international center for transdisciplinarity research has been operating since 1987 (see http://ciret-transdisciplinarity.org).

4. Reductive "theories of everything" (TOE's) are intrinsically incomplete because they presuppose actualism and reduce the real to Boolean-only logical structures; thus, such TOE's are insufficient to represent the truly integrative and inclusive framework needed to address issues of meaning and ultimate significance.

5. Contemplative Mind in Society is one organization that explores meaning, purpose and values through contemplative practice and application focused on higher education (*contemplativemind.org*, accessed October 28, 2019); similarly, Fr. Richard Rohr's *Center for Action and Contemplation* (*cac.org*) seeks to combine thoughtful practice with a more inclusive theological vision.

6. Attention to such marginalization yet hope for the future is expressed in major works by Arran Gare (1993; 2017) and Michel Weber (2016).

7. As stated by John Lango, "Creativity is, according to the 'Category of the Ultimate', the 'ultimate principle' exemplified in the coming into being of one actual entity [or Hartshornian 'dynamic particular'] from the many entities in its actual world. Moreover, the coming into being (i.e., 'becoming') of the one actual entity is the creation (i.e., 'creative advance') of a 'novel' entity . . . Thus the indeterminateness of the future is implicit in the principle of creativity" (Lango 1972, 68).

8. Consider how transformative it would be for any and all human communities if we could, at multiple levels and in all places, work toward building the spiritual foundations for a loving world, an aspiration embraced by organizations like the *Fetzer Institute* of Kalamazoo, Michigan (fetzer.org).

9. Gare calls attention to how Friedrich Schelling features intellectual intuition as "a form of knowledge gained through a reflective and imaginative experimentation and construction by the productive imagination of the sequence of forms produced by . . . the unconditioned totality, the self-organizing universe" (Gare 2018, 103). Perhaps intellectual intuition and cosmic consciousness represent two distinct integrative modes.

10. Further, speculations about ultimacies can work with speculative naturalism (*à la* Gare's work), and need not be based on any claims of supernaturalism as David Ray Griffin has argued persuasively in *Reenchantment without Supernaturalism* (Griffin 2001). A metaphysical analysis of grounding is provided by Leon Niemoczynski in *Charles Sanders Peirce and a Religious Metaphysics of Nature* (2011).

11. Roughly concurrent with the loosening ties between the British-American analytic tradition and scientism, Niemoczynski points out that "it is only recently that Continental philosophy has picked up the idea of 'nature' in its metaphysics" (2017, 135).

12. One scholarly group with particularly relevant expertise in this arena are members of the Metaphysical Society of America, founded by Paul Weiss in 1950, which maintains the journal *The Review of Metaphysics*; see *Being in America: Sixty Years of the Metaphysical Society* (Brian Henning and David Kovacs, eds. 2014).

13. Here we note that Padiyath is working within the Western religious tradition, which frequently emphasizes transcendence; this contrasts with Eastern orthodox traditions, which more often emphasizes immanence and practical faith. Non-Christian religions handle these distinctions in a multitude of ways.

14. I also intend any God concept as a pointer to a deeper reality, not some actualized entity *per se*; an evocation of a ground for the order of *potentiae*, not an exemplar of the order of actualization; a call to practical truth and creative transformation and not us-versus-them dualistic thinking.

15. A pre-space eternal present would not be confined to any simple metric representation whereas Laszlo's analogue does presume a metric representation; resolving this difference would be an important part of applying this eternal present conjecture.

16. The mapping to Whitehead's concept of prehension is close in that, as stated by Gao, "In the process of many becoming one, one is the one actual occasion and many are the many entities that enter into complex unity. Among the many entities, there are both actual entities and eternal objects [*potentiae*]. They serve as the data that are prehended by the one actual occasion that is becoming. In other words, the one prehends the disjunctive many into a conjunctive unity. It is clear that one should be mapped to Yang and many to Yin as one is active and many are passive" (Gao 2018, 136).

17. Reference to "global" in "local-Global" is here capitalized to indicate that this is a metaphysics application wherein the logic of *potentiae* is the focus; all previous usages of local-global have included both this and the logic of actualizations (Boolean logic).

18. As noted by Haipeng Gao, this 2–4–8 sequence maps directly to binary number systems with one, two, or three bits of information, which is yet another triad (Gao 2018, 133).

19. Anticipatory systems normally refer to those complex systems in which an organism is able to create and utilize a modeling framework for improved success in the competitive milieu (Robert Rosen 2012). Here "enhanced anticipatory systems" refers to the added capability of tapping pre-space potentiae to further enhance success; indeed, in addition to language, this may be a key feature that distinguishes *homo sapiens* from other advanced organisms.

20. Strictly speaking, there is no such thing as a "scientific" worldview because science is fundamentally a methodology and associated scientific practice; any worldview claim (e.g., materialism) is a philosophical or metaphysical overlay.

21. Such tapping of *potentiae* may be an embodiment of Schleiermacher's discussion of affective states of exaltation as central to religious awareness, or a type of cosmic consciousness; see Thandeka (2018) and the above section on *Aesthetics and Values*.

22. The sense of "place" is considered fully by Tim Cresswell in his book *Place* (2014).

23. Clyde Holler states that "in identifying themselves in their native tongue, native speakers tend to say 'I am Lakota/Nakota/Dakota.' When speaking English, they say instead 'I am Sioux.' The problem with this is that 'Sioux' is apparently a French term that means 'snake' or 'cutthroat,' and its use is disliked by many of the people to whom it is applied . . . Another problem is that there is no native equivalent to the term 'Indian' or 'native American,' when used in speaking of any person of aboriginal American origin. Again, the term 'Indian' is disapproved both by many of the people who use it and many to whom it is applied" (Holler 1995, xxiv). The

indigenous peoples that for millennia occupied the lands of my childhood spoke a dialect termed Dakota; thus, for my purpose here, and because the territory of my grandmother's birth was called the Dakota territory, I here use the term "Dakota" although some quotes include the term "Lakota." When making reference without specific tribal reference, I use the term "indigenous peoples" per the *Declaration of the Rights of Indigenous Peoples* (United Nations, 2007).

24. As stated in the United Nations report on the *State of the World's Indigenous Peoples*, "Of the some 7,000 languages today, it is estimated that more than 4,000 are spoken by indigenous peoples. Language specialists predict that up to 90 per cent of the world's languages are likely to become extinct or threatened with extinction by the end of the century" (United Nations 2009, 1). In addition to the "unintended" consequences of globalization and colonization, "assimilation policies lead to the destruction of languages and can thus be considered a form of ethnocide or linguistic genocide" (United Nations 2009, 58).

25. Difficulties for any systematic study of indigenous spirituality would be further enhanced with the possibility that to properly understand such lived experience would require fully "living it."

26. In his classic essay "Two Conceptions of Power," theologian Bernard Loomer distinguished two kinds of power, coercive power versus relational power, equivalent to power-over versus power-with, or unilateral power versus two-way (multi-way) power (Loomer 1976).

Appendix

Further Reading

FURTHER READING FOR CHAPTER 1: QUEST

Randall Auxier (2013) *Time, Will, and Purpose: Living Ideas from the Philosophy of Josiah Royce.* Chicago, IL: Open Court Publishing Co.

Pierfrancesco Basile (2018) *Whitehead's Metaphysics of Power.* Edinburgh: Edinburgh University Press Ltd.

Richard Campbell (1992) *Truth and Historicity.* Oxford: Oxford University Press.

Murray Code (2007) *Process, Reality, and the Power of Symbols.* Basingstoke, Hampshire: Palgrave Macmillan.

Mikhail Epstein and Igor Klyukanov (2012) *The Transformative Humanities: A Manifesto.* New York: Bloomsbury.

Arran Gare (1995) *Postmodernism and the Environmental Crisis.* New York: Routledge.

Jorge J. E. Gracia (1999) *Metaphysics and Its Task.* Albany: State University of New York Press.

William Grassie (2018) *Applied Big History: A Guide for Entrepreneurs, Investors, and Other Living Things.* New York: Metanexus Imprints.

John Haught (2006) *Is Nature Enough? Meaning and Truth in the Age of Science.* Cambridge: Cambridge University Press.

Thomas Nagel (2012) *Mind & Cosmos: Why the Materialist Neo-Darwinian Conception of Nature Is Almost Certainly False.* Oxford: Oxford University Press.

Thomas Pfau (2013) *Minding the Modern: Human Agency, Intellectual Traditions, and Responsible Knowledge.* Notre Dame, IN: University of Notre Dame Press.

Sami Pihlstrom, ed. (2017) *Pragmatism and Objectivity: Essays Sparked by the Work of Nicholas Rescher.* New York: Rutledge.

Nicholas Rescher (2000) *Process Philosophy: A Survey of Basic Issues.* Pittsburgh: University of Pittsburgh Press.

Milton Scarborough (2011) *Comparative Theories of Nonduality: The Search for a Middle Way.* London: Continuum International Publishing Group.

Santiago Sia (2015) *Society in Its Challenges: Philosophical Considerations of Living in Society.* Newcastle upon Tyne: Cambridge Scholars Publishing.

Raymond Tallis (2018) *Logos: The Mystery of How We Make Sense of the World.* Newcastle upon Tyne, UK: Agenda Publishing Ltd.

Alfred North Whitehead (1933) *Adventure of Ideas.* New York: The Macmillan Company.

FURTHER READING FOR CHAPTER 2: RELATIONS—*LOGOI*

Randall Auxier and Gary Herstein (2017) *The Quantum of Explanation: Whitehead's Radical Empiricism.* New York: Routledge.

Paul Bains (2006) *The Primacy of Semiosis: An Ontology of Relations.* Toronto: University of Toronto Press.

Philip Clayton and William Andrew Schwartz (2019) *What is Ecological Civilization?: Crisis, Hope, and the Future of the Planet.* Anoka, MN: Process Century Press.

Didier Debaise (2017) *Speculative Empiricism: Revisiting Whitehead.* Edinburgh: Edinburgh University Press.

William Desmond (2016) *The Intimate Universal: The Hidden Porosity Among Religion, Art, Philosophy, and Politics.* New York: Columbia University Press.

Timothy Eastman, Michael Epperson, and David Ray Griffin, eds. (2016) *Physics and Speculative Philosophy: Potentiality in Modern Science.* Berlin: Walter de Gruyter.

Arran Gare (2018) *The Philosophical Foundations of Ecological Civilization: A Manifesto for the Future.* Abingdon, Oxon: Routledge.

David Ray Griffin (2008) *Whitehead's Radically Different Postmodern Philosophy: An Argument for Its Contemporary Relevance.* Albany: State University of New York Press.

Leemon McHenry (2015) *The Event Universe: The Revisionary Metaphysics of Alfred North Whitehead.* Edinburgh: Edinburgh University Press Ltd.

Basarab Nicolescu (2015) *From Modernity to Cosmodernity: Science, Culture, and Spirituality.* Albany: State University of New York Press.

Nicholas Rescher (1996) *Process Metaphysics: An Introduction to Process Philosophy.* Albany: State University of New York Press.

Stephen David Ross (1983) *Perspective in Whitehead's Metaphysics.* Albany: State University of New York Press.

George Shields (2003) *Process and Analysis: Whitehead, Hartshorne, and the Analytic Tradition.* Albany: State University of New York Press.

Phillip Stambovsky (2009) *Inference and the Metaphysic of Reason: An Onto-Epistemological Critique.* Milwaukee: Marquette University Press.

Raymond Tallis (2017) *On Time and Lamentation: Reflections on Transience.* Newcastle upon Tyne, UK: Agenda Publishing Limited.

Duane Vosquil (2016) *Process and Dipolar Reality: An Essay in Process, Event Metaphysics, Rethinking Whitehead's Categoreal Scheme.* Eugene, OR: Wipf & Stock.

FURTHER READING FOR CHAPTER 3:
GORDIAN KNOT TO *LOGOI* FRAMEWORK

Karen Barad (2007) *Meeting the Universe Halfway: Quantum Physics and the Entanglement of Matter and Meaning.* Durham, NC: Duke University Press.

Timothy Eastman and Hank Keeton (2004) *Physics and Whitehead: Quantum, Process, and Experience.* Albany: State University of New York Press.

Michael Epperson and Elias Zafiris (2013) *Foundations of Relational Realism: A Topological Approach to Quantum Mechanics and the Philosophy of Nature.* Lanham, MD: Lexington Books.

John Jungerman (2000) *World in Process: Creativity and Interconnection in the New Physics.* Albany: State University of New York Press.

Ruth Kastner (2015) *Understanding our Unseen Reality: Solving Quantum Riddles.* London: Imperial College Press.

Hans Primas (2017) *Knowledge and Time.* Berlin: Springer.

Robert Rosen (2012) *Anticipatory Systems: Philosophical, Mathematical, and Methodological Foundations.* New York: Springer.

FURTHER READING FOR CHAPTER 4: CAUSATION, EMERGENCE AND COMPLEX SYSTEMS

Lawrence Cahoone (2013) *The Orders of Nature.* Albany: State University of New York Press.

Richard Campbell (2015) *The Metaphysics of Emergence.* New York: Palgrave Macmillan.

Philip Clayton (2004) *Mind & Emergence*: *From Quantum to Consciousness.* New York: Oxford University Press.

Philip Clayton and Paul Davies, eds. (2006) *The Re-Emergence of Emergence: The Emergentist Hypothesis from Science to Religion.* Oxford: Oxford University Press.

Terrence Deacon (2011) *Incomplete Nature: How Mind Emerged from Matter.* New York: W. W. Norton & Co.

George Ellis (2016) *How Can Physics Underlie the Mind?: Top-Down Causation in the Human Context.* Berlin: Springer-Verlag.

Menno Hulswit (2002) *From Cause to Causation: A Peircean Perspective.* Dordrecht: Kluwer Academic Publishers.

Stuart Kauffman (2019) *A World Beyond Physics: The Emergence and Evolution of Life.* Oxford: Oxford University Press.

George R. Lucas, Jr. (1989) *The Rehabilitation of Whitehead: An Analytic and Historical Assessment of Process Philosophy.* Albany: State University of New York Press.

Roland Omnès (2005) *Converging Realities: Toward a Common Philosophy of Physics and Mathematics.* Princeton: Princeton University Press.

Ralph Pred (2005) *Onflow: Dynamics of Consciousness and Experience*. Cambridge, MA: Bradford Books.

Joe Rosen (1995) *Symmetry in Science: An Introduction to the General Theory*. New York: Springer-Verlag.

Roberto Unger and Lee Smolin (2015) *The Singular Universe and the Reality of Time*. Cambridge: Cambridge University Press.

Michel Weber and Anderson Weekes, eds. (2009) *Process Approaches to Consciousness in Psychology, Neuroscience, and Philosophy of Mind*. Albany: State University of New York Press.

FURTHER READING FOR CHAPTER 5: INFORMATION AND SEMIOTICS

Søren Brier (2008) *Cybersemiotics: Why Information Is Not Enough*. Toronto: University of Toronto Press.

John Deely (1990) *Basics of Semiotics*. Bloomington: Indiana University Press.

John Deely (2003) *The Impact on Philosophy of Semiotics*. South Bend, IN: St. Augustine's Press.

Roland Faber, Jeffrey Bell, and Joseph Petek, eds. (2019) *Rethinking Whitehead's Symbolism: Thought, Language, Culture*. Edinburgh: Edinburgh University Press.

Jesper Hoffmeyer and Donald Favareau (2009) *Biosemiotics: An Examination into the Signs of Life and the Life of Signs*. Scranton, PA: University of Scranton Press.

Robert Logan (2014) *What Is Information?: Propagating Organization in the Biosphere, Symbolosphere, Technosphere and Econosphere*. Toronto: DEMO Publishing.

Robert Ulanowicz (2009) *A Third Window: Natural Life Beyond Newton and Darwin*. West Conshohocken, PA: Templeton Foundation Press.

James Williams (2016) *A Process Philosophy of Signs*. Edinburgh: Edinburgh University Press.

FURTHER READING FOR CHAPTER 6: COMPLEX WHOLE

David Christian (2019) "What is Big History?" In *The Routledge Companion to Big History*. London: Routledge.

David Ray Griffin (2007) *Whitehead's Radically Different Postmodern Philosophy: An Argument for Its Contemporary Relevance*. Albany: State University of New York Press.

David Grinspoon (2016) *Earth in Human Hands: Shaping Our Planet's Future*. New York: Grand Central Publishing.

Brian Henning (2005) *The Ethics of Creativity: Beauty, Morality, and Nature in a Processive Cosmos*. Pittsburgh: University of Pittsburgh Press.

Brian Henning and Adam Scarfe, eds. (2013) *Beyond Mechanism: Putting Life Back into Biology*. Lanham, MD: Lexington Books.

Stuart Kauffman (2016) *Humanity in a Creative Universe.* Oxford: Oxford University Press.

Spyridon Koutroufinis, ed. (2014) *Life and Process: Towards a New Biophilosophy.* Berlin: Walter de Gruyter.

Paul Marshall (2016) *A Complex Integral Realist Perspective: Towards a New Axial Vision.* London: Routledge.

Nicholas Rescher (2017) *Metaphysical Perspectives.* Notre Dame, IN: University of Notre Dame Press.

Michel Weber (2016) *The Political Vindication of Radical Empiricism with Application to the Global Systemic Crisis.* Anoka, MN: Process Century Press.

Alan White (2014) *Toward a Philosophical Theory of Everything: Contributions to the Structural-Systematic Philosophy.* New York: Bloomsbury.

Elizabeth Woodworth and David Ray Griffin (2016) *Unprecedented Climate Mobilization: A Handbook for Citizens and Their Governments.* Atlanta, GA: Clarity Press.

FURTHER READING FOR CHAPTER 7: PEIRCE'S TRIADS AND WHITEHEAD'S PROCESS

Pierfrancesco Basile (2017) *Whitehead's Metaphysis of Power: Reconstructing Modern Philosophy.* Edinburgh: Edinburgh University Press Ltd.

John Berthrong (1998) *Concerning Creativity: A Comparison of Chu Hsi, Whitehead, and Neville.* Albany: State University of New York Press.

James Blachowicz (2012) *Essential Difference: Toward a Metaphysics of Emergence.* Albany: State University of New York Press.

Jason Brown (2017) *Metapsychology of the Creative Process: Continuous Novelty as the Ground of Creative Advance.* Exeter, UK: Imprint Academic.

Donald Crosby (2005) *Novelty.* Lanham, MD: Lexington Books.

Guy Debrock, ed. (2003) *Process Pragmatism: Essays on a Quiet Philosophical Revolution.* Amsterdam: Radopi.

Edward Kelly, Adam Crabtree, and Paul Marshall, eds. (2019) *Beyond Physicalism: Toward Reconciliation of Science and Spirituality.* Lanham, MD: Rowman & Littlefield.

Daniel Siegel (2017) *Mind: A Journey to the Heart of Being Human.* New York: W. W. Norton & Co.

Henry Stapp (2017) *Quantum Theory and Free Will: How Mental Intentions Translate into Bodily Actions.* Cham, Switzerland: Springer International.

FURTHER READING FOR CHAPTER 8: CONTEXTUALITY—FROM EXPERIENCE TO MEANING

Lene Rachel Andersen and Tomas Björkman (2017) *The Nordic Secret: A European Story of Beauty and Freedom.* Stockholm: Fri Tanke.

Joseph Cambray (2009) *Sychronicity: Nature & Psyche in an Interconnected Universe.* College Station: Texas A&M University Press.

John B. Cobb, Jr., Richard Falk, and Catherine Keller, eds. (2013) *Reason & Reenchantment: The Philosophical, Religious, and Political Thought of David Ray Griffin.* Claremont, CA: Process Century Press.

Rem B. Edwards (2014) *An Axiological Process Ethics.* Claremont, CA: Process Century Press.

Roland Faber, Brian Henning, and Clinton Combs, eds. (2010) *Beyond Metaphysics? Explorations in Alfred North Whitehead's Late Thought.* Amsterdam: Rodopi.

Frederick Ferre (1996) *Being and Value: Toward a Constructive Postmodern Metaphysics.* Albany: State University of New York Press.

Herman Greene (2018) *The Ecozoic Way: The Foundational Papers.* Chapel Hill, NC: Center for Ecozoic Studies.

David Ray Griffin (2016) *God Exists but Gawd Does Not: From Evil to New Atheism to Fine-Tuning.* Claremont, CA: Process Century Press.

David Ray Griffin (2017) *Process Theology: On Postmodernism, Morality, Pluralism, Eschatology, and Demonic Evil.* Anoka, MN: Process Century Press.

John Haught (2015) *Resting on the Future: Catholic Theology for an Unfinished Universe.* New York: Bloomsbury Publishing.

Clyde Holler (1995) *Black Elk's Religion: The Sun Dance and Lakota Catholicism.* Syracuse, NY: Syracuse University Press.

Stuart Kauffman (2008) *Reinventing the Sacred: A New View of Science, Reason, and Religion.* New York: Perseus Books.

Ervin Laszlo (2014) *The Self-Actualizing Cosmos: The Akasha Revolution in Science and Human Consciousness.* Rochester, VT: Inner Traditions.

David Loy (1997) *Nonduality: A Study in Comparative Philosophy.* New Haven: Yale University Press.

Derek Malone-France (2007) *Deep Empiricism: Kant, Whitehead, and the Necessity of Philosophical Theism.* Lanham, MD: Lexington Books.

Steve McIntosh (2007) *Integral Consciousness and the Future of Evolution: How the Integral Worldview Is Transforming Politics, Culture and Spirituality.* St. Paul, MN: Paragon House.

Basarab Nicolescu (2015) *From Modernity to Cosmodernity: Science, Culture, and Spirituality.* Albany: State University of New York Press.

Rupert Sheldrake (2018) *Science and Spiritual Practices.* Berkeley, CA: Counterpoint.

Donald Viney and George Shields (2020) *The Mind of Charles Hartshorne.* Anoka, MN: Process Century Press.

Alfred North Whitehead (1929) *Process and Reality: An Essay in Cosmology.* New York: Macmillan; The Free Press.

Bibliography

Achtner, Wolfgang, Stefan Kunz, and Thomas Walter. 2002. *Dimensions of Time: The Structures of the Time of Humans, of the World, and of God.* Translated by Jr. Arthur Williams. Grand Rapids, MI: William B. Eerdmans Publishing Company.

Alcock, James E. 1990. *Science and Supernature: A Critical Appraisal of Parapsychology.* Amherst, NY: Prometheus Books.

Alexander, Eben. 2012. *Proof of Heaven: A Neurosurgeon's Journey into the Afterlife.* New York: Simon & Schuster.

Allan, George, and Merle Frederick Allshouse, eds. 2005. *Nature, Truth, and Value: Exploring the Thinking of Frederick Ferre.* Lanham, MD: Lexington Books.

Ames, Roger T. 2016. "Philosophizing with Canonical Chinese Texts: Seeking an Interpretive Context." In *The Bloomsbury Research Handbook of Chinese Philosophy Methodologies,* edited by Sor-hoon Tan, 37–55. London: Bloomsbury.

Andersen, Lene Rachel, and Tomas Björkman. 2017. *The Nordic Secret: A European Story of Beauty and Freedom.* Stockholm: Fri Tanke (fritanke.se).

Athearn, Daniel. 1994. *Scientific Nihilism: On the Loss and Recovery of Physical Explanation.* Albany: State University of New York Press.

Atmanspacher, Harald. 2007. "Contextual Emergence from Physics to Cognitive Neuroscience." *Journal of Consciousness Studies* 14, no. 1–2: 18–36.

Atmanspacher, Harald, and Christopher Fuchs. 2014. *The Pauli-Jung Conjecture and Its Impact Today.* Exeter: Imprint Academic.

Atmanspacher, Harald, and Hans Primas. 2003. "Epistemic and Ontic Quantum Realities." In *Time, Quantum and Information,* edited by Lutz Castell and Otfried Ischebeck, 301–321. Berlin: Springer-Verlag.

Auxier, Randall E. 2013. *Time, Will, and Purpose: Living Ideas from the Philosophy of Josiah Royce.* Chicago, IL: Open Court Publishing Company.

Auxier, Randall E., Douglas Anderson, and Lewis Hahn, eds. 2015. "The Philosophy of Hilary Putnam." In *The Library of Living Philosophers,* edited by Randall Auxier. Chicago, IL: Open Court Publishing Company.

Auxier, Randall E., and Gary L. Herstein. 2017. *The Quantum of Explanation: Whitehead's Radical Empiricism*. New York: Routledge.

Auyang, Sunny Y. 1995. *How Is Quantum Field Theory Possible?* Oxford: Oxford University Press.

Azzano, Lorenzo. 2014. "What Is the Nature of Properties?" *Rivista Italiana di Filosofia Analitica Junior* 5, no. 2: 27–42.

Baez, John C. 2020. "Noether's Theorem in a Nutshell." In *John Baez's Stuff*. Riverside, CA: University of California Riverside.

Bailey, David H. 2019. "Does Probability Refute Evolution?" *Science Meets Religion* (blog). HYPERLINK "http://www.sciencemeetsreligion.org" http://www.science meetsreligion.org.

Bains, Paul. 2006. *The Primacy of Semiosis: An Ontology of Relations*. Toronto: University of Toronto Press.

Barad, Karen. 2007. *Meeting the Universe Halfway: Quantum Physics and the Entanglement of Matter and Meaning*. Durham, NC: Duke University Press.

Barbieri, Marcello, ed. 2007. *Introduction to Biosemiotics: The New Biological Synthesis*. Dordrecht: Springer.

———. 2008. "Biosemiotics: A New Understanding of Life." *Naturwissenschaften* 95, no. 7: 577–599.

———. 2009. "A Short History of Biosemiotics." *Biosemiotics* 2, no. 3: 221–245.

Barnes, Luke A. 2012. "The Fine-Tuning of the Universe for Intelligent Life." *Publications of the Astronomical Society of Australia* 29, no. 4: 529–564.

Basile, Pierfrancesco. 2009. *Leibniz, Whitehead and the Metaphysics of Causation*. New York: Palgrave Macmillan.

———. 2018. *Whitehead's Metaphysics of Power*. Edinburgh: Edinburgh University Press Ltd.

Battista, John, and Richard Almond. 1973. "The Development of Meaning in Life." *Psychiatry: Interpersonal and Biological Processes* 36, no. 4: 409–427.

Becker, Adam. 2018. *What Is Real?* New York: Basic Books.

Berenstain, Nora, and James Ladyman. 2012. "Ontic Structural Realism and Modality." In *Structural Realism: Structure, Object, and Causality*, edited by Elaine Landry and Dean Rickles, 149–168. Dordrecht: Springer.

Berry, Thomas. 1999. *The Great Work: Our Way Into the Future*. New York: Random House.

Berthrong, John. 1998. *Concerning Creativity: A Comparison of Chu Hsi, Whitehead, and Neville*. Albany: State University of New York Press.

Bettinger, Jesse. 2015. "The Founding of an Event-Ontology: Verlinde's Emergent Gravity and Whitehead's Actual Entities." Ph.D. dissertation. Religion, Politics and Neuroeconomics, Claremont Graduate University.

Bettinger, Jesse, and Timothy E. Eastman. 2017. "Foundations of Anticipatory Logic in Biology and Physics." *Progress in Biophysics and Molecular Biology* 131 (December): 108–120.

Beuchot, Mauricio, and John Deely. 1995. "Common Sources for the Semiotic of Charles Peirce and John Poinsot." Review of Metaphysics 48, no. 3: 539–566.

Bielfeldt, Dennis. 2003. "Physicalism, Reductive and Nonreductive." In *Encyclopedia of Science and Religion*, edited by J. Wentzel Vrede van Huyssteen. New York: Macmillan Reference USA.

Birch, Charles. 1990. *On Purpose*. Sydney: University of New South Wales Press.

———. 1995. *Feelings*. Sydney: University of New South Wales Press.

Bishop, Rober, and Harald Atmanspacher. 2006. "Contextual Emergence in the Description of Properties." Foundations of Physics 36, no. 12 (December): 1753–1777.

———. 2012. "The Causal Closure of Physics and Free Will." In The Oxford Handbook of Free Will, edited by Robert Kane, 101–111. Oxford: Oxford University Press.

Blachowicz, James. 2012. *Essential Difference: Toward a Metaphysics of Emergence*. Albany: State University of New York Press.

———. 2013. "The Constraint Interpretation of Physical Emergence." *Journal for General Philosophy of Science* 44, no. 1 (July): 21–40.

———. 2016. "There Is No Scientific Method." *The New York Times–The Stone*, July 4: 1–9. https://www.nytimes.com/2016/07/04/opinion/there-is-no-scientific -method.html.

Blackburn, Patrick, Johan F. van Benthem, and Frank Wolter, eds. 2007. *Handbook of Modal Logic*. Amsterdam: Elsevier.

Blackburn, Patrick, Maarten de Rijke, and Yde Venema, eds. 2015. *Modal Logic*. Cambridge: Cambridge University Press.

Boccardi, Emiliano. 2016. "Recent Trends in the Philosophy of Time: An Introduction to Time and Reality I." *Manuscrito* 39, no. 4: 5–34.

Bogaard, Paul, and Jason Bell, eds. 2017. "The Harvard Lectures of Alfred North Whitehead, 1924–1925." In *The Edinburgh Critical Edition of the Complete Works of Alfred North Whitehead*, edited by George Lucas, Jr. and Brian Henning. Edinburgh: Edinburgh University Press Ltd.

Bohm, David, and Basil J. Hiley. 1979. "On the Aharonov-Bohm effect." *Nuov Cim A* 52: 295.

———. 1993. *The Undivided Universe: An Ontological Interpretation of Quantum Mechanics*. Abingdon, Oxon: Routledge.

Bolander, Thomas. 2002. "Self-Reference and Logic." *Phi News* 1: 9–44.

———. 2017. "Self-Reference." In *The Stanford Encyclopedia of Philosophy*, edited by Edward N. Zalta. Stanford, CA: The Metaphysics Research Lab.

Boniolo, Giovanni, and Paolo Budinich. 2005. "The Role of Mathematics in Physical Sciences and Dirac's Methodological Revolution." In *The Role of Mathematics in Physical Sciences: Interdisciplinary and Philosophical Aspects*, edited by Giovanni Boniolo, Paolo Budinich, and Majda Trobok, 75–96. Dordrecht: Springer Netherlands.

Bordeianu, Radu. 2009. "Maximus and Ecology: The Relevance of Maximus the Confessor's Theology of Creation for the Present Ecological Crisis." *The Downside Review* 127: 103–126.

Bosanquet, Bernard. 1920. *Implication and Linear Inference*. London: Macmillan.

Braasch, Gary. 2007. *Earth under Fire: How Global Warming Is Changing the World*. Berkeley: University of California Press.

Bracken, Joseph A. 2001. *The One in the Many: A Contemporary Reconstruction of the God-World Relationship*. Grand Rapids, MI: William B. Eerdmans Publishing Company.

Bradley, James. 1996. "Act, Event, Series: Metaphysics, Mathematics, and Whitehead." *The Journal of Speculative Philosophy* (January): 233–248.

———. 2003a. "The Generalization of the Mathematical Function: A Speculative Analysis." In *Process Pragmatism: Essays on a Quiet Philosophical Revolution*, edited by Guy Debrock, 71–86. Amsterdam: Radopi.

———. 2003b. "Whitehead and the Analysis of the Propositional Function." In *Process and Analysis: Whitehead, Hartshorne, and the Analytic Tradition*, edited by George Shields, 139–155. Albany: State University of New York Press.

———. 2004. "Transformations in Speculative Philosophy." In *The Cambridge History of Philosophy, 1870–1945*, edited by Thomas Baldwin. New York: Cambridge University Press.

———. 2008. "The Speculative Generalization of the Function: A Key to Whitehead." *Inflexions* no. 2 (December); first published in *Tijdschrift voor Filosofie* 64 (2002): 231–252.

———. 2009. "Philosophy and Trinity." *Canadian Journal of Continental Philosophy* 16, no. 1: 155–178.

———. 2010. "The Triune Event: Event Ontology, Reason, and Love." In *Event and Decision: Ontology and Politics in Badiou, Deleuze, and Whitehead*, edited by Henry Krips, Roland Faber, and Daniel Pettus, 97–114. Newcastle upon Tyne: Cambridge Scholars.

Brann, Eva T. H. 2011. *The Logos of Heraclitus: The First Philosopher of the West on Its Most Interesting Term*. Philadelphia: Paul Dry Books.

Brenner, Joseph. 2008. *Logic in Reality*. Berlin: Springer Science & Business Media.

Brier, Søren. 2010. "The Cybersemiotic Model of Communication: An Evolutionary View on the Threshold between Semiosis and Informational Exchange." In *Essential Readings in Biosemiotics: Anthology and Commentary*, edited by Donald Favareau, 697–729. Dordrecht: Springer.

———. 2013. *Cybersemiotics: Why Information Is Not Enough!* Toronto: University of Toronto Press.

———. 2014. "The Riddle of the Sphinx Answered: On How C. S. Peirce's Transdisciplinary Semiotic Philosophy of Knowing Links Science, Spirituality and Knowing." In *Death and Anti-Death, Volume 12: One Hundred Years After Charles S. Peirce*, edited by C. Tandy. Ann Arbor, MI: Ria University Press.

Brooks, Rodney A. 2015. *Fields of Color: The Theory that Escaped Einstein*. 2nd edition. Rodney Brooks, Silver Spring, MD: Universal Printing, LLC.

Brown, Jason. 2017. *Metapsychology of the Creative Process: Continuous Novelty as the Ground of Creative Advance*. Exeter: Imprint Academic.

Brown, Laurie, ed. 2005. *Feynman's Thesis: A New Approach to Quantum Theory*. Hackensack, NJ: World Scientific Publishing Company.

Brumbaugh, Robert Sherrick. 1982. *Whitehead, Process Philosophy, and Education.* Albany: State University of New York Press.

Brüntrup, Godehard, and Ludwig Jaskolla, eds. 2017. *Panpsychism: Contemporary Perspectives.* Oxford: Oxford University Press.

Bub, Jeffrey. 1997. *Interpreting the Quantum World.* Cambridge: Cambridge University Press.

Buchler, Justus. 1989. *Metaphysics of Natural Complexes.* Albany: State University of New York Press.

Bunge, Mario. 1966. "The Myth of Simplicity." *Philosophical Quarterly* 16, no. 62: 85–86.

———. 1977. *Treatise on Basic Philosophy: Ontology I: The Furniture of the World.* Vol. 3. Dordrecht: D. Reidel Publishing Company.

———. 2013. *Matter and Mind: A Philosophical Inquiry.* Berlin: Springer.

———. 2015. *Chasing Reality: Strife Over Realism.* Toronto: University of Toronto Press.

———. 2018. "Chance: Individual Indeterminacy or Collective Randomness?" *The Review of Metaphysics* 72, no. 2 (December): 235–255.

Burris, Stanley. 2015. "The Algebra of Logic Tradition." In *The Stanford Encyclopedia of Philosophy*, edited by Edward N. Zalta. Stanford, CA: The Metaphysics Research Lab.

Butterfield, Jeremy. 2011. "Emergence, Reduction and Supervenience: A Varied Landscape." *Foundations of Physics* 41, no. 6: 920–959.

Cahill, Reginald T. 2005. *Process Physics: From Information Theory to Quantum Space and Matter.* New York: Nova Science Publishers.

———. 2016. "Process Physics: Self-Referential Information and Experiential Reality." In *Physics and Speculative Philosophy: Potentiality in Modern Science*, edited by Timothy E. Eastman, Michael Epperson, and David Ray Griffin, 177–219. Berlin: Walter de Gruyter.

Cahoone, Lawrence. 2014. *The Orders of Nature.* Albany: State University of New York Press.

Cambray, Joseph. 2009. *Synchronicity: Nature & Psyche in an Interconnected Universe.* College Station: Texas A&M University Press.

Cammack, Richard, Teresa Attwood, Peter Campbell, Howard Parish, Anthony Smith, Francis Vella, and John Stirling Biosemiotics, eds. 2006. "Biosemiotics." In *Oxford Dictionary of Biochemistry and Molecular Biology.* 2nd edition. Oxford: Oxford University Press.

Campbell, Richard. 1992. *Truth and Historicity.* Oxford: Oxford University Press.

———. 2015. *The Metaphysics of Emergence.* New York: Palgrave Macmillan.

Canales, Jimena. 2015. *The Physicist and the Philosopher: Einstein, Bergson, and the Debate that Changed Our Understanding of Time.* Princeton, NJ: Princeton University Press.

Čapek, Milič. 1961. *The Philosophical Impact of Contemporary Physics.* New York: Van Nostrand.

———. 1971. "Bergson and Modern Physics: A Reinterpretation and Re-evaluation." Vol. VII. In *Boston Studies for the Philosophy of Science*, edited by Robert Cohen and Marx Wartofsky. Dordrecht: D. Reidel Publishing Company.

———. 1991. "The New Aspects of Time: Its Continuity and Novelties." Vol. 125. In *Boston Studies in the Philosophy of Science*. Dordrecht: Kluwer Academic Publishers.

Carlson, Stephan C. 2017. "Topology." In *Encyclopedia Britannica, Inc.*

Carroll, Sean. 2016. *The Big Picture: On the Origins of Life, Meaning, and the Universe Itself.* New York: Dutton.

Chalmers, David. 2015. "Why Isn't There More Progress in Philosophy?" *Philosophy* 90, no. 1: 3–31.

———. 2017. "The Combination Problem for Panpsychism." In *Panpsychism: Contemporary Perspectives*, edited by Godehard Bruntrup and Ludwig Jaskolla, 179–214. Oxford: Oxford University Press.

Chandler, Daniel. 2002. *Semiotics: The Basics.* London: Routledge.

Cheng, Chung-Ying. 1979. "Categories of Creativity in Whitehead and Neo-Confucianism." *Journal of Chinese Philosophy* 6, no. 3: 251–274.

Chew, Geoffrey. 2004. "A Historical Reality that Includes Big Bang, Free Will, and Elementary Particles." In *Physics and Whitehead: Quantum, Process, and Experience*, edited by Timothy E. Eastman and Hank Keeton, 84–91. Albany: State University of New York Press.

Choi, Sungho, and Michael Fara. 2018. "Dispositions." In *The Stanford Encyclopedia of Philosophy*, edited by Edward N. Zalta. Stanford, CA: The Metaphysics Research Lab.

Choudhuri, Arnab Rai. 2010. *Astrophysics for Physicists.* Cambridge: Cambridge Unviersity Press.

Christian, David. 2019. "What is Big History?" In *The Routledge Companion to Big History*, edited by Craig Benjamin, Esther Quaedackers, and David Baker, 16–34. London: Routledge.

Clayton, Philip. 2005. *Mind & Emergence: From Quantum to Consciousness.* New York: Oxford University Press.

Clayton, Philip, and Paul Davies, eds. 2006. *The Re-Emergence of Emergence: The Emergentist Hypothesis from Science to Religion.* Oxford: Oxford University Press.

Clayton, Philip, and William Andrew Schwartz. 2019a. *What is Ecological Civilization?: Crisis, Hope, and the Future of the Planet.* Anoka, MN: Process Century Press.

Clayton, Philip, and William Andrew Schwartz. 2019b. *What Is Ecological Civilization? Crisis, Hope, and the Future of the Planet.* Vol. XVIII. In *Toward Ecological Civilization* series, edited by Jeanyne Slettom. Anoka, MN: Process Century Press.

Cobb, John B., Jr. 2008a. *Whitehead Word Book.* Claremont, CA: P&F Press.

———, ed. 2008b. *Back to Darwin: A Richer Account of Evolution.* Grand Rapids, MI: William B. Eerdmans Publishing Company.

Cobb, John B., Jr., Richard Falk, and Catherine Keller, eds. 2013. *Reason & Reenchantment: The Philosophical, Religious, and Political Thought of David Ray Griffin*. Claremont, CA: Process Century Press.

Cobb, John B., Jr., and William Andrew Schwartz, eds. 2018. *Putting Philosophy to Work: Toward an Ecological Civilization*. Vol. XV. In *Toward Ecological Civilization*, edited by Jeanyne Slettom. Anoka, MN: Process Century Press.

Cobley, Paul, ed. 2010. *The Routledge Companion to Semiotics*. Abington, Oxon: Routledge.

Code, Murray. 1995. *Myths of Reason: Vagueness, Rationality, and the Lure of Logic*. Amherst, NY: Prometheus Books.

———. 1997. "On the Poverty of Scientism, Or: The Ineluctable Roughness of Rationality." *Metaphilosophy* 28, no. 1–2: 102–122.

———. 2007. *Process, Reality, and the Power of Symbols*. Basingstoke, Hampshire: Palgrave Macmillan.

Combs, Clinton. 2010. "Preface." In *Beyond Metaphysics?: Explorations in Alfred North Whitehead's Late Thought*, edited by Roland Faber, Brian Henning, and Clinton Combs, xi–xv. Amsterdam: Radopi.

Conte, Elio. 2011. "On the Logical Origins of Quantum Mechanics Demonstrated by Using Clifford Algebra." *The Electronic Journal of Theoretical Physics* 8, no. 25: 109–126.

Corfield, David. 2010. "Nominalism Versus Realism." *EMS Newsletter (European Mathematical Society)* (March): 24–26.

Cornish-Bowden, Athel, and María Luz Cárdenas. 2020. "Contrasting Theories of Life: Historical Context, Current Theories. In Search of an Ideal Theory." *Biosystems* 188 (1 February): 104063.

Corrington, Robert. 2013. *Nature's Sublime: An Essay in Aesthetic Naturalism*. Lanham, MD: Lexington Books.

Cresswell, Tim. 2014. *Place: An Introduction*. New York: John Wiley & Sons.

Croca, J. R. 2015. *Eurhythmic Physics or Hyperphysics*. Saarbrücken, Germany: Lambert Academic Publishing.

Crosby, Donald. 2005. *Novelty*. Lanham, MD: Lexington Books.

Cushing, James T. 1998. *Philosophical Concepts in Physics: The Historical Relation Between Philosophy and Scientific Theories*. Vol. 143. Cambridge: Cambridge University Press.

Damasio, Antonio R. 1999. *The Feeling of What Happens: Body and Emotion in the Making of Consciousness*. Boston: Houghton Mifflin Harcourt.

de Chardin, Teilhard. 2017. *Activation of Energy*. Mariner Books, 1963.

Deacon, Terrence. 2003. "The Hierarchic Logic of Emergence: Untangling the Interdependence of Evolution and Self-organization." In *Evolution and Learning: The Baldwin Effect Reconsidered*, edited by Bruce Weber and David Depew, 273–308. Cambridge, MA: The MIT Press.

———. 2012. *Incomplete Nature: How Mind Emerged from Matter*. New York: W. W. Norton & Co.

Deacon, Terrence, and Spyridon Koutroufinis. 2014. "Complexity and Dynamical Depth." *Information* 5, no. 3: 404–423.

Deacon, Terrence, and Tyrone Cashman. 2016. "Steps to a Metaphysics of Incompleteness." *Theology and Science* 14, no. 5: 401–429.

Debaise, Didier. 2017. *Speculative Empiricism: Revisiting Whitehead.* translated by Tomas Weber. Edinburgh: Edinburgh University Press.

Deely, John. 1982. "Introducing Semiotic: Its History and Doctrine." In *Advances in Semiotics*, edited by Thomas Sebeok. Bloomington: Indiana University Press.

———. 1990. *Basics of Semiotics.* In *Advances in Semiotics* series, edited by Thomas Sebeok. Bloomington: Indiana University Press.

———. 1994. "The Grand Vision." *The Transactions of the Charles S. Peirce Society* 30, no. 2 (Spring): 371–400.

———. 2001. *Four Ages of Understanding: The First Postmodern Survey of Philosophy from Ancient Times to the Turn of the Twenty-First Century.* In *Toronto Studies in Semiotics and Communication*, edited by Umberto Eco, Marcel Danesi, Paul Perron, and Thomas A. Sebeok. Toronto: University of Toronto Press.

———. 2003. *The Impact on Philosophy of Semiotics: The Quasi-Error of the External World, with a Dialogue betweeen a 'Semiotist' and a 'Realist.'* South Bend, IN: St. Augustine's Press.

———. 2004. "Semantics and Jacob von Uexkull's Concept of Umwelt." *Sign Systems Studies* 32, no. 1/2: 11–33.

———. 2009. *Purely Objective Reality: Semiotics, Communication and Cognition.* Vol. 4. Berlin: Walter de Gruyter.

Dembski, William II, and Robert Marks. 2010. "The Search for a Search: Measuring the Information Cost of Higher Level Search." *Journal of Advanced Computational Intelligence and Intelligent Informatics* 14, no. 5: 475–486.

de Ronde, Christian. 2007. "Understanding Quantum Mechanics through the Complementary Descriptions Approach." e-print archive arXiv:0705.3850.

———. 2011. *The Contextual and Modal Character of Quantum Mechanics: A Formal and Philosophical Analysis in the Foundations of Physics.* Ph.D. dissertation. Utrecht University.

———. 2015. "Modality, Potentiality, and Contradiction in Quantum Mechanics." In Proceedings of the 5th World Congress on Paraconsistency, edited by Mihir Chakraborty, Jean-Yves Beziau, and D. Dutta. New Delhi: Springer.

Desmet, Ronny. 2010a. "Whitehead's Philosophy of Mathematics and Relativity." Ph.D. dissertation. Center for Logic and Philosophy of Science, Free University of Brussels.

———. 2010b. "*Principia Mathematica* Centenary." *Process Studies* 39, no. 2 (Fall/Winter): 225–263.

———. 2020a. "From Physics to Philosophy, and from Continuity to Atomicity." In *Whitehead at Harvard, 1924–1925*, edited by Brian Henning and Joseph Petek, 132–153. Edinburgh: Edinburgh University Press.

———. 2020b. "Whitehead's Highly Speculative Lectures on Quantum Theory." In *Whitehead at Harvard, 1924–1925*, edited by Brian Henning and Joseph Petek, 154–181. Edinburgh: Edinburgh University Press.

Desmond, William. 1995. *Being and the Between.* In *Philosophy* series, edited by George R. Lucas, Jr. Albany: State University of New York Press.

———. 2016. *The Intimate Universal: The Hidden Porosity among Religion, Art, Philosophy, and Politics.* New York: Columbia University Press.

Dieks, Dennis. 2019. "Quantum Reality, Perspectivalism and Covariance." *Foundations of Physics* 49: 629–646.

DiPerna, Dustin. 2014. *Streams of Wisdom: An Advanced Guide to Integral Spiritual Development.* San Francisco: Integral Publishing House.

Dipert, Randall. 1997. "The Mathematical Structure of the World: The World as Graph." *The Journal of Philosophy* 94, no. 7 (July): 329–358.

Dombrowski, Daniel A. 2017. "Contingent Creativity as Necessary." *Cosmos and History* 13, no. 3: 384–400.

Douville, Victor. 2007. *Lakota Thought and Philosophy: A Universal View.* Mission, SD: Sinte Gleska University.

Doyle, Robert. 2016. *Metaphysics: Problems, Paradoxes and Puzzles, Solved?* Cambridge, MA: I-Phi Press.

———. 2001. "The Problem of Individuation." *The Metaphysicist.* metaphysicist.com. Accessed 13 October 2019.

Dubois, Daniel. 1999. "Review of Incursive, Hyperincursive and Anticipatory Systems–Foundation of Anticipation in Electromagnetism." In *Computing Anticipatory Systems: CASY'99-Third International Conference*, University of Liege, Belgium.

Duffy, Kathleen S. S. J. 2014. *Teilhard's Mysticism: Seeing the Inner Face of Evolution.* Maryknoll, NY: Orbis Books.

Dusek, Val. 1999. *The Holistic Inspirations of Physics: The Underground History of Electromagnetic Theory.* New Brunswick, NJ: Rutgers University Press.

Eames, Charles, and Ray Eames. 1977. "Powers of Ten." *Eames Office, LLC.* http://www.eamesoffice.com/eames-office/who-we-are/. Accessed 14 February 2019.

Earley, Joseph. 2002. "A Neglected Aspect of the Puzzle of Chemical Structure: How History Helps." *Foundations of Chemistry* 14, no. 3: 235–243.

———. 2016. "How Properties Hold Together in Substances." In *Essays in the Philosophy of Chemistry*, edited by Eric Scerri and Grant Fisher, 410. Oxford: Oxford University Press.

Eastman, Timothy E. 1993. "Micro- to Macro-Scale Perspectives on Space Plasmas." *Physics of Fluids B* 5 (July): 2671–2675.

———. 2004. "Duality Without Dualism." In *Physics and Whitehead: Quantum, Process, and Experience*, edited by Timothy E. Eastman and Hank Keeton, 14–30. Albany: State University of New York Press.

———. 2008. "Our Cosmos, from Substance to Process." *World Futures* 64, no. 2: 84–93.

———. 2010. "Cosmic Agnosticism, Revisited." *Journal of Cosmology* 4 (January): 655–663.

———. 2016. "Limitations, Approximations and Reality." In *Physics and Speculative Philosophy: Potentiality in Modern Science*, edited by Timothy E. Eastman, Michael Epperson, and David Ray Griffin, 233–242. Berlin: Walter de Gruyter.

Edwards, Rem. 2014. *An Axiological Process Ethics.* Claremont, CA: Process Century Press.

Ehusani, George Omaku. 1991. *An Afro-Christian Vision OZOVEHE! Toward a More Humanized World*. Lanham, MD: University Press of America.

Ellis, George F. R. 2016. *How Can Physics Underlie the Mind?: Top-Down Causation in the Human Context*. Berlin: Springer-Verlag.

———. 2020. "A Mathematical Cosmologist Reflects on Deep Ethics: Reflections on Values, Ethics, and Morality." *Theology and Science*: 1–15.

Epperson, Michael. 2004. *Quantum Mechanics and the Philosophy of Alfred North Whitehead*. New York: Fordham University Press.

———. 2009. "Quantum Mechanics and Relational Realism: Logical Causality and Wave Function Collapse." *Process Studies* 38, no. 2: 340–367.

———. 2016. "Bridging Necessity and Contingency in Quantum Mechanics." In *Physics and Speculative Philosophy: Potentiality in Modern Science*, edited by Timothy E. Eastman, Michael Epperson, and David Ray Griffin, 55–105. Berlin: Walter de Gruyter.

Epperson, Michael, and Elias Zafiris. 2013. *Foundations of Relational Realism: A Topological Approach to Quantum Mechanics and the Philosophy of Nature*. In *Contemporary Whitehead Studies* series, edited by Roland Faber and Brian Henning. Lanham, MD: Lexington Books.

Epperson, Michael, Elias Zafiris, Stuart Kauffman, and Timothy E. Eastman. 2018. "Quantum Origins of Ontic Emergence." Invited paper presented at 18th Annual Biosemiotics Gathering, University of California, Berkeley, CA, 17–20 June 2018.

Epstein, Mikhail. 2012. *The Transformative Humanities: A Manifesto*. New York: Bloomsbury.

Faber, Roland. 2011. "Introduction: Negotiating Becoming." In *Secrets of Becoming: Negotiating Whitehead, Deleuze, and Butler*, edited by Roland Faber and Andrea Stephenson, 1–49. New York: Fordham University Press.

———. 2018. *The Garden of Reality: Transreligious Relativity in a World of Becoming*. Lanham, MD: Lexington Books.

———. 2019. "Uniting Earth to the Blue of Heaven Above: Strange Attractors in Whitehead's Symbolism." In *Rethinking Whitehead's Symbolism*, edited by Roland Faber, Jeffrey A. Bell, and Joseph Petek, 56–78. Edinburgh: Edinburgh University Press.

Faber, Roland, Brian G. Henning, and Clinton Combs, eds. 2010. *Beyond Metaphysics?: Explorations in Alfred North Whitehead's Late Thought*. Amsterdam: Rodopi.

Fagg, Lawrence. 1999. *Electromagnetism and the Sacred*. New York: Continuum.

Fair, David. 1979. "Causation and the Flow of Energy." *Erkenntnis* 14, no. 3 (November): 219–250.

Fales, Evan. 1990. *Causation and Universals*. London: Routledge.

Falk, Dan. 2013. *Universe on a T-shirt: The Quest for the Theory of Everything*. New York: Skyhorse Publishing.

Favareau, Donald. 2015. "Creation of the Relevant Next: How Living Systems Capture the Power of the Adjacent Possible Through Sign Use." *Progress in Biophysics and Molecular Biology* 119, no. 3: 588–601.

Faye, Jan. 2019. "Copenhagen Interpretation of Quantum Mechanics." In *The Stanford Encyclopedia of Philosophy* (Winter edition), edited by Edward N. Zalta. Stanford, CA: The Metaphysics Research Lab.

Ferré, Frederick. 1996. *Being and Value: Toward a Constructive Postmodern Metaphysics*. Albany: State University of New York Press.

Fine, Kit. 2012. "Guide to Ground." In *Metaphysical Grounding: Understanding the Structure of Reality*, edited by Fabrice Correia and Benjamin Schnieder, 37–80. Cambridge: Cambridge University Press.

Finkelstein, David. 2004. "Physical Process and Physical Law, and Dialogue for Part III." In *Physics and Whitehead: Quantum, Process, and Experience*, edited by Timothy E. Eastman and Hank Keeton, 180–194. Albany: State University of New York Press.

———. 2013. "Nature as Quantum Computer." In *From Linear Operators to Computational Biology*, edited by M. Davis and E. Schonberg, 5–22. London: Springer.

First People. 2020. "First People of America and Canada—Turtle Island." https://www.firstpeople.us/.

Fonneland, Trude, Siv Ellen Kraft, S. J. Sutcliffe, and I. Saelid Gilhus. 2013. "New Age, Sami Shamanism and Indigenous Spirituality." In *New Age Spirituality: Rethinking Religion*, edited by Steven Sutcliffe and Ingvild Gilhus, 132–145. Durham: Acumen Publishing Ltd.

Frisch, Mathias. 2013. "Time and Causation." In *A Companion to the Philosophy of Time*, edited by Heather Dyke and Adrian Bardon, 282–300. Chichester, West Sussex: Wiley Blackwell.

Friston, Karl. 2010. "The Free-Energy Principle: A Unified Brain Theory?" *Nature Reviews Neuroscience* 11, no. 2 (February): 127–138.

Fulton, Christopher C., and Halton C. Arp. 2012. "The 2dF Redshift Survey. I. Physical Association and Periodicity in Quasar Families." *The Astrophysical Journal* 754 (1 August): 134–143.

Fung, Yiu-Ming. 2016. "Issues and Methods of Analytic Philosophy." In *The Bloomsbury Research Handbook of Chinese Philosophy Methodologies*, edited by Sor-hoon Tan, 227–244. London: Bloomsbury.

Gao, Haipeng. 2018. "A Taiji-Bagua Diagram for Whitehead's Categorial Scheme." *Process Studies* 47: 130–143.

Gare, Arran. 1993. *Nihilism Incorporated: European Civilization and Environmental Destruction*. Bungendore: Eco-Logical Press and Cambridge: Whitehorse Press.

———. 2002. "The Roots of Postmodernism: Schelling, Process Philosophy, and Poststructuralism." In *Process and Difference: Between Cosmological and Poststructuralist Postmodernisms*, edited by Catherine Keller and Anne Daniell, 31–53. Albany: State University of New York Press.

———. 2006. *Postmodernism and the Environmental Crisis*. New York: Routledge.

———. 2017. *The Philosophical Foundations of Ecological Civilization: A Manifesto for the Future*. Abingdon, Oxon: Routledge.

———. 2018. "Natural Philosophy and the Sciences: Challenging Science's Tunnel Vision." *Philosophies* 3, no. 4(33): 87–115.

———. 2019. "Consciousness, Mind and Spirit." *Cosmos and History* 15, no. 2: 236–264.

Gare, Arran, and Stuart Kauffman. 2015. "Beyond Descartes and Newton: Recovering Life and Humanity." *Progress in Biophysics and Molecular Biology* 119, no. 3: 219–244.

Gaukroger, Stephen. 2006. *The Emergence of a Scientific Culture: Science and the Shaping of Modeernity 1210–1685*. Oxford: Oxford University Press.

———. 2010. *The Collapse of Mechanism and the Rise of Sensibility: Science and the Shaping of Modernity, 1680–1760*. Oxford: Oxford University Press.

———. 2016. *The Natural & the Human: Science and the Shaping of Modernity, 1739–1841*. Oxford: Oxford University Press.

Gernert, Dieter. 2009. "Ockham's Razor and its Improper Use." *Cognitive Systems* 7, no. 2: 133–138.

Gershenson, Carlos. 2002. *Contextuality: A Philosophical Paradigm, with Applications to Philosophy of Cognitive Science*. POCS Essay, COGS, University of Sussex.

Gisin, Nicolas. 2014. *Quantum Chance: Nonlocality, Teleportation and Other Quantum Marvels*. Translated by Stephen Lyle. Heidelberg: Springer International Publishing.

Gisin, Nicolas, and Rob Thew. 2007. "Quantum Communication." *Nature Photonics* 1: 165–172.

Goedbloed, Hans, and Stefaan Poedts. 2004. *Principles of Magnetohydrodynamics: With Applications to Laboratory and Astrophysical Plasmas*. Cambridge: Cambridge University Press.

Goff, Philip. 2009. "Can the Panpsychist Get Around the Combination Problem?" In *Mind that Abides: Panpsychism in the New Millenium*, edited by David Skrbina, 129–135. Amsterdam: John Benjamins Publishing Company.

Goldstein, Sheldon. 2017. "Bohmian Mechanics." In *The Stanford Encyclopedia of Philosophy* (Summer 2017 edition), edited by Edward N. Zalta. Stanford, CA: The Metaphysics Research Lab.

Golshani, Mehdi. 2020. "Science Needs a Comprehensive Worldview." *Theology and Science*. DOI: 10.1080/14746700.2020.1786220.

Gottlieb, Anthony. 2016. "The Big Picture." Review of *On the Origins of Life, Meaning, and the Universe Itself* by Sean Carroll. Book Review (12 June) *The New York Times*.

Gracia, Jorge J. E. 1999. *Metaphysics and Its Task: The Search for the Categorial Foundation of Knowledge*. Albany: State University of New York Press.

Grange, Joseph. 1997a. *Nature: An Environmental Cosmology*. Albany: State University of New York Press.

———. 1997b. "Community, Environment, Metaphysics." *The Journal of Speculative Philosophy* 11, no. 3: 190–202.

Grant, Michael, ed. 2000. *The Raymond Tallis Reader*. Basingstoke/New York: Palgrave.

Grassie, William. 2018. *Applied Big History: A Guide for Entrepreneurs, Investors, and Other Living Things*. New York: Metanexus Imprints.

Gray, Chris G. 2009. "Principle of Least Action." *Scholarpedia* 4, no. 12: 8291. http://www.scholarpedia.org/article/Principle_of_least_action.

Gray, John. 2018. *Seven Types of Atheism*. New York: Farrar, Straus and Giroux.

Greene, Herman. 2018. "The Importance of Thomas Berry." *The Ecozoic* 5, In special issue *The Ecozoic Way: The Foundational Papers of the Center for Ecozoic Studies*, edited by H. Greene, 391, no. 5. https://www.ecozoicstudies.org.

Greyson, Bruce. 1983. "The Near-Death Experience Scale: Construction, Reliability, and Validity." *The Journal of Nervous and Mental Disease* 171: 369–375.

Grieves, Vicki. 2009. *Aboriginal Spirituality: Aboriginal Philosophy, the Basis of Aboriginal Social and Emotional Wellbeing.* Darwin: Cooperative Research Centre for Aboriginal Health.

Griffin, David Ray. 1988. "Introduction: The Reenchantment of Science." In *The Reenchantment of Science: Postmodern Proposals,* edited by David Ray Griffin, ix–xii. Albany: State University of New York Press.

———. 1989. "Charles Hartshorne's Postmodern Philosophy." In *Hartshorne, Process Philosophy, and Theology,* edited by Robert Kane and Stephen Phillips, 1–32. Albany: State University of New York Press.

———. 1997a. *Parapsychology, Philosophy, and Spirituality: A Postmodern Exploration.* Albany: State University of New York Press.

———. 1997b. "Panexperientialist Physicalism and the Mind-Body Problem." *Journal of Consciousness Studies* 4, no. 3: 248–268.

———. 2001. *Reenchantment Without Supernaturalism: A Process Philosophy of Religion.* Ithaca, NY: Cornell University Press.

———. 2007. *Whitehead's Radically Different Postmodern Philosophy: An Argument for Its Contemporary Relevance.* Albany: State University of New York Press.

———. 2013. "Responses." In *Reason & Reenchantment: The Philosophical, Religious, and Political Thought of David Ray Griffin,* edited by John B. Cobb, Jr., Richard Falk, and Catherine Keller, 261–325. Claremont, CA: Process Century Press.

———. 2015. *Unprecedented: Can Civilization Survive the CO_2 Crisis?* Atlanta, GA: Clarity Press.

———. 2016. *God Exists but Gawd Does Not: From Evil to New Atheism to Fine-Tuning.* Claremont, CA: Process Century Press.

———. 2017. *Process Theology: On Postmodernism, Morality, Pluralism, Eschatology and Demonic Evil.* Anoka, MN: Process Century Press.

———. 2018. *The American Trajectory: Divine or Demonic?* Atlanta, GA: Clarity Press.

———. 2019. *The Christian Gospel for Americans: A Systematic Theology.* Anoka, MN: Process Century Press.

Griffin, David Ray, John B. Cobb, Jr., Marcus P. Ford, Pete A. Y. Gunter, and Peter Ochs. 1992. *Founders of Constructive Postmodern Philosophy.* Albany: State University of New York Press.

Grinspoon, David. 2016. *Earth in Human Hands: Shaping Our Planet's Future.* New York: Grand Central Publishing.

Grössing, Gerhard. 2004. "From Classical Hamiltonian Flow to Quantum Theory: Derivation of the Schrödinger Equation." *Foundations of Physics Letters* 17, no. 4: 343–362.

Guigon, Ghislain. 2019. "Nominalism." In *Routledge Encyclopedia of Philosophy.* Taylor and Francis. DOI: 10.4324/9780415249126-N038-2. https://www.rep.routledge.com/articles/thematic/nominalism/v-2.

Guo, Haipeng. 2018. "A Taiji-Bagua Diagram for Whitehead's Categoreal Scheme." *Process Studies* 47, no. 1–2: 130–143.

Haag, Rudolf. 2012. *Local Quantum Physics: Fields, Particles, Algebras*. Berlin: Springer Science & Business Media.

Haig, Brian D. 2005. "An Abductive Theory of Scientific Method." *Psychological Methods* 10, no. 4: 371–388.

Haldane, John. 2015. "Philosophy, Causality, and God." In *The Philosophy of Hilary Putnam*, edited by Randall E. Auxier, Douglas R. Anderson, and Lewis E. Hahn, 683–701. Chicago: Open Court.

Hall, David, and Roger Ames. 1987. *Thinking Through Confucius*. Albany: State University of New York Press.

———. 1998. *Thinking from the Han: Self, Truth, and Transcendence in Chinese and Western Culture*. In *Systematic Philosophy* series, edited by Robert Neville. Albany: State University of New York Press.

Hallen, Barry. 2002. *A Short History of African Philosophy*. Bloomington: Indiana University Press.

Hameroff, Stuart, and Roger Penrose. 2014. "Consciousness in the Universe: A Review of the 'Orch OR' Theory." *Physics of Life Reviews* 11, no. 1: 39–78.

Hanna, Robert. 2001. *Kant and the Foundations of Analytic Philosophy*. Oxford: Clarendon Press.

———. 2006. *Kant, Science, and Human Nature*. Oxford: Oxford University Press.

———. 2020. *The Fate of Analysis: Analytic Philosophy from Frege to the Ash Heap of History, 1–449*. https://colorado.academia.edu/RobertHanna.

Hartmann, Nicolai. 2013. *Possibility and Actuality*. Berlin: Walter de Gruyter.

Hartshorne, Charles. 1958. "Metaphysical Statements as Nonrestrictive and Existential." *The Review of Metaphysics* (1 September): 35–47.

———. 1963. "Real Possibility." *The Journal of Philosophy* 60, no. 21 (10 October): 593–605.

———. 1970. *Creative Synthesis and Philosophic Method*. La Salle, IL: Open Court Publishing Company.

———. 1972. *Whitehead's Philosophy: Selected Essays, 1935–1970*. Lincoln: University of Nebraska Press.

———. 1979. "Whitehead's Revolutionary Concept of Prehension." *International Philosophical Quarterly* 19, no. 3: 253–263.

———. 2011. *Creative Experiencing: A Philosophy of Freedom*. Albany: State University of New York Press.

Haught, John F. 2006. *Is Nature Enough?: Meaning and Truth in the Age of Science*. Cambridge: Cambridge University Press.

———. 2015. *Resting on the Future: Catholic Theology for an Unfinished Universe*. New York: Bloomsbury Publishing.

———. 2017. *The New Cosmic Story: Inside Our Awakening Universe*. New Haven: Yale University Press.

Hawking, Stephen. 2005. *The Theory of Everything: The Origin and Fate of the Universe*. Beverly Hills, CA: Phoenix Books.

Heather, Michael, and Nick Rossiter. 2005. "The Universe as a Freely Generated Information System." *Against Bull ANPA* 26: 357–388.

———. 2009. *Process Categories: The Metaphysics, Methodology and Mathematics, Philosophy of Nature and Process Philosophy*. Silesia, Poland: University of Silesia.

———. 2018. "Formal Representation of Process and Reality in the Metaphysical Language of Category Theory: Whitehead's Relational Theory of Space." *ANPA-PROC-37-38*, no. 95: 217.

Hedrick, Lisa Landoe. 2019. "McDowell, Whitehead, and the Metaphysics of Agency." *The Review of Metaphysics* LXXII, no. 4 (288): 767–782.

Heft, Harry. 2001. "Ecological Psychology in Context: James Gibson, Roger Barker, and the Legacy of William James' Radical Empiricism, Resources for Ecological Psychology." In *Resources for Ecological Psychology*, edited by William Mace, Robert Shaw, and Michael Turvey. Mahwah, NJ: Lawrence Erlbaum Assoc., Inc.

Heidegger, Martin. 1996. *Being and Time (1927)*. Translated by Joan Stambaugh. Albany: State University of New York Press.

Heisenberg, Werner. 1958. *Physics and Philosophy: The Revolution in Modern Science*. London: George Allen & Unwin.

Held, Carsten. 2018. "The Kochen-Specker Theorem." In *The Stanford Encyclopedia of Philosophy*, edited by Edward N. Zalta. Stanford, CA: The Metaphysics Research Lab.

Henning, Brian. 2005. *The Ethics of Creativity: Beauty, Morality, and Nature in a Processive Cosmos*. Pittsburgh: University of Pittsburgh Press.

Henning, Brian, and Adam Scarfe, eds. 2013. *Beyond Mechanism: Putting Life Back into Biology*. Lanham, MD: Lexington Books.

Henning, Brian, and David Kovacs, eds. 2014. *Being in America: Sixty Years of the Metaphysical Society*. Vol. 272. Amsterdam: Brill-Rodopi.

Henry, Granville. 1993. *Forms of Concrescence: Alfred North Whitehead's Philosophy and Computer Programming Structures*. Plainsboro, NJ: Associated University Presses.

Henry, John. 2004. "Metaphysics and the Origins of Modern Science: Descartes and the Importance of Laws of Nature." *Early Science and Medicine* 9, no. 2: 73–114.

Hensen, Bas, H. Bernien, A. E. Dréau, A. Reiserer, N. Kalb, M. S. Blok, J. Ruitenberg, et al. 2015. "Experimental Loophole-Free Violation of a Bell Inequality Using Entangled Electron Spins Separated by 1.3 km." *arXiv preprint* (arXiv:1508.05949): 1–8.

Herstein, Gary. 2013. *Whitehead and the Measurement Problem of Cosmology*. Berlin: Walter de Gruyter.

Hey, Tony, and Patrick Walters. 2003. *The New Quantum Universe*. Revised edition. Cambridge: Cambridge University Press.

Hintikka, Jaakko. 2007. "What is Abduction? The Fundamental Problem of Contemporary Epistemology." *The Transactions of the Charles S. Peirce Society* XXXIV, no. 3 (Summer): 503–533.

Ho, Mae Wan. 2008. *The Rainbow and the Worm: The Physics of Organisms*. 3rd edition. Singapore: World Scientific.

Hoffmeyer, Justin. 1997a. *Signs of Meaning in the Universe*. Bloomington: Indiana University Press.

———. 1997b. "Biosemiotics: Towards a New Synthesis in Biology." *European Journal for Semiotic Studies* 9, no. 2: 355–376.

———. 2009. "Biosemiotics: An Examination into the Signs of Life and the Life of Signs." Vol. 2. In *Approaches to Postmodernity*, edited by Donald Favareau. Scranton, PA: University of Scranton Press.

Holler, Clyde. 1995. *Black Elk's Religion: The Sun Dance and Lakota Catholicism*. Syracuse, NY: Sycracuse University Press.

Holzner, Steven. 2012. *Quantum Physics for Dummies*. New York: John Wiley & Sons, Inc.

Horgan, John. 2015. *The End of Science: Facing the Limits of Knowledge in the Twilight of the Scientific Age*. New York: Basic Books.

Horodecki, Ryszard, Pawel Horodecki, Michal Horodecki, and Karol Horodecki. 2009. "Quantum Entanglement." *Reviews of Modern Physics* 81: 865.

Horsten, Leon. 2017. "Philosophy of Mathematics." In *The Stanford Encyclopedia of Philosophy*, edited by Edward N. Zalta. Stanford, CA: The Metaphysics Research Lab.

Houser, Nathan, and Christian Kloesel, eds. 1992. *The Essential Peirce: Selected Philosophical Writings, Vol. 1 (1867–1893)*. Vol. 1. Bloomington, IN: Indiana University Press.

Hulswit, Menno. 2002. *From Cause to Causation: A Peircean Perspective*. Vol. 90. In *Philosophical Studies* series, edited by Keith Lehrer. Dordrecht: Kluwer Academic Publishers.

Jaeger, Gregg. 2017. "Quantum Potentiality Revisited." *Philosophical Transactions of the Royal Society A* 375, no. 2106.

James, William. 2004. *The Varieties of Religious Experience (1902)*. New York: Barnes & Noble Books.

Jantsch, Erich. 1992. *The Self-Organizing Universe: Scientific and Human Implications of the Emerging Paradigm of Evolution*. Oxford: Pergamon Press.

Jones, Judith. 1998. *Intensity: An Essay in Whiteheadian Cosmology*. Nashville, TN: Vanderbilt University Press.

Juarrero, Alecia. 1999. *Dynamics in Action: Intentional Behavior as a Complex System*. Cambridge: MIT Press.

Jung, Carl G. 1981. "The Archetypes and The Collective Unconscious." In *Collected Works*, edited by Carl G. Jung and R. F. C. Hull. Abingdon, Oxon: Routledge.

———. 2010. "Syncronicity: An Acausal Connecting Principle." In *Collected Works*, edited by Carl G. Jung and R. F. C. Hull. Abingdon, Oxon: Routledge.

Jungerman, John. 2000. *World in Process: Creativity and Interconnection in the New Physics*. Albany: State University of New York Press.

Kallfelz, William. 2009. "Physical Emergence and Process Ontology." *World Futures* 65: 42–60.

Kastner, Ruth. 2013. *The Transactional Interpretation of Quantum Mechanics: The Reality of Possibility*. Cambridge: Cambridge University Press.

————. 2015. *Understanding our Unseen Reality: Solving Quantum Riddles.* London: Imperial College Press.

Kastner, Ruth, Stuart Kauffman, and Michael Epperson. 2018. "Taking Heisenberg's Potentia Seriously." *International Journal of Quantum Foundations* 4: 158–172.

Katra, Jane, and Russell Targ. 1999. *The Heart of the Mind.* Novato, CA: New World Library.

Kauffman, Stuart. 2000. *Investigations.* Oxford: Oxford University Press.

————. 2008. *Reinventing the Sacred: A New View of Science, Reason, and Religion.* New York: Perseus Books.

————. 2016. *Humanity in a Creative Universe.* Oxford: Oxford University Press.

————. 2019. *A World Beyond Physics: The Emergence and Evolution of Life.* Oxford: Oxford University Press.

Kauffman, Stuart, Robert Logan, Robert Este, Randy Goebel, David Hobill, and Ilya Shmulevich. 2008. "Propagating Organization: An Enquiry." *Biology & Philosophy* 23, no. 1: 27–45.

Kearney, Richard, ed. 2003. *Continental Philosophy in the 20th Century.* Vol. 8. In *Routledge History of Philosophy* series, edited by G. H. R. Parkinson and S. G. Shanker. Abingdon, Oxon: Routledge.

Keller, Catherine. 2014. *Cloud of the Impossible: Negative Theology and Planetary Entanglement.* New York: Columbia University Press.

Keller, John, ed. 2017. *Being, Freedom, and Method: Themes from the Philosophy of Peter Van Inwagen.* Oxford: Oxford University Press.

Kelly, Edward, Adam Crabtree, and Paul Marshall, eds. 2015. *Beyond Physicalism: Toward Reconciliation of Science and Spirituality.* Lanham, MD: Rowman & Littlefield.

Kelly, Edward, Emily Kelly, Adam Crabtree, Alan Gauld, Michael Grosso, and Bruce Greyson, eds. 2007. *Irreducible Mind: Toward a Psychology for the 21st Century.* Lanham, MD: Rowman & Littlefield Publishers, Inc.

Kelso, J. A. Scott, and David Engstrom. 2006. *Complementary Nature.* Cambridge: MIT Press.

Khrennikov, Andrei. 2014. *Beyond Quantum.* Boca Raton, FL: Pan Stanford Publishing.

Kimpton-Nye, Samuel. 2018. "Common Ground for Laws and Metaphysical Modality." Ph.D. dissertation. Philosophy, King's College London.

Kineman, John. 2008. "Fundamentals of Relational Complexity Theory." In *Proceedings of the 52nd Annual Meeting of the ISSS-2008*, Madison, Wisconsin (July).

————. 2011. "Relational Science: A Synthesis." *Axiomathes* 21, no. 3: 393–437.

————. 2017. "A Causal Framework for Integrating Contemporary and Vedic Holism." *Progress in Biophysics and Molecular Biology* 131: 402–423.

Kineman, John, Bela Banathy, and Judith Rosen. 2007. "The Atomistic Structure of Relationship: Robert Rosen's Implicate Order." In *Proceedings of the 51st Annual Meeting of the ISSS-2007*, Tokyo, Japan.

Klinger, Christopher. 2010. *Process Physics: Bootstrapping Reality from the Limitations of Logic.* Saarbrücken, Germany: VDM Verlag Dr. Müller.

———. 2016. "On the Foundations of *Process Physics.*" In *Physics and Speculative Philosophy: Potentiality in Modern Science*, edited by Timothy E. Eastman, Michael Epperson, and David Ray Griffin, 143–175. Berlin: Walter de Gruyter.

Kochen, Simon, and John Conway. 2006. "The Free Will Theorem." *Foundations of Physics* 36, no. 10: 1441–1473.

Koonin, Eugene. 2011. *The Logic of Chance: The Nature and Origin of Biological Evolution.* Upper Saddle River, NJ: Pearson Education, Inc.

Koslow, Arnold. 2003. "Laws, Explanations and the Reduction of Possibilities." In *Real Metaphysics: Essay in Honour of D. H. Mellor*, edited by Hallvard Lillehammer and Gonzalo Rodriguez-Pereyra, 169–183. London: Routledge.

Koutroufinis, Spyridon. 2013. "Teleodynamics: A Neo-Naturalistic Conception of Organismic Teleology." In *Beyond Mechanism: Putting Life Back into Biology*, edited by Brian Henning and Adam Scarfe, 309–342. Lanham, MD: Lexington Books.

———. 2014. "Beyond Systems Theoretical Explanations of an Organism's Becoming: A Process Philosophical Approach." In *Life and Process: Towards a New Biophilosophy*, edited by Spyridon Koutroufinis, 99–132. Berlin: Walter de Gruyter.

———. 2019. "Uexküll, Whitehead, Peirce: Rethinking the Concept of 'Umwelt' from a Process Philosophical Perspective." In *Metaphysical Foundations of Environmental Ethics*, edited by Dennis Soelch and Aljoscha Berve, 1–15. Cambridge: Cambridge Scholar Publishing.

Krachun, Carla. 2002. *Are Apes Conscious? An Overview of Inconclusive Evidence.* Technical Report 2002-10. No. 2002-10-07. Ottawa: Carleton University. https://ir .library.carleton.ca/pub/22367/.

Kraus, Elizabeth. 1998. *The Metaphysics of Experience: A Companion to Whitehead's Process and Reality.* 2nd edition. New York: Fordham University Press.

Krenn, M., M. Huber, R. Fickler, R. Lapkiewicz, S. Ramelow, and A. Zeilinger. 2014. "Generation and Confirmation of a (100×100)-Dimensional Entangled Quantum System." *Proceedings of the National Academy of Sciences* 111, no. 17: 6243–6247.

Kuhlmann, Meinard. 2002. "Analytical Ontologists in Action: A Comment on Seibt and Simons." In *Ontological Aspects of Quantum Field Theory*, edited by Meinard Kuhlmann, Holger Lyre, and Andrew Wayne, 99–109. River Edge, NJ: World Scientific.

Kukushkin, Alexander B., and Valentin A. Rantsev-Kartinov. 2004. "Probable Astrophysical and Cosmological Implications of Observed Self-Similarity of Skeletal Structures in the Range 10^{-5} cm–10^{23} cm." In *AIP Conference Proceedings* 703, no. 1, 409–414. College Park, MD: American Institute of Physics (AIP).

Kull, Kalevi. 2007. "Biosemiotics and Biophysics–the Fundamental Approaches to the Study of Life." In *Introduction to Biosemiotics*, edited by Marcello Barbieri, 167–177. Berlin: Springer.

———. 2014. "Physical Laws Are Not Habits, While Rules of Life are." In *Charles Sanders Peirce in His Own Words: 100 Years of Semiotics, Communication and Cognition*, edited by Torkild Thellefsen and Bent Sorensen. Berlin: de Gruyter-Mouton.

Kull, Kalevi, Silvi Salupere, and Peeter Torop. 2005. "Semiotics Has No Beginning." In *Basics of Semiotics*, ix–xxv. Tartu, Estonia: Tartu University Press.

Kundt, Wolfgang. 2001. "Book Review: 'A Different Approach to Cosmology' by Hoyle, Burbidge, and Narlikar.'" *General Relativity and Gravity* 33: 611–614.

———. 2004. *Astrophysics: A New Approach*. New York: Springer Science & Business Media.

Langer, Susanne K. 1953. *Feeling and Form*. Vol. 3. London: Routledge and Kegan Paul.

Lango, John W. 1972. *Whitehead's Ontology*. Albany: State University of New York Press.

Laszlo, Ervin. 2014. *The Self-Actualizing Cosmos: The Akasha Revolution in Science and Human Consciousness*. Rochester, VT: Inner Traditions.

———. 2016. *What is Reality?: The New Map of Cosmos, Consciousness, and Existence*. New York: SelectBooks, Inc.

Latour, Bruno. 2018. *Down to Earth: Politics in the new Climatic Regime*. English edition. Medford, MA: Polity.

Laughland, John. 2016. *Schelling Versus Hegel: From German Idealism to Christian Metaphysics*. Hampshire: Ashgate

Laughlin, Robert. 2008. *A Different Universe: Reinventing Physics from the Bottom Down*. New York: Basic Books.

Lawson, Anton. 2015. "Hypothetico-Deductive Method." In *Encyclopedia of Science Education*, edited by Richard Gunstone. Dordrecht: Springer.

Leclerc, Ivor. 1986. *The Philosophy of Nature: Studies in Philosophy and the History of Philosophy*. Washington, D.C.: Catholic University of America Press.

Lerner, Eric. 2018. "Observations Contradict Galaxy Size and Surface Brightness Predictions that are Based on the Expanding University Hypothesis." *Monthly Notices of the Royal Astronomical Society* 477, no. 3 (July): 3185–3196.

Levine, Joseph. 2001. *Purple Haze: The Puzzle of Consciousness*. Oxford: Oxford University Press.

Levy-Agresti, J., and Roger W. Sperry. 1968. "Differential Perceptual Capacities in Major and Minor Hemispheres." *Proceedings of the National Academy of Sciences* 61: 1151.

Lewis, David. 2001. *Counterfactuals*. 2nd edition. Malden, MA: Wiley-Blackwell.

Logan, Robert K. 2004. *The Alphabet Effect: A Media Ecology Understanding of the Making of Western Civilization*. Cresskill, NJ: Hampton Press.

———. 2013. "Ulanowicz's Process Ecology, Duality and Emergent Deism." *Open Journal of Philosophy* 3, no. 3: 422–428. http://openresearch.ocadu.ca/id/eprint/8 27/.

———. 2014. *What Is Information?: Propagating Organization in the Biosphere, Symbolosphere, Technosphere and Econosphere*. Toronto: DEMO Publishing.

Loomer, Bernard. 1976. "Two Conceptions of Power." *Process Studies* 6: 5–32.

Louie, Aloisius H. 2009. "More Than Life Itself: A Synthetic Continuation in Relational Biology." In *Categories*, edited by Roberto Poli. Berlin: Ontos-Verlag.

Loux, Michael. 2017. "Theories of Character." In *Being, Freedom, and Method: Themes from the Philosophy of Peter van Inwagen*, edited by John Keller, 11–31. Oxford: Oxford University Press.

Loy, David. 1988. *Nonduality: A Study in Comparative Philosophy*. New Haven: Yale University Press.

Lucas, George R., Jr. 1989a. *The Rehabilitation of Whitehead*. Albany: State University of New York Press.

———. 1989b. *The Rehabilitation of Whitehead: An Analytic and Historical Assessment of Process Philosophy*. Albany: State University of New York Press.

———. 2003. "Whitehead and Wittgenstein: The Critique of Enlightenment and the Question Concerning Metaphysics." In *Process and Analysis: Whitehead, Hartshorne, and the Analytic Tradition*, edited by George Shields, 67–93. Albany: State University of New York Press.

Lucas, J. R. 2000. *The Conceptual Roots of Mathematics: An Essay on the Philosophy of Mathematics*. London: Routledge.

MacBride, Fraser. 2016. "Relations." In *The Stanford Encyclopedia of Philosophy*, edited by Edward N. Zalta. Stanford, CA: The Metaphysics Research Lab.

———. 2018. *On the Genealogy of Universals: The Metaphysical Origins of Analytic Philosophy*. Oxford: Oxford University Press.

MacLeod, Mary C., and Eric M. Rubenstein. 2019. "Universals." In *The Internet Encyclopedia of Philosophy*. ISSN 2161-0002. HYPERLINK "https://www.iep .utm.edu" https://www.iep.utm.edu. Accessed 20 May 2020.

Mahootian, Farzad, and Timothy E. Eastman. 2009. "Complementary Frameworks of Scientific Inquiry: Hypothetico-Deductive, Hypothetico-Inductive, and Observational-Inductive." *World Futures* 65, no. 1: 61–75.

Malone-France, Derek. 2006. *Deep Empiricism: Kant, Whitehead, and the Necessity of Philosophical Theism*. Lanham, MD: Lexington Books.

Man, Kingson, and Antonio Damasio. 2019. "Homeostasis and Soft Robotics in the Design of Feeling Machines." *Nature Machine Intelligence* 1 (October): 446–452.

Marambio, José. 2010. "Natural Laws, Modality and Universals." *Epistemologia* XXXIII: 207–234.

Marcos, Sylvia. 2015. "Mesoamerican Women's Indigenous Spirituality: Decolonizing Religious Beliefs." *Journal of Feminist Studies in Religion* 25, no. 2: 25–45.

Margolis, Joseph. 2003. *The Unraveling of Scientism: American Philosophy at the End of the Twentieth Century*. Ithaca, NY: Cornell University Press.

Marquis, Jean-Pierre. 2014. "Category Theory." In *The Stanford Encyclopedia of Philosophy*, edited by Edward N. Zalta. Stanford, CA: The Metaphysics Research Lab.

Marshall, Paul A. 2016. *A Complex Integral Realist Perspective: Towards a New Axial Vision*. London: Routledge.

Martinez, David. 2004. "The Soul of the Indian: Lakota Philosophy and the Vision Quest." *Wicazo SA Review* (Fall): 79–104.

Maudlin, Tim. 2016. "Topology and the Structure of Space-Time." In *Physics and Philosophy: The Fifth Conference*, Split, Croatia, 7–8 July. http://mapmf.pmfst.u nist.hr/~sokolic/doku.php.

May, Edwin, and Sonali Marwaha, eds. 2014. Anomalous Cognition: Remote Viewing Research and Theory. Jefferson, NC: McFarland & Co.

Maxwell, Nicholas. 1999. *The Comprehensibility of the Universe: A New Conception of Science*. Oxford: Clarendon Press.

———. 2017. *Understanding Scientific Progress: Aim-Oriented Empiricism*. St. Paul, MN: Paragon House.

McHenry, Leemon. 1995. "Whitehead's Panpsychism as the Subjectivity of Prehension." *Process Studies* 24: 1–14.

———. 2011. "The Multiverse Conjecture: Whitehead's Cosmic Epochs and Contemporary Cosmology." *Process Studies* 40, no. 1: 5–24.

———. 2015. *The Event Universe: The Revisionary Metaphysics of Alfred North Whitehead*. Edinburgh: Edinburgh University Press Ltd.

———. 2017. "Whitehead and Russell on the Analysis of Matter." *The Review of Metaphysics* 71: 321–342.

McIntosh, Steve. 2007. *Integral Consciousness and the Future of Evolution: How the Integral Worldview Is Transforming Politics, Culture and Spirituality*. St. Paul, MN: Paragon House.

McLaren, Glenn. 2004. "I. Toward the Unification of Process Philosophy: The Challenge Posed by Gare's Secular Metaphysics to Fragmentary Influences Within Process Philosophy." *Academia.edu*: 43–118.

Meixner, Uwe. 2006. *The Theory of Ontic Modalities*. Vol. 13. Berlin: Walter de Gruyter.

Menkiti, Ifeanyi. 1984. "Person and Community in African Traditional Thought." In *African Philosophy: An Introduction*, edited by Richard Wright, 171–182. Lanham, MD: University Press of America.

Merriam-Webster.com Dictionary. 2020. *Internal Relation*. Accessed 20 July 2020.

Misak, Cheryl. 2017. "Forward." In *Pragmatism and Objectivity: Essays Sparked by the Work of Nicholas Rescher*, edited by Sami Pihlstrom, ix. Abington, Oxon: Routledge.

Montague, William Pepperell. 1925. *The Ways of Knowing, on the Methods of Philosophy*. New York: MacMillan Co.

Mooney, Timothy. 2002. "Derrida and Whitehead." In *Routledge Revivals: God, Literature and Process Thought*, edited by Darren J. N. Middleton, 29–46. Abington, Oxon: Routledge.

Moore, Edward. 2012. "Actuality and Potentiality." In *The Philosophy of Logical Mechanism: Essays in Honor of Arthur W. Burks, with His Responses*, edited by Merrilee Salmon, 179–190. Berlin: Springer Science & Business Media.

Moreland, J. P., and William Lane Craig. 2003. *Philosophical Foundations for a Christian Worldview*. Downers Grove, IL: InterVarsity Press.

Morris, William Edward, and Charlotte R. Brown. 2020. "David Hume." In *The Stanford Encyclopedia of Philosophy* edited by Edward N. Zalta. Stanford, CA: The Metaphysics Research Lab.

Morrison, Philip, and Phylis Morrison. 1982. *Powers of Ten: A Book about the Relative Size of Things in the Universe and the Effect of Adding Another Zero*. New York: Scientific American Library.

Moss, Ilana. 2018. "What Is the Definition of Metaphysics?" In *Metaphysics for Life: The Foundation for Creating a Mind with Heart*. http://www.metaphysics-for-life .com/definition-of-metaphysics.html. Accessed 3 February 2019.

Mou, Bo. 2003. "Becoming-Being Complementarity: An Account of the *Yin-Yang* Metaphysical Vision of the *Yi-Jing*." In *Comparative Approaches to Chinese Philosophy*, edited by Bo Mou, 86–98. Abington, Oxon: Ashgate Publishing.

Munitz, Milton, K. 1974. *Existence and Logic*. New York: New York University Press.

———. 1992. *The Question of Reality*. Princeton: Princeton University Press.

Musgrave, Cassandra. 1997. "The Near-Death Experience: A Study of Spiritual Tranformation." *Journal of Near-Death Studies* 15, no. 3 (Spring).

Nagel, Thomas. 1972. "Aristotle on Eudaimonia." *Phronesis* 17, no. 3: 252–259.

———. 1986. *The View from Nowhere*. Oxford: Oxford University Press.

———. 2012. *Mind and Cosmos: Why the Materialist Neo-Darwinian Conception of Nature Is Almost Certainly False*. Oxford: Oxford University Press.

Nakahara, Mikio. 2003. *Geometry, Topology and Physics*. Bristol: Adam Hilger Press.

Needham, Joseph, and Colin A. Ronan. 1978. *The Shorter Science and Civilisation in China: Volume 2*. Cambridge: Cambridge University Press.

Neville, Robert. 2013. *Ultimates: Philosophical Theology, Volume One*. Albany: State University of New York Press.

Nicolescu, Basarab. 2011. "The Concept of Levels of Reality and Its Relevance for Non-Reduction and Personhood." In *Consciências '04*, Portugal.

———. 2014. *From Modernity to Cosmodernity: Science, Culture, and Spirituality*. Albany: State University of New York Press.

Niemoczynski, Leon. 2011. *Charles Sanders Peirce and a Religious Metaphysics of Nature*. Lanham, MD: Lexington Books.

———. 2017. *Speculative Realism: An Epitome*. Leeds: Kismet Press.

Niiniluoto, Ilkka, and Raimo Tuomela. 2012. *Theoretical Concepts and Hypothetico-Inductive Inference*. Vol. 53. Berlin: Springer Science and Business Media.

Nobo, Jorge Luis. 1986. *Whitehead's Metaphysics of Extension and Solidarity*. Albany: State University of New York Press.

———. 1997. "Experience, Eternity, and Primordiality: Steps Towards a Metaphysics of Creative Solidarity." *Process Studies* 26/3–4 (Fall–Winter): 171–204.

———. 2004. "Whitehead and the Quantum Experience." In *Physics and Whitehead: Quantum, Process, and Experience*, edited by Timothy E. Eastman and Hank Keeton, 223–257. Albany: State University of New York Press.

———. 2008. "Metaphysics and Cosmology." In *Handbook of Whiteheadian Process Thought, Volume 1*, edited by Michel Weber and Will Desmond, 255–264. Frankfurt: Ontos-Verlag.

Nogar, Raymond J. 1966. *The Lord of the Absurd*. New York: Herder and Herder.

Norton, Stephen, and Frederick Suppe. 2001. "Why Atmospheric Modeling Is Good Science." In *Changing the Atmosphere: Expert Knowledge and Environmental Governance*, edited by Clark Miller and Paul Edwards. Cambridge: MIT Press.

Nubiola, Jaime. 2008. "Charles S. Peirce (1839–1914)." In *Handbook of Whiteheadian Process Thought*, edited by Michel Weber and Will Desmond, 481–487. Frankfurt: Ontos-Verlag.

Omnès, Roland. 1999. *Understanding Quantum Mechanics*. Princeton: Princeton University Press.

———. 2002. *Converging Realities: Toward a Common Philosophy of Physics and Mathematics*. Princeton: Princeton University Press.

Orlov, Yuri. 1994. "The Logical Origins of Quantum Mechanics." *Annals of Physics* 234: 245–259.

Ott, Walter, and Lydia Patton, eds. 2018. *Laws of Nature*. Oxford: Oxford University Press.

Padiyath, Thomas. 2014. "The Metaphysics of Becoming: On the Relationship Between Creativity and God in Whitehead and Supermind and Sachchidananda in Aurobindo." In *Process Thought*, edited by Johanna Seibt, Nicholas Rescher, and Michel Weber. Vol. 25. Berlin: Walter de Gruyter.

Papatheodorou, C., and Basil Hiley. 1997. "Process, Temporality and Space-Time." *Process Studies* 26, no. 3–4: 247–278.

Pattee, Howard. 2008. "The Necessity of Biosemiotics: Matter-Symbol Complementarity." In *Introduction to Biosemiotics: The New Biological Synthesis*, edited by Marcello Barbieri, 115–132. Dordrecht: Springer.

———. 2010. "The Physics and Metaphysics of Biosemiotics." In *Essential Readings in Biosemiotics: Anthology and Commentary*, edited by Donald Favareau, 519–540. Dordrecht: Springer.

———. 2011. "Between Physics and Semiotics." In *Towards a Semiotic Biology: Life Is the Action of Signs*, edited by Claus Emmeche and Kalevi Kull, 213–233. London: Imperial College Press.

Paul, L. A. 2013. "Categorical Priority and Categorical Collapse." In *Aristotelian Society Supplementary Volume*, 89–113. Oxford: Oxford University Press.

Paulson, Daryl. 2008. "Wilber's Integral Philosophy: A Summary and Critique." *Journal of Humanistic Psychology* 48, no. 3 (July): 364–388.

Pearl, Judea. 2000. *Causality: Models, Reasoning, and Inference*. Cambridge: Cambridge University Press.

Penrose, Roger. 2005. *The Road to Reality: A Complete Guide to the Laws of the Universe*. New York: Alfred Knopf.

Peratt, Anthony. 2015. *Physics of the Plasma Universe*. 2nd edition. New York: Springer Science & Business Media.

Petrov, Vesselin. 2010. "Dynamic Ontology as an Ontological Framework of Anticipatory Systems." *Foresight* 12, no. 3: 38–49.

———. 2016. "Milic Capek: The Bergsonian Process Philosopher." In *A. N. Whitehead's Thought through a New Prism*, edited by Aljoscha Berve and Helmut Maasen, 86–118. Newcastle upon Tyne: Cambridge Scholars Publishing.

———. 2017. *Points of Intersection between Mathematical and Process Philosophical Ideas*. Louvain, Belgium: *Les Editions Chromatika*.

Pfau, Thomas. 2015. *Minding the Modern: Human Agency, Intellectual Traditions, and Responsible Knowledge*. Notre Dame, IN: University of Notre Dame Press.

Pihlstrom, Sami, ed. 2017. *Pragmatism and Objectivity: Essays Sparked by the Work of Nicholas Rescher*. New York: Rutledge.

Pinker, Steven, Matt Ridley, Alain de Botton, and Malcom Gladwell. 2016. *Do Humankind's Best Days Lie Ahead?: The Munk Debates*. Toronto: House of Anansi Press.

Plamondon, Ann. 1979. *Whitehead's Organic Philosophy of Science*. Albany: State University of New York Press.

Poli, Roberto. 2001. "The Basic Problem of the Theory of Levels of Reality." *Axiomathes* 12, no. 3 (1 September): 261–283.

———. 2009. "Analysis-Synthesis." In *Ontological Landscapes*, edited by Vesselin Petrov, 19–42. Piscataway, NJ: Transaction Books, Rutgers University.

———. 2010. "An Introduction to the Ontology of Anticipation." *Futures* 42, no. 7: 769–776.

Pred, Ralph. 2005. *Onflow: Dynamics of Consciousness and Experience*. Cambridge, MA: Bradford Books.

Price, Lucien. 1954. *The Dialogues of Alfred North Whitehead*. Boston: Little, Brown and Company.

Primas, Hans. 2007. "Non-Boolean Descriptions for Mind-Matter Problems." *Mind and Matter* 5, no. 1: 7–44.

———. 2017. *Knowledge and Time*. Berlin: Springer.

Pugliese, Marc, and Gloria L. Schaab, eds. 2012. *Seeking Common Ground: Evaluation & Critique of Joseph Bracken's Comprehensive Worldview*. Milwaukee: Marquette University Press.

Puntel, Lorenz. 2008. *Structure and Being: A Theoretical Framework for a Systematic Philosophy*. Translated by Alan White. University Park: Pennsylvania State University.

———. 2012. *Being and God: A Systematic Approach in Confrontation with Martin Heidegger, Emmanuel Levinas, and Jean-Luc Marion*. Translated by Alan White. Evanston, IL: Northwestern University Press. Originally published as *Sein und Gott* (Tubingen: Mohr Siebeck, 2010).

Radin, Dean. 2009. *Entangled Minds: Extrasensory Experiences in a Quantum Reality*. New York: Simon and Schuster.

———. 2018. *Real Magic: Ancient Wisdom, Modern Science, and a Guide to the Secret Power of the Universe*. New York: Harmony.

Ram-Prasad, Chakravarthi. 2002. *Advaita Epistemology and Metaphysics: An Outline of Indian Non-Realism*. London: Routledge.

Ratcliffe, Hilton. 2010a. *The Static Universe: Exploding the Myth of Cosmic Expansion*. Montreal: C. Roy Keys, Inc.

———. 2010b. "Anomalous Redshift Data and the Myth of Cosmological Distance." *Journal of Cosmology* 4: 693–718.

Reich, Robert. 2018. *The Common Good*. New York: Alfred A. Knopf.

Rescher, Nicholas. 1996. *Process Metaphysics: An Introduction to Process Philosophy*. Albany: State University of New York Press.

———. 2000. *Process Philosophy: A Survey of Basic Issues*. Pittsburgh: University of Pittsburgh Press.

———. 2014. *Logical Inquiries: Basic Issues in Philosophical Logic*. Berlin: Walter de Gruyter.

———. 2017. *Metaphysical Perspectives*. Notre Dame, IN: University of Notre Dame Press.

Rodriguez-Pereyra, Gonzalo. 2016. "Nominalism in Metaphysics." In *The Stanford Encyclopedia of Philosophy*, edited by Edward N. Zalta. Stanford, CA: The Metaphysics Research Lab.

Rohr, Richard. 2015. "Meditation on Myth, Art, and Poetry-Sept 27, 2015." *Meditations: Center for Action and Contemplation*. cac.org. Accessed 15 December 2018.

———. 2018. "Listening and Learning: Meditation of Oct. 4, 2018." *Meditations: Center for Action and Contemplation*. cac.org. Accessed 15 December 2018.

Rose, Philip. 2005. "Relational Creativity and the Symmetry of Freedom and Nature." *Cosmos and History* 1, no. 1: 3–16.

Rosen, Joe. 1995. *Symmetry in Science: An Introduction to the General Theory*. New York: Springer-Verlag.

———. 2004. "The Primacy of Asymmetry over Symmetry in Physics." In *Physics and Whitehead: Quantum, Process, and Experience*, edited by Timothy E. Eastman and Hank Keaton, 129–135. Albany: State University of New York Press.

———. 2010. *Lawless Universe: Science and the Hunt for Reality*. Baltimore: Johns Hopkins University Press.

Rosen, Robert. 1991. *Life Itself*. In *Complexity in Ecological Systems* series, edited by Timothy Allen and David Roberts. New York: Columbia University Press.

———. 1996. "On the Limitations of Scientific Knowledge." In *Boundaries and Barriers: On the Limits to Scientific Knowledge*, edited by John Gasti and Anders Karlqvist, 199–214. Reading, MA: Perseus Books.

———. 2000. *Essays on Life Itself*. In *Complexity in Ecological Systems* series, edited by Timothy Allen and David Roberts. New York: Columbia University Press.

———. 2012. *Anticipatory Systems*. 2nd edition. In *Systems Science and Engineering* series, edited by George Klir. New York: Springer.

Ross, Donald, and David Spurrett. 2004. "What to Say to a Skeptical Metaphysician: A Defense Manual for Cognitive and Behavioral Scientists." *Behavioral and Brain Sciences* 27, no. 5 (October): 603–647.

Ross, Donald, James Ladyman, and David Spurrett. 2007. "In Defence of Scientism." In *Every Thing Must Go: Metaphysics Naturalized*, edited by James Ladyman and Don Ross, 1–65. New York: Oxford University Press.

Ross, Stephen David. 1980. *Transition to an Ordinal Metaphysics*. Albany: State University of New York Press.

———. 1983. *Perspective in Whitehead's Metaphysics*. In *Systematic Philosophy* series, edited by Robert Neville. Albany: State University of New York Press.

Saint-Andre, Peter. 2017. *The Ism Book*. Parker, CO: Monadnock Valley Press.

Salmon, Wesley. 1984. *Scientific Explanation and the Causal Structure of the World*. Princeton: Princeton University Press.

Salthe, Stanley. 1985. *Evolving Hierarchical Systems: Their Structure and Representation*. New York: Columbia University Press.

———. 2006. "Two Frameworks for Complexity Generation in Biological Systems." In *Evolution of Complexit, ALifeX Workshop Proceedings*, edited by Carlos Gershenson and T. Lenaerts, 99–104. Bloomington: Indiana University Press.

Sarewitz, Daniel. 1996. *Frontiers of Illusion: Science, Technology, and the Politics of Progress*. Philadelphia, PA: Temple University Press.

Scarborough, Milton. 2011. *Comparative Theories of Nonduality: The Search for a Middle Way*. London: Continuum International Publishing Group.

Schafer, D. Paul. 2014. *The Age of Culture*. Oakville, ON: Rock Mills Press.

Schaffer, Jonathan. 2003. "Is There a Fundamental Level?" *Nous* 37, no. 3: 498–517.

———. 2012. "Grounding, Transitivity, and Contrastivity." In *Metaphysical Grounding: Understanding the Structure of Reality*, edited by Fabrice Correia and Benjamin Schnieder, 122–138. Cambridge: Cambridge University Press.

Schindler, David. 2009. "Hans Urs von Balthasar, Metaphysics, and the Problem of Onto-Theology." *Analecta Hermeneutica* 1, no. 1: 102–113.

Schmitz, Kenneth. 2007. *The Texture of Being: Essays in First Philosophy*. Washington, D.C.: Catholic University of America.

———. 2010. "Semiotics or Metaphysics as First Philosophy? Triadic or Dyadic Relations in Regard to Four Ages of Understanding." *Semiotica* 179, no. 4: 119–132.

Schrijver, Carolus J., and George L. Siscoe, eds. 2009. *Heliophysics: Plasma Physics of the Local Cosmos*. Cambridge: Cambridge University Press.

Schumacher, Benjamin. 2009. "Quantum Mechanics: The Physics of the Microscopic World. Course Guidebook." In *The Great Courses*. Chantilly, VA: The Great Courses.

Schumann, John. 2012. "Symbolosphere." In *A More Developed Sign: Interpreting the Work of Jesper Hoffmeyer*, edited by Paul Cobley, Donald Favareau, and Kalevi Kull, 281. Tartu, Estonia: Tartu University Press.

Seager, William, ed. 2019. *Routledge Companion to Panpsychism*. London: Routledge.

Segall, Matthew. 2019. "Whitehead and Media Ecology: Toward a Communicative Cosmos." *Process Studies* 48, no. 2 (Fall–Winter): 239–253.

Sehon, Scott. 2007. "Goal-Directed Action and Teleological Explanation." In *Causation and Explanation*, edited by Michael O'Rourke, Joseph Campbell, and Harry Silverstein, 155–170. Cambridge: MIT Press.

Seibt, Johanna. 2002. "'Quanta,' Tropes, or Processes: Ontologies for QFT Beyond the Myth of Substance." In *Ontological Aspects of Quantum Field Theory*, edited by Meinard Kuhlmann, Holger Lyre, and Andrew Wayne, 53–97. River Edge, NJ: World Scientific.

———. ed. 2003. *Process Theories: Crossdisciplinary Studies in Dynamics Categories*. Dordrecht: Kluwer Academic Publishers.

———. 2004. "Free Process Theory: Towards a Typology of Occurrings." *Axiomathes* 14, no. 1: 23–55.

Seibt, Johanna, and Roberto Poli, eds. 2010. *Theory and Applications of Ontology: Philosophical Perspectives*. Dordrecht: Springer.

Shaviro, Steven. 2012. *Without Criteria: Kant, Whitehead, Deleuze, and Aesthetics*. Cambridge: MIT Press.

Sheldrake, Rupert. 2012. *Science Set Free: 10 Paths to New Discovery*. New York: Random House LLC.

———. 2018. *Science and Spiritual Practices*. Berkeley, CA: Counterpoint.

Shields, George W., ed. 2003. *Process and Analysis: Whitehead, Hartshorne, and the Analytic Tradition*. Albany: State University of New York Press.

———. 2010. "Eternal Objects, Middle Knowledge, and Hartshorne: A Response to Derek Malone-France." *Process Studies* 39, no. 1 (Spring–Summer): 149–165.

———. 2012. "Whitehead and the Analytic Philosophy of Mind." *Process Studies* 41, no. 2: 287–336.

———. 2016. "A Logical Analysis of Relational Realism." In *Physics and Speculative Philosophy: Potentiality in Modern Science*, edited by Timothy E. Eastman, Michael Epperson, and David Ray Griffin, 127–140. Berlin: Walter de Gruyter.

———. 2019. "Whitehead's Early Harvard Period, Hartshorne and the Transcendental Project." In *Whitehead at Harvard, 1924–1925*, edited by Brian Henning and Joseph Petek, 226–268. Edinburgh: Edinburgh University Press.

Shields, George W., and Derek Malone-France. 2010. "Introduction to Special Focus Issue on Eternal Objects and Future Contingents." *Process Studies* 39, no. 1 (Spring–Summer): 126–128.

Shields, George W., and Donald Wayne Viney. 2003. "The Logic of Future Contingents." In *Process and Analysis: Whitehead, Hartshorne, and the Analytic Tradition*, edited by George W. Shields, 209–246. Albany: State University of New York Press.

Shields, George W., and Timothy E. Eastman. 2020. "Triads as Fundamental: Triadic Asymmetry as Primal in Logic, Mathematics, and Physics." Prepared and peer-reviewed for the *Metaphysical Society of America 2020 Annual Meeting*, edited by Lawrence Cahoone. College of the Holy Cross, Worcester MA.

Short, Thomas Lloyd. 2007. *Peirce's Theory of Signs*. Cambridge: Cambridge University Press.

Sia, Santiago. 2014. *Society in its Challenges: Philosophical Considerations of Living in Society*. Newcastle upon Tyne: Cambridge Scholars Publishing.

Siebers, Johan. 2002. *An Essay on the Foundations of Whitehead's Metaphysics*. Leiden: Kassel University Press.

Siegel, Daniel. 2017. *Mind: A Journey to the Heart of Being Human*. New York: W. W. Norton & Co.

Silberstein, Michael, and John McGeever. 1999. "The Search for Ontological Emergence." *The Philosophical Quarterly* 49, no. 195 (April): 182–200.

Simpson, Christopher, ed. 2012. *The William Desmond Reader*. Albany: State University of New York Press.

Singh, Virendra. 2008. "Bohm's Realist Interpretation of Quantum Mechanics." arXiv:0805.1779 [quant-ph].

Sire, James W. 2014. *Naming the Elephant: Worldview as a Concept*. Downers Grove, IL: InterVarsity Press.

Smart, Benjamin T. H., and Karim P. Y. Thébault. 2015. "Dispositions and the Principle of Least Action Revisited." *Analysis* 75, no. 3: 386–395.

Smith, Peter. 2013. *An Introduction to Gödel's Theorems.* 2nd edition. Cambridge: Cambridge University Press.

Smith, Wolfgang. 2012. "Science and Myth: With a Response to Stephen Hawking's the Grand Design." In *Sophia Perennis*, edited by James Wetmore. Tacoma, WA: Angelico Press.

Smolin, Lee. 2019. "Have We Got the Universe the Wrong Way Round? A Radical Rethink of Quantum Theory." *New Scientist* (24–30 August): 34–37.

Snow, Charles P. 1963. *The Two Cultures: And a Second Look.* Cambridge: Cambridge University Press.

Spitzer, Robert. 2000. *Healing the Culture: A Commonsense Philosophy of Happiness, Freedom and the Life Issues.* San Francisco: Ignatius.

Stambovsky, Phillip. 2009. *Inference and the Metaphysic of Reason: An Onto-Epistemological Critique.* Milwaukee: Marquette University Press.

Stapp, Henry. 2004. "Whiteheadian Process and Quantum Theory." In *Physics and Whitehead: Quantum, Process, and Experience*, edited by Timothy E. Eastman and Hank Keeton, 92–102. Albany: State University of New York Press.

———. 2015. "A Quantum-Mechanical Theory of the Mind/Brain Connection." In *Beyond Physicalism: Toward Reconciliation of Science and Spirituality*, edited by Adam Crabtree Edward Kelly, and Paul Marshall, 157–193. Lanham, MD: Rowman & Littlefield.

———. 2017. *Quantum Theory and Free Will: How Mental Intentions Translate into Bodily Actions.* Cham, Switzerland: Springer International.

Steffen, Will, Jacques Grinevald, Paul Crutzen, and John McNeill. 2011. "The Anthropocene: Conceptual and Historical Perspectives." *Philosophical Transactions of the Royal Society A* 369: 842–867.

Stengers, Isabelle. 2014. *Thinking with Whitehead: A Free and Wild Creation of Concepts.* Cambridge: Harvard University Press.

Stoljar, Daniel. 2010. *Physicalism.* In *New Problems of Philosophy* series, edited by Jose Luis Bermudez. London: Routledge.

Stöltzner, Michael. 1994. "Action Principles and Teleology." In *Inside Versus Outside: Endo- and Exo-Concepts of Observation and Knowledge in Physics, Philosophy and Cognitive Science*, edited by Harald Atmanspacher and Gerhard Dalenoort, 33–62. Berlin: Springer-Verlag.

———. 2003. "The Principle of Least Action as the Logical Empiricist's Shibboleth." *Studies in History and Philosophy of Science Part B: Studies in History and Philosophy of Modern Physics* 34, no. 2: 285–318.

Strunk, Nathan. 2014. "Review of Alan White's Toward a Philosophical Theory of Everything." *Philosophy in Review* XXIV, no. 6: 345–348.

———. 2017. "Review of William Desmond, The Intimate Universal: The Hidden Porosity Among Religion, Art, Philosophy, and Politics." *Philosophy in Review* XXXVII, no. 4: 138–140.

Suchocki, Marjorie. 1988. *The End of Evil: Process Eschatology in Historical Context.* Albany: State University of New York Press.

Swimme, Brian. 1984. *The Universe Is a Green Dragon: A Cosmic Creation Story.* Rochester, VT: Bear & Company.

Swimme, Brian, and Thomas Berry. 1994. *The Universe Story: From the Primordial Flaring Forth to the Ecozoic Era.* San Francisco: Harper San Francisco.

Tallis, Raymond. 2017. *Of Time and Lamentation: Reflections on Transience.* Newcastle upon Tyne: Agenda Publishing Limited.

———. 2018. *Logos: The Mystery of How We Make Sense of the World.* Newcastle upon Tyne: Agenda Publishing Ltd.

Targ, Russell. 2010. *Limitless Mind: A Guide to Remote Viewing and Transformation of Consciousness.* Novato, CA: New World Library.

———. 2012. *The Reality of ESP: A Physicist's Proof of Psychic Abilities.* Wheaton, IL: Quest Books.

Taylor, Charles. 2007. *A Secular Age.* Cambridge, MA: Belknap Press.

Teel, Paul David Wilkinson. 2011. "The Metaphysics of Dappledness: Charles S. Peirce and Nancy Cartwright on the Philosophy of Science." Ph.D. dissertation. University of Victoria, Victoria, British Columbia.

Tegmark, Max. 2014. *Our Mathematical Universe: My Quest for the Ultimate Nature of Reality.* New York: Alfred A. Knopf.

Terekhovich, Vladislav. 2018. "Metaphysics of the Principle of Least Action." *Studies in History and Philosophy of Modern Physics* 62: 189–201.

Thagard, Paul, and Cameron Shelley. 1997. "Abductive Reasoning: Logic, Visual Thinking, and Coherence." In *Logic and Scientific Methods*, edited by M. L. Chiara, D. Mundici, and J. van Bentham, 413–427. Dordrecht: Kluwer.

Thalos, Mariam. 2013. *Without Hierarchy: The Scale Freedom of the Universe.* Oxford: Oxford University Press.

Thandeka. 2018. *Love Beyond Belief: Finding the Access Point to Spiritual Awareness.* Salem, OR: Polebridge Press.

Thomasson, Amie. 2014. *Ontology Made Easy.* New York: Oxford University Press.

Thomson, Iain. 2000. "Ontotheology? Understanding Heidegger's Destruktion of Metaphysics." *International Journal of Philosophical Studies* 8, no. 3 (1 January): 297–327.

't Hooft, Gerard. 2005. "Determinism Beneath Quantum Mechanics." In *Quo Vadis Quantum Mechanics?* Edited by Avshalom Elitzur, Shahar Dolev, and Nancy Kolenda, 99–112. Berlin: Springer.

———. 2016. "The Cellular Automaton Interpretation of Quantum Mechanics." In *Fundamental Theories of Physics*, edited by Henk van Beijeren, et al. Cham, Switzerland: Springer.

Tononi, Giulio, and Christof Koch. 2015. "Consciousness: Here, There and Everywhere?" *Philosophical Transactions of the Royal Society B* 370, no. 20140167. DOI: 10.1098/rstb.2014.0167.

Tooley, Michael. 1997. *Time, Tense and Causation.* Oxford: Oxford University Press.

Toulmin, Stephen. 1992. *Cosmopolis: The Hidden Agenda of Modernity.* Chicago: University of Chicago Press.

Trefil, James. 1989. *Reading the Mind of God: In Search of the Principle of Universality.* New York: Charles Scribner's Sons.

Tributsch, Helmut. 2016. "On the Fundamental Meaning of the Principle of Least Action and Consequences for a 'Dynamic' Quantum Physics." *Journal of Modern Physics* 7: 365–374.

Tritten, Tyler. 2017. *The Contingency of Necessity: Reason and God as Matters of Fact*. Edinburgh: Edinburgh University Press.

Tucker, Mary Evelyn, and Brian Swimme. 2014. *Journey of the Universe*. New Haven: Yale University Press.

Tucker, Mary Evelyn, John Grim, and Andrew Angyal. 2019. *Thomas Berry: A Biography*. New York: Columbia University Press.

Tye, Michael. 2018. "Qualia." In *The Stanford Encyclopedia of Philosophy*, edited by Edward N. Zalta. Stanford, CA: The Metaphysics Research Lab.

Tyson, Neil deGrasse. 2017. *Astrophysics for People in a Hurry*. New York: W. W. Norton & Co.

Ulanowicz, Robert. 2009. *A Third Window: Natural Life Beyond Newton and Darwin*. West Conshohocken, PA: Templeton Foundation Press.

Unger, Roberto Mangabeira, and Lee Smolin. 2015. *The Singular Universe and the Reality of Time: A Proposal in Natural Philosophy*. Cambridge: Cambridge University Press.

United Nations. 2009. *State of the World's Indigenous Peoples*, Vol. 9. Permanent Forum on Indigenous Issues and Statistical Division. United Nations Publications.

United Nations General Assembly. 2007. "United Nations Declaration on the Rights of Indigenous Peoples." *UN Wash* 12: 1–18.

Valenza, Robert. 2010. "The Origin of Forms in Later Whitehead." In *Beyond Metaphysics?: Explorations in Alfred North Whitehead's Late Thought*, edited by Roland Faber, Brian Henning, and Clinton Combs, 111–124. Amsterdam: Radopi.

Van Benthem, Johan. 2016. "Modal Logic: A Contemporary View." *Internet Encyclopedia of Philosophy*. http://www.iep.utm.edu/modal-lo.

Van Dijk, Jeroen B. J. 2011. "An Introduction to Process-Information: From Information Theory to Experiential Reality." In *Chromatikon Yearbook of Philosophy in Process*, edited by Michel Weber and Ronny Desmet, 75–84. Louvain-la-Neuve, Belgium: Les Éditions Chromatika.

———. 2017. "Process Physics, Time, and Consciousness." *Process Studies Supplement*, no. 24: 1–216.

Verlinde, Erik. 2011. "On the Origin of Gravity and the Laws of Newton." *Journal of High Energy Physics* 29: 1–27.

Viney, Donald Wayne, and George W. Shields. 2015. "Charles Hartshorne: Neoclassical Metaphysics." In *Internet Encyclopedia of Philosophy*, edited by James Fieser and Bradley Dowden. https://www.iep.utm.edu/eds/.

———. 2020. *The Mind of Charles Hartshorne: A Critical Exploration*. Anoka, MN: Process Century Press.

Voskuil, Duane. 2016. *Process and Dipolar Reality: An Essay in Process, Event Metaphysics: Rethinking Whitehead's Categoreal Scheme*. Eugene, OR: Wipf & Stock.

Wallack, F. Bradford. 1980. *The Epochal Nature of Process in Whitehead's Metaphysics*. Albany: State University of New York Press.

Walleczek, Jan, Gerhard Grössing, Paavo Pylkkänen, and Basil Hiley, eds. 2019. *Emergent Quantum Mechanics: David Bohm Centennial Perspectives*. Basel, Switzerland: MDPI.

Watzlawick, Paul, John Weakland, and Richard Fisch. 2011. *Change: Principles of Problem Formation and Problems Resolution*. New York: W. W. Norton & Co.

Weart, Spencer. 2008. *The Discovery of Global Warming*. Revised and expanded edition. Vol. 13. Cambridge: Harvard University Press.

Weber, Michel. 2013. "Polysemiality of the Concept of 'Pure Experience.'" In *Whitehead's Pancreativism: Jamesian Applications*. Vol. 8, edited by Michel Weber, 109. Berlin: Walter de Gruyter.

———. 2016. *The Political Vindication of Radical Empiricism: With Application to the Global Systemic Crisis*. Anoka, MN: Process Century Press.

Weber, Michel, and Anderson Weekes, eds. 2009. *Process Approaches to Consciousness in Psychology, Neuroscience, and Philosophy of Mind*. Albany: State University of New York Press.

Weekes, Anderson. 2009a. "Consciousness as a Topic of Investigation in Western Thought." In *Process Approaches to Consciousness in Psychology, Neuroscience, and Philosophy of Mind*, edited by Michel Weber and Anderson Weekes, 73–135. Albany: State University of New York Press.

———. 2009b. "Whitehead's Unique Approach to the Topic of Consciousness." In *Process Approaches to Consciousness in Psychology, Neuroscience, and Philosophy of Mind*, edited by Michel Weber and Anderson Weekes, 137–172. Albany: State University of New York Press.

———. 2009c. "Consciousness and Causation in Whitehead's Phenomenology of Becoming." In *Process Approaches to Consciousness in Psychology, Neuroscience, and Philosophy of Mind*, edited by Michel Weber and Anderson Weekes, 407–461. Albany: State University of New York Press.

———. 2017. "Acknowledging Ralph Pred." In *Beyond Whitehead: Recent Advances in Process Thought*, edited by Jakup Dziadkowiec and Lukasz Lamza, 67–79. Lanham, MD: Lexington Books.

Weinberg, Steven. 2017. "The Trouble with Quantum Mechanics." *The New York Review of Books* (19 January).

Weinert, Friedel, ed. 2011. *Laws of Nature: Essays on the Philosophical, Scientific and Historical Dimensions*. Vol. 8. Berlin: Walter de Gruyter.

Weiss, Eric. 2015. "Mind Beyond Body: Transphysical Process Metaphysics." In *Beyond Physicalism: Toward Reconciliation of Science and Spirituality*, edited by Adam Crabtree, Edward Kelly, and Paul Marshall, 455–490. Lanham, MD: Rowman & Littlefield.

Weissman, David. 1977. *Eternal Possibilities: A Neutral Ground for Meaning and Existence*. Carbondale: Southern Illinois University Press.

Weisstein, Eric W. 2020. "Iterated Map." In *MathWorld–A Wolfram Web Resource*. https://mathworld.wolfram.com/IteratedMap.html. Accessed 20 June 2020.

White, Alan. 2014. *Toward a Philosophical Theory of Everything*: Contributions to the Structural-Systematic Philosophy. New York: Bloomsbury.

White, Paul. 2019. "A Derivation of Space and Time." *Progress in Physics* 15: 58–63.

Whitehead, Alfred North. 1917. *The Organization of Thought: Educational and Scientific*. London: Williams and Norgate.

———. 1920. *The Concept of Nature, Tarner Lectures Delivered in Trinity College, November, 1919*. Cambridge: The University Press.

———. 1922. *The Principle of Relativity with Applications to Physical Science*. Cambridge: Cambridge University Press.

———. 1929, 1978. *Process and Reality: An Essay in Cosmology*. Corrected edition. Edited by David Ray Griffin and Donald W. Sherburne. New York: Macmillan; The Free Press.

———. 1933. *Adventures of Ideas*. New York: The Macmillan Company.

———. 1948. *Essays in Science and Philosophy*. London: Rider and Company.

Wilber, Ken. 2011. *Integral Spirituality: A Startling New Role for Religion in the Modern and Postmodern World*. Boston: Integral Books.

———. 2017. *The Religion of Tomorrow: A Vision for the Future of the Great Traditions*. Boulder: Shambhala.

Williams, James. 2016. *A Process Philosophy of Signs*. Edinburgh: Edinburgh University Press.

Williams, Richard N., and Daniel N. Robinson, eds. 2014. *Scientism: The New Orthodoxy*. London: Bloomsbury Publishing.

Williamson, Timothy. 2013. *Modal Logic as Metaphysics*. Oxford: Oxford University Press.

———. 2016. "Modal Science." *Canadian Journal of Philosophy* 46, no. 4–5: 453–492.

Wilson, Edward O. 1998. *Consilience: The Unity of Knowledge*. New York: Alfred Knopf, Inc.

Wilson, Jessica. 2015. "Hume's Dictum and Metaphysical Modality." In *A Companion to David Lewis*, edited by Barry Loewer and Jonathan Schaffer, In *Blackwell Companions to Philosophy*, 138–158. Chichester, West Sussex: John Wiley & Sons Ltd.

Wimsatt, William. 2007. *Re-Engineering Philosophy for Limited Beings*. Cambridge: Harvard University Press.

Woese, Carl. 2004. "A New Biology for a New Century." *Microbiology and Molecular Biology Reviews* 68, no. 2 (June): 173–186.

Woit, Peter. 2007. *Not Even Wrong: The Failure of String Theory and the Search for Unity in Physical Law*. New York: Basic Books.

Wuthrich, Christian. 2019. "The Emergence of Space and Time." In *The Routledge Handbook of Emergence*, edited by Robin Findlay, Hendry Sophie Gibb, and Tom Lancaster. Abingdon, Oxon: Routledge.

Zafiris, Elias. 2010. "Boolean Information Sieves: A Local-to-Global Approach to Quantum Information." *International Journal of General Systems* 39, no. 8: 873–895.

———. 2012. "Rosen's Modelling Relations via Categorical Adjunctions." *International Journal of General Systems* 41, no. 5: 439–474.

———. 2016. "Boolean Localization of Quantum Events." In *Physics and Speculative Philosophy: Potentiality in Modern Science*, edited by Timothy E. Eastman, Michael Epperson, and David Ray Griffin, 107–125. Berlin: Walter de Gruyter.

Zurek, Wojciech. 2006. "Decoherence and the Transition from Quantum to Classical-Revisited." In *Quantum Decoherence*, edited by J. Raimond, B. Duplantieer, and V. Rivasseau, In *Progress in Mathematical Physics*. Basel, Switzerland: Birkhauser.

Name Index

Subject Index

Page references for figures are italicized.

About the Author

Timothy E. Eastman obtained his doctorate in physics and geophysics from the University of Alaska Geophysical Institute (1979) and has served as a consultant in space physics, plasma sciences, and philosophy (now retired). Dr. Eastman discovered the low-latitude boundary layer of Earth's magnetosphere and, with more than forty years of experience in research and consulting, has published over 100 research papers in space physics, philosophy, and related fields. While serving as a program officer at NASA (1985–1988) and NSF (1991–1994), he was codeveloper of key foundations for major international and interagency projects, including the International Solar Terrestrial Physics program, the Interagency Space Weather program, and NSF's Basic Plasma Science and Engineering program. He created and maintains a major website for plasma science and applications at plasmas.org, and is lead editor of two volumes in philosophy and physics (*Physics and Whitehead,* SUNY, 2004; *Physics and Speculative Philosophy,* de Gruyter, 2016). Dr. Eastman's interest in philosophy and philosophy of science extends over four decades with over thirty publications in philosophy in addition to the edited volumes; further, he is on International Advisory Boards for *Process Studies* and *Studia Whiteheadiana* (Poland). For this and related scholarly research and publications, he was awarded the *Creative Advance Award* in 2009 by *The International Process Network*. His current research is focused on a synthesis of recent developments in philosophy, physics, logic, biosemiotics, and process thought as exemplified by the current work, *Untying the Gordian Knot* (Lexington Books, 2020). Such research demonstrates the limitations of simplistic reductionisms, which have often been used to dismiss all scholarly investigations into the ontological grounding of values and meaning, and top-down modes of influence. He has come to understand how the confluence of many complementary developments in science, philosophy, and related fields leads naturally to an ecological vision that more fully affirms such inclusive understandings of reality.

BOOKS BY THE AUTHOR

Eastman, Timothy E. 2020. *Untying the Gordian Knot: Process, Reality, and Context.* Lanham: Lexington Books.

Eastman, Timothy E., Michael Epperson, and David Ray Griffin, eds., 2016. *Physics and Speculative Philosophy: Potentiality, Actuality, and Process in Modern Science.* Frankfurt: Ontos Verlag.

Eastman, Timothy E. and Hank Keeton, eds., 2004, 2008. *Physics and Whitehead: Quantum, Process and Experience.* Albany: State University of New York (SUNY) Press.

Eastman, T. E. 1979. *The Plasma Boundary Layer and Magnetopause Layer of the Earth's Magnetosphere.* Ph.D. dissertation, Fairbanks: University of Alaska Geophysical Institute. [Los Alamos Scientific Laboratory Report LA-7842-T, June, 1979].